How to Write Macintosh™ Software

Scott Knaster

HAYDEN BOOKS

A Division of Howard W. Sams & Company
4300 West 62nd Street
Indianapolis, Indiana 46268 USA

Apple believes that good books are important to successful computing. The Apple Press imprint is your assurance that this book has been published with the support and encouragement of Apple Computer Inc., and is the type of book we would be proud to publish ourselves.

For Barbara and Jess

Acquisitions Editor: BILL GROUT
Developmental Editors: SCOT KAMINS/BILL GROUT
Production Editor: RONNIE GROFF
Composition and production: McFARLAND GRAPHICS & DESIGN, INC.
Cover art: GEORGE BAQUERO
Cover design: JIM BERNARD

Library of Congress Cataloging-in-Publication Data

Knaster, Scott.
　　How to write Macintosh software.

　　Includes index.
　　1. Macintosh (Computer)—Programming.　I. Title.
QA76.8.M3K68 1986　　　　005.265　　　　86-14825
ISBN 0-8104-6564-7

Macintosh is a trademark of McIntosh Laboratory, Inc., licensed to Apple Computer, Inc. Lisa, Finder, *Inside Macintosh*, MacWrite, MacPaint, and MacDraw are trademarks of Apple Computer, Inc. TMON is a trademark of ICOM Simulations, Inc.

Printed in the United States of America

	2	3	4	5	6	7	8	9	
86	87	88	89	90	91	92	93	94	YEAR

INTRODUCTION

This book is for people who want to write software for the Macintosh. It's not an introductory book; you should be experienced in (or in the process of learning) a high-level language such as Pascal or C, or assembly language. It also helps to be familiar with the basics of how Macintosh programs are written. If you've read or even skimmed **Macintosh Revealed** by Stephen Chernicoff or **Inside Macintosh** from Apple, you'll benefit from this book.

What This Book Will Tell You

What's in this book that's not in the others just mentioned? This book explains lots of the mysteries and myths about Macintosh programming that aren't really covered anywhere else. It talks about how and where things are stored in memory. It discusses what things in memory may be moved around, and teaches you how to know exactly when they may be moved. It explains how to debug your applications using available debugging tools. It shows you how to examine your program's code to learn precisely what's going on when it runs. It also gives you dozens of facts, tips, and tricks that you can use to make your software more powerful.

How This Book Was Written

In my two years in the Macintosh Technical Support group at Apple, I've worked with hundreds of programmers in helping them write and debug their software. I've tried to put as much of my experience as possible into this book. I've also put in a lot of stuff that we've taught developers in our MacCollege training course.

I wrote this book with several principles in mind:

- No mysteries. I've tried very hard to explain things that people find confusing or puzzling about Macintosh programming and to leave nothing significant unexplained that's within the book's scope.

- No fuzziness. There's nothing more irritating than a book that takes you to the brink of a great revelation, then wimps out with fuzzy, vague writing. This usually makes it obvious that the writer doesn't know any more and is trying to get on to the next topic. I've tried to avoid fuzziness by explaining things in depth.

- No wizards. Sure, some people are smarter than others. It's not right, though, to withhold potentially useful information because you don't trust people to use it correctly. I've tried to refrain from holding back information. If it's a bad idea to use a particular feature or technique, I won't just say "don't," I'll tell you why.

- All work and no fun is no fun. While we're going over all this stuff, it's a good idea to have some fun, too, so I've tried to keep the mood light enough to keep you awake, even while we work through the heavy subjects.

If you use the information presented in this book, you'll know an awful lot about the Macintosh, and your programs will be better. There's enough information presented here that you may not absorb all of it as you read it through. Don't worry about that. You can reread it as many times as you like, at no extra charge.

The Macintosh has gained quite a reputation for requiring a lot from a programmer. For various reasons, it was incredibly hard to create Macintosh software when the computer first appeared in January of 1984. In the years that have passed since then, lots of things have happened to make Macintosh programming a little easier:

- Dozens of programming languages and tools have been developed, most of them coming from outside of Apple. There are compilers for many languages, powerful debuggers, disk patching tools, and more.

- More technical material on the Macintosh has been created. Apple has produced **Inside Macintosh** and technical notes, and many good (and bad) books on Macintosh programming have appeared.

- The general level of knowledge in the programming community (wherever that may be—I think it's near Berkeley) has increased tremendously as Macintosh programmers everywhere have gotten smarter.

- The Macintosh itself has become more powerful. The first Macintosh had 128K RAM and 800K of disk space (if you had two disk drives). Today's Macintosh has up to 4 *megabytes* of RAM and as much disk storage as you want to pay for.

Still, there are some things about Macintosh programming that aren't well known and aren't written down anywhere. In this book, I've tried to gather together lots of "mysterious" things and take all the mystery out of them. As you read, you'll discover that things aren't so hard to understand after all—they're just not well known.

ACKNOWLEDGMENTS

Without these people, this book would not exist, and you would now be staring at nothing and looking very silly.

Jim Friedlander of Macintosh Technical Support helped immeasurably. He read the entire manuscript several times and kept me honest; he wrote most of the programs in Part Three; and he helped me keep up my energy level with his enthusiasm.

Martha Steffen, Apple Publishing Evangelist, helped me figure out how to get started and what was happening to me along the way.

Scot Kamins, Writéur, encouraged me, told me funny jokes, and gave me a great review. I also stole ideas from his books.

Caroline Rose inspired me by being the best technical writer I've ever known, and by writing **Inside Macintosh**, without which no other Macintosh technical books would be possible.

Cary Clark and Russ Daniels were very smart (and still are) and taught me a lot of the stuff that appears in this book.

Bryan Stearns, Ginger Jernigan, Mark Baumwell, Louella Pizzuti, Bill Dawson, and Rick Blair of Apple Technical Support put up with me whenever I rambled on about this book.

Chris Espinosa invented the tree-crash metaphor used in Chapter 4, which is used with his permission, whether he knows it or not.

Alain Rossmann gave me valuable ideas for the "Techniques" section and provided lots of enthusiasm.

Mike McGrath gave me great advice on how to write a book and get it published and loaned me his copy of **Author Law**.

Jean-Louis Gassée has encouraged creativity and fun at Apple in the post-Steve Jobs era.

Guy Kawasaki changed my life, and I have the bumper sticker to prove it.

Barbara Knaster created many of the figures, constructed Appendix E, fixed lots of stuff, and, most important, told me to do it and made me do it.

ABOUT THIS BOOK

This book is divided into three parts, plus appendices. Here's what you'll find:

Part One is called "How It All Works." This part of the book concentrates on general information about the Macintosh and how to program it, with an in-depth discussion on how things in RAM behave and misbehave.

Chapter 1, "Getting Started," talks about what makes Macintosh programming different and presents a brief overview of development tools.

Chapter 2, "Things in Memory," tells about the way things are stored in memory, what happens to them, and how you can manage them.

Chapter 3, "More about Heaps and Fragmentation," describes some common memory management problems and how to avoid them.

Part Two is called "Debugging," which kinda tells you what it's about.

Chapter 4, "Debugging Macintosh Software," introduces some general thoughts about debugging, tells about the TMON debugger, and presents information about many of the most common problems that Macintosh programmers run into.

Chapter 5, "Examining Compiled Code," shows you how to look at the object code produced by your high-level language program.

Chapter 6, "More about Compiled Code," continues directly from Chapter 5, but it would have made one big, obnoxious chapter if it had been all together, so it's not.

Chapter 7, "Real Live Debugging," presents an example program that has bugs in it and then uses an object code debugger to find and fix the problems.

Part Three is called "Tips, Tricks, and Techniques," and it's got some of each of those, including a few example programs.

Chapter 8, "General Techniques," presents stuff that's generally useful if you're writing Macintosh software.

Chapter 9, "Toolbox Techniques," contains information on some goodies that will help you make better use of the Macintosh's User-Interface Toolbox.

Chapter 10, "Operating System Techniques," covers some good things to know about various parts of the Macintosh Operating System.

Appendix A, "Assembly Language Overview," is very important if you're not familiar with 68000 assembly language. To use an object code debugger, you should be able to read 68000 code and understand what's going on. You don't have to be able to write assembly language. This appendix will tell you what all those strange instructions mean. You can read this appendix before reading Part Two or at any point that you think you need it. Even if you're already a 68000 programmer, you might want to read it to learn some fine points.

Don't forget about Appendix A. When you start to come across assembly language information that's unfamiliar to you, try reading Appendix A. It should help a lot.

Appendix B, "Common Problems," lists some of the most common (and most fatal) errors that can cause a Macintosh programmer to lose sleep.

Apppendix C, "Macintosh Plus," summarizes the new features in the Macintosh Plus computer. Although there's Macintosh Plus information throughout the book, you can use this appendix as a single source of information.

Appendix D, "A Guided Tour of Macsbug," presents detailed information about the Macsbug debugger that Apple distributes.

Appendix E, "Debugging Quick Reference Guide," contains some charts that you'll find very handy when debugging.

At the end of the book you'll find a glossary of whizzy terms.

Conventions Used in This Book

Whenever you see this typeface:

```
GetNextEvent
```

you'll know that it's the name of a call to the Macintosh User Interface Toolbox or Operating System, or a line of a Pascal, C, or assembly language program.

All words in the text that are in **boldface** can be found in the glossary, except the ones that are names of books.

Hexadecimal numbers are always preceded by a dollar sign, like this: $388   −$42 $40F7A2.

Numbers not preceded by a dollar sign are decimal numbers unless otherwise stated.

Calls to routines in the Macintosh User Interface Toolbox and Operating System are referred to as **system calls**, **ROM calls**, **traps**, or **A-traps**, depending on the context. All these terms mean the same thing.

"Workshop Pascal" is a generic term indicating either Macintosh Programmer's Workshop Pascal or Lisa Workshop Pascal.

Note for C programmers: whenever you see Pascal-specific terms, you should substitute their C equivalents. Unless otherwise noted, the information is valid for both languages. Here are some Pascal and C terms that are equivalent in this book:

Pascal	**C**
procedure or function	function
local variable	automatic variable

A paragraph that looks like this is an incidental note. It contains information that's interesting and useful, but not vital to the material.

Warning

A paragraph marked with this icon is a warning. Imagine Robby the Robot on *Lost in Space* saying, "Danger, Will Robinson!"

Macintosh Plus

This icon marks information that's specifically for the Macintosh Plus. Most of this information is also valid for the Macintosh 512K enhanced.

Looking Ahead

You'll find this crystal ball icon on paragraphs that discuss products that have been announced by manufacturers, but haven't yet (at the time of the writing) become available. For example, information about the Macintosh Programmer's Workshop from Apple is marked with this icon.

Fact

A sentence that looks like this is an important, simple truth that you should know. These sentences present facts that help to take the mystery out of Macintosh programming.

Things to Remember

This icon, found at the end of each chapter, marks a list of key points and concepts that were introduced in that chapter.

The Amazing Colossal Disclaimer

There's a lot of technical information in this book. It's been reviewed carefully by several people, and all the known problems have been fixed. Just as with software, though, there may be undiscovered bugs. Also, as the Macintosh world evolves, things change. If you find anything wrong, I would very much appreciate it if you would write to me about it in care of Howard W. Sams & Co.

What You Need to Use This Book

To make the most of this book, you should be somewhat familiar with Pascal or C. You should also have access to a copy of **Inside Macintosh**, the technical reference manual for the Macintosh computers.

In Part Two, we spend a lot of time looking at programs with a debugger. The debugger that's used for the examples is TMON, published by Icom Simulations, and it's generally regarded as the most powerful debugger available for the Macintosh. If you don't have TMON, you can do some debugging with Macsbug, the debugger that Apple distributes with a variety of software, including the Macintosh 68000 Development System and the Macintosh Software Supplement.

This book presents a lot of specific information, such as examples of how compilers compile code. Although this specific information is very useful, you should realize that this book's true mission is to tell you that you should observe your program's behavior closely and figure out for yourself what's going on. In particular, the compiled code examples given in Part Two are correct for Workshop Pascal, but may be different for other Pascal and C compilers. The only way to know how your compiler does things is to look at the code it produces.

How to Learn More

The best way to learn more about Macintosh programming is to write programs! A good source of information is your local user's group. Many user's groups have special-interest groups for programmers, and most groups publish newsletters.

You might also want to join an on-line bulletin board service. These services are frequented by Macintosh fanatics who are able to answer almost any Macintosh programming question, or at least point you in the right direction. These services also contain lots of public domain software that you can download, including the latest goodies from Apple.

There are also a number of good books available, such as books specifically for Pascal, C, or assembly language programming on the Macintosh. More books are appearing constantly, so keep checking your favorite bookstore.

One reason there's so much third-party software that runs on Apple computers is that Apple has a lot of programs that help developers in a variety of ways. These programs include marketing assistance, developer–programmer matchmaking, technical support (of course), and more. In addition, Apple distributes lots of different products, like technical documentation and software tools, through channels other than your neighborhood computer store. Apple also licenses its system software (like the Finder and the System file) so that you can ship this software on your disks.

There's so much stuff available from Apple that it can get confusing. If you need to find out anything about Apple's programs for developers or technical products, you can write to Apple Computer, Inc., Customer Relations, 20525 Mariani Avenue, Cupertino, California 95014. To find out about licensing Apple's system software, write to Apple Computer, Inc., Software Licensing, 20525 Mariani Avenue, Cupertino, California 95014.

Also, it's a good idea to develop a nice, quiet hobby unrelated to programming, so that you can relax for a while. Sky diving, for example.

Contents

PART ONE

How It All Works

Wha-a?

—*Superman*, Action Comics #1, June 1938

CHAPTER

1

Getting Started

In this chapter, we'll talk about what makes Macintosh programming different, and we'll briefly go over some of the tools available to help you write Macintosh software.

Different

Macintosh programs don't look or feel like programs on other, conventional computers. The Macintosh's user interface, which makes heavy use of graphics, gives its software a distinctive look (although that look has now become widely imitated on other personal computers).

Conventional computers have a screen format that shows 24 lines of 80 characters each and has the capability of sending those characters to a printer. If you've programmed a personal computer, you probably know how to put your display screen into a graphics mode, which allows you to draw lines and pictures in addition to (or instead of) text.

When you start to learn about Macintosh, you begin to discover that somebody has changed the rules on you. The 24-by-80 text screen is gone; instead, there are scrollable, resizable **windows**. At the top of the screen is a list of words, the **menu bar**, which suggest things that you can do, like "File" or "Edit." You've probably also noticed lots of **dialog boxes**—they're the little windows that appear and ask you about things, like what name to use when saving a document, or whether you really want to quit an application. If you've used even a couple of Macintosh applications, or programmed a few, all these user-interface goodies should be familiar to you.

One of the most famous Macintosh concepts is the icon, or picture. If you read some of the computer trade magazines, you often see Macintosh referred to as being an "icon-based" system or having an "iconic" operating system. These phrases should clue you in immediately to the fact that the writer probably hasn't used a Macintosh very much. Icons are just a part of the Macintosh user interface; most applications use them infrequently. Windows and pull-down menus are the real guts of the user interface.

The first thing most people ever see on a Macintosh is something like Figure 1-1. This screen, of course, is from the Finder, the program you see when you start up a Macintosh. The Finder uses icons to show disks, applications, documents, and folders. It also uses a trash can icon as a destination for things to be thrown away, or deleted.

Yes, the Finder uses icons. But the Finder is not Macintosh's operating system! The Finder is simply another program on the Macintosh disk, a utility program. Its purpose is to let the user move things around on disks and to start applications. It's roughly equivalent to the program that's running when you see an "A>" prompt on an MS-DOS system, though a lot friendlier for most users.

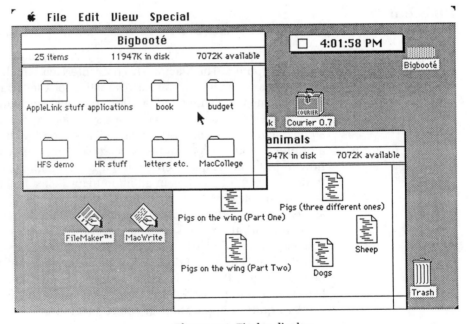

Figure 1-1 Finder display

A disk need not have the Finder in order to be usable. The only thing special about the Finder is that the Macintosh looks for a file called Finder to run when the system starts up (and even that can be changed). You can easily build a Finderless disk by using the Finder's own "Set Startup" item in the "Special" menu.

Your application can use icons, too, if you want, but you'll probably get a lot more play out of windows and menus when designing your user interface.

The ROM

If the Finder is not Macintosh's Operating System, what is the O S? What does it look like? Where is it? How is it called by programs? Well, when you're writing software, parts of the Macintosh operating system will probably look similar to other systems you may have used. There's a **File Manager**, with calls to create, delete, open, close, read from, write to, and get information about files and disks. There are **device drivers** to control the disk drives, serial ports, printer, and sound capabilities. There's a **Memory Manager** to control the allocation of chunks of RAM. Most of the Macintosh Operating System is pretty conventional (in contrast to the very unconventional user interface).

The Macintosh O S takes up part of the computer's ROM. Many computers put some low-level portion of the system in ROM and then load in more of the O S when the system is started. Macintosh roughly follows this pattern, except that it's got more of the O S in its ROM than do most systems. There's also some system stuff kept in a file on the disk called System. For a disk to boot, it has to have that file. There will be more information later on what's in the System file.

The Macintosh's Operating System takes up only a fraction of the ROM. What really makes the Macintosh unique is the code that's in the rest of the ROM. It's called the User Interface Toolbox, and it consists of hundreds of callable routines that are used to implement the windows, menus, dialog boxes, buttons, icons, and all the other familiar trappings that give the Macintosh its personality. At the heart of the User Interface Toolbox (usually just called the Toolbox) is QuickDraw, the magic artist that lets you draw almost anything you want on the Macintosh's screen.

That's what's in the Macintosh's ROM: the Operating System and the Toolbox. Notice that there's no high-level language, like BASIC, which is included in ROM in many personal computers.

Macintosh Plus

The Macintosh Plus's ROM also includes some additional things. Because it's bigger, it's able to include in ROM some things that must be provided in the System file and loaded into RAM on 64K ROM systems. For example, the 128K ROM contains the AppleTalk software, which is not in the 64K ROM and must be included in the System file on small-ROM machines. A complete list of ROM differences is given in Appendix C. Still no BASIC in ROM, though.

In Figure 1-2, you'll see the pieces of the system and where they come from. In the rest of this chapter, we'll talk about how the Macintosh uses somewhat unfamiliar techniques to accomplish familiar computing tasks in a spectacular way and how to make sure the results are what you want.

Figure 1-2 Macintosh system software

Item	Location	Comments
Operating System	ROM	Includes File Manager, Memory Manager, some device drivers, etc.
User Interface Toolbox	ROM	Includes QuickDraw, Window Manager, Menu Manager, Control Manager, etc.
ROM patches	System file	Used to fix ROM bugs and add features
Desk accessories, fonts, more device drivers	System file	Stored in System File as resources
Finder	Finder file	Contains the Finder utility program
Printing software	ImageWriter, LaserWriter files	"Chooser" desk acc. picks desired printer

Everything You Know Is Wrong

Is everything you know really wrong? No, it just seems that way sometimes when you're programming a Macintosh, especially when you're getting started. This uncomfortable feeling, common to new Macintosh programmers, arises from a sense of disorientation when beginning to write Macintosh software.

The first symptom of "Macintosh Malaise" usually comes about when you attempt to write your first program. Most folks start with a short, simple program that says "Hello, world" on the screen, or prints the integers from one to ten, or something easy like that. To accomplish this task for the first time on a Macintosh, you have to face a number of unexpected hurdles. See if any or all of these are familiar to you:

1. Understanding what a resource file is and how to create one with the right things in it.

2. Learning which "Init" calls to put in your program, and in what order.

3. Figuring out how to put text on the screen of a computer that appears to have no text mode.

4. Making sure that your program, once created on the disk, is known by the Finder to be an application, so that you can run it.

5. Figuring out how to get all those great graphics printed out on an ImageWriter or LaserWriter.

6. (Optional, for those doing Lisa cross-development) Getting the program you created onto a Macintosh disk.

These steps are necessary in addition to the usual ones required to figure out how to use a new development environment. It's easy to see why the Macintosh acquired the reputation of a machine that's hard to program (and we haven't even gotten to the hard stuff yet!).

Is Macintosh really hard to program? It's true that there's a lot for the programmer to learn. You may remember the original Macintosh commercials, in which a large instruction manual was dropped on a desk next to a computer made by you-know-who, causing the table to shake, while the Macintosh's tiny owner's guide (which most users never need and keep perpetually shrink- wrapped) flutters down next to the Macintosh. You might think of **Inside Macintosh**, Apple's comprehensive technical reference, as the table-shaker for Macintosh.

Is this deceptive on Apple's part? Not at all. The Macintosh system hides complexity from the user, but builds in enough power for developers to create programs like Jazz and Excel. Thanks to this hidden complexity, Macintosh quickly established its initial goal of being perceived as an easy-to-learn computer.

Yes, but is the Macintosh hard to program? In 1983, when the first Macintosh developers began, the answer was an unqualified yes. The development tools were few and fairly crude, the documentation was incomplete, and the sum of experience in Macintosh application development was zero.

Today, the situation is astonishingly different. There are now over 30 different development environments, representing at least a dozen different languages, including Pascal, C, assembler, BASIC, Lisp, Modula-2, Forth, and COBOL (yes, COBOL); there are disk patch tools, disassemblers, debuggers, memory-display utilities, and more; there is a complete technical manual called **Inside Macintosh**; but perhaps most important, there is the sum of more than two years of experience in application software development for Macintosh—over a thousand applications.

Obviously, we can't all learn about every technique used by developers during the past two years, but we do know enough to be light-years ahead of where we were when Macintosh was introduced. We know what different kinds of user interfaces look like; we know about several efficient memory management techniques; we know a lot about debugging. Much of this book is devoted to presenting this accumulated knowledge.

By now, you've probably figured out that I'm not going to give a straight answer to the question of whether Macintosh is hard to program (author's prerogative). Let's just say that there's more to learn, and more power to be exploited, than on a conventional system. The same amount of effort, applied in the right way to Macintosh development, can produce a result that is both easier for a user to learn and more powerful than an application program on a conventional system.

Think of it this way: imagine that you're in San Jose and that you have an hour to travel. You have a choice: you can spend the hour in your car, driving up the peninsula to San Francisco, or you can spend the hour flying in a jet plane, arriving in Los Angeles at the end of the hour (see Figure 1-3). Both are ways to travel; both trips take an hour. By using the airplane, you have a journey that is technologically more difficult, and perhaps riskier, but you get to go farther.

Writing software is the same way. Macintosh development can be tricky, but in the end you will have gone farther. You'll also have a lot more fun getting there, even if you like San Francisco better than Los Angeles.

Something that can make any task, especially writing software, seem impossible is blind ignorance and lack of information. Unfortunately, there's so much to learn when writing Macintosh software that ignorance often gets the upper hand. The only way to really solve programming problems is to understand precisely *what* is going wrong and *why*. When your Macintosh puts up a bomb, it hasn't randomly decided that it wants

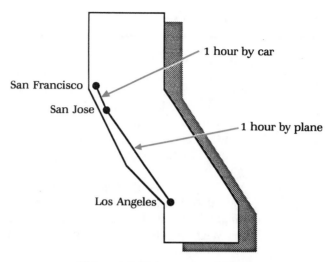

Figure 1-3 Flying versus driving

you to go to lunch—it's actually providing some clues about what went wrong.

And that's what this book is all about—to tell you what's happening when your application crashes, to teach you how to use lots of Toolbox tricks, and to give you good, solid information about what's going on inside the Macintosh when your application is running. This book is intended to enlighten you and demystify Macintosh programming for you.

What's an Open Architecture?

Apple has taken a lot of heat for making the original Macintosh a "closed system"—in other words, there are no expansion slots. However, Apple probably hasn't gotten enough credit for the openness of the Macintosh software architecture. The system provides you with **hooks** at several different levels so that you can modify the way things behave. For example, you can put in your own version of any system call; you can also implement special behavior with the low-memory global hooks (see Part Three for some examples).

How to Get There from Here

Since the Macintosh Operating System and the Toolbox are both in ROM, and since all programs have to call on the O S and Toolbox to get things done, there must be some kind of communication set up between the programming language you're using and the ROM.

The ROM contains over 600 individually callable routines. Each requires certain parameters to be passed to it and then uses these parameters to perform some action. Some routines also return values to you when you call them.

High-level languages learn how to call the ROM through the use of special codes called libraries. These libraries are programs, usually supplied on disk with language products, that define for you some or all of the Macintosh ROM calls so that your program can use them.

For example, when you use a Macintosh C compiler, you may write a statement like this:

InitFonts ();

When the compiler, which translates your source code into machine language, comes to this statement, how does it know what to do? It doesn't have statements like "InitFonts" built into it—that would make it huge and inflexible. Instead, you've probably got a statement at the beginning of your program that looks something like this:

Include Fonts;

This means that there's a file on the disk called Fonts, which has been previously created, that contains definitions for the compiler; in this case, it defines calls to the Font Manager in the Macintosh ROM, including InitFonts. So, when the compiler reaches the InitFonts line, it determines what to do by looking in the library called Fonts, which you've told it about in your "include" statement.

In the Macintosh ROM, commands like InitFonts are encoded as a single instruction to the MC68000 microprocessor that runs the Macintosh. Sometimes this instruction is produced by the compiler; sometimes it's created by the linker, if your system uses a linker. Whether the compiler or linker actually generates this ROM call instruction depends on which development system you're using and which ROM call was made.

The single-instruction machine language encoding produces several benefits:

1. The ROM routines are not required to stay fixed in a certain location from one ROM version to another, as they were, for example, with the Apple II ROM.

2. The names of the ROM routines are not present in the ROM itself; they're known by number, and the high-level language assigns the name.

3. Calls to the ROM routines are simply a special 68000 instruction which takes up just 2 bytes.

Although much of the Macintosh ROM (especially the Toolbox) was originally written with Pascal callers in mind, virtually any language can be adapted to call the ROM. All the languages available for Macintosh today provide some access to the ROM calls. For more on how ROM calls work, see the Chapter 10 section entitled "How ROM Calls Work" (appropriately enough).

Resources

Once you've compiled and linked your program, you'll probably have another development step that isn't required on other system. This step involves the creation of your program's **resources**.

To implement the user interface, the Macintosh uses lots of little pieces of data and code: a list of words in a menu; the dimensions of a window; the code that draws a scroll bar; the bits that comprise an icon. These pieces, and many others, are known as resources. Resources are so common and important in the Macintosh system that many people find it difficult to define them concisely. If you ask a Macintosh programmer what a resource is, you're likely to be told, "Everything is a resource!" That's close, but we'll try to be a little more definitive.

Every Macintosh disk file has two parts, a **data fork** and a **resource fork**. The data fork is a conventional disk file; it consists of a stream of bytes that is interpreted by the program which created it. The resource fork is also a stream of bytes, but it's got a sort of index, called the **resource map**, that allows the system to see it as a sequence of separate, discrete things: resources. The part of the Macintosh ROM called the Resource Manager understands this map and provides access to the resources in the file by name and number.

Every resource has a name, called its **type**, and a number, its **ID**, that the Resource Manager can use to get it. For example, if a program wants to display an icon that it has stored in a resource file, it does not have to know specifically where in the file the icon is stored; by knowing its type, which will probably be "ICON," and its ID number, the program can ask the Resource Manager to get the icon.

Several nice advantages that come along with the use of resources. Since just about all the standard data types used by the system are defined as resource types, you rarely have to know their format in order to use them. Another idea behind the creation of the Resource Manager is that it allows a program's logic to be separated from its data to a very high degree. This makes it a lot easier to translate an application to another language. For example, most applications have all their text—the words that show up in menus, dialogs, and windows—stored as resources. This means that a person who is not a programmer can use a resource editing tool to translate the text to the new language—no recompiling (or source code) is needed. The same person can continue using the resource editor to resize windows and dialog boxes as necessary to accommodate the new text, which may be shorter or longer.

Another interesting feature of the Resource Manager is that it provides a degree of virtual memory. A single Resource Manager call, GetResource, will first check to see if the desired resource is already in memory. If so, the call returns, simply telling the caller where in memory to find the resource; if not, the Resource Manager tries to load the resource from disk. If necessary, previously loaded resources may be unloaded from memory, making room for the new one. This means that simply using the GetResource call will automatically take advantage of larger-memory systems without changing any of your code.

There are some disadvantages to using resources. Because they're indexed, using resources is slower than using the data fork. Also, because there are so many of them and because they're so easy to summon with a GetResource call, Macintosh applications on a single-drive machine often require lots of disk swaps as the system goes back and forth between disks, reading one or two resources at a time. In fact, disk swapping, that painful shuffling between disks, is probably the leading cause of high blood pressure among Macintosh users (especially those with only one disk drive). In Chapter 8, we'll discuss some ways that you can limit disk swapping.

Why a Fork?

Many Macintosh applications put their information in resource forks. You'll find very few files that have more information in the data fork than the resource fork. If this is the case, why does the data fork exist at all? Why doesn't the Macintosh simply support resource forks? The main reason is that, as noted previously, resources require some overhead to decode resource maps, which translates into slower disk access. So the data fork is provided as a way of storing raw data that the program interprets directly.

Building Our Application

Let's say we've completed compiling and linking our application, and we've just figured out that we need to create a resource file as output. Now that we've discussed what resources are and how they fit into a resource file, it's time to figure out the relationship between a resource file and an application program on disk.

Actually, that relationship is very simple: an application is a Macintosh file, and every Macintosh file has a resource fork and a data fork (as we just discussed). What goes where, and how does it get there?

The real meat of the application, the compiled code that you've carefully crafted, goes into the resource fork. It consists of resources of type CODE (case is significant in resource types; it's CODE, not code or Code). These CODE resources are generated automatically by most development systems. For example, in Lisa Pascal, you can use the $SEG compiler directive to split your program up into separately loadable segments. When you pass the program through the Compiler and Linker, you'll get one CODE resource for each segment that you declared in your program.

Every application has at least two CODE resources in its resource fork. One of them, the CODE resource with ID 1, is a special segment called the **main segment** or **blank segment**. This segment is loaded when the application starts up and stays put until the application quits. It's used as a sort of anchor for the rest of the application's resources, which can be loaded, moved, unloaded, and reloaded as the application runs. Most development systems create CODE 1 out of whatever part of your application hasn't been directed into a specific segment. If you specify no segmentation at all, your whole program will become CODE 1. That's all right for small applications, but you'll have to segment to get the best use of the Macintosh's memory for most applications.

The other required, special CODE resource has an ID of 0. This resource actually isn't part of your program at all, but is a special table of information that is loaded into memory when your application is started. It includes information like the amount of memory that all your global variables require. We'll discuss this resource a lot more later.

These two special resources (CODE 0 and CODE 1), as well as other CODE resources, are usually generated automatically from your source code by whatever development system you're using, so you normally won't have to worry about creating them yourself. Again, most development systems use some sort of segmentation command (like $SEG in Lisa Pascal) to tell the compiler to start making a new, separately loadable, CODE resource.

An application must contain at least a CODE 0 and a CODE 1 or it will generate a system error 26 (the familiar bomb box) when it's started, but most applications have a lot more resources. Most applications have menus and store them in MENU resources; most have windows whose layout is kept in WIND resources; most have dialogs and keep the dialog information in a DLOG resource, with the dialog's item list (the things displayed in the dialog) kept in a DITL, and most have many more resources. The Finder, for example, has 12 different resource types and 32 different resources; Microsoft Word has 16 different types and 162 different resources! How are these resources created?

There are two fundamental types of resource creation tools: resource compilers and resource editors. Resource compilers work a lot like other compilers do: they take a textual, symbolic representation and produce a translated, machine-usable output file. In Figure 1-4 you'll see a sample section of input to a resource compiler such as the one supplied with Apple's 68000 Development System. This fragment describes a dialog item list (type DITL).

Resource compilers have one major drawback: they're textual representations of mostly graphical objects. Why should items be positioned by specifying coordinates? Why shouldn't we be able to see the dialog on the screen as it will appear and drag the items around with the mouse to their proper place?

These questions become even more acute when you consider that one of the promises of resources was that the separation of code from data would allow a nontechnical person to translate software from one (human) language to another. A translator who has to use a resource compiler must learn a significant amount about the Macintosh and its resources. If, on the other hand, a graphically oriented resource editor were used, the translator could get along with a lot less mucking around

Figure 1-4 Resource compiler input

```
Type DITL
, 1000
2
Button
50 220 70 300
OK
Button
90 220 110 300
Cancel
StaticText
20 200 40 300
Do you really want to?
```

in the system's internal details. Instead, the translator could enlarge a window by dragging its size box or translate a button's text by clicking on the button and typing.

The concept of a resource editor was developed early in the Macintosh's life, but creating the program itself proved to be an unimagined challenge. A resource editor is a meta-tool, since it must run in a system that is mostly composed of resources. Apple now offers a resource editor that allows you, through a painstakingly thought-out user interface, to create and modify resources that your application will use. In Figure 1-5 you can see the resource editor's version of building a dialog item list. You see the dialog as it will appear in "real life." You move items by dragging them. You change text by clicking on it and then typing. What a concept!

There is one nice advantage to resource compilers. They allow you to specify a "script", a human-readable, printable source file that can be used to re-create the resource file at any time. If you use a resource editor to create your resources, the only form you get is the "object code"—the resource file itself. If you ever lose your only copy, there's no automated way to rebuild.

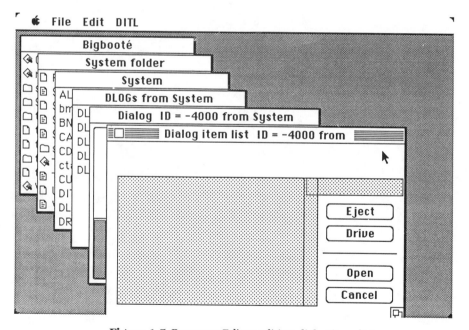

Figure 1-5 Resource Editor editing dialog item list

Fortunately, this problem is solved by a second-generation version of a resource compiler: a resource compiler/decompiler. This program can take a resource file as input and produce a text representation as output. This text representation can be printed out, put in a binder alongside your program source code, and stored in a fireproof safe to save you from disaster. As a final touch, the resource compiler/decompiler can recompile the source listing it created and produce a resource file.

So a good technique for creating a resource file is this:

1. Use the resource editor to create your MENUs, WINDs, DLOGs, and so on.

2. Use the decompiler to produce a text source.

3. As development progresses, use the resource editor to make changes and then the decompiler to make a source listing; or use a text editor to modify the source listing and use the resource compiler to produce a resource file. Figure 1-6 shows this process.

With this array of resource editing tools at your fingertips, you're way ahead of early Macintosh developers, who had nothing but a resource compiler to help their resource creativity. Three cheers for progress!

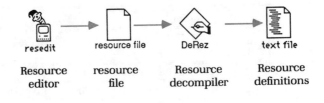

| resedit | resource file | DeRez | text file |
| Resource editor | resource file | Resource decompiler | Resource definitions |

or

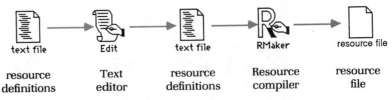

| text file | Edit | text file | RMaker | resource file |
| resource definitions | Text editor | resource definitions | Resource compiler | resource file |

Figure 1-6 Resource file development

Other Kinds of Programs

Applications are the programs most people write most of the time, but there are other kinds of programs running around inside a Macintosh. Like most other computers, the Macintosh uses **device drivers**, programs that understand how to talk to various built-in or plugged-in devices like disk drives, modems, and digitizers. But the Macintosh system also uses many other kinds of programs to do various tasks.

One special kind of Macintosh program is the **desk accessory**, which is a program that coexists with applications. The things you see in the Apple menu, like the Alarm Clock, Control Panel, and Calculator, are desk accessories. These programs must be written in a well-defined format and must follow certain rules of behavior, since they're around while application programs are running the show.

Another, less visible kind of program is the **definition function**. A definition function is a program that describes the behavior and appearance of a menu, control, or window. For example, the standard menu definition function draws menus that have one line of text per item, with options such as a checkmark to the left of the item, various text styles such as bold and italic, command key equivalents to the right of the item, and more. The Toolbox allows you to write your own definition procedures to customize the appearance of menus, controls, and windows while still taking advantage of the Toolbox structures. Again, the format of these definition functions is strictly defined.

There are additional pieces of system software called **packages** which didn't fit into the 64K ROM; for example, the Disk Initialization Package. These packages also consist of programs in a carefully defined format.

Macintosh Plus

The Macintosh Plus ROM includes some of the packages that were loaded into RAM on earlier systems. To maintain compatibility with existing software, they're still packages, even though they're now in ROM.

As you may have guessed, all these "alternative" kinds of programs are stored as resources. Device drivers and desk accessories are DRVR resources; menu, control, and window definition functions are MDEF, CDEF, and WDEF resources; packages are resources of type PACK. There are other kinds of resources that contain code; these are just a few.

If you want to write one of these special kinds of resources, you have to know how to generate the special formats required. Sometimes the way to do that isn't obvious, especially with high-level languages. One of the topics we'll play with in Chapter 9 is the creation of some of these kinds of resources with high-level languages.

Power Tools

Now that we've discussed the fundamentals of what tools are needed to do which jobs in Macintosh software development, let's take a brief look at some of the specific development systems and utilities that are available.

Looking Ahead

Computer software is an evolving thing, especially Macintosh software. Scheduling software is an arcane art, especially Macintosh software. Some of the software mentioned in this book is under development as this book is being written. Shipment dates can only be guessed at. Anything you see with the crystal ball icon is under development, but hasn't shipped yet.

Macintosh Software Supplement

When Apple first shipped the Macintosh in January 1984, the only way to develop Macintosh software was by using the Lisa Workshop system. The Lisa Workshop package did not contain the complete set of tools necessary to do Macintosh development. The off-the-shelf Workshop consisted of a Pascal compiler, a linker, an assembler, and various miscellaneous tools. But the libraries that provided access to the Macintosh ROM, a resource compiler, the program for sending the Lisa output to a Macintosh-formatted disk, the assembly language equates for Macintosh, and other tools, were not packaged with the Workshop. Instead, they were bundled into a separate package called the Macintosh Software Supplement. The original idea of the Software Supplement was that it was to contain everything necessary to complement the Lisa Workshop for the developer interested in writing Macintosh software.

Since the tools were still changing and evolving, the Software Supplement was sold on a subscription basis. Every couple of months, Apple would send out an update that contained several disks jam-packed full of tools, libraries, equates, examples, debuggers, and whatever other useful things could be gathered. Each release of the Supplement grew larger and added more tools and goodies: resource editors, new debuggers, new examples, new versions of the Pascal compiler.

As more and more native-Macintosh development systems began to appear, the Supplement began to contain more Macintosh-usable things. In early 1985, all the Supplement's text files were moved to Macintosh disks so that all Supplement purchasers could read them. By this time, the Supplement not only fulfilled its original purpose of allowing Lisa Workshop users to write Macintosh software, but also contained enough Macintosh-based tools to be valuable to all developers.

Apple has continued to issue the Software Supplement to keep programmers up to date with changes, such as the Hierarchical File System and the Macintosh Plus. This wealth of tools is vital to anyone writing Macintosh software. In Figure 1-7 you'll find a partial list of what comes with this Supplement.

Since the Supplement was updated so frequently in the past, it has never been made available through normal retail channels. You can order the Software Supplement by contacting Apple (see the "About this book.." section to find out how to do that).

Figure 1-7 Some software supplement pieces

Item	Description
Pascal libraries	Gives Pascal programs access to ROM
Equates files	Globals & ROM Calls for assembly language programs
ResEdit	Resource editor
Localizer	Configures system for different countries
Example	Sample program
Fedit	File editing utility
Macsbug	Object-code debugger
Macintalk	Software-only speech synthesizer

Inside Macintosh

Apple's comprehensive technical reference for Macintosh programmers is called **Inside Macintosh**. This manual has evolved through three different forms. Originally, beginning with Macintosh's announcement in January 1984, **Inside Macintosh** was a set of loose-leaf binders containing separate manuals for each part of the Operating System and Toolbox. As a chapter was completed or revised, it was sent to subscribers. This form of **Inside Macintosh** continued until March 1985, when Apple published the Promotional Edition of **Inside Macintosh**. This version, which resembles a telephone directory (and is nicknamed the "phone book edition"), was sold from March through December 1985. Finally, in January 1986, the "real" **Inside Macintosh** was published by Addison-Wesley Publishing Company in two versions, a three-volume softbound and a single-volume hardbound. The softbound and hardbound versions are identical in content.

The amount of work that went into producing **Inside Macintosh** was incredible. Writing the manuscript took over three years. Each chapter went through countless drafts and reviews as the book's team, led by Caroline Rose, pushed to document the complex Macintosh system definitively and accurately. In many ways, the creation of **Inside Macintosh** was as remarkable a technical achievement as the Macintosh itself. You'll find that there's no substitute for it when writing Macintosh software.

Macintosh Plus

Inside Macintosh covers the 64K ROM, not the Macintosh Plus's 128K ROM. For availability of information covering the Macintosh Plus, write to Apple.

Macintosh 68000 Development System

This package consists of a text editor, an assembler, a linker, a resource compiler, an executive processor, and a set of debuggers. It was the first native-Macintosh development environment available from Apple.

This system, called MDS for short, allows you to create multi-segment applications, desk accessories, definition procedures, or any other code you want. Resources can be generated directly from the linker or by the resource compiler. Since the resource compiler is somewhat limited, not supporting all standard Macintosh resource types, many users prefer the clumsy but more flexible method of specifying resources directly from the source. When you do it this way, your source file must specify each byte of each resource.

The MDS text editor, called Edit, has become the definitive text editor for programmers on Macintosh (that means it's the most common, not necessarily the most powerful). Several companies license this editor from Apple and ship it with their development systems. It allows up to four windows to be open at once and includes search-and-replace. Files are disk based; that is, they don't have to be small enough to fit completely in RAM.

Edit Tip

The original version of Edit doesn't respect the Hierarchical File System. Although it allows you to select files within folders, it won't open a file that is in a folder. You can get around this problem by using an undocumented feature of Edit. If you type <Command>-K, Edit enters a mode in which it will allow you to enter a file name, complete with colons to separate directory (folder) names. You won't see any echoing on the screen as you type the filename. When you're done with the filename, press Return, and Edit will load the file (if it's there). For example, to load a file named Joe in a folder named Stuff on a disk called Mine, you could type <Command>-KMine:Stuff:Joe. Not very pretty, but it makes things usable. By the way, the K in <Command>-K stands for kludge.

Looking Ahead

Macintosh Programmer's Workshop

The most significant missing link in Macintosh development tools is a set of high-level languages from Apple that run on the Macintosh itself. Apple intends to fill this gap with the Macintosh Programmer's Workshop, or MPW, which is scheduled for availability in late 1986. MPW is an environment that includes a Pascal compiler, a C compiler, and an assembler, as well as a linker and a command-scripting capability, plus miscellaneous tools. Most of the MPW tools run under a combination editor/shell program that allows the tools to run without leaving the editor.

The heart of the Pascal compiler was transplanted from the powerful Lisa Pascal compiler that developers have been using to create Macintosh software for years. It features almost total source code compatibility with Lisa Pascal. That means that you'll be able to recompile your Lisa Pascal programs with virtually no changes under the MPW Pascal compiler.

What does "virtually no changes" mean? All the Pascal example programs in the Software Supplement have been compiled successfully under a prerelease version of MPW Pascal by changing nothing but the Uses statements.

The C compiler is also a port of the Lisa Workshop tool. Since the Lisa C compiler is much newer than its Pascal counterpart, there isn't a large body of Lisa C programs, but there should be a high degree of compatibility between the Lisa and Macintosh versions.

The MPW assembler is all-new, and it's very powerful. Among its features are powerful data typing instructions that allow the use of records and fields within records. The MPW assembler is not source compatible with the Lisa Workshop assembler or the MDS assembler, but there is a utility program supplied that will convert most Lisa and MDS assembler files to MPW format.

Third-party Tools and Languages

One of Apple's wisest strategic decisions about Macintosh was to encourage third-party (that is, non-Apple) development of software and hardware add-ons. There has always been a sizable group at Apple that provides help to developers. This includes a team of "evangelists" who help developers get going and seed prototype equipment, a marketing group to assist companies in advertising and promotion, a friendly general order entry and administration group, a languages group, and an insanely great technical support team.

One pleasant result of this program is that many companies have taken up the slack in the area of Macintosh-based development systems. As we said earlier, there are now over 30 different development systems available for Macintosh. Included in this list, which you'll find in Figure 1-8, are some of the most novel and innovative tools available for any personal computer. For example, Neon, from Kriya Systems, is based on Forth, but includes extensions for creating object-oriented programs.

Figure 1-8 Macintosh system software

Company	Product
Absoft	Resource file builder
Acuity Computer	Alternative Finder
ALSoft, Inc.	Pascal Toolbox libraries
Avenue Software, Inc.	Prolog II
B/T Computing Corp.	HeapShow
Catalytix	Safe C Family
C Ware Corporation	DeSmet C
Creative Solutions, Inc.	MacForth
Consulair Corporation	Mac C
DCM Data Products	FORTRAN 77
Expertelligence	ExperLogo, ExperLisp, ExperOPS5
Faircom	C-Tree
Hippopotamus	Hippo-C
ICOM Simulations	TMON debugger
Kriya Systems, Inc.	Neon
Living Software	Living C
Magreeable Software	B-Tree Helper
Mainstay	MacAsm assembler
Manx Software Systems	Aztec C
Megamax, Inc.	Megamax C
Metaresearch, Inc.	Rascal
MicroFocus, Inc.	MacCobol
Micromotion	MasterForth
Microsoft	BASIC, Logo, FORTRAN
Modula Corporation	Modula-2
Portable Software	PortaAPL
Pterodactyl Software	BASIC compiler
Softworks, Ltd.	C Compiler
Step-Lively Software	OnStage Pascal compiler
Signature Software	McAssembly
TML Systems	Pascal compiler

MacApp

MacApp is a project of Apple's Advanced Development Group. It's a logical outgrowth of work done on the Lisa Toolkit, which was a package based on an object-oriented extension of Pascal called Clascal. The Macintosh version is called Object Pascal, but the idea remains the same: since all Macintosh applications follow the same basic rules of user interface (i.e., drag a window by its title bar, scroll things with scroll bars, etc.), all an application programmer should have to do is implement what's unique or nonstandard about the application.

When using MacApp, the basic structure and behavior of the user interface is already taken care of. This minimal application that knows all the standard behavior is called the **generic application**. The programmer must implement code that handles the special features of the program; in other words, MacApp knows that it should resize a window when the user drags the size box, so the application doesn't even have to know that this event occurred if it doesn't want to. However, since MacApp doesn't know what the application is supposed to draw in its windows, the programmer must write the code for drawing its unique views.

Smalltalk

Another project coming out of the Advanced Development Group at Apple is a Macintosh implementation of Smalltalk, the language/environment developed at Xerox Palo Alto Research Center. Although Smalltalk is not available through retail channels you can find out about getting it by contacting Apple.

Since so much software is being developed for Macintosh, you really have to keep on top of the industry to catch the new stuff. If you have a great computer store or software shop in your area, drop in frequently. You can also keep up with what's being developed by reading some of the more technical magazines, journals, user group newsletters, and on-line services that cover Macintosh and the rest of the industry.

Things to Remember

- Macintosh programming involves learning new ways of doing things, since the Macintosh user-interface concepts are so different from conventional computers.
- Much of the Macintosh's personality is defined by its ROM, which contains the Operating System and the User Interface Toolbox.
- Resources are entities that can be referred to by type and ID, in memory or in files. Many pieces of Macintosh data are resources.
- Every Macintosh application must have at least CODE resources 0 and 1.
- There are dozens of languages and tools available for writing Macintosh software.

CHAPTER

2

Things in Memory

In this chapter we'll discuss things that live in the Macintosh's memory and how they behave. If you're new to Macintosh programming, this information will help you get off on the right foot. If you've been programming the Macintosh for a while, you may find that you know some of this stuff, but not all of it, and the new information will be very useful for you, too.

Fables

In Chapter 1 we talked about the funny feeling you get when you realize that, from a programmer's point of view, just about everything on a Macintosh seems to be unlike other computers. As you progress, you begin to discover how to get things done, but you may not truly learn how and why certain things happen on a Macintosh. Eventually, this gap of knowledge rises up like a monster and bites you on the nose, stopping a project cold for hours or even days until you figure out what's going on.

These knowledge gaps have led to the existence of several popular Macintosh Programming Fables, which are stories handed down from generation to generation of Macintosh programmers, and which have in common the fact that they're absolutely false and will eventually mess up the unsuspecting programmer. One of the jobs of this book is to expose these fables.

The most popular Macintosh Programming Fable is undoubtedly the Story of the RAM That Ran Away. The story says that the Memory Manager in the Macintosh's operating system is always moving things around, like an insane electronic version of musical chairs, and that as soon as you put something somewhere in Macintosh RAM, it's not there any more. This means that you'd better take extraordinary measures to keep track of your variables, and that anything that goes wrong with your program can be blamed on something that simply "floated away" from where it belongs.

Well, it just ain't so. As with all fables, this one is based on a grain of truth and then blown completely out of proportion. The grain of truth is that the Macintosh's Memory Manager supports **relocatable blocks**, which are objects in memory that can move around *at certain well-defined times.* Unfortunately, the "well-defined" part is usually forgotten, and so a legend is born. In this chapter we'll discuss exactly what kinds of things can move in memory, exactly when they can and cannot move, and how to live with all of it.

The second most popular fable is the Tale of the Macintosh That Went to Lunch. This one says that when your program makes your Macintosh put up a system error box, or when it does something even weirder, like flashing the screen, making machine-gun sounds, or even rebooting the system, your program has gone haywire, the Macintosh went nuts, it all just sort of happened at random, and you'll never, ever find out what happened. Not true! All these happenings are distinct signals from your Macintosh as it cries out for help.

In this chapter and others we'll discuss exactly what's going on when these things happen and what you can do about them.

That Amazing Moving Memory

Everybody loves memory maps, especially old-timers. Just show 'em a memory map and they'll figure out the rest. If you like memory maps, you'll be glad to know that we've got one to help you through this discussion. The memory map, which you can see in Figure 2-1, is incredibly oversimplified, but it's a good starting point. It divides the Macintosh's RAM into five main sections:

> **System globals** area
>
> **Video/sound buffer**
>
> **System heap**
>
> **Application heap**
>
> **Stack**

The lowest part of memory, from locations 0 through $AFF (or 0 through 2815 decimal) belongs to the system. This area, called the system globals, is filled with variables that are used by various parts of the system, and you can use them too. The kinds of things that are stored in this part of memory are the pattern with which the desktop is painted (called DeskPattern), the menu ID of the currently highlighted menu

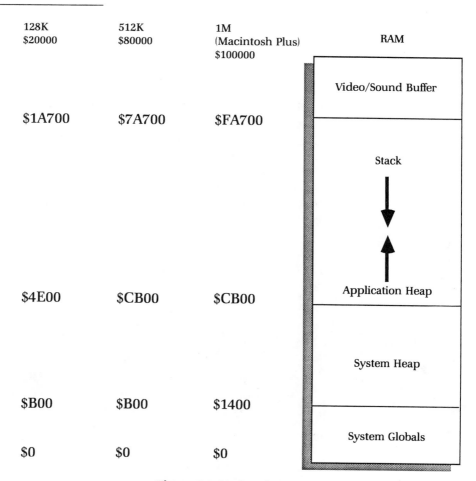

128K $20000	512K $80000	1M (Macintosh Plus) $100000	RAM
			Video/Sound Buffer
$1A700	$7A700	$FA700	
			Stack
			↓
			↑
$4E00	$CB00	$CB00	Application Heap
			System Heap
$B00	$B00	$1400	
			System Globals
$0	$0	$0	

Figure 2-1 Macintosh memory map

(TheMenu), and the name of the current application (CurApName). The information kept in the system globals area is vital, and virtually all applications will have to use it at some point.

At the top of memory is the RAM that's mapped to the screen, as well as RAM that's used for sound. Most applications never deal directly with this part of memory. In general, they draw on the screen by using QuickDraw calls, and they make sounds by using the built-in sound driver. Notice that the screen stays at the top of RAM whether you have 128K, 512K, or more. This is done to make sure that the memory that's used by programs, the application heap and the stack, is in one contiguous chunk and not split up by the video/sound area.

The next important section of RAM is the system heap, which contains objects that are used mainly by the Operating System. Unlike the system globals area, which contains mostly small variables used by the Toolbox and Operating System, the system heap contains larger data structures, such as information about open files. System heap structures are allocated dynamically as things happen in the system; for example, the system heap contains a data structure called a Volume Control Block (VCB) for every disk volume that's currently mounted by the system. If you insert a new disk, a new VCB is allocated in the system heap and filled in by the operating system.

Another difference between the system globals area and the system heap is that your application will rarely, if ever, get any information directly from the system heap.

The last two pieces of RAM are called the application heap and the stack. These are the areas that are mostly reserved for use by your application. You'll notice that the vast majority of RAM is dedicated to this purpose: over 460K on a 512K RAM system, for example.

Macintosh Plus

Notice that on the Macintosh Plus, the system globals area is larger, extending up to $13FF, with the system heap beginning at $1400. The system heap still ends at $CAFF.

The stack usually holds static variables. For example, when you declare a variable in Pascal like this:

```
VAR myResult : CHAR;
```

or like this in a C program:

```
char myResult;
```

your variable myResult will be stored on the stack. Most languages allocate stack variables in the order that they're encountered. Global variables stick around for the duration of the program. Variables that are local to a procedure or function are placed on the stack when the function starts, manipulated while the function is running, then thrown away by cutting back (shrinking) the stack when the function ends.

The final area of memory shown in Figure 2-1 is the application heap. This chunk of memory holds virtually everything used by your application except its variables, which are kept on the stack, as noted previously. Among the things kept in the application heap are all your application's resources as they're loaded into memory. Remember that an application's resources include things like MENUs, DLOGs, ICONs, and even the application's code itself (resources of type CODE).

Along with resources, the application heap holds all the objects that you create in your application when you call NewHandle or NewPtr to request memory from the Memory Manager. In fact, that's why you'll find your resources in the application heap: before a resource is loaded into memory, the Resource Manager gets a chunk of memory for it by calling NewHandle. Lots of ROM routines call NewHandle or NewPtr to get space for things in the heap, and objects created with NewHandle or NewPtr are always located in the heap.

Different Heaps

Some resources get loaded into the system heap, and sometimes NewHandle and NewPtr are used to reserve memory in the system heap. In the case of the Memory Manager calls, there's a special flavor of NewHandle and NewPtr that causes the new block to be allocated in the system heap. In addition, resources have an attribute that you can set that causes them to be loaded into the system heap instead of the application heap. Putting things in the system heap is a way to keep them around between applications, since both the stack and the application heap's contents are reinitialized when a new application starts up, but because of limited free space in the system heap, that's not a good idea. You can learn more about this subject in the "Keeping Things Around between Applications" section of Chapter 10.

Allocating Memory

As your program runs and as new things are allocated in memory, the stack and the application heap expand, as suggested by the ominous looking arrows in Figure 2-1. We've learned that the application heap holds blocks that are created with the Memory Manager calls NewHandle and NewPtr, while the stack holds a language's declared variables. How do the stack and heap allocation processes work?

First, it's important to realize the fundamental differences in creating new objects in the stack and the application heap. When a new stack object is created, usually with a variable declaration in a high-level language (as noted previously), the object is placed on the **top of the stack**. As new things are added, the size of the stack simply increases by the size of the new object. When another new object is added, it's added to the new top of the stack. The system maintains a pointer to the top of the stack called, cleverly enough, the **stack pointer**.

When an object is removed from the stack, the size of the stack is reduced and the stack pointer is adjusted to point to the top of the new, smaller stack. This kind of operation is called a **last in, first out** or **LIFO** stack; in other words, the last thing "in" (added to the stack) will be the first thing "out" (removed from the stack). This operation is pictured in Figure 2-2.

This kind of operation tells us several things about using the stack. First, it's obvious that the stack is a good place for allocating a few things at a time, using them for a while, then removing them all at once. In fact, that's exactly what you do in a high-level language when you call a procedure or function. When that function is called, it must allocate space for its local variables all at once; when it's finished, it must deallocate that space, again all at once.

High-level languages also use the stack as a place to pass parameters to routines. When you call a procedure or function, its parameters are pushed on the stack and then the routine is called. The routine can then access the parameters by looking back on the stack.

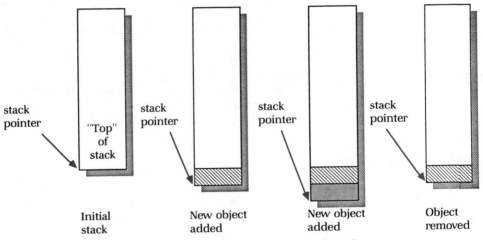

| stack pointer | "Top" of stack | stack pointer | | stack pointer | | stack pointer | |
| Initial stack | | New object added | | New object added | | Object removed | |

Figure 2-2 How a LIFO stack works

Heaps

Stacks and high-level languages were made for each other, and most procedure-oriented languages use the Macintosh stack for these purposes (among others). This is a pretty conventional use of a stack in a personal computer.

On the Macintosh, however, you also need another kind of memory allocation. Since you have an environment in which little pieces of stuff (usually resources) are constantly being loaded into memory, used, then tossed away, and since these little pieces, unlike local variables, don't necessarily correspond to a particular part of the application and often have to be loaded one-at-a-time, another way of doing things is in order, and that's where the idea of the heap comes along.

In a Macintosh heap, objects are not necessarily allocated in a neat, linear fashion as they are in the stack. Instead, the Memory Manager will attempt to put a new object wherever it has room in the heap, following certain rules of preference as to where the application would *like* the new object to go, but putting it elsewhere if it has to.

This flexibility is why the heap is the place for resources, which load into memory, then may go away, and may come back later. It's also the place for **dynamically allocated** data structures that belong to the application. For example, if your application keeps a database of information and doesn't know at runtime how many records it will need, it can allocate space for a new record in the heap whenever necessary by making a NewHandle call.

Objects in a heap may be scattered around, possibly with unused space between two heap blocks. Each block, though, must consist of consecutive bytes. You can't have a single heap block that is in pieces; all of its bytes must be together.

Heaps in Pascal

If you've used Pascal compilers on other systems, especially UCSD Pascal, you may be familiar with the term heap as an area in memory from which space can be dynamically allocated. However, the Macintosh concept of a heap is only loosely based on this idea. To avoid confusion, you should assume that a Macintosh heap behaves in a completely different way than the "other" kind of heap. Also, a terminology reminder: Macintosh heaps are also called **heap zones**. Heap = heap zone.

If you think a bit about the job a heap has to do, you can come up with some more requirements for its capabilities. For example, we've said that new objects will be loading into the heap all the time, and that old, unneeded ones may be removed if their space is needed. Let's say that we want to create three objects in memory (by calling NewHandle). We'll call them Alan, Bryan, and Cary (see Figure 2-3). Then we'll throw away (by calling DisposHandle) Bryan when we're done with him, and allocate a new, fourth object, called Donn. We're left with a gap between Alan and Cary, and if the new object is larger than the gap, the Memory Manager would have to put it after Cary, leaving an unused (and potentially unusable) space in the heap: if we never request a space smaller than or equal to the size of the gap, that space will be wasted.

If this process continues throughout the execution of the program, we could wind up with free space in little chunks all over the heap. We could have 100K bytes free, yet not be able to allocate a 10K byte object if we didn't have 10K of *consecutive* bytes free (see Figure 2-4 for a look at this situation). How can we avoid this?

Well, since the Macintosh Memory Manager was designed for just such a busy-memory system, in which new objects are constantly being created and old ones released, it includes the all-important capability of maintaining relocatable objects in a heap zone, as we mentioned earlier

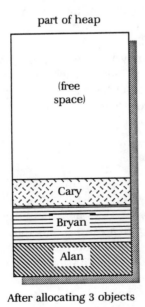

After allocating 3 objects

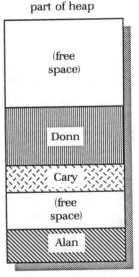

After deallocating Bryan, then allocating Donn

Figure 2-3 Allocation of objects

Heap

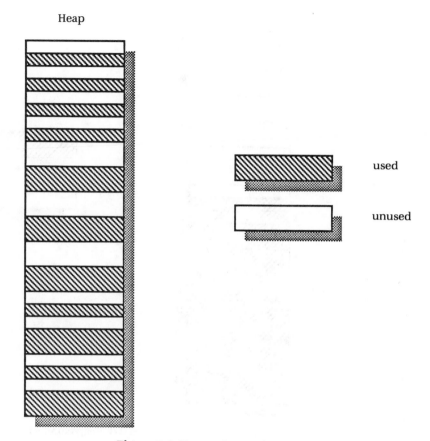

Figure 2-4 Noncontiguous free space

in this chapter. When you request some memory with the NewHandle call, the memory block that's created for you in the heap is relocatable. This allows the Memory Manager, *at well-defined times* (there's that phrase again), to move the object from one location to another within the heap. This means that we can revisit the poor, muddled heap last seen in Figure 2-4 and request our 10K block again. But as we now know (Figure 2-5), the blocks are relocatable, so the Memory Manager can put all the free space together, fulfilling our memory request.

Can you think of any obvious disadvantages in having relocatable blocks? Can you say "dangling pointer"? Sure you can, and if you're gonna go sliding things around in memory, you'd better have a pretty good way of keeping track of just where everything is and, while you're at it, letting the application know, too.

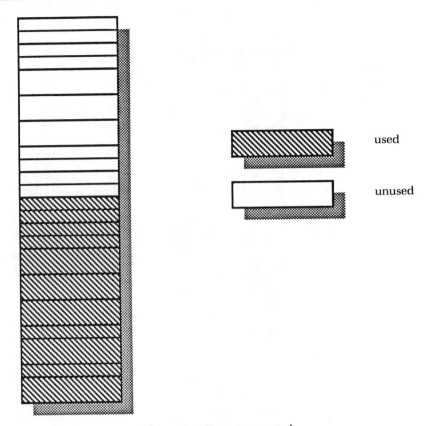

Figure 2-5 Heap compacted

The way the Macintosh Memory Manager keeps track of relocatable blocks is by creating one special pointer to each block. This pointer never moves; it's part of a nonrelocatable object in the heap. This pointer is called the **master pointer** for that block. When the Memory Manager moves the block, it changes the master pointer to indicate the block's new position.

When you call NewHandle to request a new relocatable block, the Memory Manager allocates the new block, sets up a master pointer for it, and then returns to you the address of the master pointer as NewHandle's function result. This address of the master pointer is called a **handle**. Since the Memory Manager will always keep the master pointer valid, and since the master pointer never moves in memory, the handle always provides a valid way to access the contents of the block, so no matter where it goes, there you are (see Figure 2-6, buckaroo).

In a high-level language, you can use a handle to get to an object by **double-dereferencing** it. In Pascal, it looks like this:

```
MyHandle^^
```

In C, you could write this:

```
(**MyHandle)
```

Translating from programming languages to English, these statements say that MyHandle is "a pointer to a pointer to some data," but to truly appreciate what's going on, be sure you remember that there's:

- A block in the heap that can be relocated
- A master pointer to that block, kept up to date by the Memory Manager
- A handle (MyHandle) that points to that master pointer

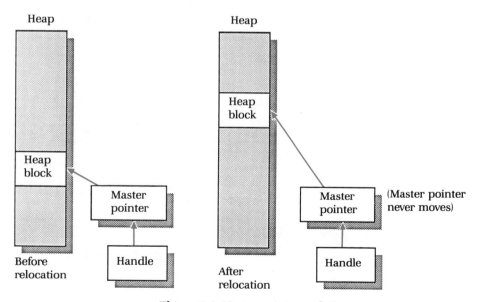

Figure 2-6 Master pointer updating

Because MyHandle holds the address of the master pointer, and the master pointer is updated by the Memory Manager whenever it moves the block, MyHandle is always good for finding the memory block. You can see an example of how this works in Figure 2-7.

What's Where?

When you allocate a new relocatable heap object, you call NewHandle, and NewHandle returns a handle as a function result. You usually wind up writing a line of code that looks like this:

```
myHandle := NewHandle (someSize);
```

Just like all objects created with NewHandle, this block is allocated in the heap. However, myHandle is a variable declared by the program, so it's on the stack. Can this be right? Sure. The variable myHandle is just a pointer to the block's master pointer, remember. So, myHandle, a variable on the stack, contains the address of a master pointer, which is in the heap; the master pointer contains the address of the relocatable block we just allocated. There's a picture of this relationship in Figure 2-8.

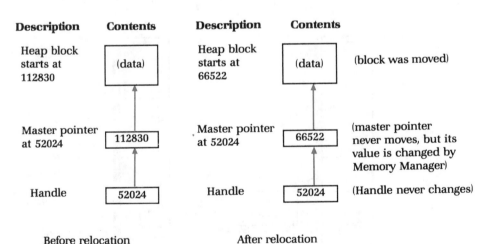

Description	Contents	Description	Contents	
Heap block starts at 112830	(data)	Heap block starts at 66522	(data)	(block was moved)
Master pointer at 52024	112830	Master pointer at 52024	66522	(master pointer never moves, but its value is changed by Memory Manager)
Handle	52024	Handle	52024	(Handle never changes)

Before relocation After relocation

Figure 2-7 How handles work

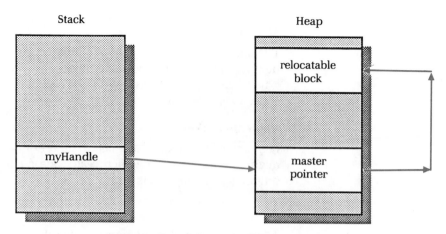

Figure 2-8 Handle on stack, object in heap

Not all the objects allocated in heaps are relocatable. In fact, when you call NewPtr, the object that's created is **nonrelocatable**. These objects are allocated and then sit there without budging until the application ends or until the application calls DisposPtr on them, whichever comes first. Since nonrelocatable objects never move, there's no master pointer for the Memory Manager to update, and no handle. When you create a new nonrelocatable object with NewPtr, you get a pointer to the object that remains valid until you dispose of the object (if you ever do).

In general, nonrelocatable objects are bad news and should be avoided for your data structures. The reason is that nonrelocatable objects are poisonous to a heap: they can reduce your available heap space by driving a stake down the middle of your precious free space. Remember that the Memory Manager can only allocate an object with consecutive bytes. If the free space in the heap becomes fragmented, as it did in Figure 2-4, you wind up with lots of free memory that's virtually useless. So, when you need to create a new object in the heap for a dynamic data structure, like a database record, make it a relocatable block by calling NewHandle, and you'll help to keep your heap nice and unfragmented.

For an in-depth discussion of using relocatable objects with random-access file I/O, see the "Random Access File I/O" section of chapter 10.

Allocation Algorithms

The Memory Manager is actually pretty smart about where it places newly allocated nonrelocatable objects. It will try very hard to put a new nonrelocatable as low in the heap as possible so as not to cause fragmentation.

Heap Allocation

Remember that a stack is a last in, first out or LIFO structure. You might say that a heap, which really doesn't maintain any kind of ordering of its objects, is a LIOF object: last in, okay, fine.

Sometimes you'll need to guarantee that an object in memory not move over some period of time. You want to be a good person and make it a relocatable object, but during some critical portion of your program, for any of several reasons (which we'll discuss later in this chapter), you have to be sure that the object stays put and is not relocated. The Memory Manager provides the flexibility for doing this by allowing you to temporarily **lock** a relocatable object. You can do this by calling the Memory Manager function HLock. Locking an object prevents it from being relocated.

You don't want to go around blindly locking objects, though, since a locked relocatable is just as immobile as a nonrelocatable. As soon as the object doesn't have to be locked down any longer, you should unlock it by calling HUnlock. This will allow it to resume being relocatable, should the Memory Manager need to move it.

Purging

Many of the relocatable objects in the heap are resources that have been loaded from disk, so the Memory Manager employs another trick to maximize the use of the space in the heap. Relocatable objects can be made **purgeable**. This means that the Memory Manager can throw them away if it needs the space. Typically, many resources are made purgeable.

At first thought, this sounds disastrous: it's not bad enough that things are getting moved around, but now they're being completely thrown away! Purged resources are usually not a problem. By using the Resource Manager call GetResource, you can ensure that a resource is actually in memory before attempting to use it (always a good idea). If the resource is already in memory, the GetResource call will simply return its handle; if not, it will be loaded. This is a very low overhead way to make sure that the resource is in memory before you use it.

Also, note that just making an object purgeable does not necessarily mean that it will be purged. It will only be purged if its space is needed for some other object that has to be loaded or created. You might say that when an object is marked purgeable it isn't immediately thrown away, but it does get sent to purgeatory.

Check That Error

When you call GetResource, the Resource Manager will return a handle to the resource, whether it's already in memory or has to be loaded from disk. If it can't find the resource at all, it'll return Nil (a handle whose value is zero) as its function result. You should always check GetResource calls for this error.

Just as you can make an object temporarily immovable by calling HLock, you can also make an object **nonpurgeable**, that is, prevent the Memory Manager from purging it. You do this with the HNoPurge call. Of course, there's a corresponding HPurge call that makes an object purgeable.

What things can safely be made purgeable? Resources have **resource attributes** that provide some information about them, and one of these attributes tells whether the resource will be purgeable or nonpurgeable when it's loaded into memory. You can set this attribute with most of the resource compilers and resource editors available for Macintosh. In addition, you can override the resource attribute after loading the resource by using the HPurge and HNoPurge calls.

Most any resource can safely be made purgeable. Resources that you don't use often are the best candidates for being made purgeable. Be careful of MENU resources. The Menu Manager assumes that MENU resources are nonpurgeable, and if you make one purgeable, you'll probably get a system error very soon after the MENU is purged.

Macintosh Plus

The 128K ROM specifically looks for and detects purged MENUs and reports them as system error 84. If you get one of these, just making your MENUs nonpurgeable with the Resource Editor should fix the problem.

Figure 2-9 Kinds of objects in memory

kind of object	location	how created	comments
static variable	stack	application declared	never moves
nonrelocatable	heap	NewPtr call	never moves
relocatable	heap	NewHandle call	can move

In general, it's not a good idea to make anything purgeable that's not a resource. If you do, you're on your own about making sure that you do the right things before the object is blown away; you may be interested in reading about the Memory Manager's PurgeProc in **Inside Macintosh**.

We can now summarize (in Figure 2-9) the three basic memory objects that are used to hold data in memory: the stack object, the relocatable heap object, and the nonrelocatable heap object. By knowing that stack objects and nonrelocatables never move, you've taken the first step toward eliminating the paranoia that surrounds the Macintosh Memory Manager.

How Relocation Works

There are still several pieces of vital information that are necessary to completely understand what's happening in memory. We said (twice!) that relocation of objects only occurs at well-defined times, and now we'll define those times.

One simple statement defines the essence of when you can expect relocation to occur:

Fact

The Memory Manager only relocates objects when it's trying to find space to create a new object or enlarge an existing one.

That's it. In other words, the Memory Manager does not relocate objects just for the hell of it (really!). It relocates objects when it's trying to allocate memory, either to a new object (as with NewHandle and NewPtr) or to an existing object (with SetHandleSize or SetPtrSize).

Even when your application makes one of these calls, there's no guarantee that relocation of any objects will take place. In particular, when the Memory Manager allocates a new relocatable object, it's not very picky about where the new object goes, since the new object can be moved in the future anyway. If the Memory Manager finds a long enough run of consecutive free bytes anywhere in the heap, it will allocate the new object there.

The Memory Manager is considerably more picky about where it puts nonrelocatable blocks, however, as we mentioned earlier. It will go to great lengths to make sure that a new nonrelocatable object is placed as low in the heap as possible so that it won't fragment the heap. It gets real zealous, relocating or even purging objects, if necessary, to achieve that goal.

So now you know that the Memory Manager will never relocate anything unless it's trying to allocate some memory. In fact, there are only eight calls in the Memory Manager that can trigger a relocation, and most applications only use four of them: NewHandle, NewPtr, SetHandleSize, and SetPtrSize. They're all listed in Figure 2-10.

Let's discuss each of them. We've already mentioned NewHandle and NewPtr; they obviously allocate new objects. SetHandleSize and SetPtrSize are used to resize existing objects. If you use either of these calls to make an object larger, memory will be allocated. These are the only commonly used calls that can trigger relocation.

Figure 2-10 Memory Manager calls that can trigger heap compaction

Commonly used:	NewHandle
	NewPtr
	SetHandleSize*
	SetPtrSize*
Less common:	ReallocHandle
	MaxMem
	CompactMem
	ResrvMem

*only if the call attempts to make the object larger.

The other four calls are rarely used, and some of them are pretty obscure. One is ReallocHandle, which is used to allocate a new relocatable block with an existing handle. The final three calls all manipulate the heap in different ways and give statistics back: MaxMem reports the largest contiguous free space in the heap after relocating and purging; CompactMem returns the size of the largest contiguous free block after relocating only (no purging); and ResrvMem tries to create a space at the lowest place in the heap by purging and compacting.

Fake-Out

Now we've got a contradiction: we said that the only calls that could cause relocation were those that allocated memory, but the last three calls, MaxMem, CompactMem, and ResrvMem don't actually allocate any space—they just move things around. It's true that these calls don't really allocate any space, but they sort of "fool" the Memory Manager into thinking that some memory is about to be allocated in order to accomplish their tasks. In any case, they can cause relocation to occur, so they complete our list.

NewPtr calls ResrvMem

The action of ResrvMem may sound familiar to careful readers. It tries to open a space at the lowest point in the heap. That sounds exactly like the description we had for NewPtr. In fact, NewPtr calls ResrvMem in the ROM to open the space low in the heap before allocating the new object. You'll find a lot of this behavior in the ROM: routines call other routines all the time.

Once you know the calls that can cause relocation, you've taken another giant step toward understanding the Memory Manager. Unfortunately, just knowing these eight calls doesn't tell you everything. Since many of the ROM routines call other ROM routines, you can easily get an indirect call to one of the relocation-triggering routines. For example, GetResource may call NewHandle, potentially causing relocation; MoreMasters calls NewPtr, which may cause relocation. Luckily, **Inside Macintosh** includes an appendix that lists all the routines that might call the relocation-triggering Memory Manager routines.

There's one other common situation in which the Memory Manager can relocate objects in the heap. It happens when your application calls a routine that is in another segment, like this fragment:

```
...
case myEvent.what of
  inMenuBar: DoCommand (MenuSelect (myEvent.where));
...
```

If DoCommand is in another segment, this call will cause that segment (a CODE resource, remember) to be loaded into memory. If there's not enough contiguous free memory in the heap for the segment, guess what happens. Of course, relocation of objects can take place. So you must add intersegment calls to the list of things that can cause relocation.

Actually, this relocation trigger fits right in with our original statement that the Memory Manager only relocates when it needs more space. When your application calls a routine in another segment, it causes a GetResource call to load in the needed CODE resource, and GetResource will call NewHandle to get space for the CODE resource if it's not already in memory.

Other Causes of Relocation

When using most development systems, only explicit calls by your application to the **Inside Macintosh** appendix routines or cross-segment calls can ever cause relocation. Some development systems may produce implicit ROM calls where you don't expect them. One place you'll find these routines is in a compiler's built-in functions. For example, a C compiler may have a printf function that, invisibly to the programmer, calls a ROM routine that could cause relocation of objects. Your development system may tell you if it has routines like this. If source code is provided, you can check for yourself. If you're not sure, see "Being Paranoid," which follows. Workshop Pascal doesn't have any routines like this that can cause relocation.

The potential causes of relocation are summarized in Figure 2-11.

By using the "evil eight" list in Figure 2-10, together with the **Inside Macintosh** appendix and your knowledge of your application's segmenting, you now have the ability to absolutely guarantee where relocation will not occur in your application. Take a moment to congratulate yourself—this is some significant knowledge!

Fig 2-11 Causes of relocation

Directly calling any of the 8 Memory Manager routines (see Figure 2-10)
Calling a system routine that calls any of the 8 Memory Manager routines
Calling a routine in another code segment of your application
  (This may call GetResource, which may call NewHandle)
Calling a development system-supplied library routine, such as printf
  (This may call a relocation-triggering ROM call)

OK, now that we've figured that out, let's discover why this new-found knowledge is so valuable and then put it to work. Since a handle is always a valid way to get an object, why should it matter when relocation occurs or what objects it happens to? In general, it's not a problem if you always use the handle to access an object.

Sometimes, though, you don't use the handle to get to a relocatable object. Instead, you may use the master pointer, which points directly to the object. Using the master pointer to access the object is also called **single-dereferencing** the handle, or just **dereferencing**. (Figure 2-12 demonstrates the difference between dereferencing and double-dereferencing.) There are two ways to dereference a handle: **explicit**

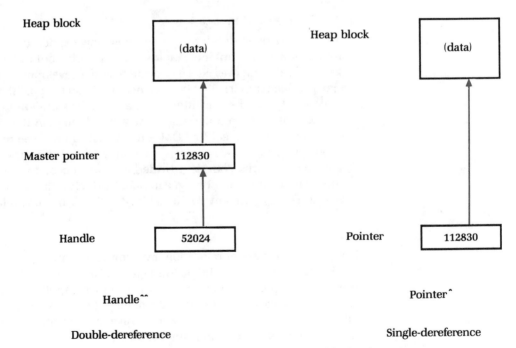

Figure 2-12 Single-versus double-dereferencing

dereferencing and **implicit dereferencing.** Aren't those impressive-sounding terms? Wait until you tell your friends that you're doing some explicit dereferencing. Don't be intimidated by these terms, though—we'll describe exactly what they mean and why they're important.

Explicit Dereferencing

An explicit dereference takes place when you make a copy of an object's master pointer and then use that copy to directly access the object. For example, consider this program fragment:

```
program Fragment;
  TYPE aRecord = record
                   myNum : integer;
                   myBool : boolean;
                   myArray : array [1..1000] of integer;
                 end;
       aPtr = ^aRecord;
       aHdl = ^aPtr;
  VAR myHdl : aHdl;
      sparePtr : aPtr;
      counter : integer;
  begin
    myHdl := NewHandle (SizeOf (aRecord));
  {Creates a relocatable object big enough for an   "aRecord"}
    for counter := 1 to 1000 do
      myHdl^^.myArray [counter] := counter;
  {Initialize each value of myArray to its index;}
  {for example, myArray [1] = 1, myArray [345] = 345, etc.}
  ...
```

Listing 2-1

This little program fragment will create a relocatable heap object that's just big enough to hold an "aRecord" (an integer, a boolean, and 1000 more integers). It then uses the for-loop to initialize the values in the array so that each value is the same as its index. In the for-loop, each assignment is done by double-dereferencing the handle to the record, so it will work fine.

Getting through the Compiler

The first line of code in this example will never make it through the compiler. Here's the problem: NewHandle is a function that returns a value of type Handle (check **Inside Macintosh**); myHdl is a variable of type aHdl (check the declaration). Although you know that Handle and aHdl are the same thing, the Pascal compiler thinks they're different, and you'll get a Type Mismatch Error if you try to compile this line.

Fortunately, Workshop Pascal provides an easy way around this problem, since it's such a common situation with Macintosh programs. You can convert a value of one type to another to make the compiler happy. In other words, we want to make the right side of this assignment statement be an expression of type aHdl. We can do this:

```
myHdl := aHdl (NewHandle (SizeOf (aRecord)));
```

Using aHdl like this causes the compiler to change the expression's type to aHdl, just like the left side of the statement. Functionally, all that this technique does is satisfy the Pascal compiler's strong type checking. This is called **type coercion** and you can read more about it in the "How to Get around Pascal's Type Checking" section in Chapter 8.

Experienced Pascal programmers may realize that there's some room for efficiency improvement here. Although the double-dereference appears to be a trivial accomplishment when written in Pascal, an experienced (or fanatically stingy) Pascal programmer will realize that the object code that the for-loop produces will double-dereference the same handle *1000 times* (every time through the loop), getting the same master pointer every time, since the object never moves while the program is in the loop. It would certainly be more efficient if we could dereference the handle only once, outside the loop. This variation on the program fragment does just that (the changes are shown in bold):

```
begin
    myHdl := NewHandle (SizeOf (aRecord));
{Creates a relocatable object big enough for an "aRecord"}
    sparePtr := myHdl^;
{Dereferences myHdl,copying the master pointer into sparePtr}
    for counter := 1 to 1000 do
        sparePtr^.myArray [counter] := counter;
{Initialize each value of myArray to its index;}
{for example, myArray [1] = 1, myArray [345] = 345, etc.}
    ...
```

Listing 2-2

This version accomplishes exactly the same function, initializing the values in the array, but it does it by dereferencing the handle only once instead of 1000 times. Is this technique safe? Let's examine exactly what's going on here. We said earlier that a handle contains the address of a master pointer and that a master pointer contains the address of a relocatable object. By writing

sparePtr := myHdl^;

we put the contents of the master pointer (that is, the address of the relocatable object) in sparePtr. Then comes the for-loop, which relies on sparePtr (1000 times!) to be a correct pointer to the record, which is a relocatable object.

Is it valid for us to assume that sparePtr, a copy of the master pointer, remains a correct pointer to the record all through the loop? The answer lies in determining if the object that the master pointer points to could be relocated. If the object is moved, the master pointer will be updated, but not copies of it (like sparePtr). So, if the object is not relocated after sparePtr gets assigned to myHdl^, then the master pointer will stay the same, and sparePtr will be correct.

Is there anything which comes between the sparePtr assignment and the use of sparePtr which would cause relocation? No. There are no calls to the Macintosh ROM, no calls to any procedures or functions in other segments, in fact no calls to anything else at all. Since there is no chance that the object will be relocated, we can count on sparePtr to continue pointing to the record throughout the loop. Listing 2-2 will work fine.

Now let's mess things up again:

```
begin
    myHdl := NewHandle (SizeOf (aRecord));
{Creates a relocatable object big enough for an "aRecord"}
    sparePtr := myHdl^;
{Dereferences myHdl,copying the master pointer into sparePtr}
    for counter := 1 to 1000 do
      begin
        sparePtr^.myArray [counter] := counter;
        DrawChar (chr (counter));
      end;
...
```

Listing 2-3

What have we done here? There's now an additional statement in the loop, a call to the ROM routine DrawChar. By looking in **Inside Macintosh's** Appendix B, we find that DrawChar is on the "routines that may move blocks in the heap" list. This absolutely destroys the credibility of sparePtr. Since DrawChar might cause things to be relocated, it could cause our record to move. This would update its master pointer, of course, *but not* sparePtr. This is the hazard of dereferencing a handle. As long as you can guarantee that the object will not be relocated while you're using a *copy* of the master pointer, everything will be fine. In this case, we can't guarantee that, because the call to DrawChar might cause any relocatable object in the heap to move.

What happens if the record moves after a DrawChar call? The next time through the loop the program will continue using sparePtr as if it still pointed to the object, although it no longer does. The program would begin assigning values to bytes in memory that *used* to belong to the record, but now are either free or are allocated to another object. This would cause your data to be messed up, at best; at worst, it could cause a system error. Figure 2-13 shows how this might look.

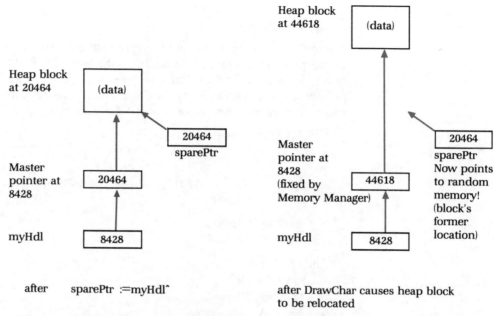

after   sparePtr :=myHdl^

after DrawChar causes heap block
to be relocated

Figure 2-13 Dangling pointer

An important question remains: why bother using a dereferenced handle? Who cares if it takes another assembly language instruction, at the cost of a few microseconds, to do the extra dereference within the loop? One answer to this question is that you may have a time-critical part of your application that needs all the time savings it can get. If you make sure that no relocation will happen while you're using the dereferenced handle, you should feel perfectly comfortable about saving time this way.

Of course, you may want to do it this way even if you're not in a time-critical part of your code. Maybe the thought of unnecessary waste of precious processor cycles just drives you nuts. Maybe you want to show off your code to your friends. That's all right, too.

But maybe you're not completely comfortable doing this . . . read on.

Where's the VAR?

You may have noticed something interesting about the fragments in the preceding section. Although we declared TYPE aRecord, we never declared a VAR of that type—yet we used a handle and a pointer to aRecord and accessed its fields (the declarations are repeated here for your convenience). What's going on here?

```
TYPE aRecord = record
                    myNum : integer;
                    myBool : boolean;
                    myArray : array [1..1000] of integer;
                 end;

     aPtr = ^aRecord;
     aHdl = ^aPtr;

VAR myHdl : aHdl;
    sparePtr : aPtr;
    counter : integer;
```

At the beginning of the program we allocated an object in the heap the size of an aRecord. This reserves the bytes in memory that we used for the record's storage. Remember that declaring a VAR means reserving space for it on the *stack*; we're reserving space in the *heap* by calling NewHandle. Even though the record is allocated on the heap, we can still use our handle and pointer to get to them. We'll discuss this technique more later; for more information on keeping your data in relocatable objects, see the "Random Access File I/O" section in Chapter 10.

Being Paranoid

As we discussed earlier in this chapter, there is a way to absolutely guarantee that a particular relocatable object will not be moved, even if one of the relocation triggers is pulled. You do it by using the HLock call. This call takes a handle as its only parameter. It sets a flag that tells the Memory Manager that this object can't be relocated.

Macintosh programmers who don't completely understand what's going on in memory (they haven't read this chapter!) use Hlock everywhere, sometimes for no apparent reason other than to satisfy their own paranoia. For example, some programmers would call HLock (myHdl) before dereferencing it in Listing 2-2 and then HUnlock (myHdl) at the end of the for-loop.

These calls would do no harm, but they would do no good either. Since we determined that nothing could trigger relocation during the period when we were using the dereferenced handle, there was no need to lock it. In Listing 2-3, however, it's a different story. When we put the DrawChar call into the loop, creating a potential for relocation, we caused sparePtr to become unreliable. But what if we had locked the object before dereferencing it, and then unlocked it afterwards?

```
begin
    myHdl := NewHandle (SizeOf (aRecord));
{Creates a relocatable object big enough for an "aRecord"}
    HLock (myHdl);
    sparePtr := myHdl^;
{Dereferences myHdl,copying the master pointer into sparePtr}
    for counter := 1 to 1000 do
      begin
        sparePtr^.myArray [counter] := counter;
        DrawChar (chr (counter));
      end;
    HUnlock (myHdl);
...
```

Listing 2-4

By locking the object, we've guaranteed that it won't move in the heap. Even if DrawChar causes relocation of heap objects to occur, our object won't be moved because we called HLock. So this example is safe, and the call to HLock is necessary to guarantee that sparePtr stays valid.

Implicit Dereferencing

Sometimes, when you least expect it, your friendly old compiler will pull an implicit dereference on you. Don't panic, though. You can easily recognize when this is happening and how to deal with it.

An implicit dereference takes place when your compiler makes a temporary copy of a master pointer, just as we did in the example in Listing 2-2, but it does so *without an explicit assignment* like sparePtr := myHdl^;. Many compilers will do this in certain situations in order to **optimize** the object code, that is, make it smaller or faster. In other cases, it happens as a normal consequence of the compiler's operation. Once again, the exact details of when these implicit dereferences take place depend on what development system you're using. We'll discuss what Workshop Pascal does.

Let's declare a simple (-minded) routine:

```
procedure setToZero (VAR aNumber:integer);

begin
    aNumber := 0; {That's all this procedure does.}
end;
```

Now let's recall our record declaration from the previous section:

```
TYPE aRecord = record
                   MyNum :  integer;
                   myBool : boolean;
                   myArray : array [1..1000] of integer;
               end;
```

Let's make a call to our simple setToZero procedure with the integer field of the record:

```
setToZero (myHdl^^.MyNum);
```

What actually gets passed to setToZero? You might expect that the value of MyNum would be passed. However, notice that the parameter to setToZero is declared as a VAR parameter, since setToZero alters its value. This is known as a variable parameter or a pass-by-reference parameter. Since setToZero is going to change the value of the thing we're passing to it, Pascal can't simply pass the value. To change the parameter, setToZero must know where it is in memory—its address. In fact, this is what every Pascal compiler does when it passes a variable parameter on the stack (see Figure 2-14).

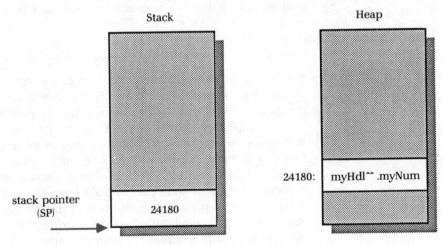

Figure 2-14 VAR parameter

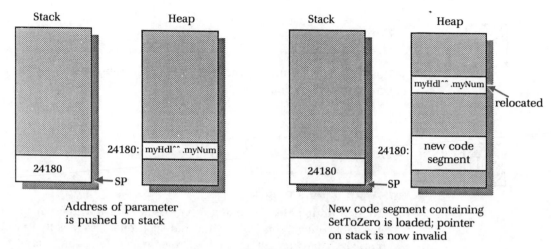

Figure 2-15 Implicit dereference

This presents an interesting problem. Pascal will pass a pointer to myHdl^^.MyNum when we call setToZero. But a pointer to myHdl^^.MyNum is a fragile thing. Since this field is part of relocatable heap object, it can move, and the pointer to it that's passed on the stack may become invalid. This can happen if (1) setToZero is in another segment, since loading its segment may cause relocation, or (2) if setToZero calls any ROM routines that can cause relocation. In our example, setToZero doesn't call any relocation-triggers, so (2) isn't applicable, but (1) could happen if setToZero is in another segment.

The moral to this story is this: although we've used an apparently safe method by starting with the handle and double-dereferencing it, the Pascal compiler foils us by implicitly dereferencing the handle; that is, relying on a pointer. This situation is illustrated in Figure 2-15.

A similar problem arises when you assign a function result to a field of a relocatable object, like this:

myHdl^^.MyNum := someFunction (someParam);

Since the result of the function will be assigned to myHdl^^.MyNum, Pascal gets a pointer to it, very much as we saw it do with a variable parameter in the previous example. Once again, this can be fatal if anything causing relocation occurs in someFunction or if someFunction is in another segment.

Didn't we say that a double-dereference was always a safe way to refer to a relocatable object? Yes, it is always safe, but in these cases the compiler has turned a double-dereference into a single-dereference. So we can now make a definitive statement:

Fact

Double-dereferencing a handle in your application will always lead you to the relocatable object.

Warning

Beware of the Compiler

Although double-dereferencing a handle is always a safe path to a relocatable object, remember that some compilers, especially Pascal compilers, may create implicit dereferences. You don't have to worry about this with most C compilers.

Interrupt Time

There are some special rules for using handles in code that executes at interrupt time. See Appendix B for more information about using handles in interrupt-driven code.

Once you're aware that these implicit dereferences are happening, they're easy to fix. The most obvious way to prevent them from being a problem is to lock the memory object by calling HLock on the handle. Remember, though, that locking the object makes it nonrelocatable and so can fragment the free space in the heap while it's locked. A way that won't mess up the heap is to make a local copy of the variable you want to pass; that is, assign it to a local variable, first for the procedure call:

```
VAR localNum : integer;
 ...
        localNum := myHdl^^.MyNum;
        setToZero (localNum);
```

and also for the function call:

```
VAR localNum : integer;
 ...
        localNum := someFunction (someParam);
        myHdl^^.MyNum := localNum;
```

By doing this, localNum is assigned its value "safely": start with the handle and then double-dereference. When we call setToZero, we use the local variable. Since it's allocated on the stack (like all local variables), it won't move. Same thing with someFunction. After the function returns, we can safely assign the returned value into the record. Easy, now that you know when to expect it!

Maybe the most insidious kind of implicit dereference takes place when you use Pascal's seemingly innocent with statement. Most Pascal programmers think that with is just a method of shorthand. Here's an example:

```
with myHdl^^ do begin
        myNum := 1234;
        myBool := true;
        myArray [1] := 1;
    end;
```

Listing 2-5

Four out of five Pascal programmers surveyed will tell you that that's just a source code shorthand way of doing this:

```
myHdl^^.myNum := 1234;
myHdl^^.myBool := true;
myHdl^^.myArray [1] := 1;
```

Ah, but that clever Pascal compiler: the with statement is not just shorthand for you, the source code author. It's also used by the compiler to optimize your code. Let's see how this works by looking at a more conventional example:

```
VAR simpleRec : record
                    first : boolean;
                    second: integer;
                    third : string [255];
                end;
    simplePtr   : ptr;

...

simplePtr := @simpleRec;
with simplePtr^ do begin
        second:= 5678;
        first   := true;
                end;
```

Listing 2-6

When you write something like with simplePtr^ do, the compiler knows that you're about to work with fields in a record pointed to by simplePtr. The compiler knows where in memory simplePtr^ is stored, and it knows how far from the beginning of the record each of its fields is stored. So, to optimize, it puts the address of the record (that is, a pointer to simpleRec) into a **register**, a special location within the 68000 itself, so that it can access it quickly. Then, when you refer to fields of the record, such as simplePtr^.second, it calculates how far from the beginning of the record second is, quickly adds this offset to the pointer it stashed in the register, and then stores 5678 there. Figure 2-16 illustrates how this works.

This is a good way for the compiler to optimize your program a little. Our example here, simpleRec, is a static (stack-based) variable, so there's no problem with saving a pointer to it—it can never move. However, as you might imagine, you can get into a little trouble when relocatable objects are about. In Listing 2-5, the record named in the with statement is a double-dereferenced handle. Once again, Pascal is doing just a little something special. To optimize the with statement, the compiler will put a *pointer* to the record in a register, as we discussed previously. But look out—the record is a relocatable object, and that pointer is extremely fragile! One relocation trigger within the body of the with statement and you can (at least potentially) wave goodbye to your record as it floats out of sight. Just because you're used to disaster by now, there's a graphic illustration of this kind of thing in Figure 2-17.

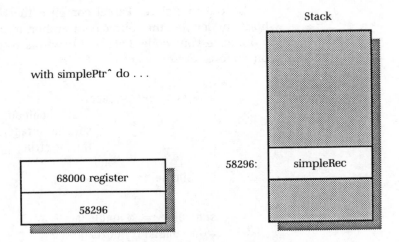

with statement puts the record's address in a
register (a memory location within the 68000 itself)

Figure 2-16 A with statement

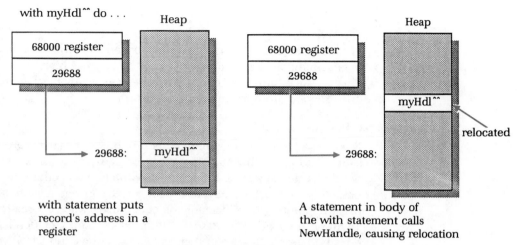

with statement puts record's address in a register

A statement in body of the with statement calls NewHandle, causing relocation

Figure 2-17 With statement causes dangling pointer

In the case of our example, Listing 2-5, we can guarantee that this problem will not happen. See if you can figure out how we know this before continuing. Go ahead . . . I'll wait.

The entire body of the with statement contains just the three assignments to MyNum, myBool, and myArray[1]. We know that these are not relocation triggers, so we know that the record will not move in the heap. Since the record won't move, we know that the pointer to the record that the compiler put in the register will be valid. If you figured this out, you deserve a cookie; if not, you should study this chapter some more.

What if there were relocation triggers in the body of the with statement, like a GetResource call or a call to a routine in another segment? Just HLock the handle before the with statement and then HUnlock it after. Remember that the locked object can fragment the heap, so you may want to skip the with altogether and just write it out longhand if you find that your heap is getting chopped up. Once again, the most important thing about this kind of implicit dereference is for you to be aware of it, able to see it coming, and able to work around it (by HLocking or avoiding the with).

Moving up

There's a Memory Manager routine called MoveHHi that takes a relocatable object and moves it up in the heap as high as possible. This is a nice thing to do to a handle before locking it, since moving it up keeps it from fragmenting the heap.

C Programmers

If you use C, you may be chuckling by now. In C, you're generally a little closer to the machine, so you get more warning when a handle is dereferenced. Whenever a pointer to something must be passed, you must specify it explicitly, so you can watch out for passing pointers to relocatable objects. Also, C doesn't really have anything analogous to Pascal's with, so that implicit dereference doesn't happen. Beware of register optimizations, though. If your C compiler can put a dereferenced handle in a register, you need to know about it.

That's about it for the problem of dangling pointers to relocatable objects. Figure 2-18 has a summary of the potential kinds of handle dereferences that can kill you and suggested remedies. To summarize:

Figure 2-18 Problem dereferencing situations

Dereferencing situation	How to avoid it
Explicit dereference: thePtr := theHdl^	Don't do it; double-dereference the handle instead: theHdl^^
Implicit dereferences: Pascal dereferences in with statement: with theHdl^^ do	Avoid relocation triggers in body of with statement; if you can't, don't use with, or HLock/HUnlock.
Parameter passed in cross-segment call: SetToZero (my Hdl^^ .myNum)	Copy the parameter into a local variable before calling, then pass the local instead: localNum := myHdl^^ .myNum; SetToZero (localNum)
Function result: myHdl^^ .myNum := aFunction (xyz)	Use a local variable as the function result, then copy it into the heap object: localNum := aFunction (xyz); myHdl^^ .myNum := localNum

Any of the situations listed in Figure 2-18 can cause a dereferenced handle to be used. If this occurs, any of the situations listed in Figure 2-11 can move the relocatable object, causing the dereferenced handle to become incorrect. To avoid this problem, use the remedies listed in Figure 2-18.

Things to Remember

- Applications use space in two memory areas, the application heap and the stack.
- Global and local variables are kept on the stack.
- Objects created with NewHandle and NewPtr, including most objects created by the Toolbox, are kept in the heap.
- Heap objects may be either relocatable or nonrelocatable.
- When you have the freedom of choice in creating a heap object, you should make it relocatable, since nonrelocatables can fragment, or clog up, your heap, and heap objects must consist of contiguous bytes.
- Relocatable objects can move, but only at well-defined, predictable times: when there's a call (directly or indirectly) to NewHandle, NewPtr, SetHandleSize, and SetPtrSize, as well as to five other, less commonly used Memory Manager calls.
- You should be careful not to single-dereference a handle and then use the dereferenced handle after a heap compaction has occurred.
- If necessary, you can ensure that a relocatable object won't move by HLocking it, but you should be sure to unlock things as soon as you can, and you should call MoveHHi on an object before locking it.

More about Heaps and Fragmentation

In this chapter we'll continue delving into how Macintosh heaps work and what happens to the things in them. We'll also talk in depth about some important data structures that you'll find associated with heap objects, including the heap zone header, heap block header, and master pointer.

We'll talk about how you can reduce fragmentation, which can make more memory available to your application. We'll also talk about using segmentation to split your program up into individually loadable pieces, which is another way of conserving memory space.

What Does "Out of Memory" Really Mean?

The memory map back in Figure 2-1 showed that the application heap and the stack occupy the same part of memory, and the arrows suggest that they move toward each other. That's true: as the stack expands, it reaches *downward* into memory; as the heap grows, it moves *upward* toward the top of the stack. If these two friendly adversaries ever collide, you're out of memory. Let's take a look at how that happens.

We discussed earlier how objects in memory are allocated. We said that stack objects are created when the high-level language programmer declares a variable, as with VAR, and that heap objects are created by calling Memory Manager routines like NewHandle and NewPtr. When an application starts up, both the stack and the heap are allotted a certain amount of RAM. Initially, the stack gets 8K and the heap gets 6K.

This allocation is controlled through the use of several global variables. Each of these variables is set by the system to a default value. Most of them can be set to different values for your application if you want to. For example, the size allotted to the stack is taken from a global variable called DefltStack. A pointer to the start of the heap is kept in the variable called ApplZone, and HeapEnd contains the address of the end of the heap. The heap begins with a 6K allocation, but the system also sets aside an area past the end of the heap that may be used by either the heap or the stack, whichever asks for it first. Since this space is usually claimed by the heap, it's often called the **growable heap space**. The end of this area is pointed to by ApplLimit. This setup is shown in Figure 3-1.

In almost every application, the bulk of RAM is taken up by the heap rather than the stack. When you ask the Memory Manager for a new object by calling NewHandle or NewPtr, it first attempts to find the space within the confines of the current heap, that is, somewhere between ApplZone and HeapEnd. If it can't allocate the requested space there, the Memory Manager will **grow** the heap by moving HeapEnd farther up in memory, if there's any "growable" space left.

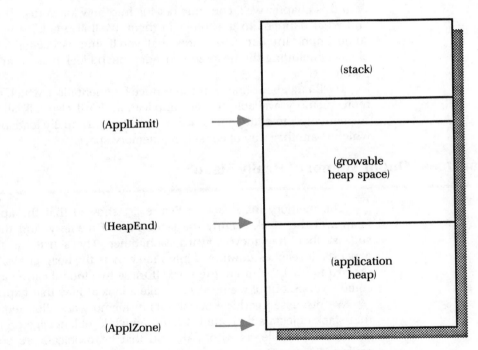

Figure 3-1 Partial Macintosh memory map

One drawback to the technique used by the Memory Manager to allocate space is that it will relocate and purge objects in the heap before attempting to grow the heap. In most applications, the initial 8K of stack space that the system sets aside is plenty, and we would prefer to pregrow the heap to its maximum size. This makes purging of objects an almost last resort technique for the Memory Manager, ensuring that it won't try to purge objects unless the heap is fully grown.

Since so many applications want to pregrow their heaps to ApplLimit, a routine called MaxApplZone is provided to do just that automatically. By calling MaxApplZone once at the beginning of your application, you will ensure that your heap is grown to its maximum size.

When the Memory Manager needs to grow the heap, it moves HeapEnd higher and higher in memory, but it can never move it higher than ApplLimit.

When you request memory from the Memory Manager and it can't find enough, even after purging purgeable objects, relocating relocatable objects, and growing the heap as far as it can, it makes one last-ditch effort to find enough memory to satisfy your request: it yells for help. This yell is in the form of a function call. This function, which you usually include in your application's code, is called a **grow zone function**.

Here's how it works: when the Memory Manager determines that there's not enough room in the heap to fulfill a request for memory, it calls your grow zone function, passing to you the number of bytes it needs to fulfill the memory request. Your application should then do something to free up some heap space, if possible. If you're able to free some memory, you set the value of your grow zone function result to a nonzero number; if you can't free up anything, you should return a zero.

If you are able to free some memory, but not enough to make the Memory Manager happy, it will call you again (it's very persistent). It will continue calling you until it gets enough memory or you signal that you can't find any more (by returning zero).

What can you do to free up memory in your grow zone function? The best thing to do is to assume in advance that the grow zone function will be called and plan for it. For example, you can run your application with some of your most important resources set to nonpurgeable. This will keep them in memory and help the application run faster, since the resources won't have to be reloaded from disk after they're purged and needed again. Then, when your grow zone function is called, and there's no more space for luxurious living, you can make them purgeable.

Don't Look Back

Note that one of the things you can't do in a grow zone function is cancel the memory allocation request that triggered the call in the first place. The Memory Manager must either find the memory or return an error (memFullErr). Asking for memory is like jumping off a cliff: once you've done it, there's no turning back.

If you've looked everywhere, even behind the couch, and just can't find a single byte of memory, you'll return a zero as the grow zone function's result. When the Memory Manager sees this result, it knows that nothing else can be done and puts up system error 25 (can't allocate requested memory block in the heap). What a terrible thing to do to users! There's a moral here: we should figure out a way to be sure that we never run out of memory this way.

One technique for doing this is to have a special "monitor" object in the heap that does nothing but tell us how the heap allocation is doing. In this technique, you allocate a relocatable object of a predetermined size, say 30K, when your application starts up. Then, if your grow zone function gets called, you know that you're within about 30K of running out of memory, minus the amount of memory requested in the grow zone call. (For this to work, your heap must be reasonably free of fragmentation.) You can then use SetHandleSize to reduce the size of your monitor object, and the newly freed memory will be allocated to the new object.

By using this technique, you can have a better handle (no pun intended) on what's going on in your heap. This way, when your monitor object starts getting small, you can issue a warning to your user, which says to do something that will free up more memory (like closing windows or saving a document), or you can have your application take some action of its own. You should also include a "final warning" for when your monitor object gets precariously small, giving the user instructions on how to free up space immediately. With careful planning, you should be able to avoid an error 25. In the worst case, when your grow zone gets a memory request that you can't fulfill, even by eliminating the monitor object, you should force the user to save any work in memory and then quit the application.

Notice that the name "grow zone function" is pretty nondescriptive about what it actually does. The function doesn't really grow the heap; it tries to create more free space by various means, but heap "growing" is done automatically by the Memory Manager.

Warning

Be careful what you try to do within a grow zone function. The function is being called because the heap is almost full, so any operations that require even a small amount of memory may fail, like putting up a dialog. The best strategy is to keep enough memory in the monitor object to handle allocation of objects needed in the "final warning" situation. In other words, if you determine that you need 2K to execute your "final warning" procedure, don't ever let the size of your monitor object get below 2K. If you can't keep it above that size, you should force the user to save and then quit.

This is just a suggestion of things you can do when you're running out of heap space. You can push the state of the art by coming up with your own techniques. Remember this guideline: a well-written program should try to save the user from ever seeing a system error 25.

Since the Macintosh has two different kinds of memory for an application, the heap and the stack, there are two distinct kinds of out-of-memory conditions. We just discussed what happens when the heap runs out of space. The stack can run out of space, too, and the result is very similar: a system error, number 28 in this case. The things that cause error 28 and the methods of prevention are a lot different, though.

All the objects in the heap are allocated by calling the Memory Manager, which is a piece of the ROM-based operating system. When it runs out of space, it signals with a system error. You might say that the heap is *tame*—everything that happens in the heap is controlled by the Memory Manager. It can never grow beyond its limit, which is kept in the system global called ApplLimit at $130.

The stack, on the other hand, is a data structure that's completely maintained by the Macintosh's 68000 microprocessor. Objects are allocated on the stack by machine language instructions, and any one of those instructions could cause the stack to grow so much that it crashes into the heap. The Memory Manager is a Macintosh concept that was invented long after the 68000 was sealed in silicon, and the 68000 doesn't know how to check before growing the stack to see if it's about to crash into the heap. Compared to the heap, the stack is *wild*.

To help tame the stack just a little, the Macintosh operating system has implemented a tiny piece of ROM-based code called the stack sniffer. The stack sniffer has the job of looking at the top of the stack every once in a while to see if it has crashed into the heap. In this case, every once in a while is every sixtieth of a second. When it checks, the stack sniffer looks to see if the top of the stack is lower than the highest block in the heap. If it is, the stack has destroyed data in the heap, we're in deep trouble, and the stack sniffer puts up system error 28. Figure 3-2 shows how this stack overflow error can happen.

There are two important things to notice here. The first is that, unlike the out-of-heap-space problem, we can't do anything when the stack runs into the heap: there's no "grow stack function." Once the problem is known, the damage is already done, and data in the heap has already been smashed by the stack. The second interesting thing is that the stack sniffer only checks things out every sixtieth of a second. This may seem like plenty often to you and me, but it's a long time to a Macintosh. A lot of processing can happen in that time, and it's possible that the stack could grow into the heap, bash a few bytes, then sneak back into the electronic vapor before a sixtieth of a second passes. In this case, the stack crash goes unnoticed, until you try to use the corrupted memory that the stack destroyed. This sounds pretty bad, but in practice it's very rare that an unseen stack overflow will cause a problem in this way. After all, it *is* just a sixtieth of a second. Just something to think about when you're debugging.

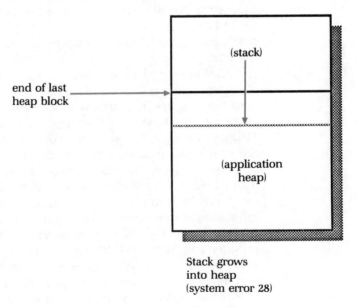

Figure 3-2 Stack overflow

What causes the stack to grow? As we've said, the stack is mainly used for local variables and for parameters passed to routines. In addition, assembly language routines (like the ones in the ROM) often use the stack as a place for keeping variables temporarily. Also, remember that stack space fluctuates: when one routine calls another, that calls a third, each routine will use space for its parameters and locals. As each routine ends, the space for its parameters and locals will be reclaimed, and the stack will shrink.

The 8K that the system gives your application for stack space is usually more than enough for the parameters and local variables used by your own routines. Usually, stack overflows are caused by particular ROM routines that use large amounts of stack space, most of which are noted in **Inside Macintosh**. If you get a stack overflow when using one of these routines, you can use the information for that routine in **Inside Macintosh** to work around the problem. If a call to one of your own routines is causing the stack overflow, you may be able to rewrite it so that it has fewer parameters or fewer local variables. You can determine how much stack space your routines use by adding up the sizes of your parameters and local variables according to the chart in Figure 3-3.

Figure 3-3 Sizes of data types

Type	Size in bytes	Comment
Integer	2	Two's complement integer (−32768 to 32767)
Longint	4	Two's complement integer (−2147483648 to 2147483647)
SignedByte	1	Two's complement integer (−128 to 127)
Boolean	1	Value in bit 0 (0 = false, 1 = true)
Char	2	ASCII code in low byte, high byte unused
Real	4	SANE single-precision format
Single	4	Same as Real
Double	8	SANE double-precision format
Extended	10	SANE extended-precision format
Comp	8	SANE computational format
String [n]	n+1	Length byte followed by ASCII codes
Byte	2	Two's complement integer, value in low byte
Ptr	4	Address of data; includes any parameters preceded by @
Handle	4	Address of master pointer; includes any kind of handle
Point	4	QuickDraw coordinate
Rect	8	QuickDraw rectangle; two points (goaltending)

Warning

If you're getting stack overflows, be sure you understand how much space your local variables and parameters are using. For example, a Pascal str255 takes 256 bytes, no matter how many characters of the string are actually used. Also, look out for obscure types like text. With many compilers, a variable of type text will take several *hundred* bytes of stack space. You should also watch out for a compiler's built-in routines. In particular, Pascal's concat call can take an enormous amount of stack space.

More Stack Space

If you've got something in your program that simply needs a lot of stack space and can't be changed, all is not lost. You can move ApplLimit lower to prevent the heap from growing. If you do this, be sure you do so before calling MaxApplZone.

Objects in Heaps

Now that you know the basics about heaps and how they work, let's explore them and their data structures a little more. We've talked about the two kinds of objects, or blocks, in a heap, relocatables and nonrelocatables. In a heap, every byte belongs to a block. Bytes that aren't allocated to a relocatable or nonrelocatable object are collected together into **free** blocks. So there are really three kinds of blocks in a heap: relocatable, nonrelocatable, and free. Figure 3-4 gives some facts about these three types of heap objects.

As we've said, all these blocks are controlled by the Memory Manager. When a program calls NewHandle, the Memory Manager finds the bytes for the new object and then creates the object in the heap. When a program calls DisposHandle, the Memory Manager changes that object into a free block.

In theory, Macintosh is a single-process system; that is, there's allegedly only one program running at a time. Even if you're not using something like Switcher, that's not really true. For example, at one time, a Macintosh can run Microsoft Word, the alarm clock desk accessory, the screen saver desk accessory, and the control panel desk accessory. There can be lots of other little programs in memory, too: the window, menu, and control definition functions, the keyboard and keypad mapping functions, and the AppleTalk drivers, just to name a few. Many of

Figure 3-4 Types of heap blocks

type	comment
relocatable	can be purgeable or nonpurgeable, locked or unlocked; can be relocated if unlocked
nonrelocatable	cannot be relocated or purged
free	may have been previously allocated; several adjacent free blocks may be combined when heap compaction occurs

these programs can allocate their own memory. Any of them could just grab a chunk of memory and use it, without going through the Memory Manager. Of course, this would create anarchy and nothing would work. So, to keep the world from falling apart, everything in a Macintosh that wants memory gets it either by asking the Memory Manager or by using the stack.

Heap Zone Header

A Macintosh heap begins with a **heap zone header**. The heap zone header gives some important information about the heap that it's attached to. A heap zone actually has a Pascal declaration, and you can see it in Figure 3-5.

A discussion of some of the important fields in this record will help understand how it works. The hFstFree field points to the master pointer that will be used for the next relocatable object that's allocated. When a new object is created, this field will be updated to point to the next available master pointer. When the last available master pointer is used up, the Memory Manager will call MoreMasters, creating another block of master pointers.

The zcbFree field contains the total number of free bytes in the heap ("zcb" stands for "zone count of bytes"). It's interesting to note that you probably can't allocate an object this big, since objects must consist of consecutive bytes, and this number is the total of all the free bytes.

The gzProc field is a pointer to our old friend, the grow zone function. The ROM call SetGrowZone lets you put the address of your application's grow zone function into this field.

```
Type
   Zone = Record
          bkLim: Ptr;              {last block in zone}
          purgePtr: Ptr;           {unlucky fellow - may be purged next}
          hFstFree: Ptr;           {first free master pointer}
          zcbFree: Ptr;            {total free bytes in zone}
          gzProc: ProcPtr;         {grow zone function}
          moreMast: Integer;       {number of master pointers allocated
                                    by MoreMasters}
          flags: Integer;          {internal use}
          cntRel: Integer;         {unused (maybe someday)}
          maxRel: Integer;         {unused (same for next 5 fields)}
          cntNRel: Integer;
          maxNRel: Integer;
          cntEmpty: Integer;
          cntHandles: Integer;
          minCBFree: Integer;
          purgeProc: ProcPtr;      {called when a block is purged}
          sparePtr: Ptr;           {in case of a flat (used internally)}
          allocPtr: Ptr;           {used internally}
          heapData: Integer;       {first byte in the heap}
      end;
```

Figure 3-5 Heap zone declaration

The moreMast field tells the Memory Manager how many master pointers to allocate at once when someone calls MoreMasters. This is set to 64 for application heap zones. If you set it to another value and then call MoreMasters, the new master pointer block will have moreMast master pointers in it. If you do this, you should be sure to change it back to 64 after you make your call, since the system will call MoreMasters itself if it ever runs out of master pointers.

The last field in the record, heapData, is very interesting. It's only declared as an integer, but it actually represents the entire heap! Here's the scoop: this record declaration exists mainly to allow high-level language programmers access to the fields of the heap zone header; that is, everything in the record except the heapData field. The heapData field is simply the first two bytes of the heap's data (the stuff beyond the header). Since the data is accessed only in assembly language by the Memory Manager, it doesn't need a record declaration.

Heap Block Header

Each block in the heap starts with a **block header**, which tells some things about the block, including which of the three types it is. Following the block header are the **contents** bytes of the block. This is where an object's actual data is kept. Finally, a block may have unused bytes at the end.

Why Unused Bytes

There are two reasons for unused bytes. One reason is that the Memory Manager will only allocate blocks with even sizes. If a program calls `NewHandle (73)`, requesting a new 73-byte object, the Memory Manager will allocate 74 bytes, with one unused byte at the end. The block maintains both a **physical size** and a **logical size**. This block's physical size is 74 bytes; that is, it actually occupies 74 bytes in memory. But its logical size is 73 bytes. That's what the program asked for, and that's all it can count on.

The second reason for unused bytes is that the Memory Manager will allocate a minimum of 12 bytes to any block, including free blocks. This means that a memory request for 6 bytes will result in a 12-byte object, though its logical size will be 6 bytes. Also, If any memory allocation would leave a free block smaller than 12 bytes, the free space is just tacked onto the end of the allocated block. For example, if the heap contained a 624-byte "gap" between two non-relocatable objects, and a new, 620-byte object was being created in the gap, the Memory Manager would make the new object's physical size 624 bytes, since it could not leave a 4-byte free block remaining.

The block header is defined and maintained by the Memory Manager, and your application will probably never delve into its contents. The main reason for studying block headers is for debugging. The contents of a block are just plain bytes to the Memory Manager. Your application may interpret a particular heap object as a page of text, a bitmap of the solar system, or one title in your compact disc collection, but that's all irrelevant to the Memory Manager. It deals with the object simply as a chunk of bytes.

Now let's take a look at the structure of a block header (just what you've been waiting for, I'm sure). As we said earlier, every heap block begins with a block header, which tells some things about the block. Block headers are always eight bytes long. The structure of a block header is shown in Figure 3-6, and we'll discuss the pieces.

The first four bits (which form the first hexadecimal digit) of the block header tell us a fundamental fact about the block: whether it's relocatable, nonrelocatable, or free. Relocatable blocks have a hex 8 in this position (binary 1000), nonrelocatables have $4 (binary 0100), and free blocks are marked with a $0 (binary 0000). The next four bits give the number of unused bytes in the block. This can also be thought of as the difference between the block's physical size and its logical size. Note that this means that there can never be more than 15 (binary 1111) unused bytes in a block. This field is called the **size correction** of the block.

The four bits that tell the type of the block and the four size correction bits together are called the block's **tag byte**. This is always the first byte of the block header.

The next three bytes in the block header give the physical size of the block in bytes. This size includes the size of the header itself. Since there are three bytes in this field, the allowable range for the physical size of a heap block is 12 to 16,777,216 ($1000000) bytes (the second number is more familiarly known as 16 megabytes). Before you chuckle and think that this should be enough room for anybody's computer, ever, remember that personal computers commonly came with 16K as recently as 1981, and that a megabyte was virtually unheard of until 1983. One of the cardinal rules of computing says that there's never enough memory.

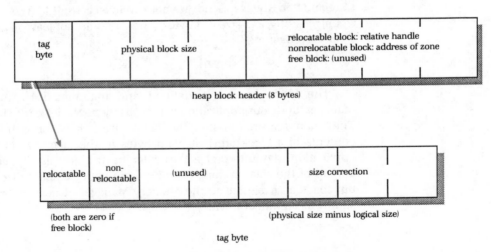

Figure 3-6 Heap block header

The final four bytes of the block header differ depending on the type of the block. If the block is a nonrelocatable, this field contains the address of the beginning of the heap zone. If the block is relocatable, this field contains (in a special format) the address of the block's master pointer.

Relativity Invitation

The address of the block's master pointer is stored in the block header as a relative offset from the beginning of the heap zone. This form is called a **relative handle**. In other words, you obtain the actual address of the master pointer by adding the relative handle to the address of the beginning of the heap zone. Adding addresses is something computers, not humans, are good at, so most debuggers that display block headers automatically show you the real (absolute) address of the master pointer in this field instead of this relative handle business.

Since debuggers decode relative handles into addresses for you, you most likely will never have to deal directly with them yourself, even when debugging. For this reason, relative handles are officially recognized as Macintosh trivia: very few people know about them, and you can now consider yourself one of the elite.

If the block is free, the last four bytes of the block header contain garbage. Officially, the last four bytes are unused for free blocks.

The Memory Manager uses the block header to keep information about the object up to date. When a new object is allocated, the Memory Manager will fill in the fields of the block header. If the object is made larger or smaller with SetHandleSize or SetPtrSize, the block header is adjusted accordingly.

Immediately following the eight-byte block header is the object's data—what we defined earlier as the contents bytes. When you create the object by calling NewHandle or NewPtr, the address (the handle or pointer) that's returned back to you is the address of the contents, not the header. This is what you want, of course: if you've allocated 250 bytes to keep your database record, you don't want to go storing into the block header. The number that you specify in the NewHandle or NewPtr call is the logical size of the block.

Futures

For compatibility with future Macintosh systems, you should only use this intricate heap zone information for debugging, and not rely on it being the same from your programs. Instead, you should try to stick to the interface provided by the Memory Manager ROM calls.

Master Pointers

Another very important data structure in the heap is the master pointer, the address of a relocatable object. A master pointer is more than simply an address, however. Since it's created and maintained by the Memory Manager, it has a very well defined form and predictable behavior, which are extremely useful to know when you're debugging.

Remember that master pointers are not relocatable, since they anchor relocatable objects. Also, since master pointers are created by the Memory Manager, they reside in the heap. Since heap objects have a minimum size of 12 bytes and master pointers really only need four bytes, it would seem like a massive waste of memory to allocate a new nonrelocatable heap object for each master pointer.

To avoid wasting space this way, master pointers come in big packages called **master pointer blocks**. As we discussed earlier, the number of master pointers in a master pointer block is specified by the moreMast field in the heap zone header, and that number is usually 64. When a program calls MoreMasters, a new block of master pointers is allocated.

When your application starts up, your heap zone contains exactly one master pointer block. How many do you need? Consider this: every relocatable object that *might* be allocated by your application would need a master pointer. This includes all your resources, all desk accessories and their resources, system resources like packages, dialog boxes, and item lists for the Standard File package, and so on.

If at any point in your application's life the Memory Manager runs out of available master pointers, it will call MoreMasters itself, creating a new nonrelocatable object possibly right in the middle of your carefully unfragmented heap! How can you prevent this disaster? Easily. Just call MoreMasters yourself in your application's initial housekeeping.

You should actually call MoreMasters several times in your initialization code. Exactly how many times to call it depends on the number of relocatable objects used by your application. A good minimum is three times, but you should determine an optimum number for your application by observing your heap zone's behavior, as we'll do in Chapter 7.

When in doubt, always allocate more master pointer blocks than you think you'll need. A master pointer block costs you 264 bytes of heap space (64 master pointers at 4 bytes each, plus 8 bytes for the block header). A master pointer block created at a random time later in your application's life will likely cost you much more by fragmenting your heap and cutting your available heap space into pieces. Don't be shy about calling MoreMasters. For example, the Finder calls it 20 times when starting up, allocating 1280 master pointers!

The actual structure of a master pointer is something that you'll rarely need to know, since most debuggers will automatically interpret master pointers for you. A master pointer is another data structure that only a ROM junkie, a debugger, or the Memory Manager could love. A diagram of its structure is shown in Figure 3-7. As you'd expect, the master pointer provides the address of the relocatable object, but it also tells us a few more important facts about the object. Since the address of the block is limited to three bytes (the 16-megabyte address range), the high byte of the master pointer is used for this extra information.

The first bit of the master pointer tells whether the relocatable object is locked or not. If it is locked, this bit is a 1. The next bit specifies whether the object is currently marked purgeable; it's a 1 if it is. The third bit indicates if the relocatable block it points to is a resource; if so, it's a 1. The remaining five bits in this byte are reserved for future magic. The first eight bits of the master pointer are called the **flags** byte.

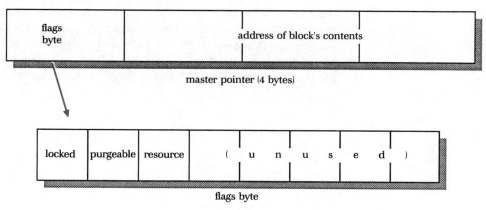

master pointer (4 bytes)

flags byte

Figure 3-7 Master pointer

Each of the three defined bits in the flag byte has a numerical value when the flag byte is expressed as a hexadecimal digit. The lock bit has the value $80, the purgeable bit is worth $40, and the resource bit adds $20. In other words, if a master pointer begins with $80, we know that it points to a locked block; if it begins with $A0, the block is a locked, non-purgeable resource ($80+$20 = $A0).

Some debuggers decode these three bits mnemonically, using L, P, and R, for locked, purgeable, and resource. Other debuggers display only the first hex digit, since the second digit is always zero (for example, displaying $8 instead of $80).

The last three bytes of the master pointer are the pointer to the block's data. Since heap blocks must always have an even number of bytes, this address is always even.

Just Setting Bits

Seeing how the Memory Manager keeps track of whether a block is locked or purgeable takes a lot of the mystery out of the HLock/HUnlock and HPurge/HNoPurge calls. In fact, they just dereference the handle passed to them and set or clear the appropriate bit. When you're doing these operations, though, you should definitely not just go and set or clear the bits yourself—please use the ROM calls. This will ensure that your application is compatible with future ROMs in case the structure of a master pointer ever changes.

Using the upper byte of a master pointer for flags limits the range of a pointer to 16 megabytes, which may not seem like much of a limit now, but could be eventually. It's likely that Apple will decide to use the full 32 bits of the master pointer, which will provide an addressing range of 4 gigabytes. This suggests that the master pointer flags will have to go somewhere else, which is another great argument (in register D0) for using the ROM calls to lock, unlock, and set purgeable status. For more information on this, see the Macintosh Plus Memory Manager calls in Appendix C.

Using the Memory Manager

The Memory Manager provides over 40 routines, but most programs will be able to get by with only a handful of the most important ones. Here's a brief list of the calls that you're most likely to use.

FUNCTION NewHandle (logicalSize: Size) : Handle;

This is probably the single most commonly used Memory Manager call. As we've already seen, NewHandle creates a new relocatable object in the heap and returns a handle to that object. You should use it to create data objects dynamically.

FUNCTION NewPtr (logicalSize: Size) : Ptr;

This call creates a new nonrelocatable object in the heap. Use it carefully and rarely since nonrelocatable objects can fragment the heap and prevent full utilization of free heap space.

PROCEDURE DisposHandle (h: Handle);

Use this call to get rid of a relocatable object after you no longer need it.

Warning

Watch out! After calling DisposHandle, any handles to the deceased heap object are now invalid. The handles are not changed—they still point to master pointers. Also, unused master pointers are kept in a linked list, each one pointing at the next unused one. So, the master pointer that these now invalid handles point to *still points to something*. Not a relocatable block any more, but another master pointer!

This means that if you call DisposHandle twice on the same handle, you will destroy the list of free master pointers, and your program will die a horrible and confusing death when it attempts to create another relocatable object. There's one weird crash in which you get a system error box with two tiny disk icons drawn in the upper-left corner of the screen. This problem can usually be traced to diposing the same relocatable object twice. Don't call DisposHandle on an already disposed object.

PROCEDURE DisposPtr (p: Ptr);

Frees up a previously allocated nonrelocatable object in the heap.

PROCEDURE MoreMasters;

Allocates a block of master pointers, usually 64 of them, getting the actual number from the moreMast field of the heap zone header. Call this several (or many) times at the beginning of your application to avoid fragmentation.

PROCEDURE MaxApplZone;

Causes the heap to be "grown" to its maximum size without relocating or purging any objects. Call this once at the beginning of your application to prevent unnecessary purging.

PROCEDURE BlockMove(sourcePtr, destPtr: Ptr; byteCount: Size);

This routine is a fast, well-tested, easy way to move bytes around in memory. You can use it to move bytes either up or down, and the source and destination ranges may overlap. This is the routine that the Memory Manager itself uses to relocate heap objects.

There are a lot more Memory Manager calls, and you'll probably use some of them in your applications, but these provide the functionality that you'll need almost everytime you sit down to write code.

Reducing Fragmentation

The key to making your applications run effectively in limited-memory environments (and what environment isn't limited-memory?) is understanding how your memory is being used and maximizing its availability. On a Macintosh, heap objects must consist of continuous bytes, and nonrelocatable objects can fragment these runs of continuous bytes, as we've seen. So reducing fragmentation in your heap involves careful management of nonrelocatable objects.

There are two common kinds of nonrelocatable objects. The first kind is the master pointer block, which we've already discussed. Master pointer blocks must be nonrelocatable objects. As we've said, the best way to avoid having master pointer blocks fragment your heap is to call MoreMasters an appropriate number of times at the beginning of your application.

The other common class of nonrelocatable objects consists of things built on the QuickDraw data structure called a **GrafPort**. A GrafPort is a drawing environment for QuickDraw operations. For example, a GrafPort holds the font to be used when drawing text, the size, shape, and pattern of the pen to be used when drawing graphics, and the rectangle in which they'll be displayed.

Almost every QuickDraw call operates on the "current," or default, GrafPort, and these calls aren't prepared to deal with GrafPort as relocatable objects. Since QuickDraw always gets to a GrafPort via a pointer, not a handle, GrafPort are nonrelocatable objects if they're in the heap (they can also be allocated on the stack).

The GrafPort is an extremely important data structure for the entire Macintosh user interface. Two other structures are built on it, and each of them must be nonrelocatable, too. The first one is the **window record**. Each window has a window record, and the window record contains a GrafPort, as well as some other information about the window, such as information about the window's title and about the window behind it on the screen. Since the first thing in the window record is a GrafPort, a window record is fundamentally a GrafPort with some extra stuff on the end, and it also is nonrelocatable.

The second data structure built on a GrafPort is the **dialog record**. A dialog record is a superset of a window record; that is, it consists of a window record, followed by additional fields, including information about the list of items in the dialog, the default button number, and more. Once again, the key here is that the first thing in the record is a GrafPort. This means that all dialog records, like GrafPort and window records, must be either nonrelocatable objects or stack objects. Figure 3-8 summarizes these common kinds of nonrelocatable objects.

Calling MoreMasters will cure the problem of fragmentation due to master pointer blocks, but as your application runs you'll create window and dialog records. How do you ensure that these records don't cause fragmentation of your heap space?

Figure 3-8 Common nonrelocatable objects

Object	Comment	Location
GrafPort	QuickDraw drawing environment	heap or stack
WindowRecord	Contains a GrafPort, so it must be nonrelocatable	heap or stack
DialogRecord	Contains a WindowRecord, so it must be nonrelocatable	heap or stack
Master pointer block	Cannot move, since master pointers "anchor" relocatables	heap

There are several different strategies you can use, some of them obvious and some not so obvious. The most obvious thing to do is simply to allocate window records and dialog records on the stack. This is very easy to do. The calls that create new windows and dialogs give the caller the option of making the new record a heap or stack object. For many applications, this method works fine. The only drawback is that window records will usually have to be declared as global variables, since they are in use most of the time. This means that if your application can show a maximum of three windows, for example, you will have to allocate three global window records, at a cost of 154 bytes per window record. Since dialog records usually only exist for a brief, well-defined period of time, you can often allocate them as local stack variables.

This technique works for some applications, but a couple of complications can spoil things. One is the problem of window records for desk accessories. If a desk accessory allocates its window on the heap, it can cause unexpected fragmentation. The best thing you can do to prevent fragmentation caused by a desk accessory is to have a heap free of locked relocatables and fragmentation.

The other problem arises if your application is capable of opening a large number of windows. If you allow the user to open, say, up to 25 windows, or maybe even an unlimited number of windows, you can't just allocate a global window record on the stack for every window you might open!

How can you avoid fragmentation when opening lots of windows? In general, you should make sure that the only time you create windows (or any other nonrelocatable heap objects) is from your application's main segment. We'll talk more about this subject later.

In addition to nonrelocatable objects, remember that locked relocatables can fragment your heap. A relocatable object becomes locked when you call HLock on it, and it stays that way until you call HUnlock on it. While it's locked, it's fragmenting your heap, and if any new objects are created while the object is locked, the newly created object can only be as large as the longest continuous run of bytes between immobile objects. As long as no new objects are allocated while the object is locked, locking it doesn't hurt you. So the rule is this: you can call HLock, if necessary, to ensure that a relocatable object won't move for a period of time; make sure that you don't allocate any new heap objects while it's locked. Before calling HLock, you should call MoveHHi on an object so that it won't fragment the heap while it's locked.

Sometimes the system will HLock objects on its own, without you telling it to do so. This may seem like a real rude thing to do, but actually it's very necessary. The system locks resources that consist of executable code while they're being executed. This includes CODE, PACK, MDEF, CDEF, WDEF, DRVR, and other resources that are made up of code. For example, your application's segments are CODE resources. When a routine in one of your segments is executing, the system automatically calls HLock on your segment. The same thing happens for the other types of resources listed when they're executing.

If you're familiar with assembly language, and you think about it, you'll see why locking executing code is absolutely necessary. The 68000 keeps track of which instruction it's executing by using a special register called the **program counter**. The program counter simply contains the address of the next instruction to be executed. Imagine what would happen if the running code called a Memory Manager routine that caused some heap objects to move, including the code itself. When the 68000 tried to return to where the program used to be, it would start running undefined bytes. To prevent this disastrous situation, code is automatically locked by the system before it's executed.

The most obvious kind of executing code is your application's CODE segments, but remember that there are lots of other little pieces of code hanging around in the Macintosh at all times, like MDEFs, CDEFs, and others (the most common ones are listed in Figure 3-9). These pieces of code are also locked by the system before they're executed and unlocked by the system after they're done executing. Note that the system does not automatically unlock CODE resources for you. We'll discuss this important fact shortly.

When resources like the ones listed in Figure 3-9 are in use and locked, it's usually because you made a ROM call in your application. For example, when you call MenuSelect, the menu's MDEF resource will be locked while the MenuSelect code uses it to draw the menus. When

Fig. 3-9 Some common resource types that contain code

Resource type	Contents
CDEF	Control definition function, used to draw controls
CODE	Application's code, one resource for each segment
DRVR	Driver or desk accessory
FKEY	"Function key"; maps <Command>-<Shift>-number
INIT	Resource loaded and executed at system startup
LDEF	List definition function, used by List Manager to draw lists
MDEF	Menu definition procedure, used to draw menus
PACK	Package, i. e. Standard File, SANE, Disk Initialization, etc.
PDEF	Printer driver code

it's done drawing the menus, the MDEF will be unlocked. In other words, the MDEF will be unlocked when your application calls MenuSelect, the system will lock it, and then unlock it before it ever returns back to the application from the MenuSelect call. This means that you'll never have to worry about the MDEF being locked over some period of your application's time.

This fast lock/unlock by the system is true of all the resource types listed in Figure 3-9 except CODE. They will be locked and unlocked during some ROM calls, but will always be unlocked when the ROM calls return. You don't have to worry about them fragmenting the heap.

Segmenting Your Application

As we mentioned earlier, the system doesn't unlock CODE resources for you automatically. This is because there's really no way for the system to tell when a CODE segment is finished executing, as it can when a ROM routine calls a resource listed in Figure 3-9. So the vital job of unlocking CODE segments is left up to you. Don't worry, it's easy, and we'll talk about it now.

Most Macintosh applications have a central core in which the application is waiting for the user to do something: type, click on something, select a menu item, and so on. This is called the **main event loop**. Based on what the user does, the application branches off into other parts of the program: a certain menu selection may cause a dialog to come up; another one may cause a new window to be created or make the document print out.

An application's external appearance usually corresponds somewhat to the internal structure of the application. There's usually a main loop that checks what the user is doing by calling GetNextEvent and performs other periodic housekeeping tasks, like calling TEIdle to keep the insertion point blinking in a TextEdit record and calling SystemTask to allow desk accessories, such as a ticking clock, to update themselves. When the main loop reveals that the user has chosen a certain menu item, the program will branch off to a different function that will handle the menu item. When it has been taken care of, control will return to the main loop.

When you're writing a Macintosh application, there's usually not enough memory to keep your entire application and all your data around. The easiest way to get past this dilemma is to break up your application into segments, with each segment being a separately loadable CODE resource. As we mentioned in Chapter 1, most development systems have some kind of directive for letting you specify segments.

How do you determine how your routines should be collected together into segments? Remember that the Macintosh system will load the entire segment into memory when you need to use any routine in that segment. This should give you a clue as to how to organize your application: put related routines together. If a certain menu item causes five different functions to be invoked, one after the other, you should probably put all five of them into the same segment. If you put them in different segments, the user may have to sit there while each of the segments is loaded from disk, spending the waiting time cursing at how slow the Macintosh and your application are.

You'll probably have routines that are so important that they're called on by many different parts of your application. There's a good place for these guys: the main segment, also called the blank segment. Remember that one piece of your application, CODE resource 1, is loaded when your application starts up, stays loaded until the application ends, and is always locked. This is the main segment. It's a real good place for commonly called utility routines, like special formatting or calculation routines. They're guaranteed to always be in memory, so you don't have to worry about a hit on the disk; but the memory that they use isn't available for anything else, since the main segment stays around forever. Don't put huge routines in the main segment unless you use them constantly; on the other hand, if you've got a fairly small routine that has to be loaded from disk a lot, putting it in the main segment will probably be a big win.

Figuring out how to collect your routines into segments is a process that will continue throughout the development of your application. As you're debugging and optimizing, you'll see where your segments need tuning and you'll move routines from one segment to another.

Unloading Your Segments

Once you've got your segmenting figured out, the hard part is over. All you have to do then is make sure that you unlock your segments correctly. This is accomplished with the UnloadSeg call. UnloadSeg actually unlocks a CODE resource and makes it purgeable. Although some application writers take great pains to unload segments only when they're sure that the segments will no longer be needed, there's a pretty efficient and much simpler way to do it that most applications use. This is simply to call UnloadSeg for all your segments every time through the main event loop.

Startup Segment

If you've put a lot of initialization code that gets executed only when the application starts up into a single segment, you don't have to waste time unloading it with UnloadSeg every time through the main event loop. Just unloading it once will do.

This works best if your application is structured along the lines we mentioned earlier; that is, the main event loop acts as a central dispatcher that calls routines in the other segments, and when those routines are done, control returns to the main event loop.

What happens if you call UnloadSeg on a segment and then call a routine in that segment? That's OK; UnloadSeg just makes the segment purgeable, it doesn't cause it to be purged. So, when the routine in the segment is called, the segment is still in memory and doesn't have to be loaded from disk. What if the segment is already unloaded or has never been loaded? That's all right, too. The operating system is smart enough to do nothing if you call UnloadSeg on an already unloaded segment.

By the way, there is also a LoadSeg call, but very few applications ever call it directly. LoadSeg is called implicitly by the system whenever your program calls a routine in another segment. LoadSeg makes sure that the segment is in memory and then locks it.

When Not to Call UnloadSeg

Is there any time that calling UnloadSeg can get you into trouble? Yes, if one segment calls another and the second segment unloads the first.

Let's say you have an application in which a routine in segment 10 calls a routine in segment 99. Then, in segment 99, you decide it's a good idea to call UnloadSeg on segment 10, just to free up its memory. Look out! When the segment 10 routine called segment 99, it left a return address on the stack so that the program would return to the right place in segment 10. By unloading segment 10, you've made it relocatable. If it moves, the return address is no longer valid (see Figure 3-10). So don't call UnloadSeg on segments that called you. The best rule is simply to put all your UnloadSeg calls in the main segment.

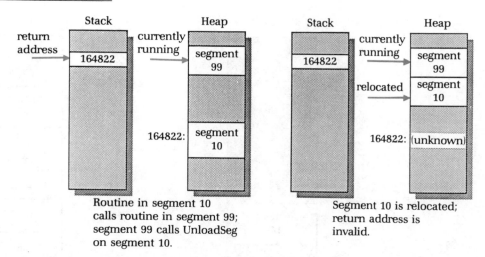

Routine in segment 10
calls routine in segment 99;
segment 99 calls UnloadSeg
on segment 10.

Segment 10 is relocated;
return address is
invalid.

Figure 3-10 Bad use of UnloadSeg

You can achieve very good segment management by just calling UnloadSeg on every segment every time through your main event loop. There is still one subtle problem that can plague you, though, even if you've done a perfect job of segmenting your code and you religiously unload your segments. This is the dreaded segment clotting problem.

Here's how it happens: the user chooses a menu item that causes you to call a routine in an infrequently used segment (let's call it segment 47) and then return to the main loop. The main loop unloads the segment and the application continues running. Since segment 47 is now unlocked, it will be relocated to make space for new objects. Since new objects tend to be allocated low in memory, segment 47 will tend to rise in memory (see Figure 3-11).

Then, as segment 47 has risen in the heap, the user chooses the menu item again, and the routine in segment 47 is called again. What does the system do? It locks segment 47 *right where it is in memory*. Now you've got a locked relocatable object right in the middle of your carefully maintained heap, and if you try to allocate any new objects from routines in segment 47, the heap's continuous bytes are fragmented by the locked CODE segment. This is segment clotting.

How do you fix this problem? One thing you can do is to confine your new-object allocation to the main loop. When the main loop is running, all the other segments are unlocked if you've called UnloadSeg on them, and so the heap will not be fragmented, even if you allocate a new nonrelocatable object.

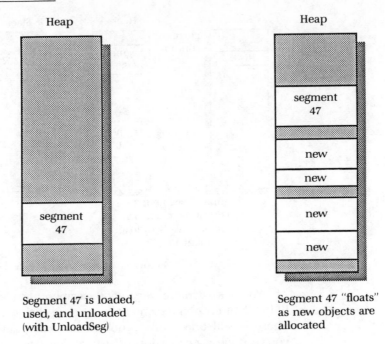

Segment 47 is loaded, used, and unloaded (with UnloadSeg)

Segment 47 "floats" as new objects are allocated

Figure 3-11 Segment clotting

Note that simply putting your memory allocation code anywhere in the main *segment* is not the same as putting it in the main *loop*. Only in the main loop do you unload the other segments. Let's say you create a main segment routine that calls NewHandle and then call that routine from your other segments to allocate new objects.

When your outlying segment calls the main segment routine, the outlying segment remains locked. You can't unlock it; if you do, the return address to it may become invalid. So, when the new object is allocated, the heap is still fragmented by the locked outlying segment. To get a real benefit, the memory allocation must be done in the main loop, after all the segments have been unloaded. See Figure 3-12 for a comparison between these two situations.

Try to do your memory allocation in the main loop when everything else is unloaded. One neat trick you can do is to allocate a nonrelocatable block the size of a window record in your main loop; then, if any of your outlying segments need a new window, they simply use the one you've already allocated, setting a flag to say that it's been used. Then the next time through your main loop you can allocate another one.

If your program's requirements don't allow you to do your memory allocations from the main loop, there are some other things you can do.

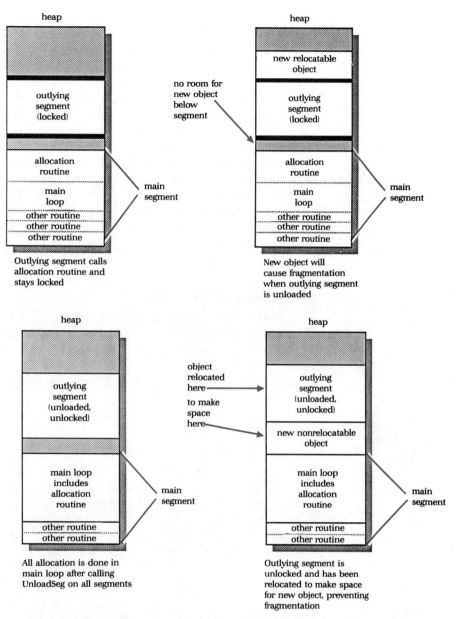

Figure 3-12 Allocation in main loop versus main segment allocation routine

Usually, the clotting problem is confined to one or two segments in specific situations. You might be able to rearrange your segmenting so that the circumstances that cause the clotting are eliminated.

The MoveHHi procedure, which takes a relocatable object and moves it to the highest point in the heap, can help. This puts it out of the way so that it doesn't fragment the heap when new objects are allocated. If you have a specific segment that's clotting in certain situations, you can call MoveHHi on it before calling any of its routines. This can be quite a hassle, however, since you then have to add the explicit MoveHHi call before calling the segment's routines. For another solution, see the following Macintosh Plus note.

The MoveHHi call can be very useful when HLocking an object. If you call MoveHHi on the object before locking it, it will be moved to the top of the heap and will not cause fragmentation, even if a new object is allocated while it's locked.

Limitations of MoveHHi

MoveHHi cannot move an object past a nonrelocatable object or a locked relocatable object. If there's one of these between the object and the top of the heap, MoveHHi relocates the object to just below the immobile object.

Macintosh Plus

In the Macintosh Plus ROM, there's a change to the LoadSeg routine that virtually eliminates the problem of segment clotting. It works like this: the LoadSeg call now checks to see if the CODE resource is locked when it gets it. If not, it calls MoveHHi on it before locking it. This means that if you're careful not to fragment your heap CODE segments won't get in the way.

If you're sure that your application will be running on a Macintosh Plus, you can mark all your CODE resources except CODE 1 as unlocked in the resource file by using a resource editor. This will allow the LoadSeg code to move the segments up when they're loaded.

If your program will be used with non-Plus Macintoshes, you can include the LoadSeg with MoveHHi as a patch in your application. This is available as a technical note from Apple.

Congratulations! If you've absorbed the information in the last two chapters, you now know more about Macintosh memory management than most of the world's Macintosh programmers. As always, the more you know about what's really going on, the better you can make your application.

Things to Remember

- Some objects must be locked at certain times. The most important of these are your application's code segments, which are locked while they're executing.

- By segmenting your application and calling UnloadSeg on each segment every time through the main event loop, you can free up memory.

- By trying to keep your memory allocations in the main event loop, when all your segments are unlocked, you can help maximize your available heap space.

- If your program can create lots of windows, your main loop can keep an extra window record allocated at all times for use by an outlying segment. When the record is used, a flag can be set so that the main loop can get another one.

- You should use MoveHHi before HLocking objects; this will move them to the top of the heap, where they won't be in the way.

PART TWO

Debugging

I could write a book, and this book would be thick enough to stun an ox.

—Laurie Anderson, *Let X=X*

CHAPTER

Debugging Macintosh Software

In this chapter, we'll talk about debugging in general and specific things you have to do when debugging Macintosh applications. We'll also go over various tools that you can use to debug your software.

We'll discuss the reasons why system errors on the Macintosh don't give you a lot of information. We'll talk about questions that you have to ask while debugging. The answers to these questions will help you find out exactly what's gone wrong so that you can fix it.

Bugs

Newly written programs usually have bugs. Even those who try to make their programs right the first time usually spend a great deal of time debugging, and many projects wind up with more debugging time than initial programming time.

The programming and debugging phases often become so tightly coupled that they flow quickly into each other, especially in light of a project's impending deadline. Your computer science professor may have outlined strict, methodical steps for design, "coding" (a word that sounds like translating messages with a secret decoder ring), and debugging, but reality is often a lot hairier than that. Most projects involve a reasonable amount of design work, but frequently the best way to compare various design alternatives is to create a few of them on the computer and test them for power and functionality.

No matter how well designed or well written the program is, it will have to be debugged. In fact, even if the program is working, you will want to improve its performance by **optimizing** the program, a process that's much the same as debugging.

93

Computer programs are complex things that truly have a life of their own. You create them, but then you turn them loose to do their work, kind of like children. You'll find that software is usually easier to debug than kids are, because it is absolutely predictable. If your program is doing something wrong, you can track down *exactly* what's happening and why and then fix the problem. It's not always easy, but it can be done.

Of course, sometimes you'll discover that the problem is not in your program, but in the Macintosh ROM, or in the compiler you're using, or in someone else's software, such as a desk accessory that your application brought up. If this is the case, you get to participate in the fascinating game of workarounds, or how to get your program to avoid somebody else's problem. It's all part of the fun. Usually, though, you find out that it's your bug.

Kinds of Bugs

There are two kinds of behavior that you'll have to fix. The first is when the program dies in a hard and fast (and sometimes spectacular) way; for example, the screen is filled with garbage, the computer reboots, funny sounds start to come out of the speaker, or a bomb (system error) dialog appears. This is called a crash. The second kind of problem is more subtle: the program isn't working properly, but it doesn't have the heart to crash. It just keeps going, not doing the right thing.

In general, bugs like the second kind are traditional logical errors in your programming, the kind programmers have been making ever since they invented FORTRAN (or thereabouts). Often, the best way to fix these bugs is the conventional computer science way: by reading through your source code as if you were a very, very slow computer and determining what you did wrong.

For the Macintosh crash, however, this method isn't always good enough. This is because of the large amount of interplay between your software and someone else's: the ROM and the other system software. The communication of errors from the system to your application is not very sophisticated. Also, the system routines tend to give the application programmer a lot of credit—credit to pass it reasonable parameters, for example. When the parameters are unreasonable, crashes can happen. For crashes, other kinds of debugging are needed, and that's the basis for most of the material in this section.

Error Checking for the ROM

Although there's not much error checking on parameters to ROM routines, there's a handy tool, called Discipline, that checks ROM call parameters for reasonableness. This public-domain utility is available through various hacker channels and user group libraries. It's also built into the TMON debugger.

One of the most important things to know about debugging is this:

Fact

A system error is the result of the execution of a single 68000 instruction.

Understanding this is the first step to fixing your program. It means that a system error is not some unapproachable random behavior, but in fact occurs for specific, well-defined reasons. To fix your program, you'll learn the reasons for the crash.

Does it sound easy? Well, it probably shouldn't sound *too* easy. The typical Macintosh programmer spends a lot of time debugging, and there are problems that can leave you totally exasperated before you solve them. But remember that there really is a reason for whatever bizarre behavior is plaguing your poor program, and that if you look long and hard enough (and get enough help) you'll find it. Remember that cheerful thought, and maybe it will keep you going on those long nights.

Understanding what's going on inside the Macintosh when your application is running is essential. The more you know, the more likely it is that you'll be able to fix and enhance your application. The more areas of mystery that you encounter without solving them, the better the chance that the program will one day exhibit a bug that will leave you wondering what in the world is happening.

Aside from just making it work, a thorough knowledge of what your application is doing will help you in the future when the inevitable revision takes place. If you really know what your code is doing, you'll have a much better shot at adding features or improving performance in the future.

Why System Errors Don't Tell You Very Much

Often your first indication that something's gone wrong is the appearance of the good ol' bomb box, which is more formally known as a system error. The system error is accompanied by a number. You might think that this would tell you a lot about the problem. Unfortunately, it tells you virtually nothing other than that something bad has happened.

Why can't we learn more from system errors? Here's a rather dramatic but effective metaphor. Imagine that you're driving down a road and you see a car smashed into a tree, burning. What happened? Was the road slippery? Was the driver drunk? Did the brakes fail? Did the driver swerve to avoid hitting a squirrel?

You can't tell. The crash and the fire have destroyed much of the evidence. To really know what happened, you'd have to have been there as the accident occurred. If you could watch it re-created, in slow motion, you might be able to see the causes, and if you were an expert, you might be able to learn what happened.

Software on the Macintosh is a lot like that. Thousands of things can go wrong: an uninitialized variable can be used as if it were valid; there can be a relocatable block that is released, but still referred to by leftover handles; or a program can neglect to check an error code, just to name a few.

Whatever the cause, the Macintosh, like the car in our metaphor, loses control and hits the tree. It's important to realize that there's no guarantee that the cause led directly to the problem; for example, the car's brakes may have been out for some time before the fateful tree was encountered. In the same way, the program may do its bad thing, like forgetting to check an error code, then run along for a while, everything apparently OK, until it does something that causes a system error.

Whatever the problem, it usually results in a system error. These occur when a variety of things happen. Each cause of a system error is discussed in this chapter.

The most important thing to remember is that a system error simply tells you that something has gone wrong, and the error number is merely a clue to learn what it was that happened. Getting a system error is the beginning of your search to find the problem, not the end.

Some errors are easily repeated. You know that if you follow a list of instructions the program will crash every time. These kinds of crashes are the programmer's friend. If you know it will crash every time, you can rerun the program and watch very carefully, in slow motion, when the error occurs.

Much tougher are the errors that seem to occur "at random." You've seen them happen, but you can't seem to come up with a script to repeat the error. These problems are usually much tougher to find, since it's hard to look back after a crash and learn much about it.

The Art of Debugging

Debugging is one of those problem-solving things that humans do real well and computers are not so good at (but the artificial intelligence folks are working to fix that). Debugging involves rules, logic, hunches, intuition, source listings, experience, tedium, and many caffeine-enriched beverages. In the typical debugging process, the programmer runs the application, uses special programs (**debuggers**) to observe and modify the application's behavior, and generally tries to figure out what's going on inside the box. It also often involves frustration, blind alleys, cursing of debuggers, and moments of supreme triumph as you finally figure out what's wrong.

In this part of the book, we'll talk about some rules and suggestions for debugging your code. As you start doing more debugging, you'll learn shortcuts, techniques, and tricks that help you along, and very soon the idea of looking at a list of "debugging rules" will be alien to you—knowing what to do will be automatic.

Also, since debugging is a problem-solving experience, there are lots of different ways to attack any situation. There's usually no way of knowing which one is best for a given situation, so you'll develop your favorites. In this chapter we'll discuss the most popular techniques.

One of the things that makes debugging difficult is that every problem is a little bit different. As you come across more and more situations, you'll figure out strange and wonderful new ways to debug your program.

High-level Language Programmers

Most Macintosh applications are written in high-level languages, but the most effective Macintosh debugging is done at the assembly language level. This is because debugging an application involves watching the application work. The more sophisticated the debugger gets, the more memory it takes and the more it intrudes on the application. This is like the old physicists' problem of wanting to observe an atomic phenomenon without disturbing it, the Heisenberg Uncertainty Principle. Low-level debuggers that let you observe an application's object code provide the least disturbance to the application.

This doesn't mean that you have to be an assembly language programmer to write or debug a Macintosh application. However, the most effective high-level Macintosh programmer will be the one who can read and follow assembly language. The ability to write assembly language is handy, but is not really required. You might call this a "read-only" knowledge of assembly language.

Reading assembly language versus writing it is kind of like being able to understand a spoken language, but not being able to speak it perfectly yourself. You might be able to listen to someone speak in, say, Spanish or Serbo-Croatian and understand what's being said, but when you try to speak, you goof up the grammar a bit. You're better off if you can speak it, too, but listening to it is a separate skill.

There are several different methods of debugging, but they all use the same basic principles. The fundamental principle, which we've already discussed, is knowing exactly what your application is doing. As we said earlier, most noncrashing bugs can be located and fixed just by working with the source, but you can use the techniques of watching your application run to debug those problems, too. Sometimes, using an object code debugger to figure out that a loop that went from 1 to 10 should have gone from 0 to 9 is overkill, but it will work.

Debugging Questions

Debugging is an information-gathering process. While you're debugging, you'll answer several important questions, like these:

- Where did the program crash?
- What specifically caused the crash?
- What assembly language instruction was the last one executed before the crash?
- What caused the offending instruction to be executed?

Fixing your bugs involves answering each of these questions. To find the answers, you'll use lots of different techniques to gather information. Each piece of information that you learn is a clue to your bug. As you gather clues, you'll start to form theories about your bugs: what they might be, where they might be located. As you think about these theories, you can do more with the debugger to test them, and you'll get still more clues. Eventually, if you do your work right, the clues will lead you to the problem.

Let's take a look at each of the questions listed and discuss how you might find the answers.

Where Did the Program Crash?

The first step in understanding what's happening to your application is finding out "where" the program was when it crashed. This means determining the last instruction it executed before the crash happened.

When the Macintosh does anything, including crashing a program, it does so because of instructions being executed by the 68000. For example, when the Macintosh puts up the system error bomb, a routine called SysError in the System Error Handler section of the ROM has been called. Why was this routine called? Either a program or subroutine determined that an error condition existed, and it called SysError, or a 68000 **exception**, such as an address error, occurred. We'll talk a lot about exceptions later in this chapter.

What routine would do a terrible thing like calling SysError? Usually, it's a ROM routine that your application called. For example, when your application calls MenuSelect, MenuSelect tries to save what's on the screen under the menu it's about to draw. It calls NewHandle to get memory to save the piece of the screen. If the NewHandle call says that there's not enough room in the heap for the saved screen, it calls SysError to report an out of memory condition.

More on SysError

SysError takes one parameter, which is the error number to report. In the preceding example, SysError is called with a parameter of 25, which means there's not enough space in the heap to allocate a requested object. SysError is documented extensively in the System Error Handler chapter of **Inside Macintosh.**

Often you'll be able to determine right away what your application's last action was before crashing. On the Macintosh, where lots of visual things are happening as the application executes, you can use visual clues to determine what code is being executed. For example, if your application is trying to bring up a dialog box with six items by calling GetNewDialog, and it draws the box and the first four items and then crashes, you have a pretty good idea that the last thing that your application did before the crash was call GetNewDialog.

Sometimes it's not that easy, of course. A crash may occur with no visual clues to what part of the application is executing. There are other techniques that you can use to find out exactly how far the application got before the crash occurred, and we'll discuss those later in this chapter.

When you determine what instruction caused the application to crash, you'll note the next important fact: was the Macintosh executing ROM code when the crash occurred, or was it running your application's code? Frequently, crashes take place in the ROM. This usually doesn't indicate a bug in the ROM (although it can); the ROM routines trust you to pass them reasonable parameters. If you don't, crashes of various kinds can occur.

What Specifically Caused the Crash?

Every crash has a specific cause. For example, routines in the ROM may cause a system error 25 if there's no heap space available. If this happens, the only fact that's immediately apparent is that a system error 25 has occurred. You'll have to do some investigative debugging to find out that it was a call to MenuSelect that triggered the error. For the purposes of terminology, we'll say that the **symptom** of this crash was an out-of-heap-space condition; the **cause** of the crash was the lack of available heap space in a MenuSelect call. The first fact, the symptom, is obvious because of the bomb dialog that appears on the screen as soon as the error takes place. The cause isn't readily apparent and requires debugging work to determine.

There are crashes other than the system error bomb dialog, of course. Another crash that happens sometimes is the one that makes machine-gun-like sounds from the speaker, usually accompanied by the screen going crazy. The cause of this problem is that data is being stored into the special Macintosh addresses that cause the screen to display different parts of memory and that cause the speaker to make various sounds. The usual reason for this crash is that the application is attempting to use data that's not valid, or the Macintosh is somehow executing code that wasn't intended to be executed; for example, the 68000 has been told by your program or one of the ROM routines you've called to begin executing code in an area of memory that's really data, not code.

Just knowing the cause of the crash will not tell you what's wrong with your program and how to fix it. If your program dies with a system error 2 after calling InsertMenu, you probably passed a bad parameter to InsertMenu, but the only way to tell how the bad parameter got there is by examining your application. Once you learn the cause of the problem, you'll have to do more legwork to discover exactly what's wrong.

At the end of this chapter, you'll find a discussion of common crashes and possible causes for each crash.

What Assembly Language Instruction Was the Last One Executed before the Crash?

Now, all you high-level language programmers out there, stay cool. By studying the information that's presented in the rest of this book, you'll be able to learn how to do this. Chapters 5 and 6 will tell you a lot about how your compiler works, and you can read Appendix A if you want an overview of how the 68000 deals with high-level languages. If you're a high-level language programmer, there's a corollary to this question: Which statement in the source generated the instruction that was executed right before the crash?

As we've said, crashes are the result of the execution of a single instruction. Although it may have taken lots of instructions to create the bad values that caused the program to crash, the actual crash can be traced to a single 68000 instruction. If the crash is a system error number 1 through 11, there was a single offending instruction that caused a 68000 exception. If the crash is a system error number greater than 11, a ROM routine called the System Error Handler by invoking the SysError trap.

The next trick in the debugging process is to find this single offending instruction. Sometimes, it's trivial; often, it's hard. If it's trivial, it's probably because you passed the wrong parameter to a ROM routine, or maybe you forgot an & when passing an object by reference from C. If it's hard and the problem is a tough one to reproduce, it may take you hours or days to find it.

One technique that's commonly used to figure out exactly which instruction caused a program to crash is rerunning the program one or more times, letting it go farther and farther each time until you watch it crash. This can be done in the source code, by inserting statements that wait until the mouse button is pressed, for example, or by using an object code debugger to set **breakpoints**: places where the debugger stops the program.

Since most Macintosh applications are so visual, you can use visual clues to help figure out how far to let the application go before setting a breakpoint. As we discussed earlier, if you see the application draw part of a dialog box and then crash, you have an excellent idea of the application's last instruction before the crash (it was probably GetNew-Dialog). Usually, the visual clues aren't quite that definitive, but they are always helpful in finding where the program was before it crashed.

If you have a nonreproducible error, you can use the **trap recording** capabilities that some debuggers have. Trap recording is a debugger feature that waits for trap calls to be executed. When trap calls are made, the debugger will record some information about the call, including which trap is being called, the location of the instruction that's calling it and the parameters to the call. This way, when the program crashes, you can see which trap calls were most recently made, which is a great help in finding the problem.

Trap recording is kind of like a security camera at a bank. Although you don't know when (or if) you'll ever need it, you install it. If the bank is robbed, you have a visual record of what went on. By turning on trap recording, you'll make sure that you have a record of what transpired if your program crashes.

What Caused the Offending Instruction to Be Executed?

This is the root of debugging and usually the hardest step. The completion of this step involves actually locating the bug. Somewhere in the application, faulty logic, bad data, or bugs in system software have caused the crash, and finding out why the crashing instruction was executed means knowing what the bug is.

Finding the bug usually involves several different techniques used together. Sometimes, an initial exploration into the bug doesn't tell you what you need to know, and you run headlong into a dead end. When this happens, you have to attack it with a different technique. Usually, you don't have to start over completely, though, because you'll be able to use the information you learned from previous efforts. Debugging is like a big logic problem, and every tidbit, fact, and clue that you pick up along the way can help you solve the puzzle.

After you've found the offending instruction, you may be able to discover the problem immediately. For example, if the crash is an address error (system error 2) that occurs in the ROM in the SelectWindow routine, you should immediately examine the values of the parameters that you passed to SelectWindow. You may find, for example, that you neglected to set up the value of the WindowPtr that you passed to SelectWindow, and it contained an odd value, thus generating the address error. If this is the case, you can probably fix the problem just by inserting a statement to set up the WindowPtr before calling the ROM.

Killing Ants with Nuclear Weapons

Note that this particular error, which is fairly typical of the kind Macintosh programmers commit, could be caught just by examining the source, without using an object code debugger. What's the easiest method? On the Macintosh, you'd probably use an object code debugger to determine, at least, the last statement that your application was able to execute. At that point, you can go to your source listing and just step through it, checking the parameters that you passed to the ROM. This method has the advantage of being mostly in the high-level language, so it's easier for most high-level language programmers. The disadvantage is that you're still looking at a piece of paper, and reality has a nasty habit of intervening between the source listing and the program's execution. What the debugger tells you is the truth (if it's a good debugger); the source listing is a couple of steps removed from that truth, so you can't always rely on it.

If you discover that one of the parameters to a ROM call was in fact causing the crash, you're not out of the woods yet. You have to find out why that parameter was passed to that particular call. If it's just a constant in your program, the answer may be easy: you just mistyped or used the wrong constant. If the bad parameter is a variable, you have to find out where and why it went bad. Maybe you simply forgot to assign it a value (sloppy you). If a variable containing a bad value was used as a parameter to an earlier ROM routine, you may find that that ROM routine placed an unexpected value in the variable. Closer investigation into the behavior of the ROM routine should reveal more about the problem.

If the crash occurred in a ROM routine and you've examined the parameters to the routine and found them all to be reasonable, there are other problems to look for. Does the ROM call rely on some global state of the system that may be set improperly? For example, does the call assume that the current GrafPort has been set to a certain value, like the frontmost window? Many of the QuickDraw calls operate on the "current port," that is, the last GrafPort that you passed to a `SetPort` call. Usually, if ROM calls require globals to be set a certain way, **Inside Macintosh** will say so.

No matter what the problem, one of the most valuable techniques for debugging involves tracing a program's execution by stepping through its instructions. This can be done either with the aid of a debugger, such as Macsbug, or by hand by stepping through your source or object code.

Don't be reluctant to try stepping through your source code yourself. When you do this, you pretend that you're the computer. Take a piece of paper and make columns for each of your variables, and maybe have a space to represent what gets drawn on the screen. If you're careful, you can make yourself almost as accurate as the computer; you will find yourself several million times slower, but don't sweat it. In school, we used to call this "playing Mr. Computer," and it's a good way to attack problems that you think are in your code. See Figure 4-1 for an example of a Mr. Computer worksheet.

Figure 4-1 Mr. Computer worksheet

Variables				
myVal	theNum	n	moe	johann
~~12~~	~~116~~	~~1~~	~~false~~	~~1.8775~~
~~-4~~	~~-8~~	~~2~~	~~true~~	~~3.24~~
~~19~~	~~3~~	~~3~~	~~false~~	~~4.4~~
~~112~~	9	~~4~~	true	~~9.345~~
~~0~~		~~5~~		104.5
−5		6		

Screen		
Window1	Window2	Window3
Empty	The text "Fünfzehn zweistimmige Inventionen"	The text "Quinze Inventions à deux parties"

Once you're familiar with the object-code debuggers, you'll use one of them to step through your program's code. This is just like playing Mr. Computer, except that the computer is actually helping you do it. When using a debugger, the computer makes itself be several million times slower than usual, just so that we humans can keep up. We'll talk more about debuggers throughout the rest of this part of the book.

Debugging Tools

You can use lots of different techniques and tools to apply the debugging principles we've discussed. Some of these are object code debuggers, source code walk-throughs, special-purpose debuggers, and diagnostic output. We'll talk about each of these and how to use them.

Source Code Walk-through

This method of debugging is the classic one, recommended by four out of five computer science professors. To debug this way, you should lock yourself in a room far away from the computer, take a printed copy of your program's source listing and notes from whatever debugging you've already done, and step through the source code, line by line, playing Mr. Computer by printing on a piece of paper the values of variables and the output that the program generates.

Walking through the source code is an important part of the debugging process, but in a complex environment like Macintosh, where dozens of different "programs" (drivers, desk accessories, ROM routines, definition procedures for menus, windows, controls, interrupt handlers, etc.) are executing all around your application, the isolation of you and your source code doesn't always provide the answers you need. However, it is a good idea to get away from the computer sometimes, relax with something to drink, and proceed at your own pace instead of the computer's for a while.

Before you retire off with your source listing, you should probably use one of the other techniques discussed next to gather more information about your application's problem. The object code debuggers are a handy way to help determine the last thing an application did before a crash; diagnostic output is good for learning where a program is when it does something unusual but doesn't crash completely.

One essential accessory to source code walk-throughs is a complete, up-to-date source listing. You should always have an accurate source listing; that's why God invented laser printers. There's nothing more frustrating than spending hours tracking down an elusive bug, only to finally discover that the bug was introduced by a program change you made since your last source listing was printed.

Object Code Debuggers

Object code debuggers seem to be the most popular tool for debugging Macintosh software. The advantages of object code debuggers are that they're right next to the action; that is, you're seeing what really happens as your application's object code is executed. There's virtually nothing that's hidden from you, no layers of complexity to keep you from observing the computer at work.

The disadvantage of object code debuggers is that they require you to read assembly language, even if you wrote your program in a high-level language. Most Macintosh high-level language programmers find the effort to get over this hump worthwhile when they see how much an object code debugger can help in programming.

Debuggers hang around in the computer's RAM just waiting for your program to crash. When it does, they take control away from the System Error Handler in the ROM, and instead of getting a bomb on the screen, you get the debugger. You can also invoke the debugger without crashing the program; most debuggers hook themselves into the interrupt switch (the rear half of the programmer's switch). By pressing this switch, you can jump into the debugger at any time and use it to examine your program and anything else that's going on inside the Macintosh.

Object code debuggers are the primary method of gaining information about your application, but there are various other ways to find out what's going on inside the Macintosh. Some of them, like the source-code walkthroughs we already discussed, are good ideas in any language; other tools and techniques require special development environments.

Warning

Beware of Debuggers

When you're running a well-written debugger, you feel like you're directly manipulating the microprocessor and the computer's memory. Sometimes you forget that the debugger itself is a program. The job of a debugger is to run without disturbing the rest of the system. This is impossible, since debuggers take up RAM, use registers, allocate stack space, and so on. Sometimes a debugger will lie to you as its operations become inadvertently mixed with the program you're debugging. It can be very frustrating, for example, when a debugger refuses to continue tracing a program that it's been tracing for an hour because of some bizarre interaction between the debugger and the program. Fortunately, this doesn't happen often, but if it happens to you, calm down and drink a nice glass of orange juice before punching out the computer.

Debuggers hook themselves into the system in a couple of different ways. One family of debuggers, collectively known as Macsbug, installs itself when the system is started up. It works like this: if you have a file named Macsbug on a startup disk, that file's contents will be installed in memory as the debugger. You've probably seen the line that says "Macsbug installed," which appears just below the "Welcome to Macintosh" message.

There have been at least ten different versions of Macsbug released over the past two years. They vary in the number of lines of information they display, the amount of memory they take up, and the place they send their output (to the screen or through a serial port). See Appendix D for more information on Macsbug.

Don't Blame This One on Apple

There are too many products in the Macintosh world that begin with "Mac." Apple certainly helped this trend by publishing MacWrite, MacPaint, and so on. However, you can't blame Macsbug on Apple. Macsbug is an acronym for Motorola Advanced Computing Systems Debugger, and it existed before the Macintosh did!

The other method of installing a debugger is through the use of an installation program, which is run just like an ordinary application. When the installation program is run, the debugger installs itself in memory. The debugger called TMON, from Icom Simulations in Wheeling, Illinois, installs itself this way. This method has the advantage of allowing you to install the debugger without having to restart the computer. A disadvantage is that this debugger cannot be used to debug code that runs before the startup application, such as boot code, since the debugger isn't installed until an application is run.

Installing a Debugger

How does a debugger "install itself"? The 68000 defines an area of low memory (locations $0 to $100) as **exception vectors**. These locations are pointers to routines that take control when the 68000 encounters one of its exceptions, for example, an address error, an illegal instruction error, a divide by zero error, and the other system errors. When the debugger is installed, it places pointers to its own code in these locations. This is how it takes control when one of these exceptions happens.

Remember that a system error can be generated in two ways: either a 68000 exception, like a system error, occurs, or a program calls the SysError routine. Some debuggers don't take control when SysError is called, only when 68000 exceptions happen. This means that you may find yourself very frustrated as a system error bomb dialog is drawn on the screen even though you have the debugger installed.

Once the debugger is installed, you can let your application run until it crashes. If the crash would normally have caused a system error, the debugger will be invoked instead of the system error. The exact display that you get depends on the debugger that you're using, of course. Figure 4-2 shows what you'll see when your application crashes with TMON installed.

Know Your Numbering System

When you're looking at debugger displays and assembly language source, be sure you don't mix up hex and decimal. Hex numbers are usually preceded by a dollar sign, but some debuggers, including TMON, assume hex as the default. Be sure to check the rules for the debugger you're using.

Since object code debuggers are so powerful and important, we'll spend some time here looking closely at the TMON debugger, the one that's used for debugging in this book. If you want to learn more about Macsbug or you don't have TMON, you should check out Appendix D, A Guided Tour of Macsbug.

```
Address error.  PC=$000116A8.
Access address: $00000715 (supervisor data), instruction: yes, mode: read.
```

Figure 4-2 TMON address error display

A Guided Tour of TMON

Macsbug in its almost infinite varieties is the most commonly used debugger, at least in part because it's easy to get: Apple has provided it with the Macintosh Software Supplement for over two years. There are other, more powerful choices. One debugger that's very popular for a number of good reasons is TMON.

Like most debuggers, TMON lurks behind the application, waiting to be called. If a system error occurs, the debugger takes control. If there's no error and you want to enter the debugger, you can do so by pressing the interrupt switch on the side of the Macintosh.

Once you're in TMON, you can get information about what's going on in the computer. If you've seen Macsbug, you'll notice a big difference here. Instead of a teletypelike display where information disappears off the top of the screen on a single display, TMON takes advantage of an almost Macintosh-like user interface. Information is displayed in scrollable windows, and the windows can be moved around on the screen. Also, there's something that looks kind of like a menu bar at the top of the screen.

The reason that TMON's version of the Macintosh user interface looks slightly mutated is related to the nature of debuggers. Because a debugger must be operable even if the system is in a disastrous state, and because a debugger must operate transparently to the system being debugged, it's a good idea to make the debugger as independent as possible; that is, it shouldn't count on the system software's data structures being in working order. TMON does a good job of this, implementing a Macintosh-like user interface, but doing so without relying on the standard system data structures being intact. Instead, it creates its own data structures to support its user interface.

The list of commands at the top of the screen make up the menu. Most of these commands create windows in which you can see various information about the state of the system.

First, let's discuss how you enter commands. In TMON, you have your choice of clicking on a menu item or typing a command key. For example, we can open a Dump window (which displays memory) by typing Command-D or by clicking on the word Dump in the menu bar.

Once we've opened a window, we can tell it what range we want displayed by typing in an address. For example, we can examine memory starting at location 1B314 by opening a Dump window and typing 1B314 on the top line. TMON displays the hex and ASCII values of subsequent memory locations. Of course, with TMON you can scroll in both directions from the location displayed. Figure 4-3 shows a sample Dump window. We'll talk more about the Dump window in a while.

```
DUMP FROM 01B314
01B314:    00 00 00 04   00 85 00 C4   00 00 00 04   00 85 00 C4   ...............
01B324:    00 00 80 02   00 10 7F FE   00 10 00 0C   00 00 00 00   ...............
01B334:    00 10 00 10   00 00 00 40   F9 A6 00 00   00 00 00 00   .......@........
01B344:    00 00 00 00   00 01 C6 C0   00 00 00 00   00 10 00 00   ...............
01B354:    CB 9C 00 00   00 00 00 FF   00 00 00 01   00 00 00 01   ...............
01B364:    00 00 00 00   D7 1E 00 00   00 00 00 00   00 00 00 01   ...............
01B374:    00 00 00 10   00 00 00 00   00 0E 00 43   6F 6E 74 72   ...........Contr
01B384:    6F 6C 86 00   00 18 00 00   00 70 00 0A   80 01 80 01   ol.......p......
```

Figure 4-3 Example of Dump window

This is probably a good time to mention another of TMON's nifty features: it's extensible. If you want some new features and capabilities, you don't have to wait for the program's author to add them: you can add your own, within some limitations, of course. This is done with a TMON feature called the **User Area**. If you look at TMON today, you'll probably find many more features than you'll read about here.

When you enter TMON, the top of the display tells what caused TMON to take control. For the rest of our guided tour, let's assume that TMON was invoked because an address error occurred, as denoted by the message "Address error." which you can see in Figure 4-2. Also, the instruction at the current program counter is displayed (that's the line that says "PC=$000116A8"). In addition, TMON tells you that the memory access that caused the address error was location $715 ("Access address: $00000715"). The other information given, which includes whether the 68000 was in supervisor mode when the error took place and whether the offending location was read or written to, is usually ignored when debugging.

Supervisor Mode

The 68000 has a supervisor mode and a user mode. In the user mode, certain instructions aren't permitted. The Macintosh always runs in supervisor mode, so it can execute all 68000 instructions.

The TMON display means that an address error occurred and that error caused the debugger to be invoked. It also says that the odd value that caused the address error was 00000715.

Help Is Available

If you're not real familiar with 68000 assembly language, don't forget about Appendix A. It's designed for high-level language programmers who want to know more about assembly language. If you fit into this category, you might want to read it right now.

To learn more about what caused the address error, we can open an Assembly window, which will disassemble 68000 code. We can open this window by clicking on the word "Asmbly" in the menu bar or by typing Command-A. By entering the offending address, 116A8, on the Assembly window's top line, we see "116A8:   OR.B (A2),A4". It says that the current program counter (PC) is at 116A8, and that the instruction at that location is OR.B (A2),A4, which means "logically-or the byte pointed to by register A2 with the contents of register A4," or "take the contents of the lowest byte of register A4, perform a logical-or between those contents and the byte pointed to by register A2 , and put the result of this operation back into A4." The debugger seems to be saying that the address error occurred after executing this statement.

Great. There's only one thing wrong with this information: there's absolutely no way that instruction could have caused an address error. Why? Well, address errors occur when word size or long word size data is accessed at an odd address (more about this later). In this instruction, the size of the operand is a byte (the .B part of OR.B). Address errors cannot occur on instructions that do not have word or long word operands.

This Window Does Two Things

The assembly window, denoted by the command Asmbly in TMON's menu bar, actually has two functions: it assembles code that you type in, which is great fun, but, more commonly, it's used to **disassemble** instructions; that is, to display them as assembly language. For this reason, this window is also sometimes called the *disassembly* window.

So what's going on? Is the debugger playing tricks on us? Is there really an address error? Yes, there is, but debuggers often misplace the program counter by a couple of instructions following an error. Part of the reason is that debuggers actually take control before executing the instruction at the current program counter. How do you find the real location of the address error?

The address error actually occurs just before the instruction displayed by the debugger, and you can use this window to list the instructions just before the one that's displayed, allowing you to see the one that caused the error.

To see the instruction that caused the address error, just press the up-arrow to scroll the disassembled listing backwards. Clicking once on the up-arrow should show you the instruction that caused the address error.

Instructions out of Synch

Since 68000 instructions are of different lengths, it's possible to use the disassembly window to start disassembling right in the middle of an instruction. This will cause a single "garbage" instruction to be displayed; then the debugger will usually get back in synchronization and start listing instructions properly. Be aware that the first instruction displayed may not be a valid one. Usually, clicking once on the up-arrow to scroll the window backwards will put the debugger back in synch.

When we scroll the window backwards, it displays the instructions that immediately precede the program counter. The listing produced is shown in Figure 4-4. The instruction we're interested in is the one right before the program counter, the line that reads MOVE.L (A3),A4. Is this instruction the one that caused the address error? Let's take a look.

The instruction says to move the long word (32-bit value) pointed to by register A3 into register A4. Since this instruction says that A3 is pointing at a long word, its contents must be even. We can find out the contents of the registers by clicking on the Regs command in TMON. This opens a window showing the values of the 68000 registers. (A nice touch is displaying the status register bits mnemonically; for example, the carry bit is displayed as an uppercase C if set and a lowercase c if clear.) If we look at the contents of A3 in this window, we see that it contains $00000715, which is indeed an odd number.

```
0116A6:    MOVE.L   (A3),A4
0116A8:    SUBQ.W   #2,A3
0116AA:    CMPI.W   #FFFF,D1
0116AE:    BEQ.S    ^$0116B4
0116B0:    CMP.W    (A3),D0
0116B2:    BNE.S    ^$0116B8
```

Figure 4-4 Example of Disassembly window

Now we can be sure that this instruction is the one that caused the address error. In fact, if you recall, the first line displayed in the debugger after the address error occurred included this number, $00000715, calling it the "access address" of the address error. This means that it was the specific odd address that caused the address error. Notice, however, that it doesn't tell you which instruction caused the error.

When a program crashes into the debugger, the first thing you'll do is find out what instruction caused the error by using the disassembly window. The next important thing to learn is what routine was being executed when the crash occurred. The disassembly window will try to tell you this by checking to see if the addresses you're looking at come just after a predefined symbol, like the name of a ROM call. If so, TMON will display the name and the offset from this defined symbol.

The most common case is that the instruction is in the ROM. Remember, this doesn't necessarily mean that there's a bug in the ROM. In fact, it rarely indicates that. Most ROM routines trust their callers to pass them reasonable parameters and often fail with system errors if the parameters are not valid. You can easily tell if the instruction is in the ROM just by looking at its address. If the address is in the range $400000 through $40FFFF, the instruction is in the ROM.

Macintosh Plus

On a Macintosh Plus, the ROM is 128K bytes long, so the range for ROM addresses is $400000 through $41FFFF.

If the crash did indeed occur in the ROM, TMON will display the name of the nearest preceding ROM call in the disassembly. At first thought, you might think that this information will enable you to determine the last ROM routine called by your application. For example, if the crash is in the ROM and the disassembly window tells you that the offending instruction is in the DrawText ROM routine, you might think that all you have to do is figure out where your program called DrawText.

Unfortunately, it's not that easy (you probably guessed that I was going to tell you that). The complication is that routines in the ROM frequently call other ROM routines to get their jobs done, sometime several levels deep. For example, when you call DisposeWindow, it calls CloseWindow, which calls DisposPtr. So, if your application crashes and the debugger tells you that the error occurred in DisposPtr, you really don't know where the DisposPtr call came from. However, a little bit later in this chapter we'll discuss another TMON command that *will* tell you the last ROM call your application made at any point.

You can use your knowledge of the Macintosh ROM to guess at what your application's last ROM call was. For example, in the preceding discussion we said that DisposeWindow eventually calls DisposPtr. If you suspect that you may have passed a bad window pointer to a DisposeWindow call, a crash in DisposPtr fits right in with that suspicion. It seems reasonable that DisposeWindow would take the window pointer you pass to it and call DisposPtr on it. If you passed an invalid pointer, an error in DisposPtr is a reasonable expectation.

What if the instruction that caused the crash is not located in the ROM? Obviously, this is the case if the offending instruction's address does not fall in the range $400000 through $41FFFF. If the crash is in RAM, which means anywhere in the vast 4-megabyte range from $0 through $3FFFFF, the offending instruction is probably in your application's code, but it may not be. Remember that there are lots of other little programs running around the Macintosh's memory with your application, and the crash may have been in one of them, too. Later in this section we'll discuss debugger commands that will tell you how to find out just what thing owns the offending instruction.

The disassembly window will also try to find symbols within your application's code. In this case, TMON will show the name of the procedure or function that the instruction resides in. How does it know this name? Some development systems, Apple's Pascal and C in particular, have an option to embed procedure and function names in the object code at the end of each procedure or function. If you invoked this option when you built the program, TMON will be able to find these names and use them. In Workshop Pascal, this feature is invoked with the D option. If your development system doesn't have this ability to embed procedure names, you won't be able to use this feature. Some development systems do this automatically. To find out if yours does, just look at some of your application's code in the disassembly window!

You can also enter the names of symbols into the disassembly window. For example, if you want to disassemble a function called DireStraits, you can type "DireStraits" (including the quotes) on the top line of the disassembly window. TMON will search for a function by this name and disassemble it from the beginning.

TMON Features TMON and other object code debuggers provide lots of different commands and displays to help you track your program's progress. Let's look at these commands now.

Many TMON commands require numbers as input, and these numbers are usually addresses. For example, the Dump command displays bytes in memory at an address that you specify, and lets you change those bytes. To allow maximum flexibility, TMON will accept expressions that include numbers in a variety of forms whenever it wants a number as input. You can enter numbers either in hexadecimal or in decimal; decimal numbers should be preceded by a period (decimal point). You can precede hex numbers with a dollar sign if you really want to, but TMON will assume hex. You can also enter ASCII strings by enclosing them in single quotes (known to punctuation fanatics as apostrophes). As we said earlier, you can use defined symbols by putting them in quotation marks.

You can also use symbols to represent the contents of the 68000 registers. You specify the contents of a data register by using the notation RDn, where n is the number of the register; address registers are indicated with RAn. For example, if you want to refer to the memory that register A2 points to, you can enter the expression RA2, which literally means "display memory beginning at the address pointed to by register A2." Since A7 is the stack pointer, you can refer to bytes on the stack with RA7. You can also refer to the program counter by using the symbol PC.

TMON will also let you perform some arithmetic in the numbers that you pass to commands. You can do addition, subtraction, multiplication, and division in your expression by using +, −, *, and /. TMON also defines the @ symbol as an "indirection operator"; in other words, it dereferences a pointer. This is most useful with system global locations that contain pointers. For example, we know that location $9D6, which is called WindowList, contains a pointer to the frontmost window. To refer to the contents of the frontmost window's windowRecord, we can use the expression @9D6, or even @"windowlist", which means "display memory at the address pointed to by location $9D6." You can use multiple @ symbols to dereference handles. For example, ScrapHandle at $964 contains a handle to the scrap (you may have guessed that). To examine the scrap, you could type @@964 or @@"ScrapHandle" into a Dump window.

As we've shown, the Dump window allows you to display memory anywhere in the Macintosh. The memory that you look at is displayed both in hexadecimal and ASCII form. This command is useful for looking at your program's data structures in memory.

The Dump window also allows to you modify the memory that you're looking at. This is handy when you want to modify the value of a variable or change one of the Macintosh global variables. You have to be careful with this, of course, since it will let you write over anything in RAM. It assumes you know what you're doing, so make sure that you do!

The TMON Registers window will allow you to examine and change the contents of the 68000's registers. To look at the values in any registers, just open the Registers window. If you want to change any of the values, just click on them in the Registers window and type in the new value. You can use any of the operators described previously when you set register values.

Execution Commands   TMON contains a set of commands for controlled execution of code. One that's frequently used is the Step command. This command executes a single 68000 instruction and then returns control to the debugger. The step command is invaluable in playing Mr. Computer as you walk through your program. This command also has the handy feature of treating ROM calls as a single instruction. In other words, if you're tracing along and you come to a ROM call, such as GetNextEvent, stepping will not trace all the 68000 instructions that GetNextEvent executes in the ROM. It will act as if GetNextEvent is a single 68000 instruction and will come back to the debugger after Get-NextEvent returns.

Usually, when you're stepping through your program, you'll want the debugger to execute ROM calls as single instructions, since their actions are usually well known and well defined. Sometimes, though, you want to actually trace through the ROM code, maybe to check subtleties of behavior, to learn more about how the call works, or perhaps just to amuse yourself (if you're a little unusual). You can do this with the Trace command in TMON. It works just like the Step command, unless the program counter is at a ROM call instruction, in which case it descends into the ROM and traces the call there.

Before using these commands, you should open a disassembly window and make sure it always displays the current program counter. You can do this by typing in (PC) as the address to disassemble from. Putting PC in parentheses tells TMON to recompute its value after every instruction is executed.

After every Step or Trace command that you execute, the disassembly window will display the program counter and disassemble the current instruction and the ones that follow. In addition, you can open any other windows that you want. For example, you may want to have a window that always displays the top of the stack. You can do this with a Dump window that displays from (A7).

If you entered the debugger by pressing the interrupt button and not because your application crashed, you may want to have your application resume executing without any further debugging. To do this, you can use the Exit command, which simply tells the Macintosh to resume normal execution at the current program counter.

Warning

Step Lightly

When you're in the debugger and you have access to registers and memory, it's pretty easy to step on some important value and completely destroy any chance of resuming your application. If you're playing around in the debugger, make sure that you haven't got any unsaved valuable data in a document in the application. When you use Exit to go back to the application after you're done messing around, you may find that you accidentally destroyed an important register value and that your applicaton quickly crashes you right back into the debugger, this time with a real error.

Sometimes when you're tracing, particularly if you're tracing through the ROM, you'll come to instructions that execute subroutines (JSR and BSR, jump to subroutine and branch to subroutine). Often, tracing through these subroutines is very tedious, and what you're really interested in is the main line code. If you come to a subroutine that you really don't want to trace through, you can use TMON's Gosub command. This command causes subroutines executed with JSR and BSR instructions to act like single instructions, much like the Step command treats ROM calls like a single instruction. If you use Gosub when the program counter is at a JSR or BSR instruction, the program will run until an RTS from the subroutine is performed. At that time, the debugger will take control again.

Often when you're debugging an application you want the debugger to be invoked when a specified part of your application's code is executed. In TMON, this is accomplished through the use of **breakpoints**. A breakpoint is an address that, when reached by the program counter, causes entry into the debugger (a "break"). To set a breakpoint, you have to know the address in your code where you want the break to occur or the name of a symbol at that address (such as a procedure name). You'll be able to determine this by examining your code with the disassembly window or by seeing code when you're tracing.

To set a breakpoint, open a Breakpoints window and type in the address where you want to set the breakpoint. The next time the computer tries to execute the instruction at that address you'll fall into the debugger. You can set up to 7 breakpoints. Remember that the debugger also knows about embedded procedure names; so if you have a procedure named Wolfgang and you want to set a breakpoint on its first instruction, you can simply enter "WOLFGANG".

You should realize that breakpoints are forever: if you set a breakpoint, it will stay set, even if you leave the application that you're debugging. If you don't want other programs, like the Finder, to stop unexpectedly, clear breakpoints before quitting an application. You can clear a breakpoint by entering a dash on top of the address and then pressing return.

No Breakpoints in ROM

When you set a breakpoint, the debugger replaces the instruction at the breakpoint address with a special instruction that calls the debugger. It saves the real contents of the location and restores them whenever you examine the location with the debugger. Since breakpoints are created this way, you can't set a breakpoint in the ROM.

Heap Information   TMON will give you important information about the system and application heap zones. The Heap window produces a display that provides you with a dizzying amount of information. Let's take a look at the sample Heap dump in Figure 4-5 and discuss what secrets it reveals.

The first line in the display tells you where the heap zone is located and how many free bytes it contains. As we discussed in Chapter 2, the first thing in the heap zone is a heap zone header, which is not displayed in the Heap window. Following the header are the objects, or blocks, in the heap. Each heap block gets one line of display.

```
Application heap is at $00CB00-$00F700.              00050E bytes free.
*$00CB3C 000100 0  Nonrel
*$00CC44 00006C 0  Nonrel              WMgrPort
*$00CCB8 00009C 0  Nonrel              Window #$00, Kind $0008
 $00CD5C 00000A 0  Handle at $00CBC0 (lpr)  (Window @$00CCB8)  VisRgn
 $00CD6E 00000A 0  Handle at $00CBBC (lpr)  (Window @$00CCB8)  ClipRgn
 $00CD80 00002C 0  Handle at $00CBB8 (lpr)  (Window @$00CCB8)  StructRgn
 $00CDB4 00000A 0  Handle at $00CC00 (lpr)  SaveVisRgn
 $00CDC6 00003B 1  Handle at $00CBC8 (lpR)  File $0020 'MENU' ID=$0081
 $00CE0A 00002A 0  Free
*$00CE3C 000B34 0  Handle at $00CC14 (LPR)  File $0020 'CODE' ID=$0001
 $00D978 0000D2 0  Handle at $00CC10 (lPR)  File $0020 'CODE' ID=$0003
 $00DA52 000000 4  Handle at $00CC20 (lpr)  Scrap
 $00DA5E 00013D 1  Handle at $00CC1C (lpr)  Resource map $0020
 $00DBA4 00004C 0  Handle at $00CC04 (lpr)  GrayRgn
 $00DBF8 000066 0  Handle at $00CBFC (lpr)  MenuList
 $00DC66 000000 4  Handle at $00CBF8 (lpr)  TEScrap
 $00DC72 0000AB 1  Handle at $00CBF4 (lpR)  File $0020 'MENU' ID=$0080
 $00DD26 000048 0  Handle at $00CBC4 (lpR)  File $0020 'MENU' ID=$0082
 $00DD76 0000D0 0  Handle at $00CC24 (lPR)  File $0002 'PACK' ID=$0007
 $00DE4E 00000A 0  Handle at $00CC0C (lpr)  (WMgrPort)         VisRgn
 $00DE60 00002C 0  Handle at $00CC08 (lpr)  (WMgrPort)         ClipRgn
 $00DE94 00000A 0  Handle at $00CBB4 (lpr)  (Window @$00CCB8)  ContRgn
 $00DEA6 00000A 0  Handle at $00CBB0 (lpr)  (Window @$00CCB8)  UpdateRgn
 $00DEB8 0002AC 0  Handle at $00CBF0 (lpR)  File $0002 'MDEF' ID=$0000
 $00E16C 0004B0 0  Handle at $00CBAC (lpR)  File $0002 'WDEF' ID=$0000
 $00E624 000009 1  Handle at $00CBA8 (lpr)  (Window @$00CCB8)  WTitle
 $00E636 00009E 0  Handle at $00CC18 (lPR)  File $0020 'CODE' ID=$0002
 $00E6DC 000080 0  Free
*$00E764 000068 0  Handle at $00CBA4 (Lpr)
*$00E7D4 000000 4  Handle at $00CBA0 (Lpr)
 $00E7E0 000AAE 0  Handle at $00CB9C (lPR)  File $0002 'FONT' ID=$018C
 $00F296 00000A 0  Handle at $00CB98 (lpr)
 $00F2A8 00044C 0  Free
```

Figure 4-5 Example of Heap window

The first column either has an asterisk or nothing. An asterisk indicates an immobile object; that is, either a nonrelocatable block or a locked relocatable block. A quick glance down this column can tell you a lot about a program's memory management. A well-managed heap will have all the asterisks gathered in two groups, one at the beginning of the heap and one at the end. If you see lots of asterisks scattered throughout the heap, you've got a fragmentation problem.

The first number in the line, 00CB3C for the first line, is the address of the contents of the heap block. Remember that each heap block starts with an eight-byte block header and that the block's contents come after the header. The address given here is the address of the block's contents, so the header begins eight bytes before that, at 00CB34. After the address is the logical size of the block, in bytes. The next number, a single digit, gives the block's size correction, that is, the difference between its physical and logical sizes, as we discussed in Chapter 2.

The next column tells whether the block is relocatable, non-relocatable, or free. If it's nonrelocatable, the word Nonrel appears; free blocks are marked with Free; relocatables have "Handle at", followed by the address of the block's master pointer.

Terminology Corner

Remember that the value of a block's handle is the address of its master pointer. Strictly speaking, TMON is wrong to label this number "Handle at . . .". Since the number given is the block's master pointer, it should say either "Handle is . . ." or "Master pointer at . . .".

Just after the "Handle at . . .", TMON shows three letters in parentheses. These represent the master pointer flags for locked, purgeable, and resource. If a block has this attribute, the mnemonic letter (l for locked, for example) will be shown in uppercase; if the block doesn't have this attribute, the letter is in lowercase.

Usually, as in our example, the first resource in the heap will be a master pointer block, which is a nonrelocatable block with a size of $100 bytes. The next thing is almost always a CODE resource with ID 1. This is the application's main segment and, as you know, it's always loaded and always locked.

At the end of each line of information, the Heap dump window tries to identify and tell you about each heap object. First it checks to see if the object is a resource. If so, it displays the file reference number of the resource file, as well as the object's resource type and ID.

If the object isn't a resource, TMON will see if it's associated with any windows in the window list. For example, it may be a window record, or one of the many regions that belong to a window, such as the visRgn or clipRgn.

If TMON can't identify the object as being associated with a window, it then checks various system globals to try to identify the object. For example, it checks the global called TEScrapHandle to identify the object that's the TextEdit scrap.

If the Heap dump window can't identify an object as a resource, a window object, or something pointed to by a system global, it simply displays nothing in the identification area.

Obviously, this identification stuff is incredibly useful in figuring out what's going on in your application. You can instantly locate any resource and check it or step through the window list to see if things are all right.

If you want to switch the Heap dump display to show the system heap, you can click in the top line of the window and then press the Enter key. To switch back, press Enter again.

Trap Commands   Another important set of TMON commands are the Trap commands. These let you work with the Macintosh's A-traps, which are the mechanism used to implement calls to the ROM- and RAM-based system software. The name comes from the fact that these calls are implemented as single 16-bit words having $A as the first digit. For the complete story on how the Macintosh implements Traps, see the "How ROM Calls Work" section of Chapter 10.

The Trap commands in TMON tell the debugger to take some action when traps are encountered. TMON includes commands that cause the debugger to record each trap as it's executed, check the heap zone after traps, cause relocatable blocks to move when traps are executed, make the program break into the debugger, and perform a checksum after traps.

Grow Your Own

All of TMON's Trap commands are defined in the user area, which is the extensible part of the debugger. It's likely that there will be even more of these as future user areas appear. You can even modify existing user areas or write your own to add more features.

All of these commands allow you to qualify when you want the specified action taken. Most let you specify the range of traps that you want the debugger to watch for. Most of them also let you designate a specific memory range in which the traps must be located.

The Trap Intercept command is like setting a breakpoint, except that instead of giving an address to break on you specify a trap (or a range of traps). Since the ROM calls itself frequently, you'll probably want to use the memory range parameter to the Trap Intercept command to tell TMON to only intercept traps that come from RAM.

All RAM addresses fall into the range 0 through $7FFFF for a 512K Macintosh (up to $FFFFF for a 1-megabyte machine). You can further narrow it down by knowing that your application's code resides in the application heap. The address of the beginning of the application heap is kept in the system global AppIZone at $2AA; a global called AppILimit at $130 contains the address of the end of the application heap's growable space. So you can specify that you're only interested in trap calls that take place between the addresses pointed to by $2AA and $130.

Given all this information, you can enter a command to tell TMON to display all the calls to GetResource made from code in the application heap zone. Just click on the Trap Intercept line in the User window and type

    _GetResource _GetResource @2AA @130

In English, this means "intercept calls to GetResource, if the call comes from code that's between the locations that $2AA and $130 point to." Note that we have to enter the name of the trap twice, because TMON expects a range of traps if we specify a range of addresses. Also, note that GetResource is preceded by an underscore (_). This is the way to tell TMON to use the trap number of the trap that's entered, which is GetResource in this case.

Other Code in RAM

Remember that there's code in the application heap other than your application's CODE resources. The system puts definition functions for controls, windows, and menus (CDEF, WDEF, and MDEF resources) in the application heap, as well as desk accessories (DRVR resources). Any of these may make ROM calls, and GetResource calls that they make will also be intercepted. So, TMON may still report some calls that you're not interested in, but there's no easy way to prevent these.

The Trap Intercept command is very useful when you're tracing through a program that you know is going to crash at a certain point. For example, if you know that the last trap an application executed before crashing was GetNewDialog, you could tell TMON to break when it saw a GetNewDialog call. Then you could examine the parameters that were passed to GetNewDialog and do further tracing, if necessary.

Another Trap command you may find useful is Trap Heap check. This command causes the heap to be checked for consistency when the given conditions are met. It can optionally take the standard address range parameters.

A variation of this command will, in addition to checking the heap for consistency, "scramble" the heap if any of the five common heap compaction triggering calls is made (these are NewPtr, NewHandle, SetPtrSize, SetHandleSize, and ReallocHandle). This is a very good way to catch bugs in your program that depend on dereferenced handles. If you use Heap Scrambling, TMON will move every unlocked relocatable object after any of the preceding five calls. Your program should be able to run under these conditions, since unlocked relocatables may move when these calls are made anyway.

This fits in nicely with what we talked about in Chapter 2: these are the only normally used traps that can cause relocation. When the specified trap and address conditions are met, the heap's unlocked relocatable blocks will be moved, thus ensuring that if you're using any improperly dereferenced handles you'll now have pointers that are no longer valid.

The Heap Scramble command is a way of enforcing a worst-case memory scenario on your heap, since you should be prepared for heap compaction whenever it might scramble things. So, if turning Heap Scrambling on causes your application to break, you're probably doing something like dereferencing a handle when it's not safe to do so. Running under normal circumstances, everything may have worked OK, but turning on Heap Scrambling is like simulating an almost full heap zone, and bad handle dereferences that may escape normal testing are often caught.

An extremely valuable TMON Trap command is the Trap Record feature. This command records the most recent traps executed that met the specifications of the parameters (that is, the right trap number and the right program counter). You can set up this command to record any number of traps.

The information you get includes the trap number, program counter where it was executed, and the value of the system global Ticks. You also get some additional information: if the last trap was an Operating System call, you'll see the contents of registers D0 and A0 at the time of the call. If the last trap was a Toolbox call, the additional information recorded will be the top 8 bytes of the stack when the call was executed. Since Toolbox calls are stack based, this information will tell you the parameters to the call when it was made.

As you might imagine, this command can be incredibly powerful in telling you what the last trap call was before the application crashed. If you suspect that your application will crash (unlikely as it may seem), you can enter a Trap Record command just in case. Then, if it does crash, you can examine the most recent trap calls, an extremely valuable piece of information in the detective work of debugging.

Another Trap command you can use is the Trap Checksum command. This command calculates a checksum for a given memory range and then recomputes the checksum periodically and compares it to the original. If the checksums don't match, it breaks into the debugger. The debugger checksums memory every time a trap within the given range is encountered. Like most of the other Trap commands, the Trap Checksum command allows you to qualify the range of traps with a specified memory range.

A final Trap command that's handy is Trap Signal. This command is similar to Trap Intercept, in which you specify a trap or range of traps and tell the debugger to break when it encounters one. With Trap Signal, you also specify the traps that you're interested in, but the debugger doesn't look for them right away. Instead, the debugger waits until you tell it to start watching by holding down the Option key while you press the interrupt switch (surely one of the most bizarre commands ever: Option-Interrupt switch). After you do this, TMON will break the *next* time it encounters the traps specified in the Trap Signal command.

This is a very handy way to interrupt the program just before it calls GetNextEvent. If you have the Trap Signal parameters set to GetNext-Event, you can simply press Option-Interrupt when you want to examine the heap. This will cause the debugger to take control when the next GetNextEvent call is reached. Since GetNextEvent is only called by the application and not the ROM, this will ensure that the break comes at a "good" time; that is, not while ROM code is executing.

Miscellaneous Commands   The File window gives you information about any open resource files. It lists all the resources within any resource map that you specify, listing each one's type, ID, and name, if any. In addition, it gives the resource's attributes (mnemonically, of course) and the location of the resource in memory, if it's currently loaded. Just to give you something else to look at, the window also tells you where in memory the resource map is and and what the file's attributes are. Figure 4-6 shows a sample File window.

There are TMON user commands to move, fill, or compare blocks of memory; to search for a particular value in memory; to display a given chunk of memory symbolically, as a window record, for example; to examine return addresses on the stack to find out what routines may have called other routines; to load any resource into memory by specifying its resource type and ID, and many more commands, which are, as they say, too numerous to name here.

As you can see, TMON provides a great deal of power for debugging. In addition, it seems to be extremely fast and reliable. In fact, the manual says that TMON performs a continual checksum of itself to ensure that

```
Resource file #$0020                      Map at $00DA5E    Attributes: rcw
'CODE'  $0000  ..P.....  Nowhere
'CODE'  $0001  ..P.....  At $00CE3C  'Main'
'CODE'  $0002  ..P..1..  At $00E636  '%A5Init'
'CODE'  $0003  ..P.....  At $00D978  '_DataInit'
'BNDL'  $0080  ........  Nowhere
'DITL'  $03E8  ........  Nowhere     'About box'
'DLOG'  $03E8  ........  Nowhere     'About box'
'FREF'  $0080  ........  Nowhere
'FREF'  $0081  ........  Nowhere
'ICN#'  $0080  ........  Nowhere
'ICN#'  $0081  ........  Nowhere
'MENU'  $0080  ........  At $00DC72
'MENU'  $0081  ........  At $00CDC6
'MENU'  $0082  ........  At $00DD26
'Scot'  $0000  ........  Nowhere
```

Figure 4-6 Example of File window

it hasn't been damaged. If you're skeptical of this (as I was), you can find TMON itself up near the top of RAM. Then use the Dump command to sneak in and change a single byte. In an instant, TMON displays the message "Warning! The monitor has been damaged. Be very careful!" Error detection that good builds a lot of confidence!

Sometimes you may want to enter the debugger programatically; that is, at someplace in your program, you may want to force the debugger to take control. You can do this with a special trap, $A9FF. If your program executes this special trap, the debugger will be invoked.

If you're using a language that allows you to generate assembly language code from your source, you can easily generate this special trap. For example, in Workshop Pascal, you can declare a procedure like this:

    PROCEDURE Debugger; Inline $A9FF;

Then, whenever you want to cause your program to invoke the debugger, you can simply call this procedure.

Limitations One complaint about TMON's implementation of windows is that there's no fast way to scroll. TMON windows only have scroll arrrows and a grow box; there's no thumb or gray scroll area. This means that the only way to peruse a heap dump is by slooooowly moving through it, a line at a time. This can be really awful if you're trying to get to the end of a heap dump.

This completes our guided tour of TMON. We now return you to your regularly scheduled discussion of object code debuggers.

MacDB

Another debugger you may have seen is Apple's MacDB (also known as the "two-Macintosh debugger"). This very interesting debugger has been shipped with the Macintosh Software Supplement and with Apple's 68000 Development System. It requires two Macintoshes hooked together by a cable between their serial ports.

The idea is that you're debugging software that's running on one Macintosh, and the debugger is displaying its information on the other Macintosh. Since most of the debugger lives in the second machine, the debugger is mostly transparent to the program being debugged.

In addition to this ingenious (if somewhat expensive) approach, MacDB has a neat user interface. It uses true Macintosh windows, menus, and controls, and can display memory dumps, heap dumps, disassemblies, and sequences of ROM calls, all in windows. In addition, if you want to display memory with an address that's showing in a window, you can just click on the address to select it, and then click a special "indirection" button in the window to display memory at that address. For example, if a window is showing the contents of a handle, you can click on the contents to select, then click on the indirection button, and you'll see the master pointer. Selecting and clicking again causes the heap object itself to be displayed. Neat!

Unfortunately, MacDB has fallen into disuse, mainly because its heap dump window provides very little information compared to Macsbug and TMON. It doesn't identify any resources or other common system objects, so you're left to figure it out for yourself if you want to look at, for example, a DITL that you've loaded. Perhaps in the future, MacDB will be enhanced so that it combines powerful debugging information with its superb user interface.

Discipline

Another interesting debugging tool that's becoming popular is one known ominously as Discipline. This program hooks into the trap dispatcher and examines the parameters to every trap call that's made by your application or by the ROM itself. It looks for things like handles that don't really point to master pointers, pointers to things that can't possibly be right (a window record in ROM, for example), and other bad situations that you might normally get away with because they might not cause an error right away. When Discipline is active, however, it will warn you of these situations.

Discipline is available in at least two forms. First, it's been distributed as a stand-alone application. When you run the application, it installs itself and watches as traps are executed. Second, Discipline has been built into some debuggers. In particular, at least one extended user area for TMON includes the discipline function and lets you choose a range of traps to watch for and a range of memory to watch. Running your application with Discipline active will often help you catch a bug or two that you may not have noticed.

Looking Ahead

In a future release, the Macintosh Programmer's Workshop from Apple will include a powerful debugger that has many of the best features of the current debuggers, including real Macintosh windows and the ability to define your own templates to look at objects in memory.

Diagnostic Output

A popular debugging technique is printing information to a window or printer. This is known as **diagnostic output**. Many programmers print out messages like "Now entering procedure FooBar" of "Setting variable Marvin to 1027" so that they can know what's going on. The more adventurous programmers will often create a special debugging window on the screen to receive this information.

However, since one goal of the debugging process is to be as invisible as possible to the running application, creating windows is usually too obtrusive a thing to do. For this reason, many programmers prefer to output this kind of information through a serial port to the printer. Another advantage in doing it this way is that you get a hard copy of your debugging efforts.

The easiest way to send diagnostic output to a printer is to open the printer port (which is named .bout) as a file and then simply to write information to it. For example, from Lisa or Macintosh Workshop Pascal, you could write

```
var
  printer : Text;

begin
  Reset (printer, '.bout');
  WriteLn (printer, 'Whatever text you want');
  ...
```

Note that the printer must not be connected via AppleTalk; it must really be plugged into the back of the Macintosh for this to work. If your printer is attached to the modem port instead of the printer port, you can use .aout instead of .bout for the file name.

> **Feeding Time**
>
> Depending on which language you're using, you may find that the printer just keeps printing over and over again on the same line. If this happens to you, just print a line feed character (ASCII code 10) after each line of text. For example, in Pascal, you would print chr (10).

Instead of a printer, you can use an external terminal if you want. If you're using one of the Termbug varieties of Macsbug, the versions that send the debugging information through a serial port instead of displaying it on the Macintosh screen, you can get your diagnostic output on the same screen as your debugging stuff. Remember that your external terminal can be a computer running a terminal program. Many an Apple III has found a home as an external terminal for a Macintosh debugger.

Some development environments predefine an output window for you. For example, Lisa Pascal has a unit called WriteLnWindow that facilitates writing information in a specially created window.

A debugging trick that's of some use is the one we'll call *diagnostic noise*. With this technique, instead of having some ouput written to a printer or window when various events of interest take place, the programmer will add code to make various beeps from the speaker when certain things happen. This can get really obnoxious when you start using one beep to mean something, two beeps to mean something else, and so on. If you were really ambitious, you could probably use Macintalk to speak the information, but that would probably be more cute than useful. As they say, the remarkable thing about the dancing bear is not how well he dances, but the fact that he dances at all.

Some of the advantages of these techniques are that they're easy to implement and that they provide information that's easy for the programmer to understand. If you know enough to write a Pascal program, you know what "Now entering procedure . . ." means. You don't have to learn assembly language or how to operate a debugger.

The disadvantages of these methods are that they often don't provide enough information. When a program crashes, you usually aren't expecting it to do so, and you need more information than just the name of the procedure that the crash occurred in. Also, since diagnostic output is created by code that's part of your application, you have to modify and rebuild your application to see the output. That's not too useful when your application has crashed right before your eyes and you want to find out why right now.

For these reasons, you'll usually use the information that you gather from diagnostic output in conjunction with an object code debugger. Adding code to write the name of every procedure as it's entered can help you narrow down a crash, but you'll probably do the nitty-gritty work with a debugger.

Special-purpose Debuggers

Some development environments provide nifty built-in debugging tools. One of the nicest of these is available with MacApp. It implements a debugger as a window that automatically traces the execution of your program, letting you know as each procedure is entered and exited, as well as providing other information.

One advantage of debuggers like this is that the debugging information presented is pretty high level; you don't have to learn a lot about assembly language and how the lowest levels of the system work in order to use them. However, most development environments don't offer the comfortably high level of presentation that MacApp affords. Usually, when writing a Macintosh application, you need to know those low-level details, as we've already discussed in great depth.

The Ultimate Debugger

The ultimate debugger is a combination of hardware and software, is amazingly sophisticated and powerful, is completely invisible to the program being debugged, and is prohibitively expensive. No, I'm not talking about hiring a Macintosh wizard—I'm referring to the magical devices known as logic analyzers and in-circuit emulators.

To use an emulator, you unplug the 68000 microprocessor from your Macintosh's motherboard and plug in the emulator. As the name implies, it then emulates the chip you just removed. But the emulator has debugging software built into it, and as the software in the computer executes, the emulator is watching what's going on very closely.

At its most primitive, the emulator acts like an object code debugger: you can do things like single-stepping through programs, recording traps, displaying and disassembling memory, and so on. However, since the emulator occupies absolutely no memory inside the Macintosh, it is truly transparent to the program that's running and thus has no effect on it.

But there's lots more to an emulator than just that. Object code debuggers are able to watch for ROM calls and take some action when they execute, such as entering the debugger or recording information. There are also commands that perform some action before each instruction is executed, like computing a checksum.

Since an emulator is actually taking the place of the 68000, it can do much better than computing a checksum after each instruction. It can literally watch the 68000's address lines and perform a desired action when a specific address is being written to. Think about that for a minute: let's say that you know that your application is trashing location 48376 once in a while, but you don't know why. With an emulator, you can tell it to watch for instructions that change the value in 48376. As soon as one executes, it'll stop and let you know.

Many object code debuggers have trap recording commands; these commands let you record the most recently executed traps so that when your application crashes, you can see which ROM calls were made most frequently. An emulator goes that one better: it can record *all 68000 instructions* and let you look at them later. Of course, a debugger could do this too, but it would be so slow that it would be unusable.

Sounds pretty great, right? Before you run down to K-Mart to buy yours, though, you'd better know about the price. In-circuit emulators usually cost in the low five figures, and all those figures are on the left side of the decimal point. They're expensive enough that they're usually available on lease, but that's not cheap, either. Oh, well. Just in case you ever need to debug a debugger, though, one of these babies sure comes in handy.

Common Crashes

For the next few pages, we'll discuss the symptoms of some common crashes and possible causes for each crash. For each crash, we'll state the symptom, its appearance to the user, some reasons why the crash may have happened, and some possible causes. This information will help you figure out what's happened when your application runs aground.

Symptom   System error (bomb dialog).

Appearance   Application stops, dialog with bomb icon, "Sorry, a serious system error has occurred.", "ID=xx" appears.

Why It Happened

1. An executing routine, usually in the ROM, has called SysError because it wanted to report a fatal error condition. These conditions include system errors with numbers greater than 11. For example, 15 is a Segment Loader error, which means that an application's code segment could not be loaded into memory; 28 means that the stack has grown into the heap; 27 means that a disk directory has been seriously damaged. See Figure 4-7 for the complete list.

2. The 68000 has detected a fatal error condition. These conditions, called **exceptions**, are then automatically reported by the System Error Handler. These are all system error numbers from 1 to 11. Examples are error 3, illegal instruction error, which means that the 68000 was told to execute an instruction that was not a valid instruction; error 2, address error, which means that the 68000 was told to get a 16-bit (word size) or 32-bit (long word size) value from an odd numbered address (these values are required to be at even-numbered addresses); error 4, zero divide, means that the 68000 executed a divide instruction with a divisor of zero. These are all listed in Figure 4-8.

Figure 4-7 System errors generated by SysError

Error number	Comment
12	Unimplemented system routine; an unknown system call
13	Spurious interrupt; no interrupt handler for an interrupt
14	I/O system error; generated various ways by Device and File Manager
15	Segment Loader error; couldn't find CODE or out of memory
16	SANE error; halt bit was set
17–24	Can't load package; couldn't find PACK or out of memory
25	Can't allocate heap block; out of memory in the heap
26	Segment Loader error; couldn't find CODE 0
27	File map destroyed; bad logical block number
28	Stack overflow; stack expanded into the heap
84	Menu purged: a MENU resource was purged

Figure 4-8 System errors caused by 68000 exceptions

Error number	Comment
1	Bus error; memory management hardware detected bad reference
2	Address error; reference to word or long word at odd address
3	Illegal instruction; attempt to execute unknown 68000 instruction
4	Divide by zero; attempt by 68000 to divide by zero
5	Check exception; CHK instruction failed (usually a Pascal range error)
6	TrapV exception; TRAPV instruction failed
7	Privilege violation; supervisor instruction in 68000 user mode
8	Trace exception; trace mode in 68000 is on
9	Line 1010 exception; trap dispatcher normally gets control here
10	Line 1111 exception; instruction $FXXX was executed
11	Miscellaneous exception; other 68000 exceptions come here

Possible Causes

1. ROM called SysError: Many of these system errors are the result of the heap being nearly full (or badly fragmented). For example, the Segment Loader attempts to load CODE resources by calling GetResource; if the GetResource call fails, it posts system error 15. Usually, GetResource fails because there's not enough room in the heap to load the requested CODE segment, but it can also fail if the CODE resource it's after has been removed from the resource file (pretty uncommon).

System error 26 is also produced by the ROM calling SysError. This error is reported if the Segment Loader got an error when calling GetResource on CODE resource 0 as it was trying to start up a new application. This indicates that the file being started up has no CODE 0; a frequent cause for this is that the development system used to create the application has spelled CODE with lower case letters, and case is significant in resource type names. You can check this with the ResEdit program.

2. 68000 exceptions: An address error (system error 2) often means that the application is relying on a handle or a pointer that has never been set up with the right value; maybe the application declared a handle but forgot to assign it a value before using it, or maybe the application called DisposHandle on a handle and then tried to use it later (oops). An illegal instruction (system error 3) can mean that the application made a ROM call that takes a ProcPtr, such as the ActionProc field in Track-Control, and that the ProcPtr has not been set up to point to a procedure.

Nesting Procedures in Pascal

Pascal users frequently have this problem when they pass a pointer to a routine whose declaration was nested within another procedure or function as a parameter of type procPtr. This happens because the Pascal compiler pushes an extra parameter on the stack so that the inner routine can use the outer routine's variables when procedure declarations are nested. The ROM routines don't know about this extra parameter, though, so the stack gets messed up and virtually any kind of error can result. For more about this, see Appendix B.

Symptom   Bizarre display and sounds.

Appearance   Screen turns to random garbage and changes rapidly, toggling between two displays; speaker makes machine-gun-like sounds.

Why It Happened   A routine is using a pointer or handle to write data into memory that is mapped to the screen, the sound buffer, or a memory I/O address that causes different parts of memory to be displayed to the screen.

Invalid Pointers

What's the difference between an invalid handle or pointer here and the one reported by system error 2 (address error)? The 68000 deals with three sizes of data: 8 bits (byte), 16 bits (word), and 32 bits (long word). Most objects in Macintosh memory are either words or long words. To provide a low level of error checking, the 68000 requires that all words and long words be located at even-numbered addresses (bytes can be addressed at odd locations). If a 68000 instruction attempts to get a word or long word from an odd address, the 68000 assumes that something has gone wrong and reports an address error. This means that the 68000 will catch roughly half of your invalid handle and pointer uses.

If you happen to use an invalid handle or pointer that's even, the 68000 cannot catch the error, and the screen-garbage crash (as well as other crashes) can occur. For example, let's assume that you've declared a handle called `myHandle`, but mistakenly neglected to initialize it in your program. So the handle contains a random value; whatever was in its location when the program started up is still there. When you use the handle on the right-hand side of an assignment statement, the Macintosh faithfully dereferences it. What happens? If the value in the handle happens to be odd, an address error will be signaled; if the value happens to be even, no error will be reported, and the assignment will take place! If the handle points to valid memory, it may write over some of your existing data; if it points to the screen, garbage may appear on the screen; if it points to the soft switch that causes a different range of RAM to be displayed on the screen, the screen can flash wildly.

So, when you have an invalid handle or pointer, you have about a 50–50 chance of getting caught by the 68000. If the handle or pointer is odd, you'll get a system error; if it's even, anything can happen, including a system error at a later time.

Possible Causes   The causes for this crash are identical to those for system errors. This crash is probably the result of an invalid pointer or handle that didn't get caught by the 68000; that is, it didn't result in an odd word or long word reference. Since the 68000 was unable to catch the error, the program was able to cruise along until it started writing to the screen or screen-switch hardware.

It's important to note that by this time, the program has already gone completely haywire and may have written over lots of memory. You may not be looking at the first damage caused by the runaway program, just the most visible. This is true, of course, of any kind of crash, as we discussed earlier.

Symptom   Macintosh reboots.

Appearance   Macintosh acts just as if you had pressed the reset button; it bongs and restarts.

Why It Happened   This, trivia fans, is called a **double bus fault**. On the 68000, the stack pointer must always be even, pointing at an even address in memory. Normally, the 68000 takes care of this for you automatically: when you push a byte-sized value onto the stack, decreasing the value of the stack pointer by 1 byte, it automatically adjusts the stack pointer by decreasing its value by one more so that it remains even. The same happens when you remove something from the stack. If the stack pointer somehow becomes odd, a double bus fault is signaled and the 68000 is reset.

Possible Causes   For a high-level language programmer, this crash is very similar to the illegal instruction error (system error 3). The only way that an odd stack pointer can be created is with an explicit 68000 instruction to put an odd value into the stack pointer register (MOVE oddValue, A7). Since most high-level languages never generate code like this, the only way such an instruction could get executed is through a bug that causes the processor to start executing undefined memory as code.

One example of such a situation is the application passing an invalid parameter as a ProcPtr to a ROM routine. If the invalid ProcPtr happens to point to a MOVE 1, A7 (or a move of any other odd value into the stack pointer), a double bus fault will result, causing the computer to reboot.

An assembly language programmer, of course, can do this much more easily. If you're manipulating the stack pointer directly rather than indirectly, you can cause this error with real code, so be careful.

The worst thing about this error is that it's so destructive. Since the computer reboots, you don't get a chance to figure out what went wrong. Luckily, it's pretty rare, especially for high-level language programmers.

Some Advice on Debugging

Most programmers have a hard time describing their debugging processes in depth. They'll tell you what debugger they use and a few tips and tricks, but the overall process of debugging software is difficult to describe in a nice, clean series of easy to follow instructions.

There are lots of reasons for this. Debugging is a problem-solving endeavor with an immense amount of information to be sought, gathered, pondered, and evaluated. Another thing that makes it hard is that no two debugging efforts are the same. Each piece of software presents unique challenges. Some kinds of software seem to be debugger resistant; that is, they present situations that confound and confuse debugging tools and make them hard to use. When you run into these you just have to try another way of attacking the problem.

The debugging process generally consists of information gathering, information evaluating, and experimentation. When your program crashes you try to learn as much as possible about the nature of the crash. You try to answer the questions we presented earlier in this chapter by gathering information that your debugging tools provide you. Then, you sift through the information and try to determine what went wrong. Sometimes, you may be able to reproduce the crash, looking more carefully this time at the sequence of events that lead up to the crash. Finally, you figure out what you think is wrong and try to fix it.

When you're in the information-gathering phase of debugging, you'll find that you can usually think of lots of different ways to attack the problem. For example, when your application crashes unexpectedly, you'll always want to know what kind of crash it was and the location of the program counter when the crash occurred, but then you'll want to find out other things. Should you try manually changing a suspected bad value and attempt to continue execution? Should you rerun the program, break somewhere before the crash, and use the debugger to single-step the program? Should you trace into the ROM, suspecting a ROM bug?

Of course, there's no single answer to these questions. You should try to answer the questions we discussed in this chapter, but you can do so in a number of different ways. Try different techniques and see which ones you feel most comfortable with. Share ideas and tips with your friends. If you have no friends, make some (it's left as an exercise for the reader). Just make sure that you gather as much information as you can and that you consider all the clues when you're figuring out the problem.

In Chapter 7, we'll debug some real programs following the rules we discussed in this chapter.

Things to Remember

- The heavy use of the Macintosh ROM makes debugging particularly interesting. The best Macintosh programmer is one who can read an object code listing, even if the program is written in a high-level language.

- System errors don't tell you very much other than that a crash has occurred. A lot more investigating is needed to know what went wrong.

- Debugging involves gathering facts by answering several questions, including:

  Where did the program crash?

  What specifically caused the crash?

  What assembly language instruction was the last one executed before the crash?

  What caused the offending instruction to be executed?

- Some popular debugging tools and techniques are object code debuggers, source code walk-throughs, diagnostic output, special-purpose debuggers, and logic analyzers.

- Macsbug is the name of a family of debuggers that Apple provides for the Macintosh. Each version has slightly different features, including the number of lines of display, whether it communicates with an external terminal, and whether it works on a Macintosh XL.

- TMON includes most of the features of Macsbug. It's missing a few of them, but it also has a lot that Macsbug doesn't, it has an interface that allows it to display more information, and it's extensible through a user area.

- MacDB, the two-Macintosh debugger, has a lot of potential power and a nice interface, but lacks the features of Macsbug and TMON.

CHAPTER

5

Examining
Compiled Code

In this chapter, we'll look at how compilers translate programs to assembly language and what the assembly language looks like. If you'd like to know more about 68000 assembly language before reading this chapter, you might want to read Appendix A, which introduces the 68000 for high-level language programmers.

Compilers

To many high-level language programmers, the compiler is a big black box that magically translates a sort-of-English program into an executing glob of machine language. How this translation takes place is of no interest to most high-level language programmers. In fact, this is why compilers were invented: to relieve programmers of the low-level details of writing a computer program.

Well, if you've come this far, you probably know that it's hard to get away with that attitude when you're creating a Macintosh application. Because you have to deal so intimately with so many details that are vital to the operation of the User Interface Toolbox, it's very difficult to completely divorce yourself from what's happening at the low level. This is why we've stated the thesis that the best Macintosh programmer is one who knows the most about what's going on in the system at all levels.

In this chapter and the next, we'll try to unlock some of the secrets of compilers so that you'll be able to recognize your program in its naked object code form. We'll discuss briefly what compilers do, and we'll spend a lot of time correlating Pascal and C statements with their resultant assembly language output.

139

Too Much Information

Most of the information that's presented in this chapter is generally applicable to high-level procedure-oriented languages like Pascal and C. However, the specific examples of object code generation were taken from Workshop Pascal. Remember that compilers evolve over time, so use the concepts presented in this book to observe your compiler's behavior if it seems to be different. Also, some enlightened compiler packages include documentation of this kind.

Since we have compilers to write assembly language programs for us, why would anyone ever want to write directly in assembly language? Although the compiler translates programs into assembly language, it's very difficult to make a compiler as smart as a human assembly language programmer. That's because the compiler is generalized; it handles lots of different cases the same way. The human will generally be able to come up with tricks and techniques that the compiler won't see. This means that human-written assembly language programs are almost always smaller or faster (or both) than compiler-generated programs, if they're written by a smart programmer.

Some compilers have intelligence built into them to look for special situations that they can exploit to make the object code smaller or faster. This process in compilers is known as **optimization**.

If this is your first journey into this sort of thing, you'll find that it's really not so bad after all. In fact, if you've got a compiler that, like the Lisa Pascal compiler, will generate assembly language source code from your Pascal source, you may soon find yourself beating the compiler by hand-optimizing its output. Yes, you!

As you know, a compiler is a program that, translates a program written in an Englishlike (usually) language like C or Pascal into an assembly language or machine language program that can be executed by a microprocessor. Compilers accept files of text as input and produce as output files that consist of a machine-language version of the program. Usually, another tool called a linker is required to put all the pieces of the program together so that it can actually be executed. On the Macintosh, the final step of the process is the creation of CODE resources. On some development systems, CODE resources are output directly from the linker; on other development systems, another tool, such as RMaker on the Lisa Workshop, takes the linker's output and converts it into CODE resources.

The process by which the compiler converts your source statements to object code is actually not all that magical (although it is pretty neat). In fact, compilers are predictable when you're trying to figure out what sort of object code will result from a given source statement.

Knowing what object code will result from your source code is important for several reasons. For one thing, if you know what the compiler's going to do when you write certain source statements, you can help to optimize your program by writing the most efficient code possible. More important for our purposes here you'll be able to navigate your way through your object code when you're debugging if you know what source statements produced the assembly language that you're looking at.

Compilers map the world of a high-level language onto the considerably lower level but vastly more efficient world of the microprocessor. In the high-level language, you can create dozens or hundreds of variables, each of them known by a real English name. They can have fancy structures, combining text with numbers in any combination, with each member of the structure having its own name.

The compiler maps these data structures into assembly language for you. When you use a variable, the compiler determines how much space in memory is needed for the variable and automatically allocates and assigns that space. When you refer to a field within a record or structure, the compiler computes the address of the field that you're interested in and writes instructions to perform the appropriate action. The compiler sees to it that procedures reserve space for their local variables when they begin executing and release that space when they're done executing. The compiler frees you from having to deal with these and hundreds of other low-level details.

Of course, high-level languages also provide a variety of statements for you to use in writing your programs. These include assignment statements; looping constructs like for, while, and repeat; control statements like goto, break, and continue; procedure and function calls; conditional statements like if...then...else and case; and more.

The job of the compiler is to create machine language equivalents for each of these statements. The 68000 has lots of instructions that were designed expressly for use by high-level languages, and most compilers take advantage of this smart design.

In some cases, source statements translate into a single assembly language instruction; in other instances, one source statement can produce a whole chunk of assembly language. Also, the compiler frequently has a choice of several different ways to accomplish the same function. For example, when you pass the value zero as a parameter to a procedure, there are several different object code instructions that the compiler could produce that would all produce the desired result.

Which one does the compiler choose when there's a choice? Good compilers will choose the option that produces the smallest instruction. Machine language instructions have different lengths, and it's possible that one option will be shorter than the others. Often the available options are the same length. In this case, excellent compilers (those recommended by Tom Peters) will choose the option that produces the fastest instruction. Machine language instructions are precisely timed, and the times, which are listed in the microprocessor's reference manual, are strictly defined, so the compiler can actually choose the fastest instruction among several options. Of course, not all compilers are well programmed enough to choose the best of several alternatives.

Future Shock

The 68020 microprocessor, which may someday become standard in future Macintosh computers, has lots of features that make it extremely difficult to time instructions precisely. The 68020 has the capability to overlap instructions in some cases and to cache instructions to execute loops more quickly.

We'll start by discussing where compilers put variables and how they keep track of them.

Allocating Space for Data

When a compiler translates your program into glorious object code, it must look through your global variable declarations and allocate space for each of them. As we discussed in Chapter 2, declared variables are placed on the stack. As the compiler looks through your list of globals, it allocates space for each of them on the stack, one by one, growing the stack as it goes. Let's look at an example.

```
PROGRAM Example;
    VAR anInteger : INTEGER;
        aLong      : Longint;
        aRecord    : RECORD
                        first, second : INTEGER;
                        myHdl : Handle;
                        myPtr : ^someType;
                     END;
        anArray    : ARRAY [1..50] of INTEGER;
    BEGIN
      {program statements here}
    END.
```

Listing 5-1

In the Workshop Pascal example in Listing 5-1, there are four global variables. The first one, anInteger, will be allocated first on the stack. Remember that, since the stack grows downward in memory, this means it will occupy the highest location of any global variable in memory. The variable anInteger will occupy two bytes in memory. Why? Because in Workshop Pascal, integers always take up two bytes. Their values can range from −32768 to 32767, which are the smallest and largest numbers that will fit into 2 bytes. It's just that simple.

Before the compiler allocates space for the first variable, it decrements the stack pointer by the size of the variable it's going to allocate, growing the stack downward by the desired amount. So, when it gets to the next variable, aLong, it must first grow the stack enough to accommodate a long integer (a Longint). In Pascal, long integers take up four bytes, so the compiler allocates four bytes for aLong.

As it allocates variables, the compiler remembers where it puts things, so that later, when it translates statements that refer to these variables, it will know where they are (so we don't have to). For example, it remembers that it placed anInteger at two bytes "below" the initial stack pointer, and when it encounters a statement that assigns a value to anInteger, it will know where the value goes.

To allocate space for the next variable, aRecord, Pascal must determine how much space the record will occupy on the stack. Doing this is easy: just add up the number of bytes used by the record's components. This record starts with two integers; at two bytes each, that's four bytes so far. Then there's a handle. Remember that a handle is the address of a master pointer. On a Macintosh, addresses are always four bytes long, so handles and pointers always occupy four bytes. The last field of the record, myPtr, is a pointer to some unknown type. In determining its size, we don't care what it points to. Since it's a pointer, it's the address of something, and it takes four bytes. Adding all this together, we come to a grand total of 12 bytes for the record. Pascal will decrement the stack pointer by 12 to reserve space for this structure.

The last global variable is the array cleverly called anArray, which consists of 50 integers. Once again, we can determine its size by computing the sizes of its components. Integers occupy two bytes each, so 50 of them will cost you exactly 100 bytes.

Figure 5-1 summarizes the global variables and their sizes.

Figure 5-1 Global variables and sizes

Variable	Type	Size in bytes
anInteger	Integer	2
aLong	Longint	4
aRecord	Record	12
anArray	Array	100

Figuring Sizes of Structures

This can be a little trickier than we've discussed here. If everything in the structure is an even number of bytes long, there's no problem. However, if you have things like chars, which can fit into one byte, and booleans, which can take as little as one *bit*, funny things can happen. High-level languages generally like to keep fields on even-address boundaries, so they'll usually allocate two bytes each for chars and booleans.

If you prefer to make your data structures as small as possible, some languages permit the word Packed in records and arrays. This causes the data to be squeezed in as tightly as possible. Even with packing, there are restrictions. If you pack an array that has two chars next to each other, they'll be packed into two bytes total; but if you have a char, followed by an integer, followed by a char, no packing will occur and each char will take up two bytes, as will the integer. Just for fun, some compilers will do some packing automatically, even without a Packed in the source. There is a reliable way to figure out how much space any data structure is using. Most languages that do packing have a built-in function called SizeOf, which takes a data structure as a parameter and returns its size in bytes. You can use this function to determine exactly how many bytes a particular data structure is really taking up.

Every data structure allowed by a compiler takes up a predetermined amount of space on the stack. Figure 5-2 lists the most common data types and their sizes.

After global variables are allocated on the stack, they stay there until the application ends. That's why they're global, of course. Local variables are allocated in much the same way, but space for them isn't reserved until the procedures or functions that declare them are executed. When the procedure ends, the space for the local variables is removed from the stack.

Figure 5-2 Sizes of data types

Type	Size in bytes	Comment
Integer	2	Two's complement integer (−32768 to 32767)
Longint	4	Two's complement integer (−2147483648 to 2147483647)
SignedByte	1	Two's complement integer (−128 to 127)
Boolean	1	Value in bit 0 (0 = false, 1 = true)
Char	2	ASCII code in low byte, high byte unused
Real	4	SANE single-precision format
Single	4	Same as Real
Double	8	SANE double-precision format
Extended	10	SANE extended-precision format
Comp	8	SANE computational format
String [n]	n+1	Length byte followed by ASCII codes
Byte	2	Two's complement integer, value in low byte
Ptr	4	Address of data; includes any parameters preceded by @
Handle	4	Address of master pointer; includes any kind of handle
Point	4	QuickDraw coordinate
Rect	8	QuickDraw rectangle; two points (goaltending)

When it compiles a procedure, the compiler generates code to make sure that space is reserved on the stack for the procedure's local variables. It reserves space just as it does for global variables. As the compiler encounters each variable declaration, it creates a location for the variable that will be on the stack when the application runs. When it compiles statements that reference local variables, it fills in the appropriate address.

Global variables take up stack space throughout the life of the program. For local variables, the compiler generates code that reserves stack space when the procedure begins; it also generates code to reduce the stack when the procedure ends. The stack is cut back just far enough to remove the local variables from it. This is how high-level languages implement the concept of scope; when a procedure ends, its local variables are no longer accessible because the stack is cut back to where it was before they were allocated.

It's also interesting to note a slight variation in the way this is done in most Pascal compilers versus most C compilers. In Pascal, you'll usually find that each procedure or function is responsible for removing its own parameters from the stack just before it ends. When you look at most C code, however, you'll find that the caller, which pushes the parameters on the stack before calling a function, is also responsible for removing the parameters after the function has been called. Once again, the only way to know how your compiler handles this is to look for yourself.

> **Constants Are a Virtue**
>
> What happens to constants when you compile a program? Constants are simply alternate ways of representing values in the source code. They take up absolutely no additional space in the object code; they're completely forgotten in the object code. Since constants don't cost you anything in the object code, you should use them liberally to help document your source.

Stack Frames

We've said that a program's variables are kept on the stack and that the compiler keeps track of each one's location. Since Macintosh programs can wind up being loaded almost anywhere in memory, they must be position independent. How does the compiler keep track of variables' locations in a position-independent way?

At first it might seem that each variable is kept at a known offset from the stack pointer. In the example in Listing 5-1, the first variable declared is an integer. It will be located at two bytes below the stack pointer, since the stack pointer will be decremented by 2 bytes to reserve space for it. But there's something wrong here: the stack pointer is decremented as each variable is allocated. So we can't say that a variable is a certain offset from the stack pointer, because the stack pointer keeps changing!

A good solution is to record the inital value of the stack pointer before any variables are allocated and use offsets from that recorded value to get to variables. If we recorded the value of the stack pointer before any variable allocations took place, we would know that the first variable, anInteger, would be stored two bytes below the recorded initial stack pointer value. We would also know the other variables' locations: aLong is at 6 bytes below the recorded value (anInteger's 2 plus aLong's 4), aRecord is at −18 from the initial value, and anArray is at −118 from the recorded value. Figure 5-3 shows the list of global variables again, but this time you can also see where each one is located in memory.

Figure 5-3 Global variables, sizes and locations

Variable	Type	Size in bytes	Starting address*	Ending address*
anInteger	Integer	2	−2	−1
aLong	Longint	4	−6	−3
aRecord	Record	12	−18	−7
anArray	Array	100	−118	−19

*addresses are relative to initial stack pointer

Ups and Downs

As we've said, the stack grows downward in memory, so each successive new variable has an increasingly larger negative number as its offset. However, the bytes in the objects themselves are stored in order from low to high memory. For example, the first element in anArray is stored at the array's lowest address, the next element is kept in the next higher bytes, and so on. That's why anArray starts at −118 and ends at −19.

This seems like a good way to keep track of global variables. You probably won't be too surprised to learn that we didn't just invent this idea. It's been around for a long time, and the Macintosh is designed to use this technique of recording the initial setting of the stack pointer and referring to global variables by their relative position to the recorded value.

Macintosh applications accomplish this by remembering the initial value of the stack pointer; it's saved in register A5. This is done automatically by the Segment Loader whenever an application is started (that is, whenever the Segment Loader trap Launch is called). The compiler assumes this fact when it compiles a program and translates all references to global variables as A5-relative references.

All global variables are allocated at a negative offset from the initial stack pointer, so it's decremented to make space for each of them (see Figure 5-4). This means that all references to global variables in the application's code will be as negative offsets from A5. In assembly language, these kinds of references are written like this: −X(A5) . In our example in Listing 5-1, we know that anInteger is −2 from A5; this would be written as −2(A5) in the object code. Assembly language hotshots around the world pronounce this "minus two off A5." It means to take the address that's in register A5 and subtract two from it. Later in this chapter we'll see how this sort of reference is used in a complete assembly language instruction.

What about local variables? Each procedure creates its own little world of variables. The compiler can't simply allocate space for each procedure's local variable on the stack at compile time, because local variables only exist during the execution of the procedure that defines them. What can we do here?

The answer is very similar to the solution for global variables. As a procedure begins executing, it should save the value of the stack pointer before any local variables are allocated. Then it can remember the location of each variable as a negative offset from this recorded value.

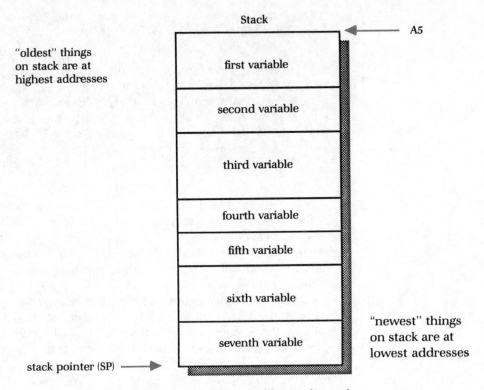

Figure 5-4 Global variables on the stack

In code produced by most Macintosh compilers, the value of the stack pointer before any local variables are allocated is saved in register A6. Then local variable references are defined as −X(A6). So we now know a quick, easy way to spot references to global and local variables in object code: anything that's −X(A5) is a global variable, and anything that's −X(A6) is a local.

As usual, there's a complication we have to consider here. What happens if one procedure calls another? The called procedure can't use A6 to hold the saved stack pointer value, because it's already in use by the calling procedure. So what happens? The answer is deceptively simple. The called procedure *saves the old value of A6 on the stack*, then puts the current stack pointer into A6, and then starts allocating space for local variables. An ingenious technique, don't you think? If you want to take a few minutes to be sure you understand what's going on, the diagram in Figure 5-5 may help.

Every procedure sets up A6 in this way before it allocates local variables. This means that A6 is used by every procedure as a base for its locals. The piece of the stack that a procedure uses for its local

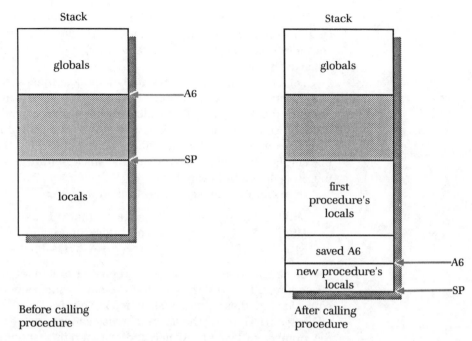

Figure 5-5 A procedure calls another procedure

variables is known as a **stack frame**. The register that's used to point to the start of the local variables, register A6, is called the **frame pointer**.

Remember that we said register A5 was used to point to the start of the global variables and that globals were found at negative offsets from A5. For this reason, A5 is sometimes called the **global frame pointer**.

A5 and A6 as Frame Pointers

Register A5 is always set up by the Segment Loader to be the value of the initial stack pointer, so almost every Macintosh language uses it as the place to start allocating global variables. However, there's nothing in the ROM that specifically supports using A6 as a local frame pointer. Virtually all Macintosh languages use A6 as their local frame pointer, but they could choose another usable register, such as A4. One good reason for using A6 is that most of the ROM routines create stack frames for their own local variables, and they all do so using A6 as the frame pointer. Since each procedure saves the previous value of A6, a debugger can use these saved A6 values to provide information about recently called procedures.

The 68000, smart little fella that it is, is designed for use by high-level languages like Pascal and C. It includes specific instructions that support common practices of high-level languages, such as creating and destroying stack frames.

Let's take a look at the assembly language that's needed to set up a stack frame. When a procedure begins executing and it creates a stack frame, it must do three things: first, it must save the value of A6 on the stack, since it's about to put a new frame pointer in that register; second, it must put the value of the stack pointer into A6, creating the frame pointer; finally, it must decrement the stack pointer to reserve space for the procedure's local variables.

In assembly language, these three things are:

```
MOVE.L A6, -(SP)        ;save current A6
MOVE.L SP, A6           ;put stack pointer in A6
SUB    #X, SP           ;reserve X bytes for locals
```

Since this operation must be repeated exactly at the start of every procedure, the 68000 has defined a single instruction that does the equivalent of these three instructions. This is the LINK instruction. It takes two parameters: the address register to use as a frame pointer, and the number of bytes by which the stack pointer should be changed to reserve space for local variables (a negative number).

So, if we were compiling a procedure that had 8 bytes of local variables, the instruction LINK A6,−8 would be generated by the compiler at the beginning of the procedure. When we run the program and execute this procedure, the LINK instruction would set up the stack frame with A6 as the frame pointer.

Notice that this just reserves the space on the stack for the variables; it doesn't give them any values. This is where "uninitialized data" errors happen: if you accidentally rely on a variable that has never been initialized, you'll get whatever value happened to be in the variable's location when the stack space was reserved. It's kind of like playing Russian roulette: you might not get shot the first time, but you will eventually.

When the procedure is finished executing, its local variables must be removed from the stack. This can be accomplished by destroying the local stack frame that was set up for the procedure. We can accomplish this in two steps: first, we put the frame pointer back into the stack pointer. This cuts the stack back to the size it was before the LINK instruction allocated local variable space. The second thing we must do is replace the old value of A6 that was saved on the stack by the LINK instruction (see the preceding discussion of LINK if you forgot that it did this).

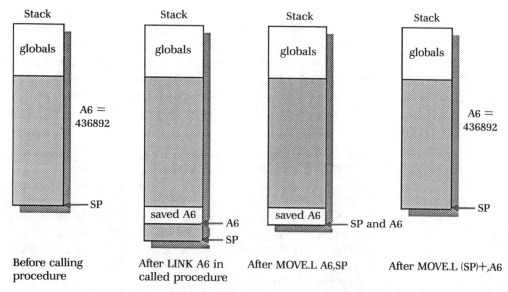

Figure 5-6 Destroying the local stack frame

In assembly language, we can accomplish this with two instructions: MOVE.L A6, SP will put the stack pointer back where it was before allocating space for locals; MOVE.L (SP)+, A6 will put the old value of A6, which LINK saved on the stack, back into A6 where it was when the procedure started. These two instructions leave things the way they were when the procedure was entered, as you can see in Figure 5-6.

Once again, the 68000 gets a gold star here. Just like the case of the LINK instruction, the 68000 defines a single instruction to handle the dismantling of the stack frame that would otherwise take two instructions. The instruction is called "unlink", and the assembler mnemonic for it is UNLK. It takes one parameter, which is the address register that was used as the frame pointer. So most of the time you'll see this at the end of a procedure: UNLK A6.

Parameters

There's one other kind of data that procedure-oriented languages work with: parameters. When a Pascal or C program calls a procedure or function, it goes through a well-defined sequence of steps. First, if it's a function, the program decrements the stack pointer to reserve space for the function's result. Then, if the procedure has any parameters, they're pushed onto the stack, one by one.

Here C and Pascal usually differ: most C's push the parameters in right-to-left order, so the last one listed in the routine's declaration is the first pushed; most Pascals push parameters the other way, left to right as they're listed in the declaration. Also, some compilers vary from these rules. In particular, some C's pass parameters in registers, rather than on the stack. To find out what your compiler does, check its documentation or better yet, take a look at the compiled code that it produces.

The ROM Is Pascal-chauvinistic

It's important to note that the routines in the Macintosh ROM follow the Pascal convention. That is, they expect their parameters pushed in left-to-right order as listed in **Inside Macintosh**. This presents a problem for C compilers. There are at least two ways to solve the problem. One rather obnoxious solution would be to define the interfaces for the ROM routines with their parameters listed backwards.

A more reasonable solution, which is used by most available C compilers, is to define an alternate, "backwards" parameter-passing convention for specified routines. For example, Workshop C and some other C's define a special keyword `Pascal` that, when used in a function declaration, tells the compiler that calls to this procedure should have their parameters passed left to right, like Pascal, instead of the normal (for C) right to left.

Also, many C compilers pass parameters to functions in registers instead of on the stack. The exact rules of passing parameters vary; you should check your compiler's documentation or take a look at the object code that the compiler produces.

After the parameters have been pushed, the routine is called. In assembly language, the actual call to the procedure or function is accomplished with a JSR (jump to subroutine) instruction. The JSR saves a return address on the stack so that the called procedure can finish execution with an RTS (return from subroutine) instruction.

What say we declare a simple procedure:

```
PROCEDURE MrCairo (friends: INTEGER);
```

This procedure takes one parameter, an integer. The code that the compiler generates to call the procedure will first push the parameter, friends, onto the stack. This is done with a MOVE N, −(SP) instruction. If the parameter is a local variable, N will be in the form −X(A6); if it's a global variable, N will be −X(A5). In both of these cases, X is the offset from the frame pointer that's computed by the compiler.

What if the parameter we send to MrCairo is a constant? In this case, the compiler simply places a constant in the instruction. For example, if we write MrCairo (7); in the source, the object code will be MOVE #7, −(SP), followed by the JSR to the procedure.

Pushing the parameter places it on the stack; JSRing to the procedure puts a return address on the stack. So, when the procedure begins executing, there are these two things already on the stack. The first thing the called procedure does is a LINK A6, −X to set up the stack frame. Figure 5-7 shows what the stack looks like while this is going on.

How does the compiler translate references to the parameters within the procedure? Notice in Figure 5-7 that parameters are always located at a positive offset from ("above") the frame pointer, register A6. So, in object code, you'll see references to the procedure's parameters in the form X(A6). [You can compare this to globals, which are −X(A5), and locals, which are −X(A6).] Also, note that the first four bytes pointed to by A6 are always the saved value of the previous A6, and the next four bytes are the return address to the calling routine, so parameters will always be at least eight bytes off A6. In our example, the parameter friends will be seen in object code as 8(A6).

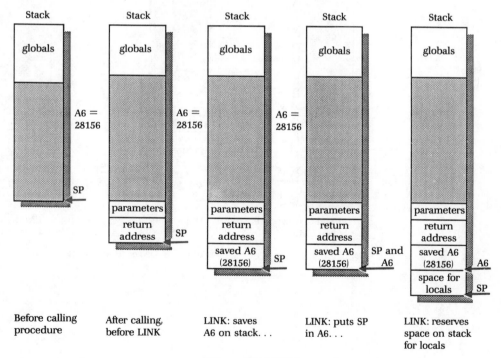

Figure 5-7 LINK instruction

Now the procedure does its thing. When it's getting ready to finish, it does an UNLK A6 to destroy the stack frame. Figure 5-8 shows what the stack looks like at this point. If the procedure executes an RTS at this point, we're in deep, deep trouble, because procedures are required to remove their parameters from the stack before returning. Before we can do an RTS, we have to cut back the stack to remove the parameters (in the case of MrCairo, that amounts to two bytes, the size of the single parameter).

How can we do this? When we needed to remove the locals from the stack, we were able to do just an UNLK, which put the stack back the way it was before the LINK instruction. UNLK knows where to put the stack pointer because the LINK instruction saved the stack pointer. We can't do that here, though. There's no saved value of the stack pointer that will cause it to point to the return address.

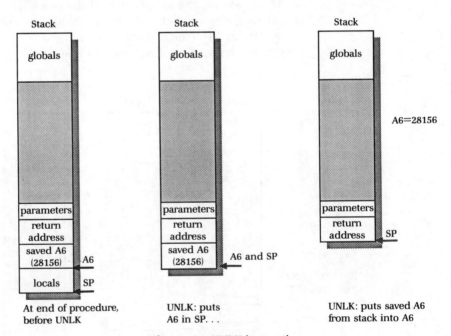

Figure 5-8 UNLK instruction

However, we really don't need such a saved value. The procedure knows how many bytes its parameters occupied. All it has to do is pop the return address off the stack, save it somewhere, and then increment the stack pointer by the size of the parameters. In assembly language, we can accomplish this with two instructions: first, we can pop the return address off the stack into a scratch register, A0, like this: MOVE.L (A7)+,A0; then we can remove the two bytes of parameters from the stack by incrementing the stack pointer by two bytes: ADDQ #2,A7. Figure 5-9 shows how the stack looks at this point. The code that removes parameters and cleans up at the end of a procedure is called the **epilog**.

Now that we've put the stack back the way we want it, we're ready to return to the code that called the procedure. But we can't do an RTS; RTS returns to the address that is on top of the stack, and we already removed our return address from the stack and put it in A0. What do we do? We could put the return address back on the stack and then execute an RTS, which would work, but there's a better way: a single instruction, JMP (A0), which means "jump to the address that's in A0." Since A0 contains the desired return address, this works great, and it saves an instruction over the other solution. Neat!

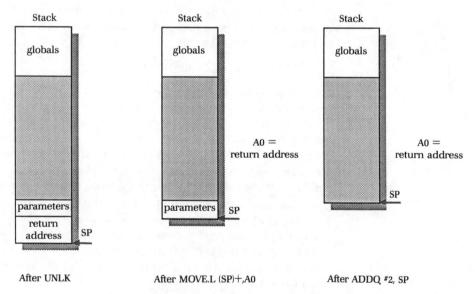

Figure 5-9 Removing parameters from the stack

C Programmers

In some C compilers, the calling function is responsible for removing the parameters from the stack, not the called function. This means that functions end by doing an UNLK and an RTS, and the caller removes the parameters it pushed.

There are a couple more interesting facts that you'll need to know about parameters. First, Pascal programmers will remember that Pascal defines two kinds of parameters, call-by-name (also known as call-by-reference), and call-by-value, also known as variable and value parameters. When a procedure uses a variable parameter, it is permitted to change the variable; when it uses a value parameter, it cannot change the value of the parameter that's passed to it.

Here's what's really going on. When you pass a value parameter, that's exactly what goes on the stack: the value that's specified. For example, let's define a procedure:

```
PROCEDURE DejaVu (david, stephen : integer; VAR neil, graham : integer;);
```

In this declaration, the first two parameters, david and stephen, are value parameters, and neil and graham are variable parameters. So, if we call the procedure like this,

```
DejaVu (int1, int2, int3, int4);
```

the first two parameters are passed by value and the next two are passed by reference. This means that the values of int1 and int2 will be pushed on the stack; DejaVu has no way of changing the values of int1 and int2. On the other hand, the procedure must be given a way to access and change the values of int3 and int4, since they're VAR parameters. So the compiler will pass *pointers* to int3 and int4 on the stack. That way, DejaVu will know where they're stored in memory, and it can change them.

When you, the programmer, write the procedure, you're completely unaware that you've been passed a pointer to variable parameters and the value of value parameters; the compiler takes care of it for you. The only thing that the average Pascal programmer knows is that a variable parameter can be changed on the left side of an assignment statement, but a value parameter cannot.

A Great, but Nerdy, Joke

Here is an apocryphal story about Niklaus Wirth, the creator of Pascal: Professor Wirth was giving a lecture, and someone inquired as to the pronunciation of his name. The professor responded, "Well, there are two correct options. You can call me by name, which is 'veert', or you can call me by value, which is 'worth'."

One last complication about parameters, and then we'll move on. If a procedure has a parameter that is more than four bytes long, the compiler doesn't push the parameter on the stack. Instead, it pushes a pointer to the parameter; then, as part of the procedure's initialization code, right after the LINK instruction, it makes a *local copy* of the parameter. It then uses this local copy in the procedure.

Why doesn't the compiler just pass the whole value on the stack, like it does for parameters of less than four bytes? The answer to this question is little known; it seems to be a remnant of older microprocessors, like the 6502, which have very small stacks. In the 6502, for example, the stack can only be 256 bytes long. To help preserve this tiny space, Pascal compilers would make a local copy of parameters longer than four bytes and pass a pointer on the stack, using only the stack space needed for a pointer. This vestige of old systems is still with us.

There are a couple of common variable types that are always passed to procedures by the "pointer on the stack, make a local copy" technique. Pascal strings, even if they're less than four bytes, are always passed by this method. Also, the Standard Apple Numerics Environment (SANE), which is the IEEE-standard numerics package that works on all Apple computers, passes its variables by pointer. These include the types Real, Single, Double, Extended, and Comp. If you want to learn more about SANE, see the Apple Numerics Manual.

Some Compilers Don't Play This Game

Some compilers, especially C compilers, don't use the "pointer on the stack, make a local copy" technique for parameters greater than four bytes. In general, C compilers will never push a parameter's address unless the caller specifies it with the ampersand (&) operator.

Figure 5-10 Sizes of parameters

Type	Size in bytes	Comment
Integer	2	Two's complement integer (−32768 to 32767)
Longint	4	Two's complement integer (−2147483648 to 2147483647)
SignedByte	2	Two's complement integer in low byte (−128 to 127)
Boolean	2	Value in bit 0 of high byte (0 = false, 1 = true)
Char	2	ASCII code in low byte, high byte unused
Real	4	Pointer to value converted to Extended
Single	4	Pointer to value converted to Extended
Double	4	Pointer to value converted to Extended
Extended	4	Pointer to value
Comp	4	Pointer to value converted to Extended
String [n]	4	Pointer to string
Byte	2	Two's complement integer, value in low byte
Ptr	4	Address of data; includes any parameters preceded by @
Handle	4	Address of master pointer; includes any kind of handle
Point	4	QuickDraw coordinate
Rect	4	Pointer to QuickDraw rectangle

You now have the complete set of rules for parameters: variable parameters are passed by a pointer to the variable; value parameters greater than four bytes, plus strings and SANE types, are passed by making a local copy and then passing a pointer to that copy; other value parameters smaller than four bytes are passed by value. Figure 5-10 lists the common data types and more explicit information on how they're passed. In the next section, we'll see some actual examples of procedure calls and the resulting assembly language.

Statements and Variables

As we discussed earlier, compilers are pretty predictable when it comes to translating statements into assembly language. In this section, we'll look at how some kinds of statements are translated and the resulting object code. With the information that you get here, you might learn enough to become a human compiler; however, computers are generally better at that than humans, so you're more likely to use this knowledge to help you trace through object code as you're debugging.

Once again, it's important to know that these descriptions and algorithms apply to the Workshop Pascal compiler. Your mileage may vary. You can take the things explained here and use them to examine your own compiler's object code. You can then determine exactly how it does things. This job is made easier if the compiler you're using has an option to produce assembly language source. Lisa Pascal and most C's have this option.

When you start looking at the object code produced by compilers, you start to appreciate how well thought out the 68000 is. Many high-level language statements translate into a short, straightforward sequence of assembly language instructions, as we'll see. Some statements can be translated into a single 68000 instruction.

Assignment Statements

One of the most common and elementary statements in any language is the assignment statement. This is the one that puts values into variables. In Pascal, it takes the form varName := expression, and in C it's varName = expression.

The assignment statement has an easy translation into assembly language. The assignment statement first computes the value of the expression on the right side and then places that value into the variable specified on the left side. In the object code, as we've discussed, a reference to a variable is translated into the address occupied by that variable; if it's a global, it's —X(A5), and so on.

So the assembly language equivalent to an assignment statement is a sequence of instructions to compute the value on the right side, followed by a single MOVE instruction to place the value into the variable's memory. Let's look at some examples of assignment statements. First, we'll assume these declarations:

```
var
    int1, int2, intResult, counter : integer;
    long1, long2 : longint;
    sing1, sing2 : single;
    ext1, ext2 : extended;
    bool1, bool2 : boolean;
    char1, char2 : char;
    string1, string2 : string[255];
    sub1, sub2 : 0..100;
    rec1 : record
        fint : integer;
        fbool : boolean;
        flong : longint;
        fpoint : point;
            end;
    array1 : array [1..20] of integer;
    ptr1, ptr2 : ptr;
```

Now let's look at some assignments to these variables.

```
int1 := 500;   {MOVE #500,−8(A5)}
```

In this example, we're simply assigning a constant to a global variable, so the object code is pretty simple, just moving an immediate value (the # in front of 500 signifies that it's an immediate) into the variable (be sure to read Appendix A if you're feeling lost in the assembly language). One thing here bears closer examination. This says that int1 is at −8(A5), but our declaration said that int1 is the first variable declared. Since it's an integer, it's two bytes long, and it should be at −2(A5). What's the deal?

The answer lies in the fact that we declared several integers on one line: int1, int2, intResult, and counter. When the Pascal compiler allocates space for variables that are declared in a bunch like this, it proceeds from right to left in the list. So the honored first space at −2(A5) is given to counter, at −4(A5) is intResult, int2 will be located at −6(A5), and space for int1 is reserved next at −8(A5).

Multiple Parameters

When we declared more than one variable on the same line, like this:

```
var
    int1, int2, intResult, counter : integer;
```

the compiler allocated space for them from right to left (counter first, then intResult, and so on). That's not the case for procedure parameters. We declared

```
PROCEDURE DejaVu (david, stephen : integer; VAR neil, graham :
integer);
```

Pascal procedure parameters are always pushed in the order that they're declared. That means that we could also declare this procedure like this:

```
PROCEDURE DejaVu (david: Integer; stephen: Integer; VAR neil: Integer;
VAR graham: Integer);
```

and the compiled code would be exactly the same. The first method requires less typing, and it's the usual way of doing it.

Pascal Units

If your application has separately compiled units that have their own global variables, they may come first below A5, before the main application's globals are allocated. Their exact placement depends on the development system you're using. In Workshop Pascal, your application's globals are allocated first, then any unit globals, including QuickDraw. To find out exactly where your variables are stored, you may want to write a dummy procedure that does nothing but assign values to all your globals; you can then look at the object code to see where each variable is.

As long as we've discovered this rule about variable allocation, let's make a chart of our global variables and their locations. You might try this one as an exercise, if you need some exercise; otherwise, you can just look at the one in Figure 5-11.

Figure 5-11 Global variables, sizes and locations

Variable	Type	Size in bytes	Starting address	Ending address
counter	Integer	2	−2(A5)	−1(A5)
intResult	Integer	2	−4(A5)	−3(A5)
int2	Integer	2	−6(A5)	−5(A5)
int1	Integer	2	−8(A5)	−7(A5)
long2	Longint	4	−12(A5)	−9(A5)
long1	Longint	4	−16(A5)	−13(A5)
sing2	Single	4	−20(A5)	−17(A5)
sing1	Single	4	−24(A5)	−21(A5)
ext2	Extended	10	−34(A5)	−25(A5)
ext1	Extended	10	−44(A5)	−35(A5)
bool2	Boolean	1	−45(A5)	−45(A5)
bool1	Boolean	1	−46(A5)	−46(A5)
char2	Char	2	−48(A5)	−47(A5)
char1	Char	2	−50(A5)	−49(A5)
string2	String255	256	−306(A5)	−51(A5)
string1	String255	256	−562(A5)	−307(A5)
sub2	0..100	1	−563(A5)	−563(A5)
sub1	0..100	1	−564(A5)	−564(A5)
rec1	Record	12	−576(A5)	−565(A5)
array1	Array	40	−616(A5)	−577(A5)
ptr2	Ptr	4	−620(A5)	−617(A5)
ptr1	Ptr	4	−624(A5)	−621(A5)

Variable Packing

The Pascal compiler will automatically pack some variables that don't require a whole word and are adjacent to each other. In particular, sub1 and sub2 are limited to the range 0 through 100, so each will fit into a single byte. They'll be packed into a single byte each. Also, the two chars and the two booleans will fit into 1 byte each, so they're packed, too.

Our next assignment:

long1 := 456789012; { MOVE.L #456789012,−16(A5) }

Again, the object code is really obvious. The MOVE instruction puts the constant value directly into the variable, which is right where we thought it would be at −16(A5). Note that the MOVE instruction specifies a long operand (that's the .L after the MOVE). This is because the value that we're moving is a long word, a four-byte value.

Next, let's look at a couple of SANE assignments.

```
ext1 := 1234.5678;  { LEA   −44(A5),A0
                      LEA   Cst0004,A1
                      MOVE.L  (A1)+,(A0)+
                      MOVE.L  (A1)+,(A0)+
                      MOVE.W  (A1),(A0) }

sing1 := 104.5;     { PEA Cst0005
                      PEA −24(A5)
                      MOVE.W  #$1010,−(A7)
                      JSR FP68K }
```

This looks pretty bizarre at first glance. In the first example, we're assigning a value to a variable of type Extended. The first instruction puts the address of ext1 into register A0. The second instruction loads the address of something called Cst0004 into register A1.

What is this Cst0004 thing? It stands for "constant #4." Whenever the Pascal compiler encounters string constants or SANE constants, it embeds them at the end of the procedure's code and marks them with a label that starts with Cst. Then, when the procedure refers to the constant, the compiler inserts a reference to the appropriate constant. So Cst0004 is the label that's attached to the constant value 1234.5678 that the compiler has embedded at the end of the procedure's code.

What's this code doing with the constant stored at Cst0004? The next three instructions cause bytes from Cst0004 to be moved into the variable's space at −44(A5). How many bytes are being moved? Well, there are two MOVE.L instructions and one MOVE.W. The long word-sized instructions each move four bytes, for a total of eight, and the word-sized move adds an additional two bytes. So the three instructions together move 10 bytes. This corresponds with what we know about variables of type Extended: they're 10 bytes long.

The assignment statement for sing1 is a little more puzzling. It begins by using PEA instructions to push the addresses of another constant (Cst0005) and the variable sing1 onto the stack. But then, instead of moving bytes from the constant to the variable, it mysteriously pushes a word (#4112, or hex $1010), onto the stack and jumps to a subroutine called FP68K. Is this right? Has the compiler gone wacko?

Of course not. Here's the scoop. To maximize accuracy and minimize the amount of code needed, SANE converts numbers to Extended before doing anything with them. So even if you declare a variable as Single, as we did with sing1, SANE must convert it to Extended before it can do anything with it. Also, whenever you use a constant of any SANE type, it's stored in Extended form until it's assigned to a variable.

> **Why Ever Use** Single?
>
> Since SANE does all its internal computation in Extended form anyway, why bother declaring your variables as Single or Double? What benefit is there? If you only need the accuracy that's indicated by single- or double-precision numbers, you save variable storage space by using Single or Double. Single precision numbers take up 4 bytes; double-precision variables use 8 bytes. Extended-precision numbers use up a whopping ten bytes of memory. So, if you have to use, for example, an array of 1000 values, and you don't need anything better than single-precision, you can save 6000 bytes by using Single instead of Extended (1000 values times 4 bytes each for Single compared to 10,000 bytes for 1000 Extended values of 10 bytes each).

In the case of a constant like 104.5 that we've used here, the compiler will embed a copy of the constant in Extended form at the end of the procedure. Before it can be assigned to the variable, it must be converted to a Single. To do this, the compiler generates code to call the SANE procedure called FX2S, which means "convert from Extended to Single."

SANE procedures are called by pushing a word on the stack that indicates which call to make and then jumping to a central dispatch point that calls the SANE package. We can see this in the object code: first, a word is pushed onto the stack, followed by a JSR to FP68K. The word, $1010, is secret code for FX2S, so this calling sequence will cause SANE to convert the Extended constant stored at Cst0005 into a Single and to put that Single into sing1 at −44(A5).

Figuring SANE Secret Codes

Officially, the word that's pushed on the stack that indicates a SANE function is called an **opword**. SANE computes the opword by adding together a **format code** and an **operation code**. The format code indicates whether a value is Single, Double, Extended, or another SANE type. For example, the format code for Single is $1000. The operation code indicates what function is being called; the operation code that means "convert from Extended" is $10. By adding these together, we come up with the opword $1010, which was pushed on the stack to indicate a "convert from Extended to Single" call to SANE. This information is definitely for fanatics and language implementors only, since most languages have SANE built in and you'll never have to know this stuff. Many assemblers even define macros for the SANE calls. If you're really interested in this sort of stuff, you can read all about it in Apple's SANE manual.

Now let's look at assignments to subrange types.

```
sub1 := 42;              { MOVE.B  #42,−564(A5) }
sub2 := sub1 * 3;        { MOVE.B  −564(A5),D0
                           EXT.W   D0
                           MULS    #3,D0
                           CHK     #100,D0
                           MOVE.B  D0,−563(A5) }
```

If you'll recall, these variables were declared as subranges of 0 to 100. This means that the compiler will make sure that no values outside this range are put into the variables. This is called **range checking**. There's a compiler option that controls range checking: putting $R− in your source turns range checking off, and $R+ turns it on. If you don't specify this option at all, the compiler will do range checking on your subrange variables.

The first subrange assignment is pretty simple. It works just like an assignment to an ordinary integer. Since we're assigning a constant, the compiler can check the constant to see if it exceeds the allowable range. If it does, the compiler stops compiling and reports a "Value out of range" error. In this case, the value 42 is within the range, so we get a nice, simple MOVE.B #42,−564(A5).

The assignment to sub2 is much more interesting for us compiler fans. It does a lot more than just put the value into the variable's space in memory. What's it up to? In this assignment, we've got an expression on the right side, which means that at compile time the compiler has no way of knowing if the value will be in range or not. It must generate code that will do the actual checking at runtime. Let's take a look at it.

The first instruction loads the value of sub1 into register D0. The next two instructions multiply the value by 3. Now the value is ready to be assigned to sub2. But wait! First, we have to make sure that it hasn't gone outside the specified subrange.

This check is performed by yet another magic 68000 instruction, CHK. This instruction compares a value in a register to a specified "boundary" value. In this case, we're comparing the newly multiplied value in D0 to the boundary value of 100. If the check fails and the value is out of range, the 68000 generates a range check error, which on the Macintosh is reported as a system error 5. In this case, of course, we humans can see that sub1 * 3 will be 42 * 3, or 126 for you nonmathematical types, which certainly exceeds the subrange boundary of 100, so we'd get a system error 5.

However, the compiler doesn't look at it that way. When it compiles this line, it's not looking at the previous line that set the value of sub1. In fact, it assumes no knowledge at all of the values of any variables already specified. Instead, it relies on the CHK instruction to perform a range check at the time the code is executed. Remember that if the CHK instruction fails, a system error 5 will occur.

After the range check is performed by the CHK instruction, the last instruction moves the computed value from D0 into the variable at −563(A5). This takes care of the assignment.

A couple more easy ones:

```
bool1 := true;     { MOVE.B  #1,−46(A5) }
char1 := 'x';      { MOVE.W  #120,−50(A5) }
```

The first assignment reveals that the Pascal compiler uses the value 1 to indicate "true" in BOOLEAN variables. You get a pat on the back if you guessed that zero represents "false."

The assignment to char1 is pretty simple, too. The compiler figures out that the character 'x' has ASCII code 120 and simply puts that value into the variable's space in memory.

Byte-sized Morsels

Both booleans and chars take up two bytes, but Pascal puts the significant part of the boolean in the high byte, while the meaningful part of the char is in its low byte. It could just as easily be the other way around; the reasons for doing it this way are mainly historical.

Short Constants

Unlike the SANE constant we saw earlier, the 'x' is not placed at the end of the procedure somewhere with a label; instead, it's just coded right in the MOVE instruction. This is because the constant is four bytes or less and can be specified completely as an operand in a MOVE instruction. Since char constants only take up one word, they're handled in this way.

Let's look at some string assignments.

```
string1 := 'Musical Youth';    { LEA   −562(A5),A0
                                 LEA   Cst0003,A1
                                 MOVE.L   (A1)+,(A0)+
                                 MOVE.L   (A1)+,(A0)+
                                 MOVE.L   (A1)+,(A0)+
                                 MOVE.W   (A1),(A0)   }

string2 := 'The quick brown cow jumped over the lazy moon.';
                               { LEA   −306(A5),A0
                                 LEA   Cst0002,A1
                                 MOVEQ   #12,D0
              Loop               MOVE.L   (A1)+,(A0)+
                                 SUBQ.W   #1,D0
                                 BGT.S   Loop }
```

Both of these statements assign constants to strings. In the first case, the constant is 14 bytes long: 13 bytes for the characters in the string, plus one byte to hold the length. The code that the compiler produces looks a lot like the assignment to the EXTENDED variable that we saw earlier. First, the address of the variable is put into register A0, and the address of the constant is put into A1. Then 14 bytes are moved from the constant into the variable. This is accomplished with three MOVE.L instructions and one MOVE.W.

The second assignment is handled a bit differently. In this case, we've got a constant that is 47 bytes long (count the characters in the string and then add one for the length byte). If the compiler generated the same kind of code as for the first assignment, there would be 12 consecutive MOVE.L statements—kind of a waste of space. So, to be more efficient, the compiler builds a neat little loop.

The code begins by loading the now familiar (see, this stuff is sinking in!) registers A0 and A1 with pointers to the variable's storage and the constant, respectively. It then moves a byte containing the number of long words to be moved (that is, the length of the constant divided by 4) into register D0. It then starts the loop by moving four bytes (a long word) from the source to the destination with a MOVE.L instruction. Since a long word is the largest operand that an instruction will take, this is the most bytes that can be moved at once.

After this, it subtracts one from the counter in D0 and does a "branch if greater than zero" (BGT.S) back to the start of the loop. Since we started with a count of 12 in D0, this will cause 12 groups of four bytes to be moved, for a total of 48. The string constant we're moving is 47 bytes long, so this will accomplish the task, with an extra unused byte at the end.

How does the compiler choose whether to use the first method of assigning a string constant or the second? It simply tries to determine which will take up the smaller amount of memory. Both of these string assignments take up six instructions. Of course, the first will execute much faster because it doesn't have to go through a loop 12 times.

Note that no matter how large the string constant is, up to its maximum of 256 bytes, it will never take more than six instructions to make the assignment. The compiler will generate "straight-line" code, like the first assignment, if it can do so in six or fewer instructions; otherwise, it will construct a loop, as in the second example. This means that constants that take up 16 bytes or less can be assigned in six instructions: two LEA instructions to load pointers into the registers and four MOVE.L to move the bytes.

Why Doesn't It Call the ROM?

Back in Chapter 3 we mentioned a nifty procedure in the Macintosh ROM called BlockMove that is used for moving bytes around in memory. If the compiler has to move bytes, why doesn't it just call BlockMove? Not a bad idea. The main reason it doesn't call Block-Move here is that the Workshop Pascal compiler can also be used to generate Lisa code, and there's no corresponding system call to move bytes in the Lisa operating system. Perhaps a future Macintosh-only compiler would call the ROM to move bytes here.

Let's look at a pointer assignment.

```
ptr1 := @int1;              { LEA −8(A5),A0
                             MOVE.L  A0,−624(A5) }
```

This seems to be pretty straightforward. In the source, we're saying that we want ptr1 to be a pointer to int1; that is, we want ptr1 to contain the address of int1.

To do this, the compiler generates two instructions. The first loads a pointer to int1 into register A0, and the second simply moves that pointer into the variable's storage at −624(A5). Neat and clean. At first glance, you might think that there would be a single 68000 instruction to accomplish this assignment. There isn't—what you'd need is an instruction that moves the address of the first operand into the memory location specified by the second operand. Maybe on the next-generation microprocessor. . . .

We've now looked at lots of examples of assignment of simple variables, plus strings, which technically are structured variables. Now that you know all about simple assignments, let's look at assignments in structured variables like arrays and records. You'll see that they're pretty similar to their simple-variable counterparts.

The first one we'll look at involves assigning the fields of a record.

```
rec1.fint := int1;                          { MOVE.W −8(A5),−576(A5) }
rec1.fbool := false;                        { CLR.B −574(A5) }
rec1.flong := 2136528028;                   { MOVE.L #2136528028,−572(A5) }
rec1.fpoint := screenbits.bounds.topLeft;   { MOVE.L −960(A5),−568(A5) }
```

The first statement assigns the value of int1 to the first field of the record. This is simply an assignment between two global integers. The value to be assigned is taken from int1 at −8(A5), and it gets stuffed into the first field, rec1.fint, at −576(A5) with a MOVE.W instruction.

For the next assignment, we need to set a boolean field to false. Booleans occupy a full word of memory when they're not packed, but only the low-order byte is significant. So the compiler sets the variable location's low byte to zero in the best way it knows how, by doing a CLR.B on it.

The third field that's assigned is a long integer constant, and it's pretty ho-hum stuff that we've already learned. The code simply moves the long word that represents the constant into the correct memory location at −572(A5).

Now that you've been lulled into a sense of false security, it's time to spring Pascal's latest surprise on you. The next assignment statement appears at first glance to be pretty simple, just moving a word-sized value, a point, from one place to another. But look more carefully. What is screenbits.bounds.topLeft?

As you probably know, it's a QuickDraw global variable. How does the compiler know about it? It knows because you have a statement that says something like uses Obj/QuickDraw at the beginning of your program. This causes the compiler to read in everything that's defined in QuickDraw's interface file, the file called Obj/Quickdraw, including its global variables and its procedures. They're defined just as if they had been part of your source.

But where does the compiler put the QuickDraw global variables? Since they're globals, it puts them on the global stack. In Workshop Pascal, space for the QuickDraw globals is allocated on the stack after all application globals have been allocated. There are 206 bytes of Quick-Draw global variables, and QuickDraw is the only piece of the Macintosh ROM that has globals that go on the stack. For your edification, Figure 5-12 lists the QuickDraw globals and their locations on the stack. Since they're allocated after your program's globals, their actual address will vary.

Figure 5-12 QuickDraw global variables, sizes and locations

Variable	Type	Size in bytes	Starts at	Ends at	Offset from thePort
thePort	GrafPtr	4	203	206	0
white	Pattern	8	195	202	−8
black	Pattern	8	187	194	−16
gray	Pattern	8	179	186	−24
ltGray	Pattern	8	171	178	−32
dkGray	Pattern	8	163	170	−40
arrow	Cursor	68	95	162	−108
screenBits	BitMap	14	81	94	−122
randSeed	Longint	4	77	80	−126
QuickDraw private globals:					
wideOpen	Handle	4	73	76	−130
wideMaster	Ptr	4	69	72	−134
wideData	Region	10	59	68	−144
rgnBuf	Handle	4	55	58	−148
rgnIndex	Integer	2	53	54	−150
rgnMax	Integer	2	51	52	−152
playPic	Longint	4	47	50	−156
playIndex	Integer	2	45	46	−158
thePoly	Handle	4	41	44	−162
polyMax	Integer	2	39	40	−164
patAlign	Point	4	35	38	−168
fontAdj	Fixed	4	31	34	−172
fontPtr	Ptr	4	27	30	−176
fontData	FMOutPut	26	1	26	−202

Starting and ending locations are relative to the first (lowest in memory) global. To access a global from assembler, use the offset from A5 after getting the address of thePort (A5 points to the location that contains thePort's address).

Where to Find QuickDraw Globals

Although Workshop Pascal puts them on the stack below your application's globals, QuickDraw globals need not be located there. In fact, they can be allocated anywhere. The only requirement is that you allocate a space of 206 bytes and then call InitGraf with the address of the 203rd byte of this allocated space. Huh? Well, InitGraf expects a pointer to thePort, the first QuickDraw global. Remember that globals are allocated downward in memory. That means that thePort is at bytes 203 through 206 of the QuickDraw space; the next global, white, is in bytes 195 through 202, and so on. Figure 5-12 lists the QuickDraw globals and their relative locations from the lowest byte of the QuickDraw global area.

The next assignment we'll look at is an array element.

```
array1 [1]:= 17;      { MOVE.W #17,−616(A5) }
```

No surprises here (surprise!). Once again, we see that assigning a value to an element of a structure is pretty much the same as a simple variable assignment. The immediate value 17 is moved directly into the variable's location. You already knew this.

Things to Remember

- Compilers translate source to object code in a predictable way. You can look at a line of source code and have a good idea what the object code will look like.
- Compilers are generalized. Smart human programmers will write better assembly language programs than compilers.
- Space for global variables is allocated on the stack, and each variable takes up a specific amount of space. Global variables are referred to by negative references from A5, like this:−xx(A5).
- Space for local variables is allocated when a procedure is executed and then released when the procedure finishes. Local variables are stored at a negative offset from A6, like this: −xx(A6).
- Most Macintosh compilers use register A6 and the LINK instruction to create local stack frames for procedures and the UNLK instruction to destroy the stack frame.
- Pascal pushes parameters onto the stack left to right. Parameters within a procedure can be found at a positive offset from A6, like this: xx(A6).
- Parameters larger than 4 bytes are passed by reference (pointer), not by value.
- Assignment statements in high-level languages translate into MOVE instructions.

CHAPTER

6

More about Compiled Code

In this chapter we'll continue to look at compiled code. We'll see how procedure calls, if statements, case statements, for, while, and repeat loops, and with statements are handled. We'll also look at linked routines, see how the jump table works, and find out how to identify unexpected things in your code.

The variables we'll use in this chapter are the same ones that were declared in Chapter 5, so you can refer back there for more information.

Procedure Calls

Now that we've pretty much covered assignment statements, let's take a look at some real live procedure calls. We'll examine both the calling sequence that the compiler sets up and the actual code in the procedure itself. As usual, we're in for a few interesting surprises, so don't go away.

Let's start with an easy little procedure that simply adds two numbers. We'll look at its declaration, a call to the procedure, and the procedure's code itself.

First, here's the declaration:

```
procedure sumNums (num1, num2: integer; VAR result : integer);
```

This procedure takes three integer parameters, two call-by-value (value parameters), and one call-by-name (variable parameter). In addition, the procedure has no local variables. Its job is simply to add the two integers passed to it and to return the sum in the third integer passed.

Here's the procedure's source code:

```
begin
    result := num1 + num2;
end;
```

Not really super hacker level stuff, admittedly, but it's better to start off with a simple one. Now let's look at source and object code for a call to this procedure.

```
sumNums (int1,int2,intResult);   MOVE.W −8(A5),−(A7)
                                 MOVE.W −6(A5),−(A7)
                                 PEA −4(A5)
                                 JSR SUMNUMS(PC)
```

The calling sequence seems to fall in line with what we've already learned. We said that procedure calls push the parameters on the stack in left-to-right order. To push the first parameter, int1, the compiler just moves the integer from its global storage location at −8(A5) onto the stack. The same thing happens for int2, that is stored at −6(A5).

Remember that the third parameter is a variable parameter. According to the rules which we carefully constructed in the last chapter, variable parameters are always passed by address. This coincides with what we see here: the PEA −4(A5) instruction causes the address of intResult to be pushed on the stack.

The actual call to the procedure is performed with a JSR instruction. The operand of the JSR is interesting. JSR SUMNUMS(PC) means "jump to the subroutine at the offset SUMNUMS from the current program counter." Another way of putting it is to say that SUMNUMS is a fixed number of bytes from the current instruction (because PC represents the current instruction).

Since Macintosh programs can be loaded almost anywhere in RAM, it's vital that they have no references to hard addresses in their code. In other words, a program cannot contain an instruction like JSR 33044, because it has no way of knowing what will be in that location at runtime. Again, the really smart folks who designed the 68000 thought of this, and they came up with a solution: PC-relative addressing.

In this scheme, programs don't refer to hard memory addresses when branching. Instead, subroutine addresses are expressed as an offset from the current program counter. Although a code segment can't be guaranteed of its location in RAM, it can be sure of a fixed offset between routines. Therefore, PC-relative addressing does a great job of solving this problem. In fact, most Macintosh assemblers automatically assume PC-relative mode for JSR instructions, since that's usually what the programmer wants.

When PC-relative Addressing Doesn't Work

The PC-relative addressing technique works great when a routine calls another routine within the same segment. Calling a routine that's in another segment presents a problem. Just think about it: two routines in the same segment can be sure of their relative location to each other, since the entire segment is loaded and relocated as a whole. However, two segments don't have a fixed relation to each other in memory, since they're loaded and relocated independently. This means that PC-relative JSR's for cross-segment calls are doomed to fail, since the calling routine has no idea at compile or assemble time where the called routine is.

Don't worry about it, though. This problem was realized and solved long before the first programmer (whoever that was) started working on a Macintosh. The solution involves the creation of a special table of routines' entry points. This table is placed at a fixed, well-defined location in memory. When a routine wants to call a different segment, it simply JSRs to the correct entry in this table, and the program is dispatched to the new segment. Simple. You've just learned the basics of the **jump table**. We'll talk much more about it later.

Meanwhile, back at the ranch, we were about to examine the code of the procedure itself.

```
begin                        LINK A6,#0
    result := num1 + num2;    MOVE.W 12(A6),D0
                             ADD.W 14(A6),D0
                             MOVE.L 8(A6),A0
                             MOVE.W D0,(A0)
end;                         UNLK A6
                             MOVE.L (A7)+,A0
                             ADDQ.W #8,A7
                             JMP (A0)
```

Let's see what's familiar and expected here. First, we see our friend the LINK A6 instruction. In this case, the operand of the LINK is zero, which means that no bytes will be reserved on the stack for local variables. Why bother to do the LINK then? Because the procedure still must have access to the parameters passed to it, and a stack frame built with a LINK is still the easiest way to do that. In Figure 6-1 you can see what the stack frame for this procedure call looks like.

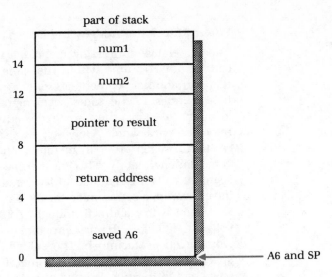

Figure 6-1 Stack frame for SumNums

After the LINK, the number crunching begins in earnest. The Pascal compiler has determined that the most efficient way to add two numbers together and put the result into a variable is to use registers to hold the sum and the destination address. This seems like a reasonable approach. First, the value of num2 is moved from its location on the stack frame into register D0 with the MOVE.W 12(A6),D0 instruction. Then the value of int1 is simply added to the value that's already in the register (ADD.W 14(A6),D0).

Now the desired value is in D0 and ready to be shipped off to the waiting memory location that holds intResult. We first get the address of intResult into another register, A0, with the MOVE.L 8(A6),A0 instruction. Then we can move the contents of D0, the sum, into this location with a MOVE.W D0,(A0). All that's left is for the procedure to clean up after itself by unlinking, popping the return address, incrementing the stack pointer to remove the 8 bytes of parameters, and returning to the caller. The section of code that cleans up the stack and returns to the caller is known as the **epilog**, as we discussed in Chapter 5. If you don't follow the epilog stuff, you can go back and reread the discussion of this technique in Chapter 5 if you want to be refreshed.

Now that we've mastered a simple procedure call, let's go completely off the deep end and play with some pretty complicated calls that show off lots of different calling conventions. First, let's declare another procedure.

```
     procedure showVal1 (valInt: integer; valLong: longint;
valSing: SINGLE; valExt: EXTENDED; valBool: BOOLEAN; valChar:
char; valString: str255);
```

This procedure is designed to include almost all the simple variable types as value parameters. Since the calling sequence is so complicated, with seven parameters, the procedure's code itself does nothing at all, just to keep things simple and almost comprehensible.

Here's a call to our do-nothing procedure that uses all constants as parameters:

```
showVal1 (1984, 2129761313, 9995.95, 12347.6683, false, 'K', 'Big');
{push valInt}                    MOVE.W #1984,−(A7)
{push valLong}                   MOVE.L #2129761313,−(A7)
{push pointer to valSing}        PEA Cst0003
{push pointer to valExt}         PEA Cst0002
{push valBool}                   CLR.W −(A7)
{push valChar}                   MOVE.W #75,−(A7)
{push pointer to valString}      PEA Cst0001
{call procedure showVal1}        JSR SHOWVAL1(PC)
```

Don't you wish all of life were this simple and straightforward? Each of these parameters is pushed with a single instruction. For the integer, long integer, and character values, a MOVE instruction is used: MOVE.W for the (word-sized) integer and character, MOVE.L for the (long word-sized) long integer.

The longer constants, the ones that don't fit into a single four-byte operand, are passed by pointer. For these, the single, extended, and string values, the compiler has embedded the constant at the end of the procedure and has used the PEA instruction here to push the address of each constant.

Finally, the compiler has used a trick to push the boolean constant "false." Instead of a MOVE.W #0,−(A7), we've got a CLR.W −(A7). Both of these instructions accomplish exactly the same result. Is the CLR faster than the MOVE.W? Evidently, the compiler thinks so. The task of finding out if it's really a faster instruction is left as an exercise for the reader (have fun!).

Finally, after all seven (gasp) parameters have been pushed on the stack, the procedure is called. Remember that this procedure literally does nothing: there's just a declaration, followed by begin and end, nothing else. Here's the source and object code listing for this procedure:

```
begin
    {create stack frame}                    LINK A6,#−266
    {make valSing a single}                 MOVE.L 20(A6),−(A7)
                                            PEA 20 (A6)
                                            MOVE.W #$1010,−(A7)
                                            JSR SANE(PC)

    {make local copy of valExt}             MOVE.L 16(A6),A0
                                            LEA −10(A6),A1
                                            TST.B (A0)
                                            MOVE.L (A0) + ,(A1) +
                                            MOVE.L (A0)+,(A1)+
                                            MOVE.W (A0),(A1)

    {make local copy of valString}          MOVE.L 8(A6),A0
                                            LEA −266(A6),A1
                                            TST.B (A0)
                                            MOVEQ #64,D0
                                            MOVE.L (A0)+,(A1)+
                                            SUBQ.W #1,D0
                                            BGT.S *−4
end;
    {standard epilog}                       UNLK A6
                                            MOVE.L (A7)+,A0
                                            ADDA.W #22,A7
                                            JMP (A0)
```

Wow! All that code for a procedure that does nothing! What's all this stuff for? Well, first, you may recall that a procedure has to make local copies of any value parameters that are more than four bytes long. This is so the procedure can change the parameter without affecting the global variable that was passed in. In this case, the parameters are all constants that can't be changed anyway, but the procedure still has to create the local copies so that the procedure can assign new values to them locally. Figure 6-2 shows the stack frame for this procedure, and you can use it to follow what's going on here.

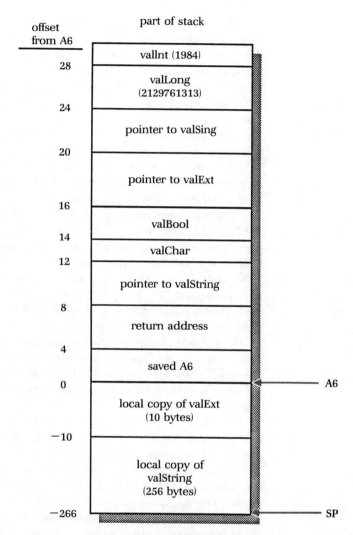

Figure 6-2 Stack frame of ShowVal1

The first thing that happens, as always, is the LINK instruction. For this procedure, there are 266 bytes allocated on the stack even though there are no local variables. This stack space is needed for local copies of parameters. So the operand in the LINK instruction is actually more than just the number of bytes needed for the local variables; it's actually the sum of the local variables plus the local copies of parameters. Close enough.

Next the procedure code starts playing around with our single parameter. First, it pushes the address of the parameter (the address of Cst0003) onto the stack; then it pushes the address of the *pointer* to the parameter at 20(A6); finally, it pushes the number $1010 on the stack and then calls SANE. What's going on here?

You may have suspected that this little song and dance is related to the fact that SANE does all its internal calculations with extended-precision numbers, no matter whether the numbers are declared as single, double or extended. This means that whenever you use a constant for a SANE variable, an extended constant is embedded in the procedure and then converted to the appropriate type whenever it's put into a variable (including a parameter). If you recall, SANE call $1010 is used to convert from extended to single, which is what we want here.

The intent of the next two operations is more obvious. In these, the procedure simply has to copy bytes from the constants to the space reserved in the stack frame for the local copies. To do this, the compiler uses the two variants of byte-moving code that we discussed earlier in assignment statements.

The first copy is an extended variable, so it's just 10 bytes. This is easily accomplished with two MOVE.Ls and a MOVE.W. In the second case, the procedure must copy a full 256 bytes, so we get a loop instead of straight-line code. The code moves 64 long words, or 256 bytes, from the address pointed to by 8(A6) to −266(A6), the space reserved in the stack frame for the local copy of Cst0001.

Since you're probably pretty observant, you probably noticed that these byte-move sequences have a little extra something that the assignment statements didn't have. After the source and destination registers are loaded up, and before any bytes are copied, there's a TST.B (A0) instruction. Then the copy proceeds.

What's the TST.B for? Well, it sets the 68000's condition codes according to the value of the first byte in the source range, which is pointed to by A0. For the extended constant, this really doesn't accomplish anything. For the string, this instruction can be used to determine whether the length of the string is zero; if so, the byte-moving operation could be skipped. This could be accomplished by putting a BEQ (branch if equal to zero) instruction right after the TST.B. Only one problem—nothing's being done in response to the test. This seems to be a half-implemented feature.

After the local copies of the long value parameters are made, the procedure would begin executing its code. In our example, the body of the procedure is empty (just a begin and an end, remember), so all that's left is for the procedure to clean up the stack and exit.

The stack-cleaning and exiting is done in the conventional way. First, the UNLK A6 destroys the stack frame and restores the previous, saved value of A6; the return address to the caller is saved in A0; the stack pointer is incremented by 22, since this procedure has 22 bytes of parameters (you can add them up if you want to double-check the compiler); and the procedure finishes up by jumping back to the caller, whose address was just saved in A0.

This example call to showVal1 used constants for all the parameters. What if we used variables instead of constants? How would things be different? Let's take a look.

```
showVal1 (int1, long1, sing1, ext1, bool1, char1, string1);

        {push int1}              MOVE.W −8(A5),−(A7)
        {push long1}             MOVE.L −16(A5),−(A7)

{do song-and-dance to push sing1}    PEA −24(A5)
                                 PEA −634(A5)
                                 MOVE.W #$100E,−(A7)
                                 JSR SANE
                                 PEA −634(A5)

        {push ext1}              PEA −44(A5)
        {push bool1}             MOVE.B −46(A5),−(A7)
        {push char1}             MOVE.W −50(A5),−(A7)

{do song-and-dance to push string1}  LEA −562(A5),A0
                                 MOVE.B (A0),−(A7)
                                 MOVE.W #255,−(A7)
                                 JSR %_SRCHK
                                 MOVE.L A0,−(A7)

        {call procedure}         JSR SHOWVAL1
```

Once again, there's more code here than we expected (isn't there always?). In the previous example, in which we used constants for all the parameters, the calling sequence was absolute simplicity. Not so this time, as you can see. Although some of the parameters are passed with a single instruction, there is some extra stuff here. What are the complications that have been introduced by using variables instead of parameters?

Some of the parameters are passed in an "obvious" way. The first two parameters, int1 and long1, are passed with simple MOVE instructions from their storage locations to the stack. The next parameter is a single, and now we're in trouble, because it has to be converted to an extended before it can be passed. So we go through the usual technique to convert it: push its address on the stack (PEA −24(A5)), followed by an address to put the converted result (PEA −634(A5)), followed by the appropriate SANE secret code, which means "convert from single to extended" (MOVE.W #$100E,−(A7)), and JSR to the SANE dispatching routine.

When the SANE routine returns, the converted number will be at −634(A5), so we can do a PEA −634(A5) to pass its address to the procedure. But what's this −634(A5) location? We said that addresses of the form −X(A5) are global variables; but if you look back in the preceding chapter at Figure 5-11, which lists all our global variables and their locations, you'll see that the last one allocated is at −624(A5). So what's going on at −634(A5)?

The answer is this: since the compiler must convert nonextended SANE types to extended before passing them to procedures, it needs some space in memory to put the converted value. Where can it find this space? In the case of a global variable, the most convenient place is the global stack, just below the application's global variables. So the compiler reserves space for an extended copy of nonextended parameters on the global stack.

The next three parameters are easy to push—they're pushovers (sorry). Passing the extended parameter requires that a pointer to it be pushed on the stack, and this is accomplished with a PEA instruction. No conversion is required, since it's already an extended. The next two, the boolean and the char, are put on the stack with MOVE instructions.

Next we have to push the string parameter, and here we get to learn a whole new game. Before we can pass the string to the procedure, we have to perform a range check on it; that is, we have to ensure that it's length hasn't exceeded the length specified for this parameter.

This check is accomplished with a little routine called %_SRCHK. No, that's not a typo. The routine's name is really percent sign–underscore–SRCHK. This is not a routine that you write; it's linked to your program automatically when you run the linker. Routines that start with this odd prefix are Pascal **run-time library** routines. They come from the file called paslib.

As we said, the range-checking routine checks the length of the string against the parameter's declared maximum. The calling sequence here first puts the address of the string into A0 and then pushes the string's length byte, the first byte in the string, onto the stack, followed by the constant 255. The 255 comes from the fact that this parameter was declared as type string[255]. After these pushes, the procedure calls %_SRCHK.

From this calling sequence, we can infer that %_SRCHK expects two values on the stack and performs a range check (CHK instruction, remember?) to ensure that the first parameter is less than or equal to the second one; in this case, that means checking to see that the length byte of the string does not exceed 255.

The showVal1 procedure will be expecting a pointer to the string on the stack, since strings are always passed by pointer. After the range check subroutine returns, presumably having removed its two parameters from the stack but not having modified any registers, the calling code pushes A0 on the stack. Since A0 still contains a pointer to the string, this will serve to pass the string parameter.

You might also have realized that there really doesn't have to be a check here. Since the string can be 255 bytes long, and the maximum value that you can put in a byte anyway is 255, there's no way the CHK could fail. Apparently, this is a compiler optimization that could be added.

No Branch after the Range Check

You might be surprised at first to see that the range-check subroutine apparently doesn't return a result indicating whether the check succeeded or failed, since there's no BNE or something to an error-handling routine. Well, remember that the range check is performed with a CHK X,Y instruction. If the CHK instruction results in a value out of range (if the second operand is larger than the first), the 68000 generates an exception, which becomes a system error on the Macintosh. You can trap such errors with the System Error Handler's resume procedure, which you can read about in **Inside Macintosh**, or by directly stealing the CHK interrupt vector at location $18, which you can read about in the Motorola 68000 manual.

Now that all the SANE-converting and range checking are done, we can call the procedure with a JSR SHOWVAL1. You can clearly see how using parameters that are variables compares with using constant parameters. For some parameters, there's virtually no difference: just a single MOVE instruction in either case. However, when the parameter is a string or a SANE type other than extended, there's code necessary to do some extra work.

Once again, it's important to remember that the compiler generates all this unexpected special code for you automatically. We're studying it here not to learn how to write a compiler, but to understand what we're looking at when debugging programs. Don't worry if you don't remember every nuance and rule of parameter passing—that's the compiler's job. Your job is to able to look at the code put out by the compiler and say, "Oh yeah, I see what's going on here."

Debugging Compilers

I almost hate to point this out, but compilers are big, complex programs, and they can have bugs, too. I'm not talking about the compiler generating two instructions where one would do. I mean real-live, rip-roaring, break-my-program bugs. Bugs like this tend to be rare, especially in mature products like the Workshop Pascal compiler, which has been around for many years, but they do happen.

As you get better and better at this, you may come to a point where you're absolutely sure that you're doing everything right and that you've found a place where the compiler goofed and generated bad code. If this happens, you should contact the software manufacturer, who should be able to tell you if you've got a real bug or to tell you why you're wrong. Finding a real bug in a compiler is always a thrill (unless you've been going nuts for a week trying to find it).

Now that we've learned all there is to know about passing simple variable-type parameters, let's expand our knowledge and look at structured variables. We'll declare a new procedure:

```
procedure showVal2 (valRec: myRecType; valArray: myArrayType; valPtr: ptr);
```

This procedure takes three parameters. Two of these are structures, a record of type myRecType and an array of type myArrayType, and the third is a pointer of type ptr. Since the record and the array are more than four bytes long, pointers to these structures will be passed to the procedure, and the procedure will make local copies of the structures.

Let's now look at the calling sequence created by a call to this procedure.

```
showVal2 (rec1, array1, ptr1);
        {push pointer to rec1}        PEA −576(A5)
        {push pointer to array1}      PEA −616(A5)
        {push ptr1}                   MOVE.L −624(A5),−(A7)
        {call the procedure}          JSR SHOWVAL2
```

There's nothing unexpected or surprising here. First, pointers to the record and the array are pushed onto the stack with PEA instructions. Then the value of ptr1 is pushed in from its location at −624(A5). A JSR instruction completes the calling sequence.

Now let's look at the code of the procedure itself. You'll find that the procedure is our usual do-nothing, empty procedure.

```
begin
        {make stack frame}           LINK A6,#−52
        {make local copy of rec1}    MOVE.L 16(A6),A0
                                     LEA −12(A6),A1
                                     TST.B (A0)
                                     MOVE.L (A0)+,(A1)+
                                     MOVE.L (A0)+,(A1)+
                                     MOVE.L (A0)+,(A1)+

        {make local copy of array1}  MOVE.L 12(A6),A0
                                     LEA −52(A6),A1
                                     TST.B (A0)
                                     MOVEQ #10,D0
                                     MOVE.L (A0)+,(A1)+
                                     SUBQ.W #1,D0
                                     BGT.S *−4
end;
        {tear down stack frame}      UNLK A6
        {save return address}        MOVE.L (A7)+,A0
        {pop off 12 bytes of params}  ADDA.W #12,A7
        {go back to caller}          JMP (A0)
```

Once again, there's nothing going on here that we haven't talked about already. First, the stack frame is created with the LINK instruction. Next, the local copy of rec1 is made in the usual way. You may remember that way back toward the beginning of Chapter 5 we figured out that type myRecType took up 12 bytes. So the procedure here copies 12 bytes into the local stack frame with three MOVE.L instructions.

Next, the procedure has to make a local copy of array1. Since this array is 40 bytes long, the local copy is made by looping 10 times, copying four bytes each time.

If the procedure had any statements in its body, they would be executed at this point, but it ain't got no body, so the next thing that happens is the procedure's epilog. This code, which by now should be very familiar to you, unbuilds the stack frame, saves the return address, increments the stack pointer past the 12 bytes of parameters, and jumps through register A0 back to the caller.

For this procedure, we don't have to examine what happens when constants are passed instead of variables, because Pascal doesn't support constants of structured types like records and arrays.

Congratulate Yourself

We've now covered so much information that we were able to step through that last procedure call without having to learn a single new fact. If you've been keeping up, you should feel a great sense of accomplishment now. Please go reward yourself with a new compact disc, something to eat, or some other treat of your choice.

We've saved the best for last. So far all the parameters we've looked at have been value parameters. None of the parameters to either of the procedures we've studied so far have been variable (VAR) parameters. Earlier in this chapter we said that VAR parameters are always passed by pointer. Let's declare a procedure with VAR parameters and examine it.

```
procedure showVar1 (VAR varInt: integer; VAR varLong:
longint; VAR varSing: SINGLE; VAR varExt : EXTENDED; VAR varBool:
BOOLEAN; VAR varChar: char; VAR varString: str255);
```

It may look complicated, but we'll dissect it completely in a few minutes. This procedure's declaration is basically the same as showVal1 that we played with earlier, except that all the parameters here are VAR instead of value. Now let's look at a sample call to the procedure.

```
showVar1 (int1, long1, sing1, ext1, bool1, char1, string1);
    {push pointer to int1}                     PEA −8(A5)
    {push pointer to long1}           PEA −16(A5)
    {push pointer to sing1}           PEA −24(A5)
    {push pointer to ext1}                     PEA −44(A5)
    {push pointer to bool1 (yawn)}    PEA −46(A5)
    {push pointer to char1}           PEA −50(A5)
    {push pointer to string1}         PEA −562(A5)
    {call procedure}                           JSR SHOWVAR1
```

Didn't I say that I saved the best for last? See how easy this stuff is? Since all the parameters are VAR, the procedure wants a pointer to each one to be pushed. This is easy. In turn, a pointer to each parameter is pushed with a PEA instruction, and the procedure is called with a JSR, as usual.

No Constants

Of course, the caller can't use a constant where a VAR parameter is required; it must be a real live variable.

Here's the code of the procedure showVar1:

```
begin
    {create stack frame}      LINK A6,#0
    {nothing else to do!}
end;
    {destroy stack frame}         UNLK A6
    {save return address}         MOVE.L (A7)+,A0
    {pop off parameters}      ADDA.W #28,A7
    {jump back to caller}         JMP (A0)
```

Nothing there! Our procedure with no source has finally produced no object code! Since all the parameters are VAR, that means that the procedure has been given direct access to the global variables, and there's no need to make local copies of anything. So the procedure simply creates the stack frame, does its thing (which, in this example, is nothing), and then goes through the standard epilog.

Next let's look at a procedure with VAR structured variables as parameters.

```
procedure showVar2 (VAR varRec: myRecType; VAR varArray:
myArrayType; VAR varPtr: ptr);
```

This procedure is the same as showVal2 except that all the parameters here are VAR parameters. Here's a call to this procedure:

```
showVar2 (rec1, array1, ptr1);
     {push pointer to rec1}        PEA −576(A5)
     {push pointer to array1}  PEA −616(A5)
     {push pointer to ptr1}        PEA −624(A5)
     {call procedure}             JSR SHOWVAR2
```

Again, everything here follows the rules we've already learned. And now, here's the code of the procedure itself:

```
begin
     {create stack frame}         LINK A6,#0
     {nothing else to do!}
end;
     {destroy stack frame}        UNLK A6
     {save return address}        MOVE.L (A7)+,A0
     {pop off parameters}         ADDA.W #12,A7
     {jump back to caller}        JMP (A0)
```

Just as in the previous example, the procedure doesn't have to do any setup at all except for the LINK instruction. There are no local copies to be made.

These examples raise several questions. Using VAR parameters for types longer than four bytes is obviously far more efficient than using value parameters. What are the advantages and disadvantages of each method? A VAR parameter of more than four bytes will require less stack space than a value parameter, since no local copy will be made. Also, the procedure will execute more quickly if it doesn't have to make local copies of parameters. Plus, there's less obscure code to dig through when you're debugging.

The obvious disadvantage of VAR parameters is the chance of side effects; that is, a global variable may get changed when you didn't want it to. In fact, this is one of the reasons for the invention of value parameters in the first place. So if you start using lots of VAR parameters to speed things up and to save stack space, that's fine, but be careful of accidentally blowing up the value of one of your globals. You decide.

Conditional Statements

Now that we know what procedure calls look like, let's take a guided tour of some standard statements used in languages like Pascal and C. We'll see how each of these statements shows up in object code.

The first set of statements we'll look at are the conditional statements. These include if . . . then . . . else and case . . . otherwise.

Let's start with some if statements. Here's the source and object code for one example:

```
if intResult <> 17
        {compare intResult to 17}      CMPI.W #17,−4(A5)
        {branch ahead to "else" if equal} BEQ.S L0003
    then int2 := 3
        {not equal to 17, assign int2}  MOVE.W #3,−6(A5)
        {branch around "else" clause}   BRA.S L0004
    else int2 := 294;
L0003   {assign 294 to int2}            MOVE.W #294,−6(A5)
L0004   {next statement in program}     . . .
```

This if statement compares the global variable intResult to 17. If it is not equal to 17, int2 is assigned the value 3; otherwise, int2 gets 294. The assembly language strategy used by the compiler is very straightforward.

First, there's a CMPI.W instruction that compares 17 to intResult's value and sets the 68000's condition codes register (CCR) accordingly. In particular, the Z (zero) flag of the CCR is set if this comparison is true (in other words, if intResult equals 17) and cleared if the comparison fails. After this comparison, there's a BEQ (branch if equal) instruction. Whether this branch is taken depends on the state of the Z flag. If it's set, the branch will be taken; otherwise, it will not be taken. The destination of the branch, L0003, is simply a label that the compiler has put on the code of the else clause so that it knows where to branch.

If the CMPI.W finds that intResult is equal to 17, the Z flag will be set and the BEQ will be taken, skipping to the else clause, just like we wanted. See how that works? The compiler's general technique on if statements is this:

1. Do the comparison, usually with a CMP instruction, to set the condition codes.

2. Use a Bcc (branch on condition code) instruction to branch to the "else" part of the statement (or to the next statement, if there's no else) if the values compared don't have the desired relationship.

3. Fall through into the "then" part if the branch is not taken. If there's an else part, branch around it to the next statement.

The mnemonic Bcc is a shorthand for any one of several different branch instructions. These include BEQ for "branch if equal," BNE for "branch if not equal," and a whole bunch more. There's a complete listing of the most common conditional branches in Figure 6-3.

Figure 6-3 Conditional branches and
high-level operators

Branch instruction	High-level binary operator
BNE	=
BEQ	<>
BLE	>
BGE	<
BGT	<=
BLT	>=

Big Science

Note that in this scheme the branch is taken if the comparison *fails*; that is, the branch skips around the "then" part of the statement. This means that the branch instruction that tests the condition codes must actually test the *inverse* of the desired condition. For example, in the case we looked at, the test we were performing was inequality (intResult <> 17), but the branch was taken if it found equality (BEQ). You'll see this in our next example and in your own code. Figure 6-4 gives an example of how this principle works.

Figure 6-4 "If" statement logic

Source code	Object code
if IntResult <> 17	Compare intResult to 17.
	Are they equal?
	Yes, jump to "else" part
	No, fall into "then" part
then int2 := 3	"then" part:Assign 3 to int2; jump past "else"
else int2 := 294;	"else" part: Assign 294 to int2

Here's another if statement.

```
if intResult = 8
            {compare intResult to 8)}      CMPI.W #8,−4(A5)
            {if not equal, branch ahead}   BNE.S L0004
            {otherwise, fall into "then" code}
then begin
      int2 := sizeOf (rec1);
            {assign value to int2}         MOVE.W #12,−6(A5)
      int1 := int2;
            {assign value to int1}         MOVE.W −6(A5),−8(A5)
      end {if};
L0004          {next statement in program}    ...
```

This statement is similar to the first one, except that the comparison is for equality instead of inequality, and the body of the "then" part of the statement is a compound statement; that is, it has a begin and an end. This really doesn't make any difference to the form of the if statement; it just makes sure that the "then" part gets executed if the conditions are right. Also, note that this statement has no else; if the if is false, there's a branch to the next statement.

For this if statement, the first step is comparing the value of intResult to the constant value 8. This sets the condition codes according to the comparison. Then the BNE instruction skips to the next statement if the value of intResult was not equal to 8. If intResult was 8, the compound statement that comprises the "then" part is executed; that is, the two assignments are performed.

Next let's look at a fancier kind of conditional statement: the case statement.

```
            case int1 of
                {get value of int1 in D0}          MOVE.W −8(A5),D0
                {is it a 1?}                       SUBQ.W #1,D0
                {yes, branch to case 1}            BEQ.S L0005
                {not 1, subtract 1 more}           SUBQ.W #1,D0
                {if zero, branch to case 2}        BEQ.S L0006
                {subtract 1 again}                 SUBQ.W #1,D0
                {if zero, it's case 3}             BEQ.S L0007
                {subtract yet again}               SUBQ.W #1,D0
                {and branch to case 4 if zero}     BEQ.S L0008
                {one last subtraction}             SUBQ.W #1,D0
                {branch if zero to case 5}         BEQ.S L0009
                {not 1-5, branch to next statement} BRA.S L0010
            1 : int2 := 5;
  L0005         {put 5 in int2}                    MOVE.W #5,−6(A5)
                {jump to next statement}           BRA.S L0010
            2 : int1 := 906;
  L0006         {put 906 in int1}                  MOVE.W #906,−6(A5)
                {jump to next statement}           BRA.S L0010
            3 : bool1 := NOT bool1;
  L0007         {put bool1 in D0}                  MOVE.B −46(A5),D0
                {flip bit 1 of D0, negating it}    EORI.B #1,D0
                {put NOT bool1 in bool1}           MOVE.B D0,−46(A5)
                {jump ahead}                       BRA.S L0010
            4 : sub1 := 99;
  L0008         {put 99 in sub1}                   MOVE.B #99,−564(A5)
                {it's a constant, so no range check is needed}
                {jump away}                        BRA.S L0010
            5 : rec1.fint := 3 * (5 + int2);
  L0009         {put int2 in D0}                   MOVE.W −6(A5),D0
                {add 5 to D0}                      ADDQ.W #5,D0
                {multiply the whole schmeer by 3}  MULS #3,D0
                {put the result into rec1.fint}    MOVE.W D0,−576(A5)
            end
  L0010       {next statement}                     ...
```

This statement branches to one of several different locations (called **case labels**) depending on the value of int1, which is called the **case selector**. The strategy used is this:

1. Begin by putting the value of the case selector into a register.

2. Subtract from this the value of the first case label. In other words, if the first case label used is 1, subtract 1. If the result is zero, we know that the case selector was a one, so branch to the first case label.

3. If the result was not zero, subtract again. The amount to subtract is the difference between the first and second case labels. If the result of the subtraction is zero, branch to the second case label.

4. Keep subtracting and checking for zero, branching if zero is obtained, until the maximum possible case label value has been tested. In other words, if the highest case label used is 16, keep subtracting until you've subtracted a total of 16 from the original case selector.

5. Following the last subtraction and BEQ, insert a BRA (branch always) to the next statement, or, if the case statement has an otherwise clause, branch to it. This takes care of case selectors that don't match any case label.

Alternate Form of Case Statement

If there are a lot of case labels, the compiler will produce a different-looking case statement. Instead of straight-line subtraction from the case selector and branches, the alternate form builds a table of dispatch addresses to the various case labels. It takes the case selector and uses it to select the appropriate address from the table, then jumps to that address. This is similar in principle to the technique used in copying bytes for local parameter copies: the compiler is smart about choosing the more efficient method depending on the situation.

Improving on the Compiler

By now you've probably noticed that there are places where the compiler appears to be doing some silly, inefficient things in its code generation. We discussed earlier how compilers aren't always able to see the same optimizations as humans, even if they're pretty obvious. In the preceding case statement, you may have noticed that case 3, which assigns NOT bool1 to bool1, uses three instructions where a single instruction would suffice (EORI.B #1,−46(A5)). By using the option in the Workshop compiler that generates assembly language source, you can actually hand-optimize your programs to make them smaller and faster. You can do this by taking the assembly language source that the compiler generates and assembling it with the assembler. Beating the compiler at its own game is a lot of fun and is a character-building experience.

Repetitive Statements

Another important group of high-level language statements are the repetitive statements, also known as looping statements. In C and Pascal, the looping statements are while and for; Pascal also uses repeat. We'll look at Pascal examples of each of these.

First, let's look at a sample repeat statement.

```
      repeat
         int2 := int2 * 5;
L0010       {put 5 in D0}                         MOVEQ #5,D0
            {multiply the 5 in D0 by int2}        MULS −6(A5),D0
            {put the product back in int2}        MOVE.W D0,−6(A5)
      until int2 >= 2000;
            {check int2 against 2000}             CMPI.W #2000,−6(A5)
            {branch if less than back into loop}  BLT.S L0010
```

When you use repeat, the statements in the loop are always executed once before any test to end the loop. As you see here, the statement in the loop multiplies int2 by 5. Then the until part, which is the test to end the loop, checks to see if int2 is greater than or equal to 2000. If not, the loop is executed again (the BLT.S L0010 is not some kind of sandwich, but a "branch if less than" to label L0010, which is the body of the loop). If the comparison finds that int2 has exceeded 2000, the program will fall through the loop into the next statement.

Once again, just like in the if statement, the strategy is to branch if the test fails. So the Pascal test ">=" (greater than or equal to) is implemented in assembly language with a BLT (less than), the inverse.

Let's examine the second kind of looping statement.

```
      while int2 < 2000
L0013       {compare int2 to 2000}               CMPI.W #2000,−6(A5)
            {branch out if > or =}               BGE.S L0011
         do int2 :=int2 * 5;
            {put multiplier in D0}               MOVEQ #5,D0
            {Sweden is lovely this time of year} MULS −6(A5),D0
            {put result where it belongs}        MOVE.W D0,−6(A5)
            {branch always to start of loop}     BRA.S  L0013
L0011       {next statement}                       . . .
```

What's different about this loop? Mainly one thing: the test to exit the loop, the comparison of int2 to 2000, occurs before the body of the loop has been executed. It's possible that the body of the loop will not be executed at all. If you use a repeat statement, the body will be executed once before the loop boundary test is performed.

Again, you see that the branch that's produced is the inverse of the condition specified in the source. The source uses a "less than" comparison to determine if the statement in the loop should be executed; the object code uses a "greater than or equal to" comparison to determine if the loop should be exited.

Now let's look at the last kind of loop, the for statement.

```
for counter := 2 to 20 do
                {put 2 in the control variable}         MOVE.W #2,−2(A5)
                {jump to loop test}                     BRA.S L0001
        array1 [int1] := int1 + 6;
L0002           {put int1 in D0}                        MOVE.W −8(A5),D0
                {also put it in D1 (smart!)}            MOVE.W D0,D1
                {adjust zero-based to one-based}        SUBQ.W #1,D1
                {range check on array subscript}        CHK #19,D1
                {turn index into array offset in D0}    ASL.W #1,D0
                {put int1 back in D1}                   MOVE.W −8(A5),D1
                {add 6 to int1}                         ADDQ.W #6,D1
                {put start of array into A0}            LEA −618(A5),A0
                {store at start (A0) + offset (D0)}     MOVE.W D1,0(A0,D0.W)
                {increment loop control variable}       ADDQ.W #1,−2(A5)
L0001           {compare loop variable to 20}           CMPI.W #20,−2(A5)
                {if < or =, re-loop at L0002}           BLE.S L0002
```

The for statement starts out a little strangely. It begins by initializing the loop variable to 2. Then it immediately jumps to the end of the loop where the test for the loop boundary takes place. Why do this? It's done to ensure that the initial value specified for the loop variable isn't greater than the boundary value, for example, if you said for feyd := paul to 100 do {something}, and the value of paul is 110. The loop will not be executed at all, since the initial test of the boundary condition will fail.

More Compiler Stuff

You might also be interested in looking at the code that the compiler uses to compute the address of array1[int1]. The basic technique is to put the address of the beginning of the array into an address register and the offset into the array to the element we want in a data register. The compiler can then use one of the 68000's more esoteric addressing modes, which adds the contents of an address register, the contents of a data register, and an immediate value (zero in the preceding example). For the 68000 trivia fans among you, this addressing mode is called "address register indirect with index." Remember that, because there will be a quiz later.

With **Statements**

The next kind of statement that we'll look at is the with statement. Here's one now, by golly.

```
with rec1 do
  begin
    fint := fint div 6;
        {put rec1.fint into D0}        MOVE.W −576(A5),D0
        {prepare D0 for division}      EXT.L D0
        {divide D0 by 6}               DIVS #6,D0
        {put result back into fint}    MOVE.W D0,−576(A5)
    bool1 := fbool OR bool2;
        {put bool2 into D0}            MOVE.B −45(A5),D0
        {OR rec1.fbool with D0}        OR.B −574(A5),D0
        {put ORed value in bool1}      MOVE.B D0,−46(A5)
    fpoint.v := 37;
        {oh c'mon—this one's easy!}    MOVE.W #37,−568(A5)
  end;
```

That covers most of the common statement types. Remember that this information is just a guideline to understanding compilers' output. You'll certainly find variations on the behavior we've discussed in this chapter. But once again, you can use the information that we've discussed here as a clue to figuring out just what the heck your compiled code means.

Linked Routines

Every time you compile a program that runs on the Macintosh, you have to specify a uses or include statement that tells which of the Macintosh **libraries** you're going to be using; for example, Workshop Pascal programmers type something like this:

```
uses {$U Interfaces.p:MemTypes.p} MemTypes,
     {$U Interfaces.p:QuickDraw.p} QuickDraw,
     {$U Interfaces.p:OSIntf.p    } OSIntf,
     {$U Interfaces.p:ToolIntf.p  } ToolIntf;
```

What does this do, exactly? Well, we know that it reads in the contents of each of these files and declares them as if they were declared by our program. But what's really happening? In particular, how does the program call procedures and functions within these libraries? What do these calls look like in object code? To be smart debugging folks, we need to know the answer to these and other questions.

Shortcut

In Macintosh Programmer's Workshop Pascal, you can simply use the $U+ command to read in all the standard Macintosh libraries.

The process of figuring out how to call routines in the library files involves cooperation between the compiler and the linker. At compile time, when the compiler encounters a call to a library procedure, the compiler first checks to make sure that the procedure was in fact declared in one of the libraries that appeared in the uses statement; if so, it simply generates a JSR in the object code to the procedure.

There is a catch, though. At the time it compiles, the compiler knows some things about the library procedures: it knows their names and their parameters. It does not, however, know where in memory the procedures will reside. So how is it able to generate a JSR if it doesn't even know where the procedure will be?

Here's where the compiler–linker cooperation takes place. The compiler generates a dummy JSR, reserving space for a real one, and sets a flag telling the linker that it needs help. Then, when you run the linker after compiling, you again specify the names of the library files. One of the linker's jobs is to attach library routines to the code file; therefore, it knows where the library routines are located in the code segment. The linker looks for the compiler's dummy JSR's to library routines and fills them in with the proper references. Figure 6-5 symbolically illustrates this process, from compiler to linker.

The flag that the compiler sets to tell the linker that it needs an outside routine's address filled in is called an **external reference**. It simply means that the compiler is assuming that a procedure or function will be linked in later, and that the linker will fill in its address at that time. If the linker can't find an externally referenced routine at link time, it generates an error message, which you've probably seen more than once. If this happens, the linker gives up and refuses to generate a CODE resource.

We said that the library routines get attached to the code and become part of the CODE resources that are created. Specifically, where do they get linked? What CODE resource do the library routines get attached to and how are they referenced when they're called?

Figure 6-5 External references

Source code	Object code
Program example;	
Procedure A;	;Procedure A
begin	
(code)	;(code)
end;	;end
Procedure B;	
external;	
Procedure C;	;Procedure C
begin	
A;	JSR A(PC) ;call A (PC-relative)
B;	JSR 0(PC) ;reserve space for call to B
	; (when we find out where it is)
end;	;end
begin {main program}	;main
A;	JSR A(PC)
B;	JSR 0(PC) ;external reference, to be
	;fixed by the Linker
C;	JSR C(PC)
end.	;end

After compiling

```
                    ;Procedure A
                    ;(code)
                    ;end
                    ;Procedure C
                    JSR A(PC) ;call A (PC-relative)
                    JSR B(PC) ;fill in address of B (in same segment)
                    ;end
                    ;main
                    JSR A(PC)
                    JSR B(PC) ;fill in the address here, too
                    JSR C(PC)
                    ;end
```

After linking

Which CODE resource they get attached to depends on the development system you're using, but usually library routines get stuck in with CODE 1, the main segment. On some systems, you can specify which CODE resource gets the library routines; sometimes you only get to do this for library routines you write yourself, not those that are provided for you, like the Macintosh interface libraries.

After you run the linker, the library routines are just like any other procedure or function calls. If one of them is called from the same segment as the caller, the call will appear as a PC-relative JSR; that is, it will be in the form JSR routine(PC). If the call is in a different segment from the library routine, the call will look like any intersegment call; that is it will jump to an address in the jump table.

If you're paying close attention, you may recall that we very briefly discussed the jump table earlier in this chapter. We said that when the program had to call routines in another segment it did so through a structure called the jump table, which is at a fixed, well-known memory location. Where is the jump table, and what do these cross-segment calls look like?

The jump table is allocated in high memory, above the stack. The official way to find the start of the jump table is to add the value of the global variable called CurJTOffset (stored at $934) to the contents of register A5. In practice, CurJTOffset is always equal to $20, so the jump table begins at $20 bytes above the address that A5 points to; in 68000-ese, this is 20(A5).

Since the jump table is located at an A5-relative address, references to things in the jump table are also A5-relative expressions. So jumps to routines in other segments look like this: JSR routine(A5). In this case, routine is the offset from A5 to the appropriate jump table entry for that routine. There's one jump table entry for every routine that's called by another segment. Later in this chapter we'll discuss jump tables in greater detail so that you can learn everything there is to know about them.

Now we'll compare two different kinds of linked routines: "standard" library routines and Macintosh ROM interface routines.

Standard Library Routines

Standard library routines are functions and procedures that appear to be built into the compiler, but are actually added in at link time. In fact, these routines are sometimes called built-in procedures and functions. Some classic examples of standard routines include the fillChar procedure, which fills an array with values; the length function, which returns the length of a string variable; and the concat function (sometimes named cat), which combines two strings.

When a program uses these or other built-in functions, the compiler treats it as an external reference; that is, it puts in a dummy JSR that it expects the linker to fill in later. The linker finds these standard functions and procedures in one of the libraries that you link with; in Workshop Pascal, the file's called Paslib.

When you run the linker, it resolves references to the built-in routines by pulling them out of the standard library (Paslib) and putting them into your code file. Usually, they're added to the main segment, as we discussed earlier.

Forgetting to Link with the Standard Library

If you've ever forgotten to link a program with the standard library, you probably got an error message telling you that some bizarrely named routine that you never heard of resulted in an unresolved external reference. This is because standard library routines are pretty invisible to the average programmer. How can you tell that length or concat are library functions and not part of the compiler, unless the documentation says so or you look at the object code? There is no way to tell.

In addition, other compiler functions may be implemented in the standard library; for example, range checking on strings, as we saw earlier, is done through a library routine called %_SRCHK. If you tried to link that program and forgot to link with the standard library, the compiler would report that it couldn't find %_SRCHK, which certainly should be a finalist in the Cryptic Error Message of the Year competition.

ROM Interface Routines

Every program that uses the Macintosh ROM routines must have some way of calling those routines. Of course, the routines are always there in ROM, but the high-level language programmer must have a method of communicating parameters to the ROM and actually calling the routines.

Since the ROM routines are set up to act like procedures and functions, it seems like the easiest thing to do would be to convince the compiler that the ROM routines are simply procedures and functions in some other library that we can call. How can we do this?

As you probably know, a call to the Macintosh ROM is made with a single 68000 instruction. Each routine in the ROM is assigned a number, called the **trap word**, and that word is used as the instruction to call the routine. For example, the trap word for CloseDialog is $A982, so an

$A982 in your code is an instruction to call CloseDialog in the ROM. Note that this is not an address to JSR to—it's the actual machine language instruction. For more on exactly how this works, see "How ROM Calls Work" in Chapter 10.

Before the trap is called, we must ensure that its parameters are pushed onto the stack properly. In the case of CloseDialog, there's one parameter to be pushed, a DialogPtr to the dialog to be closed. So, if we were to write the assembly language necessary to make a call to CloseDialog, we could write

```
MOVE.L theDialog,-(A7)      ; push dialog pointer
.WORD $A982                 ; call CloseDialog
```

Can we simulate these instructions from Pascal? If we declared a procedure that took a single parameter of type DialogPtr, that would certainly push the parameter on the stack, but Pascal procedure calls are done with JSR's. How can we get the compiler to embed a trap word in the code instead of doing a JSR?

Since it's such an obvious need, it happens that there's a method to do exactly this in most compilers available for the Macintosh. In Workshop Pascal, there's a special directive called Inline that you can use in procedure and function declarations. This directive tells the compiler that it shouldn't generate a JSR to call this procedure or function, but instead should embed a specified byte or bytes directly in the code.

The format of an Inline directive is this:

Procedure XXXXX (param1: type; {more params}); Inline $YYYY;

When the compiler encounters a call to this procedure, it will push the parameters on the stack. Then, instead of a JSR to somewhere to call the procedure, the compiler will simply place the word specified by $YYYY directly in the code. This means that Macintosh ROM calls that take their parameters from the stack, which includes virtually all of the User Interface Toolbox, can be called in this way.

To continue with our example, we could specify a procedure to call CloseDialog like this:

Procedure CloseDialog (theDialog: DialogPtr); Inline $A982;

What will happen if we call this procedure? First, the parameter we pass will be pushed on the stack; then there should be a $A982 embedded in the code, which will cause a call to CloseDialog in the ROM. Perfect! So perfect, in fact, that this is exactly the way it's done.

Workshop C has a similar facility, with slightly different syntax. In C, instead of Inline, the magic word is extern. If you specify extern followed by a trap word where the body of the function would normally be, you'll accomplish the same result as the Pascal Inline.

Since most programmers want to have access to the Macintosh ROM routines, most development systems come with predefined libraries for the ROM calls. For example, the Workshop comes with a library, ToolIntf, that defines all the User Interface Toolbox calls. If you look at this file, you'll see that after the constant and type declarations it's mostly a long list of procedure and function declarations with Inline numbers.

There's nothing magical about these declarations. If you want, you can even define your own Inline procedures. The syntax allows for any number of words after the Inline; so if you have a handy, very short assembly language routine that you'll be using, you can avoid having to specify it in a separate file that will have to be linked in. Just declare the procedure and specify the object code with an Inline.

This takes care of ROM calls that take their parameters on the stack, which includes most of the Toolbox routines. But what about the Operating System routines, most of which take their parameters in registers, not on the stack? How can a Pascal or C communication to these routines be set up?

Let's take a look at this problem with a sample register-based ROM call. For our example, we'll choose the function GetTrapAddress. This Operating System function is used to find out the address of a Macintosh trap; given a trap word, it returns the address of that trap.

To call GetTrapAddress, you specify the desired trap word in register D0. After calling, the address of that trap will be returned in register A0. We can use the Inline directive to produce the trap word to call GetTrapAddress, but how can we get Pascal to put the parameter into register D0 instead of on the stack? And once the function returns, how can we obtain the result that's in A0?

Most Pascals, including Workshop Pascal, always push their procedure and function parameters on the stack. There's absolutely no way to declare a function that puts parameters into registers instead of on the stack. So one way to call register-based routines would be to first declare a Pascal procedure to push the parameters on the stack, like this:

```
Function GetTrapAddress (trapNum: Integer) : Longint;
```

Then we need a way in the procedure itself to take the trapNum parameter off the stack and put it in register D0 (where the ROM expects it), make the ROM call, then move the result from register A0 (where the ROM puts it) onto the stack for Pascal. To better understand the problem, let's look at the object code that the compiler will generate for a call to this function.

```
CLR.L  −(A7)              ; make space for function result
MOVE.W trapNum,−(A7)      ; push trapNum parameter
JSR GetTrapAddress        ; jump to a routine which will
                          ; resolve stack vs. registers
```

Here we see that the compiler will first reserve four bytes of stack space for the function result, since it's a longint, then will push the one parameter, and then will JSR somewhere to a routine called GetTrapAddress.

Wherever this GetTrapAddress routine is, it must remove the trapNum parameter from the stack and put it in D0, call the ROM, and then move the function result from A0 onto the stack. Let's write an assembly language routine to do just that.

```
GetTrapAddress
     MOVE.L (A7)+,A1  ; save return address to caller
     MOVE.W (A7)+,D0  ; put trapNum in D0 for call
     .WORD $A146      ; this calls GetTrapAddress
     MOVE.L A0,(A7)   ; put call result onto stack
     JMP (A1)         ; return to caller
```

This routine takes care of putting the parameter and the function result in the right places. When this routine gets control, it has been called by the Pascal calling sequence for GetTrapAddress, and the stack looks like Figure 6-6. To get to the parameter, we must start by popping the return address; we stash it in A1 so that we can use it later. Next we move trapNum off the stack and into D0, which is where the ROM call to GetTrapAddress will expect to find it. Next is the word that actually calls GetTrapAddress, $A146.

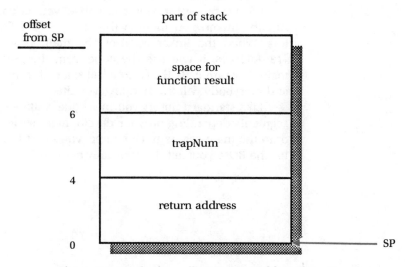

Figure 6-6 Stack after calling GetTrapAddress from Pascal

After we call the ROM, the function result is in A0. We move it onto the stack to the space reserved by Pascal for the function result with a MOVE.L instruction. Finally, we can return to the caller by jumping through the return address saved in A1.

A routine like this, which mediates between a stack-based compiler and a register-based ROM call, is known as a **glue routine**, or simply **glue**. The glue routines allow us to solve this sticky problem.

This seems like a reasonable solution. If we can get the compiler to use this routine when it calls GetTrapAddress, everything will work right. How can we tell the compiler to use this assembly language routine for GetTrapAddress?

Once again, there's a Pascal feature to the rescue. Another Pascal directive, called External, is used to allow assembly language routines to be linked to Pascal programs. Here's how it works: first, you declare the routine, using the word External after the parameter declaration.

Function GetTrapAddress (trapNum: integer): longint; External;

The external directive tells the compiler to generate an external reference for calls to this function. This means that the linker will have to fill in the reference at link time. For this to work, you have to have another code file that defines a procedure called GetTrapAddress. So you would create a file that includes the source to the assembly language glue routine, plus an assembler directive to name the function Get-TrapAddress; in the Workshop Assembler, this would be a statement like Func GetTrapAddress at the beginning of the glue source.

After creating the glue source file, you assemble it. Then, when you run the linker, you include the glue's object file as one of the files to link. When the linker resolves the main program's reference to Get-TrapAddress, it will use the code from the glue routine. So, when the main program calls GetTrapAddress, a call to the glue will be generated, and everybody will live happily ever after.

Like standard library routines, glue routines get linked into different segments depending on your development system. Usually, they're glued onto the main segment. Of course, you don't have to write glue routines for the ROM yourself. They usually come with the development system.

Sniffing Glue

If you're interested in seeing what various glue routines look like, you can use the Workshop's DumpObj program to disassemble routines in the glue files. This can be an interesting and highly educational experience. It can also help you debug when you're not sure what's happening when your program jumps to a ROM call's glue.

Inline Glue

The Pascal Inline feature is normally used to embed a single word, a trap word, into the code. Actually, Inline can be used to emit any number of bytes. So why couldn't we simply write a glue routine to go right in the code, assemble it to learn its machine language equivalent, and then just use an Inline? Let's see ... the glue routine we wrote was designed to be called by a JSR. Let's modify it to be used inline.

```
GetTrapAddress
        MOVE.W (A7)+,D0    ; put trapNum in D0 for call
        .WORD $A146        ; this calls GetTrapAddress
        MOVE.L A0,(A7)     ; put call result onto stack
```

Since the routine is being used inline, there will be no JSR to it, so there's no return address to save and jump through. If we crank this routine through the assembler, we find that the object code looks like this:

```
MOVE.W (A7)+,D0    ; $301F
.WORD $A146        ; $A146 (obviously)
MOVE.L A0,(A7)     ; $2E88
```

So, instead of having glue, we could declare GetTrapAddress like this:

```
Function GetTrapAddress (trapNum: integer): longint;
Inline $301F, $A146, $2E88;
```

This would work just fine. So why aren't all OS calls done this way, instead of with glue? Two main reasons. The first reason is historical. Inline in the Pascal compiler is a relatively recent invention, and the ROM interface libraries were written before the Inline feature existed. The second reason is that most glue routines are more complex than this. For example, all Memory Manager routines report their error code to a global called MemErr, which adds a little code to the glue. When you have glue, the glue code is only linked to the application once, and so it takes up a minimum of space if you call a particular ROM routine many times. When you use Inline, you use space for the stack/register manipulation code every time you call the routine.

So, in the end, most Inline routines will cost more memory than glue if you call the routine more than once. Still, for some routines with simple calling sequences, like GetTrapAddress, an Inline would be more efficient than glue. Also, inlines are easier to debug than glue, since you don't have to jump off to another part of the code when you're tracing. It's possible that in future versions some of the calls in Apple's interface libraries will have been rewritten to use Inline routines instead of glue.

The Jump Table

We've mentioned the jump table a couple of times. Now it's time to reveal all its secrets.

Just to recap for those of you who came in late, the jump table exists so that routines in one segment can call routines in another segment. When routines are in the same segment, the call is done with a PC-relative JSR instruction, since the difference between the current location (the PC) and the routine to be called is always the same. When a routine in one segment calls another segment, however, it can't be sure of the offset between the routines.

To solve this little problem, the system creates a jump table, which is a table of entry points. There's one entry in the jump table for each routine that's referenced by a routine in another segment. Figure 6-7 illustrates the use of the two different methods for same-segment and cross-segment calls.

The jump table always begins at $20 bytes above A5. Cross-segment calls look like this in your program: JSR routine(A5), where routine is the offset from the beginning of the jump table to the desired entry, plus $20.

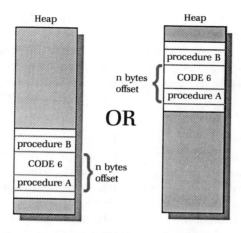

Procedure A calls B: JSR n(PC)

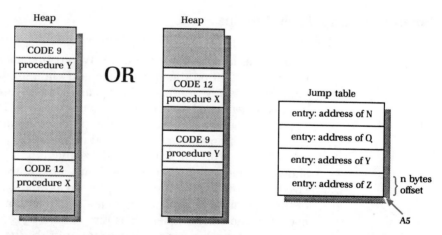

Procedure X calls Y: JSR n(A5)
(when CODE segments move, jump table is updated)

Figure 6-7 Calling procedures and functions

The jump table is created by the linker. As the linker puts the pieces of the program together, it notes each routine that's referenced outside its own segment and starts building the jump table. When it has linked the entire program, it sorts the jump table entries by segment number. The linker spits out the jump table as part of CODE resource 0.

There's another interesting problem that crops up when you're calling routines in a different segment. It's possible that the segment you're calling won't be in memory at the time you make the call, so the system better make sure that the segment is brought in before diving into it. We'll talk about how this happens.

Format of Jump Table Entries

What is the format of a jump table? Would I be able to recognize one if I bumped into it on the street? Each entry in a jump table is eight bytes long. There are two forms of jump table entries: **loaded** and **unloaded**. A loaded segment is currently in memory and is locked. An unloaded segment is purgeable, is unlocked, and may be in memory. We'll discuss shortly how segments get loaded and unloaded.

When a program starts up, all segments are unloaded. Figure 6-8 shows the format of an unloaded jump table entry. The first two bytes give the location of the routine, expressed as an offset from the beginning of the segment. The next six bytes are actual executable code; this is the code that the cross-segment calls jump into.

What does this code do? It simply pushes the segment number of this routine's segment onto the stack and then calls the Operating System routine `LoadSeg`. `LoadSeg` reads in the specified code segment and locks it. It then proceeds to change the jump table entry to the loaded entry format.

Loading the segment, of course, loads all the routines in the segment. Since there's a jump table entry for each routine in a segment that's referenced externally, it's possible that there's more than one entry for a given segment. So `LoadSeg` goes through the jump table and courteously changes all the "unloaded" entries for the segment it just loaded into "loaded" entries. Figure 6-9 illustrates this process.

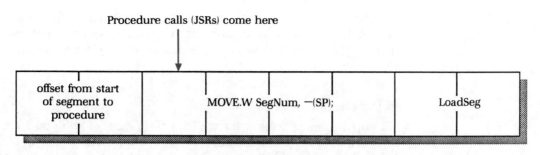

8 bytes

Figure 6-8 Unloaded jump table entry

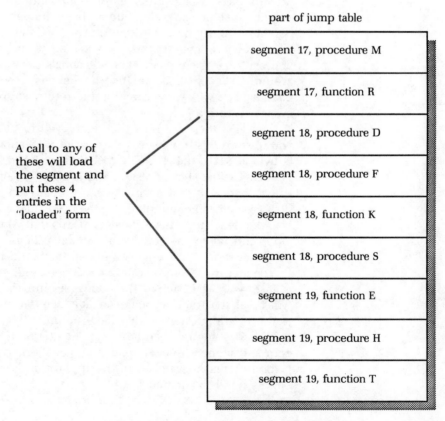

Figure 6-9 LoadSeg fixes jump table entries

Finally, when LoadSeg has finished changing all the jump table entries for this segment, it jumps to the called routine, using the offset that it got from the first word of the unloaded jump table entry.

MacCharlie on the MTA

Suppose you're tracing through your application and you trace a call to another, unloaded segment. As you trace into the jump table, eventually the next instruction will be a LoadSeg call. Usually, when you're debugging and you reach a trap call, you don't want to trace the trap into the ROM—you just want to get past it. So most debuggers have commands that return control after executing the trap; in Macsbug, for example, this command is T (trace).

LoadSeg presents a unique problem, though: it never "returns." Instead of finishing its job by returning to the code that called it, it ends by jumping into the newly loaded segment. This means that you can't use a command like Macsbug's trace command to trace around a LoadSeg. If you try to, the debugger will execute the LoadSeg and will wait forever for it to return, slipping it sandwiches every now and then.

Luckily, there's a neat trick employed in LoadSeg that allows you to solve this problem. There's a global location called LoadTrap (a byte at $12D) that is a flag to LoadSeg. It works like this: when LoadSeg is just about finished and is about to jump to the routine it just loaded, it first checks to see if LoadTrap is nonzero. If it is nonzero, instead of jumping into the newly loaded routine, it breaks into the debugger. This is great! It means that you can trace merrily along and, when you come to a LoadSeg call, just use the debugger to set location $12D to something other than zero. Then, just exit the debugger (G from MacsBug or <command>-E from TMON). In a flash, you'll be back in the debugger, and the program counter will be at the last instruction in LoadSeg. You can then continue to trace right into the newly called routine.

There's another handy use for LoadTrap. If you set it to non-zero and launch a new application, you'll enter the debugger just before the first instruction in the application is executed. This can be very handy sometimes.

Now let's look at the format of a loaded jump table entry and compare it to what we've already learned. Figure 6-10 shows your average loaded jump table entry. The last six bytes of the entry are still executable code, just like before. This time, instead of calling LoadSeg, the code simply does a JMP (jump) to the start of the routine.

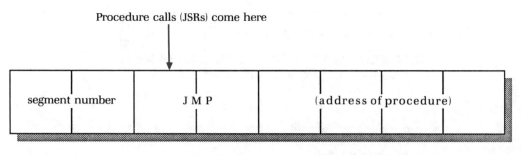

8 bytes

Figure 6-10 Loaded jump table entry

When LoadSeg changed the jump table entries from unloaded style to loaded style, it replaced the LoadSeg instruction in the last six bytes with a direct, absolute address jump to the routine. An absolute jump works, because once the segment is loaded, it's locked. LoadSeg computes this address dynamically at the time it modifies the jump table entry by getting the newly loaded segment's handle, double-dereferencing it, and adding the offset to the desired routine, which it gets from the other 2 bytes in the jump table entry. Figure 6-11 shows how this process works.

Note that when the jump table entry is in the loaded state the first two bytes are used to keep the segment number. This is done so that later, when the segment is unloaded, the entry can be restored to its unloaded state (MOVE.W segnum,−(A7); LoadSeg).

A segment gets unloaded when the application calls UnloadSeg. When you call UnloadSeg, the process of loading the segment is reversed. First, UnloadSeg unlocks the segment. Then it looks through the jump table for all entries for routines in this segment and changes each one to the unloaded state. It does not change the purgeable status of the segment; since most segments are normally marked purgeable when they're created by the development system, unloaded segments may be purged.

The unloaded jump table entry keeps the offset to the routine it represents in the first two bytes of the entry. It stashes this information so that it can be used when LoadSeg is called on the segment.

Also, note that no matter which of the two states a jump table entry is in the application's call looks the same: it's a JSR routine(A5), and the address that's jumped to is the third byte of a jump table entry. If the entry is unloaded, this will cause LoadSeg to be called; if the entry is already loaded, this will simply be a JMP to the desired routine.

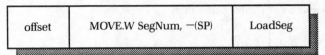

Unloaded jump table entry when LoadSeg is called

- Load Seg gets the segment number off the stack and calls GetResource on it,
- HLocks the segment,
- double-dereferences it,
- adds the offset,
- stores a JMP to that address in the jump table entry's last 6 bytes,
- stores the segment number in the jump table entry's first 2 bytes,
- repeats the last 3 steps for each of this segment's entries,
- then jumps to byte 3 in the jump table entry

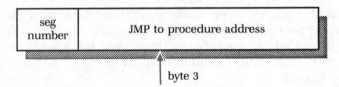

byte 3

Figure 6-11 LoadSeg

LoadSeg **Calls** GetResource

In the incestuous tradition of the ROM, LoadSeg calls GetResource to load in the desired CODE resource. You probably know that GetResource is smart: it first looks to see if the resource is already in memory. If so, it simply returns a handle to it. If not, it loads it from disk and then returns the handle. That means that LoadSeg is a pretty inexpensive call, as is UnloadSeg. In fact, it's not a bad idea to use UnloadSeg to unload all your segments every time through the main event loop. That way they're made purgeable in case memory is needed. They're also unlocked, so they can be relocated if necessary. If their memory space isn't required, they won't be purged, and the next call to one of them won't have to hit the disk to reload it.

Unexpected Things in Your Object Code

As you look through your application's object code, you'll find some things that look completely out of place and off the wall. This is often "behind the scenes" code that the compiler generates to set things up for the application. Usually, this code is there to support the compiler's built-in procedures and functions. For example, if a compiler's built-in library includes text reading and writing (like printf in C and writeln in Pascal), it may generate some code to initialize internal data structures used by these routines.

An application need not do any global setup to execute on a Macintosh. By the time the application executes its first instruction, space for global variables has already been allocated on the stack, so the procedure doesn't have to set up any registers. It can just begin with its own code.

Sometimes your compiled output will have strange things in it for historical reasons. In particular, the Workshop Pascal compiler was originally created to produce code that executed in the Lisa native environment, not Macintosh. Lisa applications had a few different rules. For one thing, Lisa applications were required to create their own global stack frame in A5; in other words, the application did a LINK A5 when it started up. In addition, Lisa programs had to adjust the stack pointer by subtracting from it a system global variable that was located above A5.

When you look at your compiled output, you'll see the vestiges of these requirements. All programs produced by the Lisa Pascal compiler generate this setup code. Since Macintosh programs don't want to start this way, the compiler inserts a call to a special built-in routine to destroy the setup done by this code whenever you use the Macintosh built-in library. So, at the beginning of your Pascal program's main code, you'll find something like the following bizarre sequence of instructions:

```
JSR %_BEGIN          ; Lisa setup routine
LINK A5,#NNNN        ; Lisa global stack frame
SUB.L 10(A5),A7      ; Lisa global setup
JSR %_INIT           ; special Macintosh routine
                     ; which undoes all this stuff!
```

Yes, it's weird, but reality is like that sometimes. The important thing to know is that the net result of all this code is to leave things as they were before it was executed. So this code basically does nothing. You might then wonder why the code is put into your object file. It's probably because the compiler is still capable of generating code to be executed on a Lisa, and this is the easiest way to be compatible with both.

At the end of the program, there's a similar little charade that's done to clean up from the program. Once again, a Macintosh program need not do anything to the registers when it ends. The stack and A5 are automatically fixed by the ROM when it loads the next application. But Lisa applications created a global stack frame, which they had to destroy when the application ended. So the compiler must once again insert a special procedure call to fix things up.

```
JSR %_TERM        ; special Macintosh procedure
                  ; which does a LINK A5...
UNLK A5           ; so that this Lisa code
                  ; can unlink it!
JSR %_END         ; Lisa cleanup procedure
RTS
```

Once again, the net result of this code is nothing. It's presented here so that you'll be familiar with it when you see it at the end of your application.

A somewhat more useful trick that you'll see the compiler using is register optimization. This is where the compiler takes a commonly used variable, such as a loop control variable, and places it in a register for the duration of the loop. This is done because operations like addition and subtraction are faster in the 68000 if they're done on registers.

The compiler ensures that registers D3 through D7 and A2 through A4 are not changed by Pascal routines. This doesn't mean that the routine can't use these registers—it simply means that the compiler will automatically save them on the stack at the beginning of the procedure and restore them at the end if it uses any of them.

So, if you have a procedure that includes a for loop, the compiler may put the loop control variable into a register, probably D7. If it optimizes more than one variable, it can also use D3 through D6 and A2 through A4.

You can tell which registers the compiler has used for optimizations in a procedure if you look at the first instruction after the LINK. If there are any register optimizations, there will be an instruction of the form MOVEM.L D3–D7/A2–A4, –(A7), where the registers listed will correspond to the registers actually used by the procedure. For example, if the procedure contains three for statements that are optimized into registers, you'll probably see a MOVEM.L D5–D7,–(A7) instruction at the beginning of the procedure, which saves these three registers on the stack. Then, near the end of the procedure, there will be a corresponding MOVEM.L (A7)+,D5–D7, which will put things back the way they were.

Summary

Remember that the descriptions of algorithms and techniques we've discussed in this chapter are pretty general; your actual compiler may vary. Use the information that we've learned here to navigate through your compiler's object code. By stepping through unfamiliar code with your source listing as your guide, you should be able to figure out what the compiler's doing. Then you'll really know what's going on!

Things to Remember

- Procedure and function calls translate into JSR instructions.
- Procedures in the same segment are called with PC-relative JSR instructions, like this: JSR xx(PC).
- Procedures in other segments are called with jumps into the jump table, which look like this: JSR xx(A5).
- Conditional statements are implemented with CMP instructions followed by Bcc (branch conditionally) instructions. The branch test is the opposite of the condition specified in the source.
- Tests to end repetitive statements are also done with CMP instructions followed by conditional branches.
- Linked routines are compiled separately and then added to the object file by the linker.
- ROM interface routines can be very simple, especially for Toolbox calls, or they may have to move things between registers and the stack for O S calls.
- The jump table contains one entry for every procedure that's called from outside its own segment. It can be in one of two forms, depending on whether its segment is loaded or not.
- Some weird things can show up in your object code. Many of these are remnants of earlier systems that are still in the compiler.

CHAPTER

7

Real Live Debugging

$\mathbf{I}$n this chapter, we're going to take everything we've learned and use it in some actual debugging situations. We'll take an example program with some bugs and proceed to run it, observe problems, and then use a debugger and our knowledge to find and eliminate the bugs.

What We'll Do

The program that we'll use is a modified version of the tiny program Sample that appears in the Road Map chapter of **Inside Macintosh**. This program, as modified, allows the user to open any number of nonresizable, nonscrollable (we're talking no frills here) windows and type text into them. The program supports standard text editing in the windows, and it also supports desk accessories, with cut and paste between all windows. Listing 7-1 is the source code for the sample program, which is called Showoff.

The debugger we'll be using is TMON, which we discussed in Chapter 4. All the debugger displays that you see in this chapter were produced with TMON.

For this chapter, we'll assume the role of the programmer who is testing the program, since it's much less embarrassing to catch our own mistakes than to have someone else do it for us. We'll run Showoff and try its features, waiting for something bad to happen. When it does, we'll decide on a course of action and eventually fix the problem.

217

```
program Showoff;

   uses
      {$U HD:MPW:Interfaces.p:MemTypes.p } MemTypes,
      {$U HD:MPW:Interfaces.p:QuickDraw.p} QuickDraw,
      {$U HD:MPW:Interfaces.p:OSIntf.p   } OSIntf,
      {$U HD:MPW:Interfaces.p:ToolIntf.p } ToolIntf,
      {$U HD:MPW:Interfaces.p:PackIntf.p } PackIntf;

   const
      appleID = 128;    {resource IDs/menu IDs for Apple, File and Edit menus}
      fileID  = 129;
      editID  = 130;

      appleM = 1; {index for each menu in myMenus (array of menu handles)}
      fileM  = 2;
      editM  = 3;

      menuCount = 3;        {total number of menus}

      aboutItem = 1;        {item in Apple menu}

      undoItem  = 1;        {Items in Edit menu}
      cutItem   = 3;
      copyItem  = 4;
      pasteItem = 5;
      clearitem = 6;

      newItem = 1;       {items in File menu}
      closeItem = 3;
      quitItem = 5;

      wName = 'Window ';   {prefix for window names}

      windDX = 25;         {distance to move for new windows}
      windDY = 25;

      leftEdge = 10;       {initial dimensions of window}
      topEdge = 42;
      rightEdge = 210;
      botEdge = 175;

   var
      myMenus: array [1..menuCount] OF MenuHandle; {handles to the menus}
      dragRect: Rect;          {rectangle used to mark boundaries for dragging window}
      txRect: Rect;            {rectangle for text in application window}
      textH: TEHandle;         {handle to Textedit record}
      theChar: char;           {typed character}
```

Listing 7-1

```
    extended: boolean;         {true if user is Shift-clicking}
    doneFlag: boolean;         {true if user has chosen Quit Item}
    myEvent: EventRecord;      {information about an event}
    wRecord: WindowRecord;     {information about the application window}
    myWindow: WindowPtr;       {pointer to wRecord}
    myWinPeek : WindowPeek;    {another pointer to wRecord}
    whichWindow: WindowPtr;    {window in which mouse button was pressed}
    nextWRect: Rect;           {portRect for next window to be opended}
    nextWTitle: Str255;        {title of next window to be opened}
    nextWNum: Longint;         {number of next window (for title)}
    savedPort: GrafPtr;        {pointer to preserve GrafPort}
    menusOK: boolean;          {for disabling menu items}
    scrapErr: Longint;
    scrCopyErr: Integer;

procedure SetUpMenus;
{ set up menus and menu bar }

  var
    i: Integer;

  begin
    myMenus[appleM] := GetMenu(appleID); {read Apple menu}
    AddResMenu(myMenus[appleM],'DRVR');  {add desk accessory names}
    myMenus[fileM] := GetMenu(fileID);   {read file menu }
    myMenus[editM] := GetMenu(editID);   {read Edit menu }

    for i:=1 to menuCount do
      InsertMenu(myMenus[i],0);  {install menus in menu bar }
    DrawMenuBar;  { and draw menu bar}
  end;  {SetUpMenus}


procedure OpenWindow;
{ Open a new window }

  begin
    NumToString (nextWNum, nextWTitle); {prepare number for title}
    nextWTitle := concat (wName, nextWTitle); {add to prefix}
    myWindow := NewWindow (Nil, nextWRect, nextWTitle, True, noGrowDocProc,
      Pointer (-1), True, 0);   {open the window}
    SetPort (myWindow);         {make it the current port}
    txRect := thePort^.portRect;{prepare TERecord for new window}
    InsetRect (txRect, 4, 0);
    textH := TENew (txRect, txRect);
    myWinPeek := WindowPeek (myWindow);
    myWinPeek^.refcon := Longint (textH); {keep TEHandle in refcon!}
    OffsetRect (nextWRect, windDX, windDY);{move window down and right}
```

Listing 7-1 (*continued*)

```
  if nextWRect.right > dragRect.right  {move back if it's too far over}
    then OffsetRect (nextWRect, -nextWRect.left + leftEdge, 0);
  if nextWRect.bottom > dragRect.bottom
    then OffsetRect (nextWRect, 0, -nextWRect.top + topEdge);
  nextWNum := nextWNum + 1;   {bump number for next window}
  menusOK := false;
  EnableItem (myMenus [editM],0); {in case this is the only window}
end; {OpenWindow}



procedure KillWindow (theWindow: WindowPtr);
{Close a window and throw everything away}

  begin
    TEDispose (TEHandle (WindowPeek (theWindow)^.refcon));
                              {throw away TERecord}
    DisposeWindow (theWindow);  {throw away WindowRecord}
    textH := NIL;               {for TEIdle in main event loop}
    if FrontWindow = NIL        {if no more windows, disable Close}
      then DisableItem (myMenus[fileM], closeItem);
    if WindowPeek (FrontWindow)^.windowKind < 0
                                {if a desk acc is coming up, enable undo}
      then EnableItem (myMenus[editM], undoItem)
      else DisableItem (myMenus[editM], undoItem);

  end; {KillWindow}



function MyFilter (theDialog: DialogPtr; var theEvent: EventRecord;
    var itemHit: Integer): Boolean;

  var
    theType: Integer;
    theItem: Handle;
    theBox: Rect;
    finalTicks: Longint;
```

Listing 7-1 (*continued*)

```
  begin
    if (BitAnd(theEvent.message,charCodeMask) = 13) {carriage return}
      or (BitAnd(theEvent.message,charCodeMask) = 3) {enter}
      then
        begin
          GetDItem (theDialog, 1, theType, theItem, theBox);
          HiliteControl (ControlHandle (theItem), 1);
          Delay (8, finalTicks);
          HiliteControl (ControlHandle (theItem), 0);
          itemHit := 1;
          MyFilter := True;
        end {if BitAnd...then begin}
      else MyFilter := False;
  end; {function MyFilter}


procedure DoAboutBox;

  var
    itemHit: Integer;

  begin
    myWindow := GetNewDialog (1000, @MyFilter, pointer (-1));
    repeat
      ModalDialog (Nil, itemHit)
    until itemHit = 1;
    DisposDialog (myWindow);
  end; {procedure DoAboutBox}


procedure DoCommand (mResult: LONGINT);
{Execute Item specified by mResult, the result of MenuSelect}

  var
    theItem: Integer; {menu item number from mResult low-order word}
    theMenu: Integer; {menu number from mResult high-order word}
    name: Str255;     {desk accessory name}
    temp: Integer;
```

Listing 7-1 (*continued*)

```
begin
  theItem := LoWord(mResult);  {call Toolbox Utility routines to set }
  theMenu := HiWord(mResult);      { menu item number and menu number}

  case theMenu of            {case on menu ID}

    appleID:
      if theItem = aboutItem
        then DoAboutBox
        else
          begin
            GetItem(myMenus[appleM],theItem,name);
            {GetPort (savedPort);}
            scrapErr := ZeroScrap;
            scrCopyErr := TEToScrap;
            temp := OpenDeskAcc(name);
            EnableItem (myMenus [editM],0);
            {SetPort (savedPort);}
            if FrontWindow <> NIL
              then
                begin
                  EnableItem (myMenus [fileM], closeItem);
                  EnableItem (myMenus [editM], undoItem);
                end; {if FrontWindow then begin}
            menusOK := false;
          end;  {if theItem...else begin}
    fileID:
      case theItem of

        newItem:
          OpenWindow;

        closeItem:
          if WindowPeek (FrontWindow)^.windowKind < 0
            then CloseDeskAcc (windowPeek (FrontWindow)^.windowKind)
            {if desk acc window, close it}
            else
              begin
                DisposeWindow (FrontWindow); {if it's mine, blow it away}
                KillWindow (FrontWindow);
              end; {if WindowPeek...else begin}


        quitItem:
          doneFlag := TRUE; {quit}

      end; {case theItem}
```

Listing 7-1 (*continued*)

```
    editID:
      begin
        if not SystemEdit(theItem-1)
          then
            case theItem of {case on menu item number}

              cutItem:
                TECut(textH); {call TextEdit to handle Item}

              copyItem:
                TECopy(textH);

              pasteItem:
                TEPaste(textH);

              clearItem:
                TEDelete(textH);

            end;     {case theItem}
        end;     {editID begin}

    end;     {case theMenu}
    HiliteMenu(0);
  end; {DoCommand}


procedure FixCursor;

  var
    mouseLoc: point;

begin
  GetMouse (mouseLoc);
  if PtInRect (mouseLoc, thePort^.portRect)
    then SetCursor (GetCursor (iBeamCursor)^^)
    else SetCursor (arrow);
end; {procedure FixCursor}
```

Listing 7-1 (*continued*)

```
begin           {main program}

  InitGraf(@thePort);
  InitFonts;
  FlushEvents(everyEvent,0);
  InitWindows;
  InitMenus;
  TEInit;
  InitDialogs(NIL);
  InitCursor;

  SetUpMenus;
    with screenBits.bounds do
      SetRect(dragRect,4,24,right-4,bottom-4);
      doneFlag := false;

  menusOK := false;
  nextWNum := 1;    {initialize window number}
  SetRect (nextWRect,leftEdge,topEdge,rightEdge,botEdge);
                    {initialize window rectangle}
  OpenWindow;       {start with one open window}

{ Main event loop }
  repeat
    SystemTask;
    if FrontWindow <> NIL
      then
        if WindowPeek (FrontWindow)^.windowKind >= 0
          then FixCursor;
    if not menusOK and (FrontWindow = NIL)
      then
        begin
          DisableItem (myMenus [fileM], closeItem);
          DisableItem (myMenus [editM], 0);
          menusOK := true;
        end; {if FrontWindow...then begin}
    TEIdle(textH);

    if GetNextEvent(everyEvent,myEvent)
      then
      case myEvent.what of

        mouseDown:
          case FindWindow(myEvent.where,whichWindow) of

            inSysWindow:
              SystemClick(myEvent,whichWindow);
```

Listing 7-1 (*continued*)

```
inMenuBar:
  DoCommand(MenuSelect(myEvent.where));

inDrag:
  DragWindow(whichWindow,myEvent.where,dragRect);

inContent:
  begin
    if whichWindow <> FrontWindow
      then SelectWindow(whichWindow)
      else
        begin
          GlobalToLocal(myEvent.where);
          extended := BitAnd(myEvent.modifiers,shiftKey) <> 0;
          TEClick(myEvent.where,extended,textH);
        end;  {else}
  end;  {inContent}

inGoAway:
  if TrackGoAway (whichWindow, myEvent.where)
    then KillWindow (whichWindow);

end;    {case FindWindow}

keyDown, autoKey:
  begin
    theChar := CHR(BitAnd(myEvent.message,charCodeMask));
    if BitAnd(myEvent.modifiers,cmdKey) <> 0
      then DoCommand(MenuKey(theChar))
      else TEKey(theChar,textH);
  end;  {keyDown, autoKey begin}

activateEvt:
  begin
  if BitAnd(myEvent.modifiers,activeFlag) <> 0
    then  {application window is becoming active}
      begin
        SetPort (GrafPtr (myEvent.message));
        textH := TEHandle (WindowPeek (myEvent.message)^.refcon);
        EnableItem (myMenus[fileM],closeItem);
        DisableItem(myMenus[editM],undoItem);
        if WindowPeek (FrontWindow)^.nextWindow^.windowKind < 0
          then scrCopyErr := TEFromScrap;
      end {if BitAnd...then begin}
```

Listing 7-1 (*continued*)

```
      else  {application window is becoming inactive}
        begin
        TEDeactivate(TEHandle(WindowPeek(myEvent.message)^.refcon));
        if WindowPeek (FrontWindow)^.windowKind < 0
          then
            begin
              EnableItem (myMenus[editM], undoItem);
              scrapErr := ZeroScrap;
              scrCopyErr := TEToScrap;
            end {if WindowPeek...then begin}
          else DisableItem (myMenus[editM], undoItem);
        end;  {else begin}
    end;  {activateEvt begin}

  updateEvt:
    begin
      BeginUpdate(WindowPtr(myEvent.message));
      EraseRect(WindowPtr(myEvent.message)^.portRect);
      TEUpdate(WindowPtr(myEvent.message)^.portRect,
        TEHandle(WindowPeek(myEvent.message)^.refcon));
      EndUpdate(WindowPtr(myEvent.message));
    end;  {updateEvt begin}

  end;  {case myEvent.what}

  until doneFlag;
end.
```

Listing 7-1 (*continued*)

Since this is the first time the program has ever been run, we should approach this assuming that the program will fail. This means that we should enable Trap Record, the debugger feature that records traps as they're executed. With TMON, you can record up to 2047, surely more than we'll want to sift through. For debugging purposes, it's usually sufficient to record ten traps. If we enter the Trap Record command in TMON and tell it to record ten traps, we'll always know the ten most recently executed trap calls.

Also, since the ROM calls ROM traps a lot, and we're usually just interested in tracking the traps our program calls, we need to tell TMON to only record traps that our application executes. The best way to do this is to specify limits of @ApplZone and @ApplLimit; this will ensure that traps are recorded only from code executed in the application heap zone, which should include all of the application's code.

Entering the Debugger

The easiest way to get into the debugger is to press the interrupt button on the programmer's switch. However, when we do this, we might interrupt at a bad time, like right in the middle of a heap block being relocated. While this is not necessarily harmful, it may mess us up if we try to do certain things, like looking at a heap dump: the heap may appear inconsistent. Also, register A5 may be invalid; it may have been saved off by a ROM routine and not yet restored.

Since the system's state may be inconsistent, we can use a special debugger feature called Trap Signal to ensure that we avoid this problem. Trap Signal enters the debugger only when a specified trap is encountered. Most applications call GetNextEvent frequently, so if we set Trap Signal to GetNextEvent, then press option-interrupt, which means "break when the trap specified in Trap Signal is encountered," the program will stop at the next GetNextEvent call, a clean and consistent time.

Here are the actual commands to set up this trap recording. First, open the User window. Then, on the Record line, type 0 A <return>; then, on the Trap Record line, type 0 FFF @"ApplZone" @"ApplLimit". This will cause the last ten (hexadecimal $A) traps that are executed from the range pointed to by ApplZone through ApplLimit (that is, everything in the application heap zone) to be recorded. The 0 FFF parameters mean to record traps with numbers $0 through $FFF, that is, all traps.

A Hands-on Experience

You'll find this chapter most valuable if you actually debug along (just follow the bouncing mouse). If you don't have TMON, you can use Macsbug to do many of the things we'll do. Translating commands between these two debuggers is also a good exercise in understanding exactly what the debugging commands do, although some TMON commands don't really have Macsbug counterparts.

Running the Program

Let's crank 'er up! We double-click the program, and it begins by displaying a single window entitled "Window 1." Right off the bat, there's something wrong: there should be a blinking insertion point in the window, but there's not. So we begin keeping a list of observed problems by noting this as problem number one.

At this point, we, the programmer–debugger, can either work on finding out what's causing the no-insertion point problem, or we can continue running the program normally and see if we can discover any other bugs. Since one bug can often cause a number of different problems to appear as symptoms, it's usually a good idea to do some detective work on a bug as soon as you see it. However, this time we'll continue running the program normally to see what other problems we observe, for two reasons: (1) this is the first time we've run the program, so we'd like to see whether it works at all, and (2) since this problem is evident just by starting the program, it's apparently very easy to duplicate, so we can check it out whenever we want.

The first feature of the program that we'll try out is the ability to type text into a window. When we type, the text does appear in the window, although there's still no insertion point visible. Also, we can select text, and cut, copy, and paste seem to work correctly, both from the Edit menu and with keyboard command key combinations.

After selecting text, we find another funny problem. When we make a selection in the text and then make a different selection, the first selection stays highlighted, as you see in Figure 7-1. This problem may be related to the no-insertion-point problem. This becomes problem number two on our list.

The next thing we'll try is dragging the window around the screen. This seems to work fine. If we drag the window so that part of the text is off the screen and then drag it back onto the screen, the text is redrawn properly. At least something is working right!

Now we'll try opening additional windows with the File menu's New command. If we choose the New item, another window appears on the screen, just below and to the right of the first window's original location; the new window's title is "Window 2"; the new window is highlighted as the front window, and the first window is unhighlighted. All this is just as we'd wanted it, so things seem to be going a little better. Still no insertion point in the new window, though. Also, when we highlight another window, the text in the first window is staying highlighted, even though it shouldn't be. This is number three on our problem list.

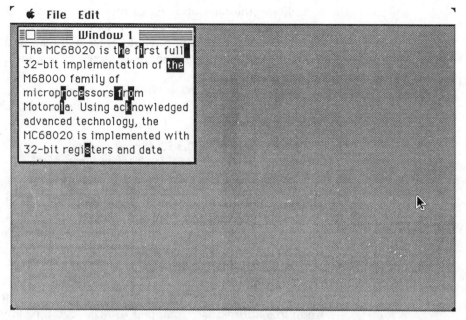

Figure 7-1 Screen display showing multiple selection bug

Once again, even though there's no insertion point in the new window, typed text still appears properly, and the text can be edited by selecting it and using the editing commands. We can drag the second window around, too, and we can even copy and paste between the two windows (we're on a winning streak here).

We shouldn't get too cocky, though, because there are some more problems. When we drag Window 1 so that it covers part of Window 2, then uncover Window 2, Window 1 goes blank! The same thing happens if we cover Window 1 with Window 2 and then drag away Window 2: as soon as the partially hidden window is exposed, the frontmost window's contents go blank. This is problem four on our list.

Next let's try opening some desk accessories. This seems to work right: the desk accessories we choose open, we can use them, we can drag them around the screen, and we can close them either by clicking in their close box or by choosing Close from the File menu. We can even copy and paste between application windows and desk accessories or between two desk accessory windows. We're still getting the top window erased, though.

We also have to observe the behavior of the Undo and Close menu items. We want Undo to be enabled if and only if the frontmost window is a desk accessory, and we want Close to be enabled if there are any windows open, desk accessories included. If we open several windows, including some desk accessories then click on various windows, we see that Undo seems to know what to do, being active for desk accessories and inactive for application windows. Also, the application doesn't seem to mind if we open several more windows, except for the problems we've already seen.

Next we try closing a window by typing command-W . . . and it's crash time. There's been a system error, and the debugger takes over with this message:

```
Address error.    PC=$0040F850
Access address: $4E494C73 (supervisor data)
```

This greeting from the debugger tells us that we've suffered an address error, meaning that a 68000 instruction tried to get a word or long word operand from an odd address, which is a no-no, of course. The debugger also tells us that the program counter was at $40F850 when the address error occurred, and that the actual address that the instruction was attempting to access was $4E494C73.

The bad address, $4E494C73, is indeed odd, but we human debuggers can also see that it's not a reasonable address to be reading data from: this address isn't mapped to ROM, RAM, or anything else on the Macintosh, as you can tell by checking our simplified memory map in Figure 7-2.

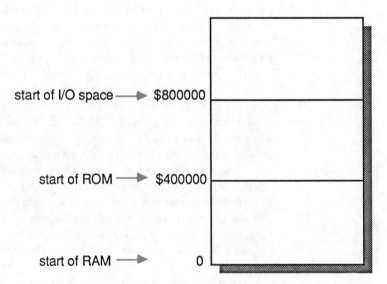

start of I/O space ⟶ $800000

start of ROM ⟶ $400000

start of RAM ⟶ 0

Figure 7-2 Partial Macintosh memory map

```
DISASSEMBLY FROM 40F850
40F850:P  !_TEClick+0312    ORI.W   #$2F0A,(A2)
40F854:   !_TEClick+0316    _SetPort
40F856:   !_TEClick+0318    SUBQ.W  #4,A7
40F858:   !_TEClick+031A    _NewRgn
40F85A:   !_TEClick+031C    MOVE.L  (A7),$0008(A7)
40F85E:   !_TEClick+0320    MOVE.L  (A7),-(A7)
```

Figure 7-3 Disassembly from Program Counter

Since the program is hosed, we can stop looking for more bugs and investigate this one a little more thoroughly as long as we're here. So we start playing detective and see how much information we can gather about the crash.

The first step is to look at the offending instruction at $40F850. We can tell that this instruction is in the ROM, because it's in the range $400000 through $40FFFF. We can see what the instruction is by opening a disassembly window and looking at this address. This window is shown in Figure 7-3.

The P in the first column after the address means that this is the location the program counter is pointing to. The !_TEClick+0312 means that this instruction is located at 312 bytes beyond the start of the TEClick trap code in the Macintosh ROM. Following this information is the instruction itself, ORI.W #$2F0A,(A2).

To see exactly why this program has crashed, we have to look at the contents of register A2, which should be an odd value. But surprise, surprise: if we examine A2 by opening a Registers window (see Figure 7-4), we see that it contains $68850, an even, valid number. What's going on?

```
REGISTERS                  PC=0040F850      SR='t.S..000...xnZvc'  USP=4A696D46
            0        1        2        3        4        5        6        7
DATA  00000000 FFFFFFF8 00000000 0000FFFE 00000000 0000FFFE 0000FFFE 00000000
ADDR  000698E2 000697D4 00068850 4E494C21 00000000 00069EA2 00068896 000697CA
```

Figure 7-4 Register display

```
DISASSEMBLY FROM 40F84E
40F84E:    !_TEClick+0310    MOVEA.L  $0052(A3),A2
40F852:    !_TEClick+0314    MOVE.L   A2,-(A7)
40F854:    !_TEClick+0316    _SetPort
40F856:    !_TEClick+0318    SUBQ.W   #4,A7
40F858:    !_TEClick+031A    _NewRgn
40F85A:    !_TEClick+031C    MOVE.L   (A7),$0008(A7)
```

Figure 7-5 Disassembly from just before Program Counter

As we mentioned back in Chapter 4, an address error is sometimes reported just beyond the location where it actually occurred. This is because the processor increments the PC before the address error happens. So, to see the instruction that really caused the address error, we have to subtract a word (two bytes) from the program counter and look at the resulting instruction. The result is shown in Figure 7-5.

This is more like it. The instruction at $40F84E moves a long word from 52 off A3, and we see from the registers window that A3 has the wacko value $4E494C21, which is odd. When the 68000 tried to reference the location 52(A3), the effective address produced was $52+$4E494C21, or $4E494C73, which is odd and is the "access address" that was reported by the debugger when the crash occurred. This seems to verify that the address error really occurred as the debugger told us.

"Skewed" Disassemblies

Notice that the "instruction" at $40F850 is not really an instruction at all! It's the last two bytes of the real instruction that begins at $40F84E, plus the instruction that begins at $40F852. In raw bytes, these locations look like this:

40F84E: 24 6B 00 52 2F 0A

The first four bytes here, 24 6B 00 52, form the instruction MOVEA.L $0052(A3),A2 ; the next two bytes, 2F 0A, are machine language for MOVE.L A2,—(A7) (you can look it up). When we told the debugger to start disassembling at $40F850, we forced it to interpret 00 52, the last half of the MOVE instruction, as a complete instruction itself. The disassembler has no way of knowing that this really isn't an instruction, so it begins disassembling right where we told it, and it finds that 00 52 2F 0A is a valid instruction, ORI.W #$2F0A,(A2). This is kind of like telling a computer to look at the phrase "the unforgettable fire" starting with the thirteenth character; the computer would interpret the last two words as "table fire," both perfectly valid words, but not at all what we meant. When this happens, the disassembler is said to be **skewed**. The debugger is usually able to correct itself within a couple of instructions.

Crimefighter's Notebook

The opcode for the ORI instruction always begins with a zero. Many Macintosh addresses also begin with a zero. Therefore, an ORI instruction is often the sign of a skewed disassembly. If you think this might be happening to you, just back up the disassembly window by two bytes.

The next interesting fact is the debugger's telling us that the program crashed within the TEClick trap (that's what ⌐TEClick+0310 in front of the instruction means). But the only time we call TEClick is when the user clicks in the window. In this example, all we did was type command-W; there's no way TEClick should have been called. What's going on here?

The answer is that when you display a disassembly in the ROM the debugger searches backwards for the first trap it can find and then displays instructions as an offset from that location. In this case, TEClick starts at $40F53E, and the location we're displaying is $40F84E; so TEClick is the closest trap address without going over (sort of like bidding on "The Price is Right").

However, most of the Managers in the ROM have subroutines that are called on to perform common tasks, just like applications. These subroutines are usually called with BSR or JSR instructions. The subroutines are located at various places in the ROM, and just because a subroutine is closer to a certain trap does not necessarily mean that it is actually a part of that trap. So the disassembled code that we're looking at isn't really a part of TEClick at all. See Figure 7-6 for a picture of this.

TEClick is at $40F53E, but a TextEdit common routine begins at $40F840:

```
40F84E:    !_TEClick+0310    MOVEA.L $0052(A3),A2
40F852:    !_TEClick+0314    MOVE.L  A2,-(A7)
40F854:    !_TEClick+0316    _SetPort
40F856:    !_TEClick+0318    SUBQ.W  #4,A7
40F858:    !_TEClick+031A    _NewRgn
40F85A:    !_TEClick+031C    MOVE.L  (A7),$0008(A7)
```

TMON reports the nearest trap, which is TEClick. It doesn't know about common routines that are not traps.

Figure 7-6 TMON reports nearest trap

When the PC is in one of these common subroutines, how do we tell what trap really was called? There are a couple of techniques. First, one ROM Manager rarely calls subroutines within another, so the fact that the nearest trap is TEClick says that we're almost certainly somewhere in TextEdit. Also, since we used the Trap Record feature, we can simply look at the most recently executed trap to see what it was.

Stack Addresses

If we hadn't turned on trap recording, another technique we could have used is the Stack addresses feature in the TMON User window. This handy feature looks back on the stack, from newest to oldest stack locations, for possible return addresses to routines that executed JSRs or BSRs.

Let's look at the traps TMON recorded with Trap record. The User window tells us that the traps are recorded starting at location $3370, so we'll open a dump window at that address (see Figure 7-7). The recorded traps are in a somewhat cryptic format. Each trap that's recorded takes 16 bytes, or one line of the dump display. The first two bytes indicate the trap word that was executed. The next two bytes contain the value of the global variable Ticks at the time the trap was executed; this variable holds the number of ticks (sixtieths of a second) since the system was started up.

```
DUMP FROM 003370
003370:V   A9 DA 38 7A  00 00 D3 56  00 00 00 00  00 40 4D 0E   ..8z...V.....@M.
003380:    A9 3A 38 7A  00 00 D3 4A  00 00 00 00  CB C4 00 40   .:8z...J.......@
003390:    A9 3A 38 7A  00 00 D3 42  00 03 00 00  CB C8 00 40   .:8z...B.......@
0033A0:    A9 24 38 7A  00 00 D3 2C  00 00 00 00  00 00 00 01   .$8z...,........
0033B0:    A9 24 38 7A  00 00 D3 0A  00 00 00 00  00 40 4D 0E   .$8z.........@M.
0033C0:    A9 B4 38 7A  00 00 D3 06  00 40 4D 0E  78 18 00 06   ..8z.....@M.x...
0033D0:    A9 38 38 7A  00 00 D2 2E  00 00 00 00  FF FF 00 00   .88z............
0033E0:    A9 3A 38 7A  00 00 D0 14  00 01 00 00  CB C4 00 06   .:8z............
0033F0:    A9 24 38 7A  00 00 CF F6  00 00 00 00  00 06 97 F8   .$8z............
003400:    A9 3A 38 7A  00 00 CF F2  00 03 00 00  CB C8 00 06   .:8z............
```

Figure 7-7 Dump of Trap Record information

The next four bytes contain the value of the program counter at the time the trap was executed. This allows us to see where the traps were called from. The next eight bytes contain different information depending on whether the trap was stack based or register based. For stack-based calls, these bytes contain the top eight bytes of the stack; for register-based calls, these bytes are the contents of registers D0 and A0, in that order.

Putting all this together, we can determine that the last trap called by the application before it crashed was $A9DA, which is TEIdle. It was called from location $D356, which we can now disassemble. We can see in Figure 7-8 that the TEIdle call occurs just before a call to GetNextEvent. Since these calls occur only once in our program, it's easy to find them in the source program: they're right at the start of the main event loop.

```
DISASSEMBLY FROM 00D356
00D356:     "SHOWOFF "+00CC    _TEIdle
00D358:     "SHOWOFF "+00CE    CLR.W    -(A7)
00D35A:     "SHOWOFF "+00D0    MOVE.W   #$FFFF,-(A7)
00D35E:     "SHOWOFF "+00D4    PEA      $FFCC(A5)
00D362:     "SHOWOFF "+00D8    _GetNextEvent
```

Figure 7-8 Disassembly from Showoff

The TEIdle trap takes one parameter, a handle to a TextEdit record. Looking at the last eight bytes of the trap record in Figure 7-7, we can see that this parameter, which was the top long word on the stack at the time of the trap call, was 00 00 00 00, or Nil. This is the cause of the crash! In the ROM, TEIdle attempted to use 0, or Nil, as a handle to a TextEdit record. Like most of the ROM, TextEdit doesn't check for Nil handles, and when it dereferenced the handle, it simply treated the value zero as if it were the address of a master pointer. So it got the value in location 0 and attempted to use it as a pointer to a TextEdit record. Since this value happened to be odd ($4E494C21), an address error was generated.

As a general rule, whenever your program dies with an address error and the access address is something like $4E494C21, you've usually tried to dereference a Nil handle.

What If Location 0 Has an Even Value?

Attempting to double-dereference a Nil handle is a fairly common error. If the value in location 0 is odd, you'll get an address error, which is good, because double-dereferencing a Nil handle is a problem you need to fix. If the value in 0 happens to be even, no address error will be generated, and the program will get random data, whatever location 0 happened to be pointing to; and it will probably run for a while with bizarre things happening before another error (maybe an address error) causes it to crash.

Of course, the second situation is much harder to diagnose than the first, since the program may continue to run for a while before crashing. To help ensure that dereferencing a Nil handle causes an address error, TMON does you a favor: it puts a long-word odd value into location 0, which is normally unused on the Macintosh. This guarantees that dereferencing a Nil handle will cause an address error instantly. Since location 0 is unused, it usually stays at the value set even when these subsequent applications are executed.

Remember that address errors only happen when a word or long word is accessed at an even address. If the value being accessed is byte sized, which is pretty rare, odd addresses are OK and the problem will slip through. Often, it'll be caught soon thereafter, though.

For Your Amusement

Why does TMON put $4E494C21 in location 0, and not something simple like $FFFFFFFF or just $00000001, which would have the same effect? See what $4E494C21 spells in ASCII for the answer.

Discovering that we called TEIdle (Nil) is a major step in getting rid of this bug. Now we have to determine why we called TEIdle with this bad value. Looking at the source listing, we see that the code reads TEIdle (textH). Apparently, textH is being set to Nil and the TEIdle call is causing the crash. We have to find out where and why this is happening so that we can prevent it.

Since this crash occurred so readily, just by closing a window, we can make a reasonable assumption that it's repeatable. We'll try running the program again, this time under a closer watch. Before rerunning the program, we should do some final looking around just to see if there are any more interesting clues to this problem.

One thing we should certainly do is check to see if the heap has been trashed. The User window contains a function that performs a consistency check on the heap, making sure that, for example, each block has a proper header. A heap check reveals that the heap seems to be OK.

Finding no other clues to the nature of this problem, we can now restart the program and take a closer look. Since the system has crashed with an address error, we probably won't be able to exit normally, so we'll use the User window function that runs the Finder.

Warning

After an application has crashed, the system is in an uncertain state. System globals or system heap objects may be damaged. If you use the debugger to exit to the Finder, everything may appear to be in good shape, but beware. The safest thing to do is to reboot after a system error. If you save your disk just once, you won't regret the small inconvenience of rebooting.

Watching More Closely

When we restart the application, we'll again try closing a window, but this time we'll watch things much more closely. In particular, we'll trace through the program as it handles the Close command to see exactly what's going on.

Since the problem occurs when we close a window, we can start the application normally. Then we need to pick an easily found spot to stop the program and enter the debugger. There are two strategies for this: find a fairly unique ROM call in the program and tell the debugger to break on that ROM call or find the right spot in the source program and set a breakpoint there.

One thing we could do is tell the debugger to break every time it encounters the GetNextEvent trap. Since we know that the application calls GetNextEvent, this will certainly give control to the debugger. However, if you try this, you'll see why it's a bad idea that can lead to insanity: because GetNextEvent is called so frequently (every tick or so), the program is constantly being interrupted, and there's no way to get it to stop when we really want it to. What we need is a more restrictive way of breaking into the debugger.

In this example, we know that the main event loop calls the program's procedure DoCommand whenever there's a MouseDown event in the menu bar. If we're confident that the program is working at least this far (that is, the DoCommand procedure is in fact getting called when we select a menu item), we can set a breakpoint at the location called DoCommand.

The Workshop Pascal compiler thoughtfully embeds procedure and function names in compiled code so that debuggers can use these names as symbols. So we can open a Breakpoint window at tell TMON to set a breakpoint at "DoCommand". It will respond by figuring out where DoCommand is (it's at $D102) and then setting a breakpoint there. We can then return to the application with the Exit command. The application will run normally until it hits the breakpoint, that is, until we do something that causes DoCommand to be executed, like pulling down a menu and choosing the Close command, which is exactly where we want it to stop.

So we start up the application and then use the File menu to open a couple more windows. At this point, the screen has three windows called "Window 1", "Window 2", and "Window 3". We then press the interrupt button to get into the debugger and set the breakpoint at DoCommand. After typing command-E to exit the debugger, we pull down the File menu and choose Close. The Close item blinks, the menu goes away, and we're instantly zapped into the debugger. This time, though, instead of the dread Address Error message, the debugger tells us "Breakpoint at $0000D102." Nothing has gone wrong; the debugger has just followed our instructions by taking control upon reaching a certain location.

As we trace through the application, we should always keep the phrase "reality check" in mind. This means that, as often as possible, we should examine the parameters to ROM calls and their effects to make sure that what's happening is exactly what we intended. It's very important to keep our minds on red alert while we're doing this. Don't take anything for granted. Think hard about the code that's being executed, and check out anything questionable or unexpected.

Now we're going to trace through the program to see precisely what's happening. Before we begin, we'll open several windows in the debugger. First, we'll open a Disassembly window and tell it to disassemble instructions at (PC); this will cause it to always display the instruction at the current program counter as we trace. Next we'll open a Dump window that we'll anchor to (A7) so that it will always display the top of the stack. Below that we'll open another Dump window, which we'll use generically to display different memory locations. Next we'll open a Registers window to watch the contents of the 68000 registers. Below that we'll place a Heap window to observe the application heap. Finally, we'll open a Number window that will allow us to figure expressions, such as effective addresses and hex-to-decimal conversions. This setup is shown in Figure 7-9.

```
REGISTERS            PC=0000D362      SR='t.S..000...xNzvc'   USP=9FFD7FFE
             0         1         2         3         4         5         6         7
DATA   00000004 00000000 0000FFFF 0000FFFF 00000000 0000FFFF 0000FFFF 00000000
ADDR   0000D358 00408EB4 00068850 00069EC4 0000FD42 00069EA2 00068896 000697FC

DISASSEMBLY FROM 000000(PC)
00D362:P  "SHOWOFF "+00D8    _GetNextEvent
00D364:    "SHOWOFF "+00DA    MOVE.B   (A7)+,D0
00D366:    "SHOWOFF "+00DC    BEQ      ^$00D546              ;"SHOWOFF "+02BC

DUMP FROM 000000(A7)
0697FC:S   00 06 9E 6E  FF FF 00 00   00 40 4D 0E  78 18 00 06  ...n.....@M.x...
06980C:    9E C2 00 06  00 00 00 00   00 40 4D 0E  00 00 00 00  .........@M.....
06981C:    00 00 00 00  00 00 00 00   00 00 00 00  00 00 00 00  ................

DUMP FROM 014356
014356:    2F 0A 61 00  FB F8 42 20   6F 20 72 20  69 20 73 20  /.a...B  o  r  i  s
014366:    74 20 68 20  65 20 20 53   20 70 20 69  64 20 65 72  t  h  e  S  p id er
014376:    00 38 D1 AD  F2 FA 52 6D   F3 16 60 00  D0 5E 59 4F  .8....Rm..`..^YO

Application heap is at $00CB00-$00F700.                   000520 bytes free.
*$00CB3C 000100 0  Nonrel
*$00CC44 00006C 0  Nonrel                      WMgrPort
*$00CCB8 00009C 0  Nonrel                      Window #$00, Kind $0008
 $00CD5C 00000A 0  Handle at $00CBC0 (lpr)    (Window @$00CCB8) VisRgn
 $00CD6E 00000A 0  Handle at $00CBBC (lpr)    (Window @$00CCB8) ClipRgn
 $00CD80 00002C 0  Handle at $00CBB8 (lpr)    (Window @$00CCB8) StructRgn

NUMBER
$00000000 +.0000000000(+.00000) '....' _Open
```

Figure 7-9 TMON windows setup

It may seem this is a lot of window opening to do before beginning to trace the program. Actually, we can open the windows at any time in the debugging process, but you may find it easier and less distracting to open them all before you begin. Also, you might decide that you prefer a different collection and placement of windows when you're debugging. That's OK—that's why they call it a personal computer.

Now we can start tracing through DoCommand, with our source code close at hand. Figure 7-10 shows the Disassembly window displaying the first part of DoCommand. We can move through DoCommand with either the Trace command or the Step command. In general, we'll use Step, because it treats ROM calls as single instructions. If we need to follow an instruction into the ROM, we can use the Trace command. As we trace, we'll look at the source code so that we know more about what's going on.

```
DISASSEMBLY FROM 00D102
00D102:P  "DOCOMMAN"+0000    LINK     A6,#$FEFA
00D106:   "DOCOMMAN"+0004    MOVEM.L  D5-D7,-(A7)
00D10A:   "DOCOMMAN"+0008    CLR.W    -(A7)
00D10C:   "DOCOMMAN"+000A    MOVE.L   $0008(A6),-(A7)
00D110:   "DOCOMMAN"+000E    _LoWord
00D112:   "DOCOMMAN"+0010    MOVE.W   (A7)+,D7
00D114:   "DOCOMMAN"+0012    CLR.W    -(A7)
00D116:   "DOCOMMAN"+0014    MOVE.L   $0008(A6),-(A7)
00D11A:   "DOCOMMAN"+0018    _HiWord
00D11C:   "DOCOMMAN"+001A    MOVE.W   (A7)+,D6
00D11E:   "DOCOMMAN"+001C    MOVE.W   D6,D0
00D120:   "DOCOMMAN"+001E    SUBI.W   #$0080,D0
00D124:   "DOCOMMAN"+0022    BEQ.S    ^$00D134         ;"DOCOMMAN"+0032
00D126:   "DOCOMMAN"+0024    SUBQ.W   #1,D0
00D128:   "DOCOMMAN"+0026    BEQ.S    ^$00D1A0         ;"DOCOMMAN"+009E
00D12A:   "DOCOMMAN"+0028    SUBQ.W   #1,D0
00D12C:   "DOCOMMAN"+002A    BEQ      ^$00D1E8         ;"DOCOMMAN"+00E6
```

Figure 7-10 Disassembly from DoCommand

Warning

Be careful about using the Trace command to trace a trap through the ROM. Many trap calls do a lot of processing, like several hundred instructions worth. Unless you really think tracing into the ROM will give you important information, you should avoid doing it or you might be tracing for a long, long time.

If you do get stuck in the ROM and you decide you want to get out, you can do so by looking back at the point in your program where you called the ROM. When the ROM call is finished, it will return to the next instruction in your application. This means that you can set a breakpoint on that next instruction and then just Exit the debugger. When the ROM call is finished, the debugger will take control on the breakpoint.

Stepping through the first two instructions, we see that Pascal begins the procedure with the usual Link instruction and then saves three registers (D5 through D7), which it will no doubt use for optimization in the procedure. It then calls LoWord and HiWord on the parameter mResult and puts the results into D7 and D6, respectively. Then it begins the grand production of a case statement. It begins by copying the value of the variable theMenu, the case selector, into register D0. Since the case statement labels are appleID, fileID, and editID (128, 129, and 130), it then subtracts 128 (which is hex $80) from this value to "normalize" it, that is, to put it into the range 0 through 2. This leaves a 1 in D0.

There's a BEQ instruction that will execute the appleID portion of code if the selector is zero. In our case, the selector is one, so the branch is not taken. The next instruction, SUBQ.W #1,D0, leaves D0 at zero, so the branch-if-equal to $D1A0 is taken. This corresponds to taking the fileID branch of the case statement in the object code.

As we're stepping through the object code in this way, we're following along in the source code listing to see if anything unexpected is happening, like a branch to the wrong label or surprising results from an assignment statement. So far everything has happened as we expected it to.

The fileID branch of the theMenu case is another case statement: case theItem of. Figure 7-11 shows the object code for this case statement. You may recall that the compiler stashed theMenu in register D7 when it called LoWord at the start of the procedure. Here the compiler prepares for the case statement by copying this value into scratch register

```
DISASSEMBLY FROM 00D1A0
00D1A0:P  "DOCOMMAN"+009E  MOVE.W  D7,D0
00D1A2:   "DOCOMMAN"+00A0  SUBQ.W  #1,D0
00D1A4:   "DOCOMMAN"+00A2  BEQ.S   ^$00D1B0              ;"DOCOMMAN"+00AE
00D1A6:   "DOCOMMAN"+00A4  SUBQ.W  #2,D0
00D1A8:   "DOCOMMAN"+00A6  BEQ.S   ^$00D1B6              ;"DOCOMMAN"+00B4
00D1AA:   "DOCOMMAN"+00A8  SUBQ.W  #2,D0
00D1AC:   "DOCOMMAN"+00AA  BEQ.S   ^$00D1E0              ;"DOCOMMAN"+00DE
00D1AE:   "DOCOMMAN"+00AC  BRA.S   ^$00D22C              ;"DOCOMMAN"+012A
```

Figure 7-11 Disassembly from DoCommand

D0, since it's about to start subtracting from it to find the right case to branch to. In our program, D0 is set to 3, the value of closeItem, which is the item we selected from the menu.

The cases of this case statement are newItem, closeItem, and quitItem, constants that have the values 1, 3, and 5, respectively. So the case statement first tests for newItem (1) by subtracting 1 from D0 and branching to the appropriate code if equal. In our example, this leaves 2 in D0, so the branch is not taken. The next instruction subtracts 2 from D0, leaving it at zero for the BEQ test at $D1A8, so the branch is taken. In the source code, this will cause the closeItem code to be executed.

Just in Case

Why did the case statement code first subtract 1, then 2, in testing the case selector? The compiler knows that the difference between the first two case labels (newItem and closeItem, or 1 and 3) is 2. There's no point in testing for theItem = 2, since there's no case label set up to handle it; the compiler just tests for values that are used. One brownie point for the compiler.

The branch to $D1B6 has taken us to the code for the closeItem case (see Figure 7-12). First, the program calls FrontWindow and checks that window's WindowKind field to see if it's less than zero (TST.W $006C(A0)), since WindowKind is $6C bytes from the start of the window record). In our case it's not, and the next instruction (BGE) causes a branch to the "else" part of the if statement. This code, starting at $D1D0, first calls DisposeWindow on the frontmost window and then calls the program's procedure KillWindow with FrontWindow as a parameter.

```
DISASSEMBLY FROM 00D1B6
00D1B6:P  "DOCOMMAN"+00B4   CLR.L    -(A7)
00D1B8:   "DOCOMMAN"+00B6   _FrontWindow
00D1BA:   "DOCOMMAN"+00B8   MOVEA.L  (A7)+,A0
00D1BC:   "DOCOMMAN"+00BA   TST.W    $006C(A0)
00D1C0:   "DOCOMMAN"+00BE   BGE.S    ^00D1D0          ;"DOCOMMAN"+00CE
00D1C2:   "DOCOMMAN"+00C0   CLR.L    -(A7)
00D1C4:   "DOCOMMAN"+00C2   _FrontWindow
00D1C6:   "DOCOMMAN"+00C4   MOVEA.L  (A7)+,A0
00D1C8:   "DOCOMMAN"+00C6   MOVE.W   $006C(A0),-(A7)
00D1CC:   "DOCOMMAN"+00CA   _CloseDeskAcc
00D1CE:   "DOCOMMAN"+00CC   BRA.S    ^00D22C          ;"DOCOMMAN"+012A
00D1D0:   "DOCOMMAN"+00CE   CLR.L    -(A7)
00D1D2:   "DOCOMMAN"+00D0   _FrontWindow
00D1D4:   "DOCOMMAN"+00D2   _DisposWindow
00D1D6:   "DOCOMMAN"+00D4   CLR.L    -(A7)
00D1D8:   "DOCOMMAN"+00D6   _FrontWindow
00D1DA:   "DOCOMMAN"+00D8   JSR      ^00CFCA          ;"KILLWIND"+0000
00D1DE:   "DOCOMMAN"+00DC   BRA.S    ^00D22C          ;"DOCOMMAN"+012A
00D1E0:   "DOCOMMAN"+00DE   MOVE.B   #$01,$FFDC(A5)
00D1E6:   "DOCOMMAN"+00E4   BRA.S    ^00D22C          ;"DOCOMMAN"+012A
```

Figure 7-12 Disassembly from DoCommand

Now let's trace into the KillWindow procedure (Figure 7-13). After the usual LINK instruction to create the local stack frame, the code calls TEDispose on the window record's TextEdit record. Then the program calls DisposeWindow on the window record. Wait a minute—deja vu! Didn't we just call DisposeWindow on this window a few instructions ago, back in DoCommand, before we even called KillWindow? Yep, we sure did.

So what are we disposing of here? To find out, all we have to do is look at the parameter we just pushed on the stack. Before calling DisposeWindow, the top of the stack contains a pointer to the window we're about to dispose of. The top of the stack contains $CD5C. We can use the User window's Template command to display this window record. You can see this display in Figure 7-14.

The window we're about to dispose of is "Window 2"; we can tell by looking at the "title" field of the Template display. But when we selected Close, "Window 3" was the frontmost. Why are we now disposing of a different window?

For clues, we need to look at the source listing. The source line that generated this code is DisposeWindow (theWindow) in the KillWindow procedure. Where did theWindow come from? It's the parameter that was passed to KillWindow by the caller, DoCommand.

```
DISASSEMBLY FROM 00CFCA
00CFCA:P   "KILLWIND"+0000    LINK      A6,#$0000
00CFCE:    "KILLWIND"+0004    MOVEA.L   $0008(A6),A0
00CFD2:    "KILLWIND"+0008    MOVE.L    $0098(A0),-(A7)
00CFD6:    "KILLWIND"+000C    _TEDispose
00CFD8:    "KILLWIND"+000E    MOVE.L    $0008(A6),-(A7)
00CFDC:    "KILLWIND"+0012    _DisposWindow
00CFDE:    "KILLWIND"+0014    CLR.L     $FFE0(A5)
00CFE2:    "KILLWIND"+0018    CLR.L     -(A7)
00CFE4:    "KILLWIND"+001A    _FrontWindow
00CFE6:    "KILLWIND"+001C    TST.L     (A7)+
00CFE8:    "KILLWIND"+001E    BNE.S     ^$00CFF4              ;"KILLWIND"+002A
00CFEA:    "KILLWIND"+0020    MOVE.L    $FFF8(A5),-(A7)
00CFEE:    "KILLWIND"+0024    MOVE.W    #$0003,-(A7)
00CFF2:    "KILLWIND"+0028    _DisableItem
00CFF4:    "KILLWIND"+002A    CLR.L     -(A7)
00CFF6:    "KILLWIND"+002C    _FrontWindow
00CFF8:    "KILLWIND"+002E    MOVEA.L   (A7)+,A0
00CFFA:    "KILLWIND"+0030    TST.W     $006C(A0)
00CFFE:    "KILLWIND"+0034    BGE.S     ^$00D00C             ;"KILLWIND"+0042
00D000:    "KILLWIND"+0036    MOVE.L    $FFFC(A5),-(A7)
00D004:    "KILLWIND"+003A    MOVE.W    #$0001,-(A7)
00D008:    "KILLWIND"+003E    _EnableItem
00D00A:    "KILLWIND"+0040    BRA.S     ^$00D016             ;"KILLWIND"+004C
00D00C:    "KILLWIND"+0042    MOVE.L    $FFFC(A5),-(A7)
00D010:    "KILLWIND"+0046    MOVE.W    #$0001,-(A7)
00D014:    "KILLWIND"+004A    _DisableItem
00D016:    "KILLWIND"+004C    UNLK      A6
00D018:    "KILLWIND"+004E    MOVE.L    (A7)+,(A7)
00D01A:    "KILLWIND"+0050    RTS
```

Figure 7-13 Disassembly of KillWindow

```
Template {WindowRecord @00CD5C} (addr):00CCB8
:address=07A700:rowBytes=40:bounds=FFBD FFDD 0113 01DD:portRect=0000 0000 0085 0
:visRgn=00CB98:clipRgn=00CB94:windowKind=0008:invisible:hilited:goAway:
:strucRgn=00CB90:contRgn=00CB8C:updateRgn=00CB88:defProc=00CBAC:dataHandle=00000
:controlList=000000:nextWindow=00CCB8:refCon=0000CB80:title="Window 2":
```

Figure 7-14 Window template display

Let's backtrack and see how DoCommand passed the wrong window pointer to KillWindow. Looking back in the source at the line that called this procedure, we see that it says KillWindow (FrontWindow). Reality check time. What's FrontWindow? It's a ROM function that returns the frontmost window. Isn't that what we wanted to pass to KillWindow? Think about it: before we called KillWindow, we'd already called DisposeWindow on the frontmost window ("Window 3"); this caused "Window 2" to move up to the front. When KillWindow (FrontWindow) was executed, FrontWindow had become "Window 2". That's why KillWindow is about to dispose of it: DoCommand called it with a screwy parameter. So paying attention has enabled us to catch a bug we hadn't even noticed yet. We'll resolve to watch ROM-call parameters even more closely from now on.

We're Not So Smart

If we had been in superparanoid mode, we might have noticed this bug when we called KillWindow (if you did—congratulations!). If we were doing strong reality checks, we could have checked the window pointer returned by FrontWindow with the Template function and seen that it wasn't the window we expected. In practice, though, this kind of vigilance is hard to maintain. It takes a long time to check every parameter to every call. If you're looking for an elusive bug, though . . . .

The problem here is that we're calling DisposeWindow twice, where once would do. Which one should we leave in? If we dispose of the window before calling KillWindow, the window pointer that we pass to KillWindow is invalid, because the window record has been deallocated. For this reason, we should fix this problem by removing the DisposeWindow call before calling KillWindow.

Could this silly bug have caused the address error we got the first time? It doesn't seem likely; we haven't yet run into any code that would cause an address error. All that happens as a result of this bug is that the two front windows get disposed, instead of just the frontmost. So we need to keep tracing to find the address error bug. Onward.

Looking for the Address Error

After disposing of "Window 2", the code sets the variable hText to Nil, since there's no longer an active TextEdit record. Then it checks to see if FrontWindow is Nil, that is, if there are no windows. Since there is still another window, even though our mad program has closed two for the price of one, FrontWindow is not Nil and the BNE to $CFF4 is taken (see Figure 7-13).

Here the if statement that ends KillWindow is executed. It checks to see if the new frontmost window is a desk accessory by looking at its windowKind field; if this value is less than zero, it's a desk accessory. In our example, of course, it's not a desk accessory, so we jump to the "else" part of the statement, which disables the Undo menu item, since it's only supported for desk accessories. Then the procedure finishes up by unbuilding the stack frame and incrementing the stack pointer past the parameter—standard stuff.

Now that we're done with KillWindow, we've returned to the end of DoCommand (Figure 7-15). The last statement in DoCommand is HiliteMenu (0), and then the procedure packs up and goes home.

Well, we've now traced all the way through DoCommand and KillWindow and we haven't found the address error yet. Debugging requires persistence, so don't get tired yet. It's not unheard of to have to trace for hours to find a bug (that probably doesn't surprise you, though).

When DoCommand returns, it returns to the end of the main event loop, to the until doneFlag test, which is the end of the giant repeat-until loop that forms the main event loop. This test fails, of course, since doneFlag is false, so the program branches back up to the beginning of the main event loop to do it all again. So will we.

```
DISASSEMBLY FROM 00D22C
00D22C:P   "DOCOMMAN"+012A    CLR.W    -(A7)
00D22E:    "DOCOMMAN"+012C    _HiliteMenu
00D230:    "DOCOMMAN"+012E    MOVEM.L  (A7)+,D5-D7
00D234:    "DOCOMMAN"+0132    UNLK     A6
00D236:    "DOCOMMAN"+0134    MOVE.L   (A7)+,(A7)
00D238:    "DOCOMMAN"+0136    RTS
```

Figure 7-15 Disassembly from DoCommand

The next chunk of code is displayed in Figure 7-16. The first thing in the loop, as confirmed by our source listing, is a call to SystemTask. Since this call takes no parameters, there's nothing that can go wrong. The program next checks to see if FrontWindow is Nil; it's not, so it then looks to see if the frontmost window is an application window. Since it is, it calls the FixCursor procedure.

You can see FixCursor's object code in Figure 7-17. It looks pretty harmless, but we'll trace through it just in case. It begins by calling GetMouse and then tests to see if the coordinate returned by GetMouse is in the current GrafPort's port rectangle. If so, it sets the cursor to the I-beam; if not, the cursor is set to an arrow. The procedure then does its epilog and returns to the caller. Hmmm . . . guess it was harmless after all.

```
00D306:P   "SHOWOFF "+007C   _SystemTask
00D308:     "SHOWOFF "+007E   CLR.L     -(A7)
00D30A:     "SHOWOFF "+0080   _FrontWindow
00D30C:     "SHOWOFF "+0082   TST.L     (A7)+
00D30E:     "SHOWOFF "+0084   BEQ.S     ^$00D320         ;"SHOWOFF "+0096
00D310:     "SHOWOFF "+0086   CLR.L     -(A7)
00D312:     "SHOWOFF "+0088   _FrontWindow
00D314:     "SHOWOFF "+008A   MOVEA.L   (A7)+,A0
00D316:     "SHOWOFF "+008C   TST.W     $006C(A0)
00D31A:     "SHOWOFF "+0090   BLT.S     ^$00D320         ;"SHOWOFF "+0096
00D31C:     "SHOWOFF "+0092   JSR       ^$00D244         ;"FIXCURSO"+0000
00D320:     "SHOWOFF "+0096   MOVE.B    $FE13(A5),D0
00D324:     "SHOWOFF "+009A   EORI.B    #$01,D0
00D328:     "SHOWOFF "+009E   MOVE.L    D0,-(A7)
00D32A:     "SHOWOFF "+00A0   CLR.L     -(A7)
00D32C:     "SHOWOFF "+00A2   _FrontWindow
00D32E:     "SHOWOFF "+00A4   MOVE.L    (A7)+,D1
00D330:     "SHOWOFF "+00A6   MOVE.L    (A7)+,D0
00D332:     "SHOWOFF "+00A8   TST.L     D1
00D334:     "SHOWOFF "+00AA   SEQ       D1
00D336:     "SHOWOFF "+00AC   AND.B     D1,D0
00D338:     "SHOWOFF "+00AE   BEQ.S     ^$00D352         ;"SHOWOFF "+00C8
00D33A:     "SHOWOFF "+00B0   MOVE.L    $FFF8(A5),-(A7)
00D33E:     "SHOWOFF "+00B4   MOVE.W    #$0003,-(A7)
00D342:     "SHOWOFF "+00B8   _DisableItem
00D344:     "SHOWOFF "+00BA   MOVE.L    $FFFC(A5),-(A7)
00D348:     "SHOWOFF "+00BE   CLR.W     -(A7)
00D34A:     "SHOWOFF "+00C0   _DisableItem
00D34C:     "SHOWOFF "+00C2   MOVE.B    #$01,$FE13(A5)
00D352:     "SHOWOFF "+00C8   MOVE.L    $FFE0(A5),-(A7)
00D356:     "SHOWOFF "+00CC   _TEIdle
00D358:     "SHOWOFF "+00CE   CLR.W     -(A7)
00D35A:     "SHOWOFF "+00D0   MOVE.W    #$FFFF,-(A7)
00D35E:     "SHOWOFF "+00D4   PEA       $FFCC(A5)
00D362:     "SHOWOFF "+00D8   _GetNextEvent
```

Figure 7-16 Disassembly from Showoff

```
DISASSEMBLY FROM 00D244
00D244:P   "FIXCURSO"+0000   LINK     A6,#$FFFC
00D248:    "FIXCURSO"+0004   PEA      $FFFC(A6)
00D24C:    "FIXCURSO"+0008   _GetMouse
00D24E:    "FIXCURSO"+000A   CLR.W    -(A7)
00D250:    "FIXCURSO"+000C   MOVE.L   $FFFC(A6),-(A7)
00D254:    "FIXCURSO"+0010   MOVEA.L  $FA40(A5),A0
00D258:    "FIXCURSO"+0014   PEA      $0010(A0)
00D25C:    "FIXCURSO"+0018   _PtInRect
00D25E:    "FIXCURSO"+001A   MOVE.B   (A7)+,D0
00D260:    "FIXCURSO"+001C   BEQ.S    ^$00D272              ;"FIXCURSO"+002E
00D262:    "FIXCURSO"+001E   CLR.L    -(A7)
00D264:    "FIXCURSO"+0020   MOVE.W   #$0001,-(A7)
00D268:    "FIXCURSO"+0024   _GetCursor
00D26A:    "FIXCURSO"+0026   MOVEA.L  (A7)+,A0
00D26C:    "FIXCURSO"+0028   MOVE.L   (A0),-(A7)
00D26E:    "FIXCURSO"+002A   _SetCursor
00D270:    "FIXCURSO"+002C   BRA.S    ^$00D278              ;"FIXCURSO"+0034
00D272:    "FIXCURSO"+002E   PEA      $F9D4(A5)
00D276:    "FIXCURSO"+0032   _SetCursor
00D278:    "FIXCURSO"+0034   UNLK     A6
00D27A:    "FIXCURSO"+0036   RTS
```

Figure 7-17 Disassembly of FixCursor

Stamina Check

Don't bail out yet! I know it seems like we've been tracing for a long time and haven't found the address error yet. After a little practice, and without having to read this narrative, you'll be able to do all the tracing we've done so far in about 10 minutes, so this is still considered a lightweight debugging session. Go get something to drink, then continue.

Next, back in Figure 7-16, the program checks the global menusOK. This variable is used to help adjust the menus if there are no windows open. The code looks at menusOK to see if it's false (zero) and then calls FrontWindow. If menusOK is false and there are no windows, it does some menu fixing; in our case, FrontWindow is not Nil, so the BEQ to the next statement is taken.

The next statement in the source calls TEIdle with the parameter textH. Hold on—we know that the address error is caused by calling TEIdle with a Nil handle, and, yes, we did set textH to Nil a while ago. Let's do a reality check: examine the parameter textH [−20(A5)] after it's pushed on the stack. Sure enough, it's zero, which is the value for Nil. We found it! Just to make sure (another reality check), let's try to single-step through the TEIdle. As soon as we do, we get the same address error we got before.

Now that we've found the problem, we have to decide how to fix it. What's the value that should have been passed to TEIdle? Well, TEIdle is called with the currently active TextEdit record. At the moment, we don't have an active TextEdit record: we just closed a window, and we'll get an active TextEdit record when the new frontmost window's activate event is handled. So we don't know what TextEdit record to activate. Also, consider the case of the last window on the screen. When we close it, there's no TextEdit record to idle until another window is opened.

It seems like a reasonable thing to do is to test textH to see if it's Nil and, if not, to call TEIdle. If it is Nil, there's nothing to do. So we'll change the TEIdle (textH) statement to if textH <> Nil then TEIdle (textH). This should fix the address error problem.

At some point in debugging a program that still has several bugs to be chased, you have to decide when to end a debugging session and rebuild the program with the fixes you've decided on. It's usually a good time to do this when you fix a fatal bug that has no workaround. In this case, we've just fixed a fatal bug that we can work around by not closing any windows.

Whether to rebuild now is a judgment call. Some programmers like to implement fixes and rebuild their programs after every minor change; most, however, find this too time consuming and save up several changes to add at one time. You decide.

Magic

Sometimes it's useful or fun to try a potential fix to a program without rebuilding the program. If you're pretty comfortable writing assembly language or you like to experiment, you can do this by applying a **patch** to the program. This means that you actually modify the object code right before your very eyes. Obviously, this is hard to do if it's not a simple change. But if it is an easy change, such as a constant 10 that should have been 20, you can use the debugger's ability to change bytes in memory to modify the program. Some debuggers even have built-in assemblers, as in TMON's Disassembly window, so you can actually modify the instruction, not just data. Patching your code on the fly like this is interesting and can be useful in testing proposed changes, but don't forget to rebuild the program with the change applied to the source code!

In this case, we won't rebuild the application right now. We'll just rerun it and avoid closing any windows.

Finding the Text Bug

We can use the debugger to restart the application after quitting to the Finder. Just to refresh your memory, we observed two other problems that we need to track down. The first was the odd behavior of text in windows: no blinking insertion point and no unhighlighting of old selections when a new selection was made. The second problem was windows going blank when we dragged other windows around.

Let's think about the first problem for a moment. The instruction that makes the insertion point blink is TEIdle. We've already discovered that we've been calling TEIdle with a Nil handle after closing a window. Could that bug be causing this problem too? One way to find out is to instruct the debugger to record TEIdle calls and then examine the calls.

We enter the debugger in the usual way, by pressing the interrupt button. We then tell the Trap Record command that we want to record TEIdle calls that come from RAM-based (that is, our application) code. We exit the debugger, let the application run for a few seconds then press interrupt again. We can then use a Dump window to examine the recorded traps (see Figure 7-18).

```
DUMP FROM 003370
003370:V    A9 DA 16 97    00 00 D3 56    00 00 CB A4    00 40 4D 0E    .......V.....@M.
003380:     A9 DA 16 94    00 00 D3 56    00 00 CB A4    00 40 4D 0E    .......V.....@M.
003390:     A9 DA 16 94    00 00 D3 56    00 00 CB A4    00 40 4D 0E    .......V.....@M.
0033A0:     A9 DA 16 93    00 00 D3 56    00 00 CB A4    00 40 4D 0E    .......V.....@M.
0033B0:     A9 DA 16 93    00 00 D3 56    00 00 CB A4    00 40 4D 0E    .......V.....@M.
0033C0:     A9 DA 16 92    00 00 D3 56    00 00 CB A4    00 40 4D 0E    .......V.....@M.
0033D0:     A9 DA 16 92    00 00 D3 56    00 00 CB A4    00 40 4D 0E    .......V.....@M.
0033E0:     A9 DA 16 91    00 00 D3 56    00 00 CB A4    00 40 4D 0E    .......V.....@M.
0033F0:     A9 DA 16 90    00 00 D3 56    00 00 CB A4    00 40 4D 0E    .......V.....@M.
003400:     A9 DA 16 90    00 00 D3 56    00 00 CB A4    00 40 4D 0E    .......V.....@M.
```

Figure 7-18 Trap Record display

Remember that the first two bytes are the trap word; in this case, they're all $A9DA, which is TEIdle. The next two values, Ticks and the program counter at the time the trap was executed, aren't of interest to us here. The third set of four bytes is what we're after. This is the value at the top of the stack. In the case of TEIdle, which takes one parameter, it's the handle to the TextEdit record.

In every case we've recorded in this table, the TEIdle call was passed $0000CBA4 as its parameter. A quick check with the User window's Template command shows that this appears to be a good handle to a real TextEdit record. Also, our recording shows that we're not calling TEIdle (Nil) as long as there's an active TextEdit record. So it seems that the lack of a blinking insertion point can't be blamed on bad calls (or lack of calls) to TEIdle.

What else could be going wrong? Let's think about the basics of displaying text with TextEdit. We can use **Inside Macintosh** for help. According to the "Using TextEdit" section of **Inside Macintosh's** Text-Edit chapter, we start by calling TEInit; we call TENew to allocate a new TextEdit record; TEIdle is used to make the insertion point blink; and TEActivate is used to highlight the text or display an insertion point when the window becomes active. That's all there is to it.

Are we doing these things? A quick check of the beginning of the main program shows that we do call TEInit; let's set up the debugger to catch calls to the other traps. We'll use the Trap intercept command in the User window to look for TENew. After setting up this command, we return to the application and then open a new window. As the window opens, we enter the debugger with a "Trap intercepted" message. The Disassembly window is shown in Figure 7-19, along with the top of the stack.

```
DISASSEMBLY FROM 00CF44
00CF44:P ⌐"OPENWIND"+009A    _TENew
00CF46:    "OPENWIND"+009C    MOVE.L  (A7)+,$FFE0(A5)
00CF4A:    "OPENWIND"+00A0    MOVE.L  $FF2C(A5),$FF28(A5)


DUMP FROM 000000(A7)
0695D2:S   00 06 9E 86   00 06 9E 86   00 00 00 00   08 57 69 6E   ............Win
```

Figure 7-19 Disassembly from OpenWindow and top of stack

We can single-step through the TENew call to see if it returns a valid handle. After stepping through TENew, there's a reasonable looking handle, $CB7C, on the top of the stack. Doing a reality check on this handle by looking at it with the User window's Template function shows that it's a real TextEdit record, so the call to TENew seems to have worked.

Now that we know that TENew is being called properly, we need to check to make sure that TEActivate is getting called when the new window's activate event is handled. To do this, we set the Trap intercept function to look for TEActivate and return to the application. It should zap right back into the debugger when in encounters the TEActivate . . . but it doesn't! Is the program hung? No, it still seems fully functional: we can drag windows, pull down menus, and type normally.

So what happened to TEActivate? For some reason, it was never called. To see if we can figure out why, let's take a look at the source code for the activate event-handling case of the main event loop.

A quick look at the source listing shows why TEActivate isn't getting called: it's not there! Apparently we just forgot to put it in the program! Nice bug, eh? It seems like we can fix this one just by adding a TEActivate call to the activate event-handling code.

This kind of numb-brained error is often called a **gross bug** because it's so massive and obvious. Of course, I've never created a bug like this, and neither have you. Right?

Finding the Window-erase Bug

Now we can go looking for the other problem that we discovered: the front window getting erased when we drag it off another window. Let's think: what can cause a window's text to be erased? One likely cause is an inadvertent call to EraseRect. The application calls EraseRect in its update event-handling code. Maybe we're erasing the wrong rectangle.

```
DUMP FROM @RA7
00CCC8:        00 00 00 00   00 85 00 C8
```

Figure 7-20 Rectangle pointer on stack

To find out, we can tell the debugger to intercept EraseRect calls that are made from code in the application heap. First, we open two windows. We type some text into each window and then drag "Window 2" on top of "Window 1", making "Window 2" the frontmost. Then we drag "Window 2" away, uncovering "Window 1". When we do this, the debugger kicks in with a "Trap intercepted" message as soon as it finds the EraseRect call in the update event-handling code.

Before we step through the EraseRect, let's do a reality check on its parameter, which is the rectangle that's about to be erased. The top of the stack holds a pointer to this rectangle. To see the rectangle, we can open a Dump window (see Figure 7-20). The rectangle's coordinates appear to have the proper dimensions for one of our window's port rectangles (0,0, $85, $C8).

Something else that's important to many QuickDraw calls, including EraseRect, is the current GrafPort. EraseRect erases the specified rectangle in the current GrafPort, so we should check the current GrafPort. Since the program should be updating the window that was just uncovered, "Window 1", it should be the current GrafPort.

We can check the value of the current port in the global called thePort; you might remember from Chapter 6 that register A5 contains the address of a pointer to thePort. By using a Dump window, we see that thePort is $CD5C. To see which window this indicates, we can use the User window's Template function. The result of this is shown in Figure 7-21.

```
Template {WindowRecord @00CD5C} (addr):00CCB8
:address=07A700:rowBytes=40:bounds=FFBD FFDD 0113 01DD:portRect=0000 0000 0085 0
:visRgn=00CB98:clipRgn=00CB94:windowKind=0008:invisible:hilited:goAway:
:strucRgn=00CB90:contRgn=00CB8C:updateRgn=00CB88:defProc=00CBAC:dataHandle=00000
:controlList=000000:nextWindow=00CCB8:refCon=0000CB80:title="Window 2":
```

Figure 7-21 Window template display

The interesting field here is "title". It says that the current port is "Window 2", not "Window 1" as we had expected. This means that the `EraseRect` that is about to happen will erase "Window 2"'s port rectangle! That's our bug!

Let's analyze what's going wrong here. We're in the update event-handling code. What we want to do here is erase the port rectangle of the window that's being updated. Looking at the source code, we had the right idea by calling `EraseRect (WindowPtr (myEvent.message)^.portRect)`. That's the right rectangle, since `myEvent.message` contains a pointer to the window that needs to be updated. But for `EraseRect` to work, we have to set `thePort` to point at this window. Also, it would be nice if the setting of `thePort` at the beginning of the update event-handling code were restored at the end, so that any other drawing code in the application isn't confused; this is a standard good practice, called **preserving the port**.

What we'll do is add to the beginning of the update event-handling code a `GetPort` call, which will save the current port, followed by a `SetPort (myEvent.message)`, which will set the port to the window that needs updating. At the end of the code, we'll add a `SetPort` call, which sets the port back to the one preserved at the start of the code. This should fix our "erasing the wrong window" bug.

Looking for More Bugs

We've now found all the bugs that we'd discovered previously (hooray for us), so it seems like this is a pretty good time to rebuild the application. Then we'll run it again to make sure we fixed the bugs we thought we fixed and see if we can find any more.

The new, fixed version of the program is shown in Listing 7-2. Let's run it and see if the bugs have really been fixed. As the program starts up, we see a good sign: "Window 1" now has a blinking insertion point, which says that adding TEActivate seems to have worked (you should always think in nonabsolute, vaguely negative terms like this when dealing with debugging—you never know when the computer might be reading your mind).

```
program Showoff;

  uses
    {$U HD:MPW:Interfaces.p:MemTypes.p } MemTypes,
    {$U HD:MPW:Interfaces.p:QuickDraw.p} QuickDraw,
    {$U HD:MPW:Interfaces.p:OSIntf.p    } OSIntf,
    {$U HD:MPW:Interfaces.p:ToolIntf.p } ToolIntf,
    {$U HD:MPW:Interfaces.p:PackIntf.p } PackIntf;

  const
    appleID = 128;   {resource IDs/menu IDs for Apple, File and Edit menus}
    fileID  = 129;
    editID  = 130;

    appleM = 1; {index for each menu in myMenus (array of menu handles)}
    fileM  = 2;
    editM  = 3;

    menuCount = 3;       {total number of menus}

    aboutItem = 1;       {item in Apple menu}

    undoItem  = 1;       {Items in Edit menu}
    cutItem   = 3;
    copyItem  = 4;
    pasteItem = 5;
    clearitem = 6;

    newItem = 1;       {items in File menu}
    closeItem = 3;
    quitItem = 5;

    wName = 'Window ';   {prefix for window names}

    windDX = 25;        {distance to move for new windows}
    windDY = 25;

    leftEdge = 10;      {initial dimensions of window}
    topEdge = 42;
    rightEdge = 210;
    botEdge = 175;
```

Listing 7-2

```
var
   myMenus: array [1..menuCount] OF MenuHandle; {handles to the menus}
   dragRect: Rect;          {rectangle used to mark boundaries for dragging window}
   txRect: Rect;            {rectangle for text in application window}
   textH: TEHandle;         {handle to Textedit record}
   theChar: char;           {typed character}
   extended: boolean;       {true if user is Shift-clicking}
   doneFlag: boolean;       {true if user has chosen Quit Item}
   myEvent: EventRecord;    {information about an event}
   wRecord: WindowRecord;   {information about the application window}
   myWindow: WindowPtr;     {pointer to wRecord}
   myWinPeek : WindowPeek;  {another pointer to wRecord}
   whichWindow: WindowPtr;  {window in which mouse button was pressed}
   nextWRect: Rect;         {portRect for next window to be opended}
   nextWTitle: Str255;      {title of next window to be opened}
   nextWNum: Longint;       {number of next window (for title)}
   savedPort: GrafPtr;      {pointer to preserve GrafPort}
   menusOK: boolean;        {for disabling menu items}
   scrapErr: Longint;
   scrCopyErr: Integer;

procedure SetUpMenus;
{ set up menus and menu bar }

   var
     i: Integer;

   begin
     myMenus[appleM] := GetMenu(appleID); {read Apple menu}
     AddResMenu(myMenus[appleM],'DRVR');  {add desk accessory names}
     myMenus[fileM] := GetMenu(fileID);   {read file menu }
     myMenus[editM] := GetMenu(editID);   {read Edit menu }

     for i:=1 to menuCount do
        InsertMenu(myMenus[i],0);  {install menus in menu bar }
     DrawMenuBar;  { and draw menu bar}
   end;  {SetUpMenus}
```

Listing 7-2 (*continued*)

```
procedure OpenWindow;
{ Open a new window }

  begin
    NumToString (nextWNum, nextWTitle); {prepare number for title}
    nextWTitle := concat (wName, nextWTitle); {add to prefix}
    myWindow := NewWindow (Nil, nextWRect, nextWTitle, True, noGrowDocProc,
      Pointer (-1), True, 0);    {open the window}
    SetPort (myWindow);              {make it the current port}
    txRect := thePort^.portRect;{prepare TERecord for new window}
    InsetRect (txRect, 4, 0);
    textH := TENew (txRect, txRect);
    myWinPeek := WindowPeek (myWindow);
    myWinPeek^.refcon := Longint (textH); {keep TEHandle in refcon!}
    OffsetRect (nextWRect, windDX, windDY);{move window down and right}
    if nextWRect.right > dragRect.right   {move back if it's too far over}
      then OffsetRect (nextWRect, -nextWRect.left + leftEdge, 0);
    if nextWRect.bottom > dragRect.bottom
      then OffsetRect (nextWRect, 0, -nextWRect.top + topEdge);
    nextWNum := nextWNum + 1;    {bump number for next window}
    menusOK := false;
    EnableItem (myMenus [editM],0); {in case this is the only window}
  end; {OpenWindow}


procedure KillWindow (theWindow: WindowPtr);
{Close a window and throw everything away}

  begin
    TEDispose (TEHandle (WindowPeek (theWindow)^.refcon));
                              {throw away TERecord}
    DisposeWindow (theWindow);  {throw away WindowRecord}
    textH := NIL;               {for TEIdle in main event loop}
    if FrontWindow = NIL        {if no more windows, disable Close}
      then DisableItem (myMenus[fileM], closeItem);
    if WindowPeek (FrontWindow)^.windowKind < 0
                              {if a desk acc is coming up, enable undo}
      then EnableItem (myMenus[editM], undoItem)
      else DisableItem (myMenus[editM], undoItem);

  end; {KillWindow}
```

Listing 7-2 (*continued*)

```
function MyFilter (theDialog: DialogPtr; var theEvent: EventRecord;
    var itemHit: Integer): Boolean;

  var
    theType: Integer;
    theItem: Handle;
    theBox: Rect;
    finalTicks: Longint;

  begin
    if (BitAnd(theEvent.message,charCodeMask) = 13) {carriage return}
      or (BitAnd(theEvent.message,charCodeMask) = 3) {enter}
      then
        begin
          GetDItem (theDialog, 1, theType, theItem, theBox);
          HiliteControl (ControlHandle (theItem), 1);
          Delay (8, finalTicks);
          HiliteControl (ControlHandle (theItem), 0);
          itemHit := 1;
          MyFilter := True;
        end {if BitAnd...then begin}
      else MyFilter := False;
  end; {function MyFilter}


procedure DoAboutBox;

  var
    itemHit: Integer;

  begin
    myWindow := GetNewDialog (1000, Nil, pointer (-1));
    repeat
      ModalDialog (@MyFilter, itemHit)
    until itemHit = 1;
    DisposDialog (myWindow);
  end; {procedure DoAboutBox}


procedure DoCommand (mResult: LONGINT);
{Execute Item specified by mResult, the result of MenuSelect}

  var
    theItem: Integer; {menu item number from mResult low-order word}
    theMenu: Integer; {menu number from mResult high-order word}
    name: Str255;     {desk accessory name}
    temp: Integer;
```

Listing 7-2 (*continued*)

```
begin
  theItem := LoWord(mResult); {call Toolbox Utility routines to set }
  theMenu := HiWord(mResult);     { menu item number and menu number}

  case theMenu of              {case on menu ID}

    appleID:
      if theItem = aboutItem
        then DoAboutBox
        else
          begin
            GetItem(myMenus[appleM],theItem,name);
            {GetPort (savedPort);}
            scrapErr := ZeroScrap;
            scrCopyErr := TEToScrap;
            temp := OpenDeskAcc(name);
            EnableItem (myMenus [editM],0);
            {SetPort (savedPort);}
            if FrontWindow <> NIL
              then
                begin
                  EnableItem (myMenus [fileM], closeItem);
                  EnableItem (myMenus [editM], undoItem);
                end; {if FrontWindow then begin}
            menusOK := false;
          end;  {if theItem...else begin}
    fileID:
      case theItem of

        newItem:
          OpenWindow;

        closeItem:
          if WindowPeek (FrontWindow)^.windowKind < 0
            then CloseDeskAcc (windowPeek (FrontWindow)^.windowKind)
            {if desk acc window, close it}
            else KillWindow (FrontWindow);
            {if it's one of mine, blow it away}

        quitItem:
          doneFlag := TRUE; {quit}

      end; {case theItem}
```

Listing 7-2 (*continued*)

```
      editID:
        begin
          if not SystemEdit(theItem-1)
            then
              case theItem of {case on menu item number}

                cutItem:
                  TECut(textH); {call TextEdit to handle Item}

                copyItem:
                  TECopy(textH);

                pasteItem:
                  TEPaste(textH);

                clearItem:
                  TEDelete(textH);

              end;      {case theItem}
          end;      {editID begin}

      end;      {case theMenu}
      HiliteMenu(0);
  end;   {DoCommand}


procedure FixCursor;

  var
    mouseLoc: point;

begin
  GetMouse (mouseLoc);
  if PtInRect (mouseLoc, thePort^.portRect)
    then SetCursor (GetCursor (iBeamCursor)^^)
    else SetCursor (arrow);
end; {procedure FixCursor}
```

Listing 7-2 (*continued*)

```
begin          {main program}

   InitGraf(@thePort);
   InitFonts;
   FlushEvents(everyEvent,0);
   InitWindows;
   InitMenus;
   TEInit;
   InitDialogs(NIL);
   InitCursor;

   SetUpMenus;
     with screenBits.bounds do
       SetRect(dragRect,4,24,right-4,bottom-4);
       doneFlag := false;

   menusOK := false;
   nextWNum := 1;      {initialize window number}
   SetRect (nextWRect,leftEdge,topEdge,rightEdge,botEdge);
                       {initialize window rectangle}
   OpenWindow;         {start with one open window}

{ Main event loop }
   repeat
     SystemTask;
     if FrontWindow <> NIL
       then
         if WindowPeek (FrontWindow)^.windowKind >= 0
           then FixCursor;
     if not menusOK and (FrontWindow = NIL)
       then
         begin
           DisableItem (myMenus [fileM], closeItem);
           DisableItem (myMenus [editM], 0);
           menusOK := true;
         end; {if FrontWindow...then begin}
     if textH <> Nil
       then TEIdle(textH);

     if GetNextEvent(everyEvent,myEvent)
       then
       case myEvent.what of
```

Listing 7-2 (*continued*)

```
mouseDown:
  case FindWindow(myEvent.where,whichWindow) of

     inSysWindow:
        SystemClick(myEvent,whichWindow);

     inMenuBar:
        DoCommand(MenuSelect(myEvent.where));

     inDrag:
        DragWindow(whichWindow,myEvent.where,dragRect);

     inContent:
        begin
          if whichWindow <> FrontWindow
            then SelectWindow(whichWindow)
            else
              begin
                GlobalToLocal(myEvent.where);
                extended := BitAnd(myEvent.modifiers,shiftKey) <> 0;
                TEClick(myEvent.where,extended,textH);
              end;  {else}
        end;  {inContent}

     inGoAway:
        if TrackGoAway (whichWindow, myEvent.where)
          then KillWindow (whichWindow);

  end;    {case FindWindow}

keyDown, autoKey:
  begin
    theChar := CHR(BitAnd(myEvent.message,charCodeMask));
    if BitAnd(myEvent.modifiers,cmdKey) <> 0
    then DoCommand(MenuKey(theChar))
    else TEKey(theChar,textH);
  end;  {keyDown, autoKey begin}
```

Listing 7-2 (*continued*)

```
activateEvt:
  begin
  if BitAnd(myEvent.modifiers,activeFlag) <> 0
    then  {application window is becoming active}
      begin
        SetPort (GrafPtr (myEvent.message));
        textH := TEHandle (WindowPeek (myEvent.message)^.refcon);
        TEActivate(textH);
        EnableItem (myMenus[fileM],closeItem);
        DisableItem(myMenus[editM],undoItem);
        if WindowPeek (FrontWindow)^.nextWindow^.windowKind < 0
          then scrCopyErr := TEFromScrap;
      end {if BitAnd...then begin}
    else  {application window is becoming inactive}
      begin
      TEDeactivate(TEHandle(WindowPeek(myEvent.message)^.refcon));
      if WindowPeek (FrontWindow)^.windowKind < 0
        then
          begin
            EnableItem (myMenus[editM], undoItem);
            scrapErr := ZeroScrap;
            scrCopyErr := TEToScrap;
          end {if WindowPeek...then begin}
        else DisableItem (myMenus[editM], undoItem);
      end;  {else begin}
  end;  {activateEvt begin}

updateEvt:
  begin
    GetPort (savedPort);
    SetPort (GrafPtr (myEvent.message));
    BeginUpdate(WindowPtr(myEvent.message));
    EraseRect(WindowPtr(myEvent.message)^.portRect);
    TEUpdate(WindowPtr(myEvent.message)^.portRect,
    TEHandle(WindowPeek(myEvent.message)^.refcon));
    EndUpdate(WindowPtr(myEvent.message));
    SetPort (savedPort);
  end;  {updateEvt begin}

end;  {case myEvent.what}

until doneFlag;
end.
```

Listing 7-2 (*continued*)

Next we'll try opening another window, typing text into the two windows, and then dragging them on top of each other and away from each other. This is working OK, too, so it looks like our SetPort fix in the update event-handler was the right thing to do.

Now we're ready for the big one: closing a window. If you remember, there were two problems here: two windows were getting disposed of, and we were getting an address error when the program called TEIdle with a Nil handle.

When we close a window now, everything seems to be working fine. The window we close goes away, and the window behind it becomes the new frontmost window. Only one window is being closed, and no address errors in sight. Success!

All the bugs we found seem to be fixed. We should now spend a few minutes exercising the application to see if we can find anything else wrong. In fact, just to give you something to do, I've left a really vicious bug in the program for you to seek and destroy. All I'll tell you about this bug is that it causes a system error, is easily accessible and reproducible, and should be found if you're careful to try out all the program's features (and there aren't that many features to try). If you want another clue, here's how to make the problem appear (use your debugger to translate hex into ASCII):

$4F 70 65 6E 20 41 62 6F 75 74 20 42 6F 78 20 74 77 69 63 65

Isn't this fun?

Know What You're Doing

One unfortunate symptom of sloppy programming is the magical bug fix. That is, you've got a problem somewhere in your program and you know that if you insert some blessed line of code somewhere the problem goes away. You don't fully understand what the problem is, you don't know why the magical line of code fixes it, but you're happy, since it's one less bug for you to worry about. Don't fall into this trap! If you're in this situation, you're dooming yourself in two ways. First, you've added code to your program that you don't really understand. Second, and more important, you probably haven't fixed the bug. If a magical line of code seems to make the problem go away and you don't understand why, it'll probably come back later and kill you (or your customers). What do you do then?

Debugging and understanding what your code really does is the key to avoiding this situation. Obviously, if you really know what your code is doing, you can figure out what it takes to fix it. Understand that magical bug fix code is like a secret incantation: it seems to work, but you don't know why.

It's important to realize that not all short pieces of code that fix problems are bad. Frequently, a bug will be fixed by a single instruction or parameter change. That's great—just be sure you know what the problem was and why the fix works, or you can bet that you'll get it in the end.

Optimizing with the Debugger

Once you get rid of a program's bugs, you can use a debugger to help you optimize the program, that is, make it run faster and smarter by eliminating waste and doing a better job of memory management. There are two basic categories of problems: bad practices in code and bad management of data. If you're using a compiler, there are some things you can do to get better code, but, in general, you pretty much have to live with what the compiler generates. If it's a fairly smart compiler, like Workshop Pascal, this isn't so bad. You can always write the most crucial pieces of the application in assembly language and link them as external routines.

Management of your data objects, on the other hand, is up to you. To demonstrate some of the atrocities that people inflict on their data, we can use a debugger to examine the application heap zone while running a program. The program we'll use is a version of the one we've been using in this chapter that's been slightly modified to be atrocious. It's shown in Listing 7-3.

```
program Showoff;

  uses
    {$U HD:MPW:Interfaces.p:MemTypes.p } MemTypes,
    {$U HD:MPW:Interfaces.p:QuickDraw.p} QuickDraw,
    {$U HD:MPW:Interfaces.p:OSIntf.p   } OSIntf,
    {$U HD:MPW:Interfaces.p:ToolIntf.p } ToolIntf,
    {$U HD:MPW:Interfaces.p:PackIntf.p } PackIntf;

  const
    appleID = 128; {resource IDs/menu IDs for Apple, File and Edit menus}
    fileID  = 129;
    editID  = 130;

    appleM = 1; {index for each menu in myMenus (array of menu handles)}
    fileM  = 2;
    editM  = 3;

    menuCount = 3;       {total number of menus}

    aboutItem = 1;       {item in Apple menu}

    undoItem  = 1;       {Items in Edit menu}
    cutItem   = 3;
    copyItem  = 4;
    pasteItem = 5;
    clearitem = 6;

    newItem = 1;         {items in File menu}
    closeItem = 3;
    quitItem = 5;

    wName = 'Window ';   {prefix for window names}

    windDX = 25;         {distance to move for new windows}
    windDY = 25;

    leftEdge = 10;       {initial dimensions of window}
    topEdge = 42;
    rightEdge = 210;
    botEdge = 175;
```

Listing 7-3

```
var
   myMenus: array [1..menuCount] OF MenuHandle; {handles to the menus}
   dragRect: Rect;          {rectangle used to mark boundaries for dragging window}
   txRect: Rect;            {rectangle for text in application window}
   textH: TEHandle;         {handle to Textedit record}
   theChar: char;           {typed character}
   extended: boolean;       {true if user is Shift-clicking}
   doneFlag: boolean;       {true if user has chosen Quit Item}
   myEvent: EventRecord;    {information about an event}
   wRecord: WindowRecord;   {information about the application window}
   myWindow: WindowPtr;     {pointer to wRecord}
   myWinPeek : WindowPeek;  {another pointer to wRecord}
   whichWindow: WindowPtr;  {window in which mouse button was pressed}
   nextWRect: Rect;         {portRect for next window to be opended}
   nextWTitle: Str255;      {title of next window to be opened}
   nextWNum: Longint;       {number of next window (for title)}
   savedPort: GrafPtr;      {pointer to preserve GrafPort}
   menusOK: boolean;        {for disabling menu items}
   scrapErr: Longint;
   scrCopyErr: Integer;
   dummy: Handle;


{$S InitSeg}
procedure SetUpMenus;
{ set up menus and menu bar }

   var
      i: Integer;

   begin
      myMenus[appleM] := GetMenu(appleID); {read Apple menu}
      AddResMenu(myMenus[appleM],'DRVR');  {add desk accessory names}
      myMenus[fileM] := GetMenu(fileID);   {read file menu }
      myMenus[editM] := GetMenu(editID);   {read Edit menu }

      for i:=1 to menuCount do
         InsertMenu(myMenus[i],0);  {install menus in menu bar }
      DrawMenuBar;   { and draw menu bar}
   end;   {SetUpMenus}
```

Listing 7-3 (*continued*)

```
{$S Main}
procedure OpenWindow;
{ Open a new window }

  begin
    NumToString (nextWNum, nextWTitle); {prepare number for title}
    nextWTitle := concat (wName, nextWTitle); {add to prefix}
    myWindow := NewWindow (Nil, nextWRect, nextWTitle, True, noGrowDocProc,
      Pointer (-1), True, 0);   {open the window}
    SetPort (myWindow);           {make it the current port}
    txRect := thePort^.portRect;{prepare TERecord for new window}
    InsetRect (txRect, 4, 0);
    textH := TENew (txRect, txRect);
    Hlock (Handle (textH));
    myWinPeek := WindowPeek (myWindow);
    myWinPeek^.refcon := Longint (textH); {keep TEHandle in refcon!}
    OffsetRect (nextWRect, windDX, windDY);{move window down and right}
    if nextWRect.right > dragRect.right  {move back if it's too far over}
      then OffsetRect (nextWRect, -nextWRect.left + leftEdge, 0);
    if nextWRect.bottom > dragRect.bottom
      then OffsetRect (nextWRect, 0, -nextWRect.top + topEdge);
    nextWNum := nextWNum + 1;   {bump number for next window}
    menusOK := false;
    EnableItem (myMenus [editM],0); {in case this is the only window}
  end; {OpenWindow}


{$S InitSeg}
procedure Initialize;
{ One-time set up of everything }
  begin

    InitGraf(@thePort);
    InitFonts;
    FlushEvents(everyEvent,0);
    InitWindows;
    InitMenus;
    TEInit;
    InitDialogs(NIL);
    InitCursor;

    dummy := NewHandle (4000000);

    SetUpMenus;
      with screenBits.bounds do
        SetRect(dragRect,4,24,right-4,bottom-4);
        doneFlag := false;
```

Listing 7-3 (continued)

```
      menusOK := false;
      nextWNum := 1;      {initialize window number}
      SetRect (nextWRect,leftEdge,topEdge,rightEdge,botEdge);
                          {initialize window rectangle}
      OpenWindow;         {start with one open window}

   end; {procedure Initialize}


{$S Killseg}
procedure KillWindow (theWindow: WindowPtr);
{Close a window and throw everything away}

   begin
      TEDispose (TEHandle (WindowPeek (theWindow)^.refcon));
                                   {throw away TERecord}
      DisposeWindow (theWindow);   {throw away WindowRecord}
      textH := NIL;                {for TEIdle in main event loop}
      if FrontWindow = NIL         {if no more windows, disable Close}
        then DisableItem (myMenus[fileM], closeItem);
      if WindowPeek (FrontWindow)^.windowKind < 0
                                   {if a desk acc is coming up, enable undo}
        then EnableItem (myMenus[editM], undoItem)
        else DisableItem (myMenus[editM], undoItem);

   end; {KillWindow}

{$S Main}
function MyFilter (theDialog: DialogPtr; var theEvent: EventRecord;
     var itemHit: Integer): Boolean;

   var
      theType: Integer;
      theItem: Handle;
      theBox: Rect;
      finalTicks: Longint;
```

Listing 7-3 (*continued*)

```
    begin
      if (BitAnd(theEvent.message,charCodeMask) = 13) {carriage return}
        or (BitAnd(theEvent.message,charCodeMask) = 3) {enter}
        then
          begin
            GetDItem (theDialog, 1, theType, theItem, theBox);
            HiliteControl (ControlHandle (theItem), 1);
            Delay (8, finalTicks);
            HiliteControl (ControlHandle (theItem), 0);
            itemHit := 1;
            MyFilter := True;
          end {if BitAnd...then begin}
        else MyFilter := False;
    end; {function MyFilter}


{$S Main}
procedure DoAboutBox;

  var
    itemHit: Integer;

  begin
    myWindow := GetNewDialog (1000, Nil, pointer (-1));
    repeat
      ModalDialog (@MyFilter, itemHit)
    until itemHit = 1;
    DisposDialog (myWindow);
  end; {procedure DoAboutBox}


{$S Main}
procedure DoCommand (mResult: LONGINT);
{Execute Item specified by mResult, the result of MenuSelect}

  var
    theItem: Integer; {menu item number from mResult low-order word}
    theMenu: Integer; {menu number from mResult high-order word}
    name: Str255;     {desk accessory name}
    temp: Integer;


  begin
    theItem := LoWord(mResult); {call Toolbox Utility routines to set }
    theMenu := HiWord(mResult);    { menu item number and menu number}

    case theMenu of              {case on menu ID}
```

Listing 7-3 (*continued*)

```
appleID:
  if theItem = aboutItem
    then DoAboutBox
    else
      begin
        GetItem(myMenus[appleM],theItem,name);
        {GetPort (savedPort);}
        scrapErr := ZeroScrap;
        scrCopyErr := TEToScrap;
        temp := OpenDeskAcc(name);
        EnableItem (myMenus [editM],0);
        {SetPort (savedPort);}
        if FrontWindow <> NIL
          then
            begin
              EnableItem (myMenus [fileM], closeItem);
              EnableItem (myMenus [editM], undoItem);
            end; {if FrontWindow then begin}
        menusOK := false;
      end;  {if theItem...else begin}
fileID:
  case theItem of

    newItem:
      OpenWindow;

    closeItem:
      if WindowPeek (FrontWindow)^.windowKind < 0
        then CloseDeskAcc (windowPeek (FrontWindow)^.windowKind)
        {if desk acc window, close it}
        else KillWindow (FrontWindow);
        {if it's one of mine, blow it away}

    quitItem:
      doneFlag := TRUE; {quit}

  end; {case theItem}

editID:
  begin
    if not SystemEdit(theItem-1)
      then
        case theItem of {case on menu item number}

          cutItem:
            TECut(textH); {call TextEdit to handle Item}
```

Listing 7-3 (*continued*)

```
            copyItem:
               TECopy(textH);

            pasteItem:
               TEPaste(textH);

            clearItem:
               TEDelete(textH);


         end;      {case theItem}
      end;      {editID begin}


   end;      {case theMenu}
   HiliteMenu(0);
 end;   {DoCommand}



{$S Main}
procedure FixCursor;

  var
    mouseLoc: point;

begin
  GetMouse (mouseLoc);
  if PtInRect (mouseLoc, thePort^.portRect)
    then SetCursor (GetCursor (iBeamCursor)^^)
    else SetCursor (arrow);
end; {procedure FixCursor}



begin            {main program}

  Initialize;
{ Main event loop }
  repeat
    SystemTask;
    if FrontWindow <> NIL
      then
        if WindowPeek (FrontWindow)^.windowKind >= 0
          then FixCursor;
    if not menusOK and (FrontWindow = NIL)
      then
```

Listing 7-3 (*continued*)

```
    begin
      DisableItem (myMenus [fileM], closeItem);
      DisableItem (myMenus [editM], 0);
      menusOK := true;
    end; {if FrontWindow...then begin}
if textH <> Nil
  then TEIdle(textH);

if GetNextEvent(everyEvent,myEvent)
  then
  case myEvent.what of

    mouseDown:
      case FindWindow(myEvent.where,whichWindow) of

        inSysWindow:
          SystemClick(myEvent,whichWindow);

        inMenuBar:
          DoCommand(MenuSelect(myEvent.where));

        inDrag:
          DragWindow(whichWindow,myEvent.where,dragRect);

        inContent:
          begin
            if whichWindow <> FrontWindow
              then SelectWindow(whichWindow)
              else
                begin
                  GlobalToLocal(myEvent.where);
                  extended := BitAnd(myEvent.modifiers,shiftKey) <> 0;
                  TEClick(myEvent.where,extended,textH);
                end;  {else}
          end;  {inContent}

        inGoAway:
          if TrackGoAway (whichWindow, myEvent.where)
            then KillWindow (whichWindow);

    end;    {case FindWindow}
```

Listing 7-3 (*continued*)

```
keyDown, autoKey:
  begin
    theChar := CHR(BitAnd(myEvent.message,charCodeMask));
    if BitAnd(myEvent.modifiers,cmdKey) <> 0
      then DoCommand(MenuKey(theChar))
      else TEKey(theChar,textH);
  end;  {keyDown, autoKey begin}

activateEvt:
  begin
  if BitAnd(myEvent.modifiers,activeFlag) <> 0
    then  {application window is becoming active}
      begin
        SetPort (GrafPtr (myEvent.message));
        textH := TEHandle (WindowPeek (myEvent.message)^.refcon);
        TEActivate(textH);
        EnableItem (myMenus[fileM],closeItem);
        DisableItem(myMenus[editM],undoItem);
        if WindowPeek (FrontWindow)^.nextWindow^.windowKind < 0
          then scrCopyErr := TEFromScrap;
      end {if BitAnd...then begin}
    else  {application window is becoming inactive}
      begin
      TEDeactivate(TEHandle(WindowPeek(myEvent.message)^.refcon));
      if WindowPeek (FrontWindow)^.windowKind < 0
        then
          begin
            EnableItem (myMenus[editM], undoItem);
            scrapErr := ZeroScrap;
            scrCopyErr := TEToScrap;
          end {if WindowPeek...then begin}
        else DisableItem (myMenus[editM], undoItem);
      end;  {else begin}
  end;  {activateEvt begin}

updateEvt:
  begin
    GetPort (savedPort);
    SetPort (GrafPtr (myEvent.message));
    BeginUpdate(WindowPtr(myEvent.message));
    EraseRect(WindowPtr(myEvent.message)^.portRect);
    TEUpdate(WindowPtr(myEvent.message)^.portRect,
    TEHandle(WindowPeek(myEvent.message)^.refcon));
    EndUpdate(WindowPtr(myEvent.message));
    SetPort (savedPort);
  end;  {updateEvt begin}

end;  {case myEvent.what}
```

Listing 7-3 (*continued*)

```
UnloadSeg (@Initialize);

   until doneFlag;
end.
```

Listing 7-3 *(continued)*

We'll run this program, open a few windows, type some stuff, open the "about box," close some windows, and then interrupt it and go into the debugger to spy on it. We press the interrupt button to get into the debugger. The main thing we're interested in here is the application heap zone, which is shown in Figure 7-22.

The first thing to look for when examining a program's heap for bad things is **fragmentation**. This is when there are nonrelocatable objects scattered throughout the heap, as we discussed in the first part of this book (remember, so long ago?). Just to remind you, this is bad because objects in the heap consist of consecutive bytes, and nonrelocatables reduce the number of consecutive free bytes in the heap, effectively limiting the amount of available memory.

Fragmentation is easy to spot with a debugger. All you have to do is look down the first column of the heap dump. The objects that start with asterisks are nonrelocatables and locked relocatables; they're the ones that can cause fragmentation. The ideal heap zone will have all the starred items collected in two groups, one at the beginning of the heap and one at the end (it's also OK if they're all at the beginning). If all the asterisks are together in these two places, there's no fragmentation and the program is doing a great job.

The average program won't be quite this good. It's likely to have a collection of asterisks at each end of the heap, with a few more scattered around in the middle. This is a sign that the program's memory management can be improved. Some programs will have really awful fragmentation problems: they'll have asterisks all over the place. These programs are doomed to run out of memory before their time.

It's the Thought That Counts

Remember that it doesn't matter how large the nonrelocatable or locked relocatable objects are. Even if they're only 10 bytes, they still do their damage by splitting the heap's available free space.

```
Application heap is at $00CB00-$0677F8.                        05802C bytes free.
*$00CB3C 000100 0  Nonrel
*$00CC44 000A5E 0  Handle at $00CC18 (LpR)   File $0020 'CODE' ID=$0001
*$00D6AA 00006C 0  Nonrel                    WMgrPort
*$00D71E 00009C 0  Nonrel                    Window #$01, Kind $0008
 $00D7C2 00009C 0  Free
*$00D866 00009C A  Nonrel                    Window #$00, Kind $0008
 $00D914 00002C 8  Handle at $00CC04 (lpr)   (WMgrPort)          ClipRgn
 $00D950 00006E 0  Free
*$00D9C6 000100 0  Nonrel
 $00DACE 000048 0  Handle at $00CBC0 (lpR)   File $0020 'MENU' ID=$0082
 $00DB1E 00000A 0  Handle at $00CBB0 (lpr)   (Window @$00D71E) ContRgn
 $00DB30 00000A 0  Handle at $00CBAC (lpr)   (Window @$00D71E) UpdateRgn
 $00DB42 0002AC 0  Handle at $00CBEC (lpR)   File $0002 'MDEF' ID=$0000
 $00DDF6 00000A 0  Handle at $00CBFC (lpr)   SaveVisRgn
 $00DE08 000024 0  Handle at $00CBBC (lpr)   (Window @$00D71E) VisRgn
 $00DE34 00000A 0  Handle at $00CC08 (lpr)   (WMgrPort)          VisRgn
 $00DE46 0001FA 0  Free
*$00E048 000072 0  Handle at $00CBA0 (Lpr)
 $00E0C2 00000A 6  Handle at $00CB70 (lpr)   (Window @$00D866) ClipRgn
 $00E0DA 0004B0 0  Handle at $00CBA8 (lpR)   File $0002 'WDEF' ID=$0000
 $00E592 000009 1  Handle at $00CBA4 (lpr)   (Window @$00D71E) WTitle
 $00E5A4 00002C 2  Handle at $00CB6C (lpr)   (Window @$00D866) StructRgn
 $00E5DA 000000 4  Handle at $00CBF4 (lpr)   TEScrap
 $00E5E6 000000 4  Handle at $00CC20 (lpr)   Scrap
 $00E5F2 0000AB 1  Handle at $00CBF0 (lpr)   File $0020 'MENU' ID=$0080
 $00E6A6 000009 1  Handle at $00CB60 (lpr)   (Window @$00D866) WTitle
 $00E6B8 00000A 0  Handle at $00CB74 (lpr)   (Window @$00D866) VisRgn
 $00E6CA 00000A A  Handle at $00CB68 (lpr)   (Window @$00D866) ContRgn
 $00E6E6 00000A 2  Handle at $00CB64 (lpr)   (Window @$00D866) UpdateRgn
 $00E6FA 000165 1  Handle at $00CC1C (lpr)   Resource map $0020
 $00E868 00004A 0  Free
*$00E8BA 000072 0  Handle at $00CB5C (Lpr)
 $00E934 00000A 0  Handle at $00CBB8 (lpr)   (Window @$00D71E) ClipRgn
 $00E946 00002C 0  Handle at $00CBB4 (lpr)   (Window @$00D71E) StructRgn
 $00E97A 000010 0  Handle at $00CB9C (lpr)
 $00E992 000066 0  Handle at $00CBF8 (lpr)   MenuList
 $00EA00 00000F 7  Handle at $00CB58 (lpr)
 $00EA1E 00029A 0  Handle at $00DAB2 (lPR)   File $0002 'CDEF' ID=$0000
 $00ECC0 00003B 1  Handle at $00CBC4 (lpR)   File $0020 'MENU' ID=$0081
 $00ED04 000044 0  Handle at $00CB4C (lPR)   File $0002 'CURS' ID=$0001
 $00ED50 00004C 0  Handle at $00CC00 (lpr)   GrayRgn
 $00EDA4 000AAE 0  Handle at $00CB98 (lPR)   File $0002 'FONT' ID=$018C
 $00F85A 00001F 1  Handle at $00CB54 (lpR)   File $0020 'DLOG' ID=$03E8
 $00F882 00006A 0  Handle at $00CB50 (lpR)   File $0020 'DITL' ID=$03E8
 $00F8F4 0000FA 0  Handle at $00CC10 (lPR)   File $0020 'CODE' ID=$0003
 $00F9F6 0000D0 0  Handle at $00CC24 (lPR)   File $0002 'PACK' ID=$0007
 $00FACE 000526 0  Free
*$00FFFC 000060 0  Handle at $00CB48 (LPR)   File $0020 'CODE' ID=$0004
 $010064 057788 0  Free
```

Figure 7-22 Application heap display

Objects in the Heap

What about our heap? It's in pretty bad shape. Following the cluster of nonrelocatables that start the heap, there are quite a few asterisks that clutter up the heap. Several of them, like the objects at $E048 and $E8BA, are locked relocatable objects. What are these things?

Let's take a look at one of them. There's a dump of one of them in Figure 7-23. Does it look familiar? Not really. If it's one of the standard Macintosh data structures, we should be able to get some clues as to its identity by its size and its contents. The heap dump tells us that it's $72 (decimal 114) bytes long. Looking at the first part of its contents, we see 00 00 00 04 00 85 00 C4. If we translate this into decimal integers, we get 0 4 133 196, which you may recognize as the dimensions of the rectangles that we passed to TENew. Could this be a TextEdit record?

TextEdit records always start out $68 bytes long (104 bytes decimal) and then grow as more text is typed into the record. The first things in a TextEdit record, as we can see by looking at its declaration, are the destination and view rectangles. This memory block begins with two identical rectangles, and we called TENew with identical rectangles in the program's OpenWindow procedure. That confirms it: this is a TextEdit record.

Knowing the size and characteristics of various common Macintosh data objects can help you identify them when you find them in the heap. Most objects have recognizable patterns that hint at the type of object, like the two rectangles that begin a TextEdit record. You can think of this pattern as a **signature** for that type of object. Another big clue to an object's identity is its size. Figure 7-24 lists some common types and their signatures.

```
DUMP FROM 00E048
00E048:    00 00 00 04   00 85 00 C4   00 00 00 04   00 85 00 C4   ................
00E058:    00 00 80 02   00 10 7F FE   00 10 00 0C   00 00 00 00   ................
00E068:    00 10 00 10   00 00 00 40   F9 A6 00 00   00 00 00 00   .......@........
00E078:    00 00 00 00   00 01 C6 C0   00 00 00 00   00 10 00 00   ................
00E088:    CB 9C 00 00   00 00 00 FF   00 00 00 01   00 00 00 01   ................
00E098:    00 00 00 00   D7 1E 00 00   00 00 00 00   00 00 00 01   ................
00E0A8:    00 00 00 10   00 00 00 00   00 0E 00 43   6F 6E 74 72   ...........Contr
00E0B8:    6F 6C 86 00   00 18 00 00   00 70 00 0A   80 01 80 01   ol.......p......
```

Figure 7-23 Locked heap block

Figure 7-24 Common data structures in the heap

Data structure	Hex size	Dec size	Signature (first few bytes)
AlertTemplate	C	12	Rectangle, such as 00 64 00 74 01 12 01 20
BitMap	E	14	Address, such as 00 07 A7 00
ControlRecord	28+title	40+title	ControlHandle followed by WindowPtr
Cursor	68	104	Bits of cursor
*DialogRecord	AA	170	Window Record
*GrafPort	6C	108	00 00 00 07 A7 00 or 00 00 00 0F A7 00
*Master Ptr Block	100	256	Addresses in heap (entire block)
Pattern	10	16	Patterned bytes, such as AA or 55
Print record	78	120	Small integer, such as 00 02
Region	A	10	00 0A followed by rectangle
TERecord	68**	104**	Two rectangles (record grows with more text)
*WindowRecord	9C	156	GrafPort (00 00 00 07 A7 00)

*nonrelocatable object
**object gets larger as more text is entered

Why are these TextEdit records locked? They certainly don't have to be locked; this is an example of what happens when the programmer suffers from paranoia about things in memory moving away. If you look in the `OpenWindow` procedure's source, you'll see that the TextEdit record is locked right after it's created and stays locked forever. Obviously, the fix for this is simply not to lock the thing.

What are the other fragmenting objects in this heap? There's a window record at $D866 that's caused a tiny bit of fragmentation. Look at the size of the free "hole" between the two windows: it's $9C bytes, exactly the size of a window record. This hole was created because we just closed a window. Since the Memory Manager automatically forces nonrelocatable objects as low as possible when it allocates them, the next window we open will fit into this hole. To prove it, we can exit the debugger, open another window, and then return to the debugger. Sure enough, the new window record fills the gap (see Figure 7-25), so this can't really be called fragmentation; it's just a normal occurrence for applications that allow any number of windows to be opened.

Now that we've identified the starred objects that are clogging up the heap, let's look at the ones that aren't in the middle of things, just for fun. The first object in the heap, as always, is a master pointer block. We know this because it's always the first object in a heap! Also, the fact that its size is $100 (decimal 256) bytes is a dead giveaway.

```
Application heap is at $00CB00-$0677F8.                    057E94 bytes free.
*$00CB3C 000100 0  Nonrel
*$00CC44 000A5E 0  Handle at $00CC18 (LpR)   File $0020 'CODE' ID=$0001
*$00D6AA 00006C 0  Nonrel                    WMgrPort
*$00D71E 00009C 0  Nonrel                    Window #$02, Kind $0008
*$00D7C2 00009C 0  Nonrel                    Window #$00, Kind $0008
*$00D866 00009C A  Nonrel                    Window #$01, Kind $0008
 $00D914 00000A 0  Handle at $00CC04 (lpr)   (WMgrPort)          ClipRgn
 $00D926 00002C 2  Handle at $00CB84 (lpr)   (Window @$00D7C2)   StructRgn
```

Figure 7-25 Start of application heap

Why a Duck?

Yes, the first thing in an application heap zone is always a master pointer block, but why? The application heap zone is created when the application starts up, when Launch is called. At this point, the heap is completely empty. The first thing that goes in the heap is the application's CODE 0, when Launch calls GetResource. Since CODE 0, like all resources, is a relocatable object, it needs a master pointer, but there are no master pointers in the application heap. So the Memory Manager automatically calls MoreMasters to create one. (See the Chapter 10 section entitled "Play by Play: An Application Is Launched" for more information about what Launch does.)

The next object is identified by the debugger as CODE 1, the main segment. This is standard, too. The main segment is always loaded and always locked, as we've discussed previously. The third object is the window manager port, which was created when the application called InitWindows. It's usually found right where we see it here, after the main code segment. Following it are the three window records. All these objects have a legitimate right to be here.

There's another locked object. It's at $FFFC, and it's identified as CODE resource #4. We can find out which CODE resource this is by opening a File window and looking up CODE 4's name (see Figure 7-26): it's the KillSeg segment. A quick look through our source code shows that we've never called UnloadSeg on this segment. If we don't call UnloadSeg, it will remain loaded and locked until the end of the universe, or until the application quits, whichever comes first. Oops. It's taking up memory. It should be unloaded so that it can be purged, if necessary. This is easily fixed by putting in an UnloadSeg (@KillWindow) call at the end of the main event loop.

```
Resource file #$0020                              Map at $00D820     Attributes: rcw
'BNDL'   $0080   ........   Nowhere
'DITL'   $03E8.  ........   Nowhere     'About box'
'DLOG'   $03E8   .......    Nowhere     'About box'
'FREF'   $0080   ........   Nowhere
'FREF'   $0081   ........   Nowhere
'ICN#'   $0080   ........   Nowhere
'ICN#'   $0081   ........   Nowhere
'MENU'   $0080   ........   At $00E4D0
'MENU'   $0081   ........   At $00DAFE
'MENU'   $0082   ........   At $00DB42
'Scot'   $0000   ........   Nowhere
'CODE'   $0000   ..P.....   Nowhere
'CODE'   $0001   ...L.1..   At $00CC44  'Main'
'CODE'   $0002   ..P..1..   Nowhere     '%A5Init'
'CODE'   $0003   ..P..1..   At $00D98E  'InitSeg'
'CODE'   $0004   ..P.....   Nowhere     'Killseg'
'CODE'   $0005   ..P.....   Nowhere     '_DataInit'
```

Figure 7-26 Application resource map

The last nonrelocatable object is the one at $D9C6 that's $100 bytes long. Nonrelocatable blocks of $100 bytes are almost always master pointer blocks and that's what this guy is. Why is it there? When you run out of available master pointers, the Memory Manager calls MoreMasters, which creates another master pointer block. This can be a problem if the heap is fragmented, since you're never really sure when the system will run out of master pointers. To avoid this problem, you should call MoreMasters yourself a few times in your initialization code.

Going, Going . . . Gone!

Master pointers are used up more quickly than you may realize. When you create a new window, for example, at least six master pointers are used up, one for each of the window record's five regions and one for its title, which is kept as a relocatable heap block. How many times should you call MoreMasters? The easiest thing to do is run your application and really exercise it, opening lots of windows and desk accessories, and then use the debugger to see how many master pointer blocks the system created. You can then call MoreMasters that many times at the start of your application.

> For the real fanatics, that method is a little wasteful. After all, why create hundreds of master pointers that may never be used? A flashier and more efficient technique is to monitor the number of free master pointers and then call `MoreMasters` yourself when you're running low. One way to do this is to step through the free master pointer list every time through the main event loop, counting the number of available master pointers (the first free master pointer's address is kept in the heap zone header; see Chapter 3 for more information).

There's another nasty thing that our application is doing to the heap that isn't obvious. In our startup segment, we cleverly attempt to grow the heap to its maximum possible size by asking for an impossibly large handle (4,000,000 bytes). We do this because the Memory Manager purges objects before growing the heap; so if we force it to be grown now, we can prevent purging later. The problem with this is that the Memory Manager goes through its usual allocation process before figuring out that it doesn't have 4 million bytes of free space. This process includes purging all purgeable objects. So any objects that have the preload attribute set, which means that they're loaded when the resource file is opened, are purged now. This doesn't cause anything to break, but it does destroy the intent of marking things as preloaded.

You can make the heap grow to its fullest size by calling `MaxApplZone` when the application starts up. This will add all the growable heap space without purging anything.

Looking at Resources

We're still not done checking for inefficiencies. Now we're going to identify heap objects, checking to see if there's anything we can improve on.

We'll start with the resources. First is old faithful CODE 1, which, as we've already noted, will always be there. Next are the MENUs, in various places in the heap. The lowercase p tells us that these resources are nonpurgeable. That's OK; the system always expects menus to be non-purgeable and will die otherwise.

The next resource is MDEF 0, which is the standard menu definition procedure. It's nonpurgeable. Most people like it that way. If it were purged and the user pulled down a menu, the disk would spin and there would be an annoying delay while the MDEF was loaded.

The next resource is the standard window definition function, WDEF 0. It's marked nonpurgeable, which is a good idea since it's used all the time. Most applications need it constantly, so you probably don't want to change it with HPurge.

The next resource is CDEF 0, the standard control definition function for buttons, which was loaded to handle the button in the "about" dialog. Notice that it's marked purgeable, unlike the MDEF. Again, this makes sense: users expect instant reaction when they pull down menus, so MENUs and MDEFs aren't purgeable; controls, on the other hand, aren't used as commonly, so CDEFs are marked purgeable in the System file. Of course, if you disagree violently and think this is all baloney, you can simply call HNoPurge on the CDEFs to keep them around.

System resources like CDEFs and MDEFs are kept in the resource file called System. Their attributes are marked in that file, for example, purgeable or nonpurgeable. Since the System file is shared by all the applications on a disk, you shouldn't change the attributes of resources in the file. However, you can customize attributes for your application by calling HPurge or HNoPurge on resources whose attributes you want to change. These calls will affect the resource attributes only until the application quits, so your changes won't bother anyone else.

Next is CURS 1, which is the I-beam cursor. Notice that it's marked purgeable (it has an uppercase P in its attributes). Most people find it kind of annoying when the computer has to whir the disk just to change the cursor to an I-beam, and it's only 68 bytes; so many applications load the I-beam and call HNoPurge to make sure that it stays around.

The next resource in the heap is FONT $18C, which is Geneva 12, the standard application font. Note that it's purgeable by default, like all fonts except the system font. Once again, you can change that by calling HNoPurge if you want to.

The next two resources in the heap are the DLOG and DITL that were used to display the "about" box. Even though the program will rarely use these things (only when the user chooses the "About . . ." menu item), they're not marked purgeable. They should be! Although they're tiny, they should be made purgeable so that their space can be used if it's needed. Since these resources belong to the application and not the System resource file, we don't have to call HPurge from the application; we can make them purgeable by using ResEdit to set their resPurgeable attribute bits.

The next resource we see is CODE 3, which the File window (Figure 7-26) says is called "InitSeg", our startup segment. Didn't we call Unload-Seg on this guy? Yes, we did, and that's why it's marked purgeable (uppercase P in the attributes) and unlocked (lowercase l). Purgeable objects aren't immediately thrown away; they just fade away, getting deallocated when their space is needed.

Next is PACK 7. This is the binary-decimal utilities package, which we called to help build our window titles. It's marked purgeable, as we would want. Finally, at the end of the heap is CODE 4, which we've already complained about.

Identifying the Remaining Heap Objects

We've now identified and pondered almost every object in this heap. Let's take a stab at the remaining ones. The most common bunch of things are the various objects associated with windows. These include a visible region (visRgn), clip region (clipRgn), update region (updateRgn), content region (contRgn), structure region (structRgn), and window title string (wTitle) for each window. The nice debugger automatically identifies each of these for us. There's not really anything we can do to check these for efficiency, since they're managed automatically by the Window Manager.

There are several objects that the system uses. These include the window manager port and its regions, some special window manager regions called GrayRgn and SaveVisRgn, the menu list, the desk scrap, the TextEdit scrap, the parameter text strings used by the Dialog Manager, and resource maps. The debugger automatically identifies all these objects for us.

The only remaining unidentified objects are at $E97A and $EA00. A quick visual examination of these objects with a Dump window shows that they contain the text that's in each window. These are the hText fields of the TextEdit records. We can double-check this fact by using the Template function to display the TextEdit records; one of the fields will be the hText handle.

That's it! We've now identified and been skeptical about every single object on the heap. What did we learn? Even in a small, virtually useless program like this, we learned a lot and found a few surprises. For example, we saw how windows and other nonrelocatable objects are forced low when they're allocated, preventing some possible fragmentation. As we discussed in Chapter 2, this means that we should always make sure code segments are unloaded and relocatable objects not locked whenever we allocate a new nonrelocatable object, like a window.

Macintosh Plus

Remember that Macintosh Plus ROMs automatically move code segments to the highest part of RAM when they're loaded, so we can allocate new nonrelocatables from any segment with a minimum of fragmentation, as long as we call `MaxApplZone` when the application starts up to grow the application heap zone to its fullest. Even on a Macintosh Plus, we have to be sure that we don't have any locked relocatable objects clogging the heap when we allocate new nonrelocatables.

By examining the heap, we also discovered several ways to improve the efficiency of our memory management. Sure, this program contained some intentionally obnoxious examples of bad things to do, but it's a really small program, so just imagine the atrocities that big programs can commit.

When you're writing a program, it's a great feeling to find and fix that last bug. With most programs, you can find and fix the "last" bug every few days.

Special Free Bonus

At no extra charge, you'll find here in Listing 7-4 a C translation of Listing 7-2, the "good" version of our program. It's a very faithful translation: in most cases, the code has been directly transformed to C, without a lot of optimizing for the new language. It'll be especially helpful to those of you who are Pascal programmers and are just learning C. Have fun!

```
#include <types.h>
#include <quickdraw.h>
#include <fonts.h>
#include <events.h>
#include <controls.h>
#include <windows.h>
#include <menus.h>
#include <textedit.h>
#include <dialogs.h>
#include <desk.h>
#include <toolutils.h>
#include <scrap.h>

/*resource IDs/menu IDs for Apple, File and Edit menus*/
#define     appleID  128
#define     fileID   129
#define     editID   130

/*index for each menu in myMenus (array of menu handles, 0-based in C!!!!)*/
#define     appleM   0
#define     fileM    1
#define     editM    2

/*total number of menus*/
#define     menuCount  3

/*item in Apple menu*/
#define     aboutItem  1

/*Items in Edit menu*/
#define     undoItem   1
#define     cutItem    3
#define     copyItem   4
#define     pasteItem  5
#define     clearItem  6

/*items in File menu*/
#define     newItem    1
#define     closeItem  3
#define     quitItem   5

/*default name for windows */
#define     WindName "Window "

/*distance to move for new windows*/
#define     windDX  25
#define     windDY  25
```

Listing 7-4

```
/*initial dimensions of window*/
#define     leftEdge  10
#define     topEdge   42
#define     rightEdge  210
#define     botEdge   175
.


/* global variables */

MenuHandle     myMenus[menuCount];   /*handles to the menus*/
Rect           dragRect;             /*rectangle used to mark boundaries for dragging window*/
Rect           screenRect;           /*to hold screenbits.bounds */
Rect           txRect;               /*rectangle for text in application window*/
TEHandle       textH;                /*handle to Textedit record*/
Boolean        extendedCH;           /*true if user is Shift-clicking*/
Boolean        doneFlag;             /*true if user has chosen Quit Item*/
EventRecord    myEvent;              /*information about an event*/
WindowRecord   wRecord;              /*information about the application window*/
WindowPtr      myWindow;             /*pointer to wRecord*/
WindowPeek     myWinPeek;            /*another pointer to wRecord*/
WindowPtr      whichWindow;          /*window in which mouse button was pressed*/
Rect           nextWRect ;           /*portRect for next window to be opended*/
long           nextWNum;             /*number of next window (for title)*/
GrafPtr        savedPort;            /*pointer to preserve GrafPort*/
Boolean        menusOK;              /*for disabling menu items*/
long           scrapErr;
short          scrCopyErr;

main(argc,argv)                 /*main program*/
int       argc;
char      **argv;
{
extern struct qd qd;


    InitGraf(&qd.thePort);
    InitFonts();
    FlushEvents(everyEvent,0);
    InitWindows();
    InitMenus();
    TEInit();
    InitDialogs(nil);
    InitCursor();

    SetUpMenus();   /* local procedure */
    screenRect = qd.screenBits.bounds;
    SetRect(&dragRect,4,24,screenRect.right-4,screenRect.bottom-4);
    doneFlag = false;
```

Listing 7-4 (*continued*)

```
    menusOK = false;
    nextWNum = 1;      /*initialize window number*/
    SetRect (&nextWRect,leftEdge,topEdge,rightEdge,botEdge);
                            /*initialize window rectangle*/
    OpenWindow();            /*start with one open window*/

/* Main event loop */
    do {
        SystemTask();
    /* An exercise for the reader: */
    /* add variable 'curFrontWindow' here instead of making all these calls */
        if (FrontWindow() != nil)
            if (((WindowPeek)FrontWindow())->windowKind >= 0)
                FixCursor();

        if (!menusOK && (FrontWindow() == nil))
        {
            DisableItem (myMenus [fileM], closeItem);
            DisableItem (myMenus [editM], 0);
            menusOK = true;
        }
        if (textH != nil)
            TEIdle(textH);

        if (GetNextEvent(everyEvent,&myEvent))
            switch (myEvent.what)
            {

                case mouseDown:
                    switch (FindWindow(&myEvent.where,&whichWindow))
                    {

                        case inSysWindow:
                            SystemClick(&myEvent,whichWindow);
                            break;
                        case inMenuBar:
                            DoCommand(MenuSelect(&myEvent.where));
                            break;
                        case inDrag:
                            DragWindow(whichWindow,&myEvent.where,&dragRect);
                            break;
```

Listing 7-4 *(continued)*

```
            case inContent:
                if (whichWindow != FrontWindow())
                    SelectWindow(whichWindow);
                else
                {
                    GlobalToLocal(&myEvent.where);
                    extendedCH = ((myEvent.modifiers & shiftKey) != 0);
                    TEClick(&myEvent.where,extendedCH,textH);
                } /*else*/
                break;
            case inGoAway:
                if (TrackGoAway (whichWindow, &myEvent.where))
                    KillWindow (whichWindow);
                break;
        }   /*switch FindWindow*/
        break;
    case keyDown:
    case autoKey:
        if ((myEvent.modifiers & cmdKey) != 0)
                DoCommand(MenuKey(myEvent.message & charCodeMask));
            else TEKey((char)(myEvent.message & charCodeMask),textH);
        break;
    case activateEvt:
        if (myEvent.modifiers & 01)
        {           /*application window is becoming active*/
            SetPort((GrafPtr)myEvent.message);
            textH = ((WindowPeek)myEvent.message)->refCon;
            TEActivate(textH);
            EnableItem (myMenus[fileM],closeItem);
            DisableItem(myMenus[editM],undoItem);
            if (((WindowPeek)FrontWindow())->nextWindow->windowKind < 0)
                scrCopyErr = TEFromScrap();
        }   /*if myEvent.modifiers*/
        else  /*application window is becoming inactive*/
        {
            TEDeactivate(((WindowPeek)myEvent.message)->refCon);
            if (((WindowPeek)FrontWindow())->windowKind < 0)
            {
                EnableItem (myMenus[editM], undoItem);
                scrapErr = ZeroScrap();
                scrCopyErr = TEToScrap();
            }/*if WindowPeek*/
            else
                DisableItem (myMenus[editM], undoItem);
        } /*else*/
        break;
```

Listing 7-4 (*continued*)

```
            case updateEvt:
                    GetPort(&savedPort);
                    SetPort((GrafPtr)myEvent.message);
                    BeginUpdate(((WindowPtr)myEvent.message));
                    EraseRect(&((WindowPtr)myEvent.message)->portRect);
                    TEUpdate(&((WindowPtr)myEvent.message)->portRect,
                        ((WindowPeek)myEvent.message)->refCon);
                    EndUpdate((WindowPtr)myEvent.message);
                    SetPort(savedPort);
                    break;
            }   /*switch myEvent.what*/

    }while (!doneFlag);

    return(0);
} /*of main*/




SetUpMenus()
    /* set up menus and menu bar */
{
    short i;

    myMenus[appleM] = GetMenu(appleID); /*read Apple menu*/
    AddResMenu(myMenus[appleM],(ResType)'DRVR');  /*add desk accessory names*/
    myMenus[fileM] = GetMenu(fileID);   /*read file menu */
    myMenus[editM] = GetMenu(editID);   /*read Edit menu */

    for (i=0;i<menuCount;++i)
        InsertMenu(myMenus[i],0);  /*install menus in menu bar */
    DrawMenuBar(); /* and draw menu bar*/
} /*SetUpMenus*/


OpenWindow()    /* Open a new window */
{
    char  wNameDef[256];        /* to hold our default window title */
    char  nextWTitle[256];      /* title of next window to be opened*/
    char  *wName;

    NumToString (nextWNum, nextWTitle);    /* prepare number for title -- returns C string?*/
    strcpy((char *)wNameDef,WindName);     /* WindName is a #define */
    wName = strcat((char *)wNameDef,(char *)nextWTitle);
```

Listing 7-4 (*continued*)

```
   myWindow = NewWindow (nil, &nextWRect, wName, true, noGrowDocProc,
       (WindowPtr)-1, true, 0);        /*open the window*/
   SetPort (myWindow);                 /*make it the current port*/
   txRect = qd.thePort->portRect;/*prepare TERecord for new window*/
   InsetRect (&txRect, 4, 0);
   textH = TENew (&txRect, &txRect);
   myWinPeek = (WindowPeek)myWindow;
   myWinPeek->refCon = (long int)textH;   /*keep TEHandle in refCon!*/
   OffsetRect (&nextWRect, windDX, windDY);/*move window down and right*/
   if (nextWRect.right > dragRect.right)     /*move back if it's too far over*/
      OffsetRect (&nextWRect, -nextWRect.left + leftEdge, 0);
   if (nextWRect.bottom > dragRect.bottom)
      OffsetRect (&nextWRect, 0, -nextWRect.top + topEdge);
   nextWNum++;     /*bump number for next window*/
   menusOK = false;
   EnableItem (myMenus [editM],0); /*in case this is the only window*/
} /* OpenWindow */


KillWindow(theWindow)    /*Close a window and throw everything away*/

WindowPtr        theWindow;

{

   TEDispose (((WindowPeek)theWindow)->refCon);
                                        /*throw away TERecord*/
   DisposeWindow (theWindow); /*throw away WindowRecord*/
   textH = nil;                         /*for TEIdle in main event loop*/
   if (FrontWindow() == nil)            /*if no more windows, disable Close*/
      {
         DisableItem (myMenus[fileM], closeItem);
         SetCursor(&qd.arrow);
      }
   else /* FrontWindow() != nil */
   {
     if (((WindowPeek)FrontWindow())->windowKind < 0)
         /*if a desk acc is coming up, enable undo*/
      {
         EnableItem (myMenus[editM], undoItem);
         SetCursor(&qd.arrow);
      }
     else
         DisableItem (myMenus[editM], undoItem);
   } /* else */
} /*KillWindow*/
```

Listing 7-4 (*continued*)

```
/*    function MyFilter (theDialog: DialogPtr; var theEvent: EventRecord;*/
/*       var itemHit: Integer): Boolean; */

pascal Boolean MyModalFilter(theDialog,theEvent,itemHit)
DialogPtr           theDialog;
struct EventRecord  *theEvent;
short               *itemHit;

{
   short   theType;
   Handle  theItem;
   Rect    theBox;
   long    finalTicks;

   if (((theEvent->message & charCodeMask) == 13) || /*carriage return*/
   ((theEvent->message & charCodeMask) == 3)) /*enter*/
   {
      GetDItem (theDialog, 1, &theType, &theItem, &theBox);
      HiliteControl((ControlHandle)theItem, 1);
      Delay(8, finalTicks);
      HiliteControl((ControlHandle)theItem, 0);
      *itemHit = 1;
      return(true);
   }   /*if BitAnd...*/
   else
      return(false);
}  /* MyModalFilter */


DoAboutBox()

{
   short   itemHit;


   myWindow = GetNewDialog(1000, nil, (WindowPtr) -1);
   do {
      ModalDialog (MyModalFilter, &itemHit);
      }
   while (itemHit != 1);
   DisposDialog (myWindow);
} /*DoAboutBox*/
```

Listing 7-4 *(continued)*

```
    /*Execute Item specified by mResult, the result of MenuSelect*/
DoCommand(mResult)
long      mResult;

{
    short      theItem;     /*menu item number from mResult low-order word*/
    short      theMenu;     /*menu number from mResult high-order word*/
    char       name[256];   /*desk accessory name*/


    theItem = LoWord(mResult);          /*call Toolbox Utility routines to set */
    theMenu = HiWord(mResult);          /* menu item number and menu number*/

    switch (theMenu)                        /*switch on menu ID*/
    {
        case appleID:
            if (theItem == aboutItem)
                DoAboutBox();
            else
            {
                GetItem(myMenus[appleM],theItem,name);
                /*GetPort (&savedPort);*/
                scrapErr = ZeroScrap();
                scrCopyErr = TEToScrap();
                (void) OpenDeskAcc(name);
                EnableItem (myMenus [editM],0);
                /*SetPort (savedPort);*/
                if (FrontWindow() != nil)
                {
                    EnableItem (myMenus [fileM], closeItem);
                    EnableItem (myMenus [editM], undoItem);
                } /*if FrontWindow*/
                menusOK = false;
            } /*if theItem...else*/
            break;
        case fileID:
            switch (theItem)
            {
                case newItem:
                    OpenWindow();
                    break;
                case closeItem:
                    if (((WindowPeek)FrontWindow())->windowKind < 0)
                        CloseDeskAcc(((WindowPeek)FrontWindow())->windowKind);
                        /*if desk acc window, close it*/
                    else
```

Listing 7-4 (*continued*)

```
                    KillWindow(FrontWindow());
                    /*if it's one of mine, blow it away*/
                break;
            case quitItem:
                doneFlag = true; /*quit*/
            break;
        } /*switch theItem*/
        break;
    case editID:
        if (!SystemEdit(theItem-1))
            switch (theItem)  /*switch on menu item number*/
            {
                case cutItem:
                    TECut(textH);  /*call TextEdit to handle Item*/
                    break;
                case copyItem:
                    TECopy(textH);
                    break;
                case pasteItem:
                    TEPaste(textH);
                    break;
                case clearItem:
                    TEDelete(textH);
                    break;
            }   /*switch theItem*/
}    /*switch theMenu*/
HiliteMenu(0);

} /*DoCommand*/


FixCursor()

{
Point    mouseLoc;

    GetMouse (&mouseLoc);
    if (PtInRect (&mouseLoc, &qd.thePort->portRect))
        SetCursor(*(GetCursor(iBeamCursor)));
    else
        SetCursor(&qd.arrow);

}
```

Listing 7-4 (*continued*)

Things to Remember

- Debuggers are a great help in finding bugs, and they can also be used to examine your program's behavior very closely to see how you can make it better, stronger, and faster.

- Debugging requires a mixture of intelligence, logic, intuition, experimentation, and deduction (sounds pretty dramatic).

- When debugging, you're a fact gatherer. You should constantly make sure that things are what they appear to be; you should take very little for granted.

- You'll often find yourself running down blind alleys when debugging, but you just have to stick with it and use the information you've already gathered to help find the problems.

PART THREE

Tips, Tricks, and Techniques

There's a light in the darkness of everybody's life.

—Brad and Janet, "Over at the Frankenstein

Place"

CHAPTER

8

General Techniques

In Part Three, we'll discuss specific tips and techniques that you can use in your programs. Some techniques will discuss little known goodies in the Macintosh ROM, many of which are well documented in **Inside Macintosh** but have just been lost in the shuffle of learning about the Macintosh. Other techniques aren't specifically documented in **Inside Macintosh**, but are very useful. For a few tips and techniques, we'll present a complete example program.

This section is divided into three chapters: General Techniques, which are things that are generally useful when writing Macintosh programs; and Toolbox Techniques and Operating System Techniques, which give you examples of fancy and clever things you can do with those parts of the ROM.

Have fun!

Preflighting

Many of the Macintosh ROM calls return to you some kind of error status. For example, when you make any Resource Manager calls, there will be an error code placed in the global ResErr, which you can read with the function called ResError. Similarly, the Memory Manager posts an error code in the global MemError after every Memory Manager call.

If you make a ROM call from your application that results in an error, you can deal with it in a friendly way; for example, if the user asks for another record in your database, you call NewHandle, and it tells you that there's not enough memory left, you can tell the user that you can't create any more records.

297

Remember that the ROM itself makes lots of ROM calls; for example, when LoadSeg is called, it calls GetResource to load in the new CODE segment. If this GetResource call fails for any reason, such as lack of memory or the resource not being found, LoadSeg will put up system error 15. It doesn't bother trying to report an error to the application. How would it report it? Most application programmers aren't even aware when LoadSeg is being called and certainly aren't prepared to deal with an error from it.

There are lots of situations like this in the ROM, often dealing with memory allocations. It works like this: your application makes a ROM call, which in turn makes a memory request with NewHandle or NewPtr. If the request fails, the ROM puts up a system error.

How can you prevent these situations from happening? If there were some way for you to detect beforehand that the error was going to occur, you could avoid starting the operation at all. You don't have to be psychic to do this, although it helps; you just have to anticipate what possible system problems could happen when you do something in your program. This is called "preflight checking," or just **preflighting**: checking things out before you take off. Preflighting is a good idea in general, because it's better to find out about a potential problem before you take off than while you're in mid-air.

For example, let's say you're about to put up a dialog. If you call GetNewDialog, the ROM will attempt to load the DLOG and DITL resources for the dialog with GetResource. What if the call to load the DLOG fails? The GetNewDialog call, which, like much of the ROM, has less than robust error checking, fails to detect the error, and you're likely to crash quickly with an address error.

How can you prevent this? Before calling GetNewDialog, you can anticipate that the system is going to try to load the DLOG and DITL resources, so you can try to load them yourself with GetResource. If a GetResource call returns a Nil handle, it failed, and your program can gracefully report the error to the user. If your GetResource calls are successful, you can proceed with the GetNewDialog call. The resources will already be in memory, so it won't have to load them again.

The important thing here is that you anticipated a situation where the ROM was going to make some ROM calls itself and ignore the error results. By calling GetResource yourself, you preempted the ROM and made sure that the resources were really there.

You can preflight all sorts of situations. When you're about to do something that will require memory to be allocated, you can try to make sure that you have enough memory to complete the whole operation before you find yourself stuck halfway through it. For example, when you ask the Finder to copy a bunch of files from one disk to another and there's not enough room for the copy, it tells you so before it ever starts copying. This is because it preflights the copy; that is, it checks to make sure that the destination disk has enough space on it to receive the copies before ever starting.

Often, trying to preflight a situation will be tricky. Let's say that the user has chosen a desk accessory from the Apple menu, and you want to preflight to make sure that there's enough memory to open the desk accessory. What can you do? Your first instinct might be to find out how big the desk accessory (the DRVR resource) is. Then you could see if a block of that size is available in the heap.

In general, this is a pretty good strategy, but it has one problem: the desk accessory may allocate memory of its own in the heap, and it may also load in other resources. If you want to be a real fanatic about it, you can find all the resources in the system resource file that are ''owned'' by this desk accessory; the system applies a special numbering convention to resources that belong to desk accessories (see **Inside Macintosh** for details).

However, no matter what you do, you have no way of knowing how much additional space the desk accessory will try to allocate with direct NewHandle or NewPtr calls. It's actually a pretty nasty thing for a desk accessory to try to allocate a great chunk of memory; after all, a desk accessory is the application's guest and it shouldn't do anything rude, like ask for a ton of memory.

So about the best preflighting you can do before opening a desk accessory is to get the size of the DRVR resource and see if there's enough room in the heap to accommodate it. If you want, you can also check the sizes of all the resources owned by the desk accessory, too.

Sometimes you may have to preflight situations that require the enlargement of an already existing heap object. For example, when you call PutScrap, you're increasing the size of a relocatable object, the global scrap. You might think that all you have to do is check to see if there's enough free heap space to accommodate the additional bytes in the object. But this won't necessarily work: when you're resizing an existing object, not creating a new one, you're under some additional limitations. In particular, if you're making a relocatable object larger, it can't move past a nonrelocatable object if it's relocated. If you're making a non-relocatable larger, the restrictions are even greater, since it can't move at all.

How can you predict if growing the object will succeed? The surest way to do it is to actually call SetHandleSize or SetPtrSize and check the returned error code to see if the call succeeded. If it didn't, your program can fail gracefully; if it did, you can call SetHandleSize or SetPtrSize again to shrink the object back down and then go ahead with your operation (such as calling PutScrap).

These are some hints about how to preflight in different situations. In practice, you'll come up with lots of different times when it's appropriate to preflight before doing something. When you're preflighting, try to think each situation through clearly, understanding what's really happening when you do something, and then check for possible problems before you start. That way you'll have the best chance at saving your users from disaster, and they'll appreciate it.

Switch Launching and Disk Swapping

In the early days of the Macintosh, all users had 128K of RAM and most had only one disk drive. In addition to great graphics, ease of use, and innovation, the Macintosh quickly became known for its disk swapping. This occurred when the system needed to load in some piece of a disk file from a disk that had been ejected.

At the low level, this is a pretty impressive capability: the system keeps track of disks even when they're ejected, and if it needs a disk back, it ejects the one it has and asks for the other one. In real life, though, it gets to be pretty annoying, having to keep switching disks around (imagine what it would have been like if Macintosh disk drives had doors on them, and you had to pull the disk out yourself!).

When external disk drives and 512K RAM became more common, the disk switch problem was alleviated a bit, but it's still really frustrating to be asked for a disk when you can't imagine why the computer needs it back. Worst of all is when the disk that's asked for has already been stuck into another Macintosh and modified—the disk that the first computer wants back doesn't exist any more!

Several other developments have helped reduce the disk switching problem. The Finder got smarter about launching applications, working to eliminate disk swaps when an application on a different disk was started up. The Macintosh Plus helps get rid of this problem: since it has some common resources in ROM, they never have to be loaded from disk. Also, the Macintosh Plus allows the user to escape from the dreaded disk switch message just by pressing <Command>-<period>. This can be dangerous, though, because many applications aren't prepared to deal with not getting the disk back that they asked for. They become very disappointed and sometimes take out their frustrations by crashing.

Despite these improvements in the situation, disk swapping still happens, and it's still annoying. What can you do in your application to help prevent disk swaps? To answer this question, we have to understand why disk swaps take place. When the system needs to load something from a disk that's not in any drive, it presents the disk switch alert.

When the disk switch alert appears, it tells you which disk it wants, of course, but not what file or what specific thing it's looking for. Usually, the disk switch happens when there's a `GetResource` or `LoadResource` call. Imagine this scenario: on a system with one disk drive, you start up the system with a system disk. Then you want to run an application that's on another disk, so you eject the first disk, insert the second disk, and run the application. As the application starts up, it repeatedly ejects the program disk and requests the system disk again.

What's going on? Well, remember that although all the application's resources are contained in its resource file, the application also needs resources from the system file now and then. These resources include packages (PACK), definition procedures (WDEF, MDEF, CDEF), and more. Whenever one of these resources is needed, it must be read from the system disk.

As a partial solution to the problem of needing system resources, the Finder uses a technique called a **switch launch** when it launches an application. It works like this: if the Finder is launching an application that's not on the same disk as the Finder (that is, not the system disk), it will check the disk that has the application that it's launching. If that disk has a file named System and a file named Finder, the Finder will go through an intricate routine that changes the system disk to the disk that contains the application. It closes the system file on the old system disk, opens it on the new disk, changes the system global `BootDrive` to indicate the new disk, and launches the application.

Changing System Files Is Tricky

To close the system resource file, you call `CloseResFile (0)`. In addition to closing the system file, this call closes all other open resource files, too. That includes the file that contains the CODE resource that you're running! Closing the resource file causes all the resources in the file to be released, including the running CODE. This means that the CODE resource is suddenly sitting in a deallocated heap block and may be clobbered by any calls that allocate new memory. To prevent the CODE from getting stuck in no-man's land like this, the Finder calls `DetachResource` on the CODE before calling `CloseResFile`. This removes the CODE from the resource map in memory so that it doesn't get thrown away when the files are closed by `CloseResFile`.

The Finder Doesn't Always Switch Launch

Early versions of the Finder always switch launched if the disk containing the application being launched contained a Finder and a System. This feature is really annoying, though, if you've got a hard disk. Since the hard disk will always be there, there's no need to ever close the system file on it. Also, hard disk owners tend to put all their favorite fonts and desk accessories in the hard disk's system file, and switch launching away from this disk makes these unavailable. By the time Apple shipped Finder version 5.0 with the Hard Disk 20 in late 1985, the Finder was smart enough not to switch launch away from hard disks, unless the user held down the Option key while launching.

What can you do in your applications to avoid disk swapping? To reduce the number of disk swaps, you have to be conscious of which of your calls cause disk reads to occur. Since most of these disk reads are for resources, this involves figuring which resources must be loaded for which ROM calls. Sometimes, the answer can be surprising.

For example, see if you can figure out how many resources must be loaded by a single SFGetFile call. Any guesses? How about ten? Every time you call SFGetFile, at least ten resources must be loaded. First, of course, is the code for the package itself, PACK 3. Once it's in, it calls GetResource for each of the other resources needed. First, it loads DLOG −4000 and DITL −4000, the dialog template and item list for the dialog; it also needs WDEF 0, the standard window definition function so that it can draw the dialog, CDEF 0 to draw the Eject, Drive, Open, and Cancel buttons, and CDEF 1 to draw the scroll bar; it loads CURS 4, the wristwatch cursor; it also needs FONT 12, which is the system font (Chicago) in 12-point size to draw the text in the dialog; finally, the scroll bar definition procedure loads PAT 11, which is the gray pattern used in the scroll area.

If you could name all those, congratulations. Of course, if any of them are already in memory before calling SFGetFile, they won't have to be loaded from disk, but if they're not in memory (and not in ROM, as the WDEF is in the Macintosh Plus), they'll cause a disk read. If the system disk isn't in a drive, a disk switch will happen.

> **How to Find This Out**
>
> Did I get this list of resources by guessing, by consulting a fortune teller, or just by knowing? None of the above. You can find out by using a debugger, like TMON. I set it to intercept `Pack3` (Standard File) calls and then returned to the application and chose Open from the File menu. Back in the debugger, I set it up to intercept `GetResource` calls. As each one was intercepted, I checked the top of the stack to see what it was going after. Of course, you can do that, too, with your favorite calls.

The way to avoid disk swaps is to anticipate when resources will have to be loaded and try to load them all at once. For example, if your application calls Standard File, you might want to explicitly call `GetResource` on the resources listed previously when your application first starts up. This may cause extra disk activity at application startup time; but if you've got enough memory for some of the resources to stay around, you may have less disk swapping when you call Standard File in the middle of your application. Of course, this technique relies on future versions of Standard File using the same resources, which may not be the case.

This example is actually a pretty extreme case. Most system calls don't cause anywhere near this many resources to be loaded. In fact, many disk swaps occur on explicit `GetResource` calls by your application, not indirect ones loaded by ROM calls. By knowing when you're causing resources to be loaded, you can group important resource-getting code together at the start of the application. If you then use `HNoPurge` to make the resources that are most important to your application nonpurgeable, you might be able to avoid a few disk swaps.

How to Get Around Pascal's Type Checking

On the Macintosh, lots of information is kept in the low-memory globals. Sometimes you have to read the information that's stashed away in these globals; sometimes you have to change them. From assembly language or C, that's no problem. But what can you do from Pascal?

As you may know, Apple's Workshop Pascal and the other Pascals that run on the Macintosh aren't exactly standard—they've got some neat extensions to make them more useful on a Macintosh. One of the most powerful of these extensions is something called **explicit type coercion**, which is a great idea that's stolen from C. With explicit type coercion, you can actually assign values of one type to variables of a different type.

Not only is this feature useful for Macintosh programmers, it's absolutely essential.

Here's how it works: let's say you need to create a new relocatable heap object that's 50 bytes long. You want the handle to this object to be in a variable called myJoeHandle, which you've declared like this:

```
type
   Joe = Record
             int1, int2: integer;
             str1: string[5];
         end; {joe}
   JoePtr = ^Joe;
   JoeHandle = ^JoePtr;

var
   myJoeHandle: JoeHandle;
```

You have to call NewHandle to create the new heap object, but NewHandle returns a variable of type Handle. If you try to write myJoeHandle := NewHandle (50), the compiler will refuse to compile it, saying that it's a type mismatch error.

You know that myJoeHandle and the generic type Handle returned by NewHandle have exactly the same format; unfortunately, the compiler doesn't know that. You can convince the compiler that it's OK, even though you're mixing types. It's done with explicit type coercion.

It's amazingly simple. All you have to do to coerce a variable of one type to another type is use the desired type as if it were a function call. For example, you can make the result of the NewHandle call look like type Joehandle just by writing this: myJoeHandle := JoeHandle (NewHandle (50)). This sends a message to the compiler saying, "Yes, I know that NewHandle and myJoeHandle have different types, but I know what I'm doing, I'm over 18 (or whatever), so let me do it." For more about this technique, see the next section, "Random Access File I/O".

You can also use explicit type coercion to change or get the value of any memory location. To do this, you should first declare a variable of a pointer type. Exactly which pointer type depends on the size of the thing in memory that you want to look at or change. As an example, let's get the value of HeapEnd, which is a global located at address $114. HeapEnd is a long word (4 bytes), so we need to declare a pointer to a four-byte object, like a Pascal Longint:

```
var
   thePtr: ^Longint;
```

Next, we have to declare a variable to hold the value of HeapEnd. This is an ordinary Longint:

```
theValue: Longint;
```

Now we're ready. First, we have to make `thePtr` point to the right location, which is $114. We can do this with a type-coerced assignment statement:

```
thePtr := pointer ($114);
```

A couple of things here need explanation. First, $114 is a real, live, legal Workshop Pascal number. Any number that begins with a dollar sign is treated as a hexadecimal constant. The other curious part of this assignment is the `pointer` around $114. What is this? It's type coercion, as you might have guessed. But we said that explicit type coercion required a specific type name. Usually, it does; however, `pointer` is a special case. It's sort of a generic type coercion function. It coerces the value in parentheses to whatever type is necessary to make the compiler happy. In this case, it makes the value of `thePtr` be $114; in other words, it makes `thePtr` point to $114.

Now that our pointer is set up, all we have to do is dereference it and assign it to the Longint:

```
theValue := thePtr^;
```

That's all there is to it. The variable `theValue` now contains the LongInt value from location $114, which is `HeapEnd`. You can use this technique to access any byte in memory.

A very similar technique is used when you want to change the value of any byte in memory. This can be very useful, for example, when installing routines into any of the various low-memory hooks, like `DragHook` or `MenuHook`.

Let's say you want to have a routine installed in `DragHook`, which is a pointer at $9F6. When the user drags a window around, the system looks to see if there's an address of a routine stored in `DragHook`; if so, it calls that routine while it's dragging.

To use `DragHook`, we first declare the routine we want to install there.

```
procedure MyDragHook;

  begin
    SystemTask;
end; {MyDragHook}
```

This little procedure simply calls `SystemTask`, which is the ROM call that makes sure that desk accessories perform their periodic actions; for example, the alarm clock desk accessory uses this to update the time that it's displaying. By calling `SystemTask` from `DragHook`, the alarm clock should be able to update its display even while windows are being dragged. Usually, of course, the clock stops ticking while you're dragging windows.

Now we have to put myDragHook's address in the global DragHook location. Here's the code to do that:

```
thePtr := pointer ($9D6);    {make thePtr point to DragHook}
thePtr^ := @myDragHook;   {put address of myDragHook in $9D6}
```

This makes the DragHook global point to our myDragHook procedure. You can use this technique to change the value of any byte in memory. Remember, the compiler is trusting you, so behave yourself. You can easily use this feature to trash your program if you want or if you're not careful.

Patching Traps

Everybody knows that the Macintosh has a whole bunch of routines in ROM. What a lot of folks don't realize is that the Macintosh's ROM is probably the least permanent read-only memory ever made. It's not that the particles within the Macintosh ROM will decay after time; although the code for the system calls is indeed located in unalterable ROM, the table that says where each and every ROM call begins is located in RAM and is quite changeable.

There's absolutely no reason why the addresses in this table can't be addresses of routines in RAM. In fact, this is how bugs in the ROM are "fixed." When the system starts up, the system loads in a special resource of type PTCH from the system resource file. This resource includes patches to a number of traps. The appropriate addresses in the trap dispatch table are modified to point to these new routines, and that's that.

> **Before Macintosh Plus**
>
> On older systems, the PTCH resource did not exist. Instead, the patches to traps were stored in the system file's data fork.

In some cases, traps are patched not to fix bugs, but to add features. For example, in the Macintosh Plus ROM, TextEdit has patches to support arrow keys. Why weren't these features put directly into the ROM? They simply weren't done in time to include them in the ROM, so they're patched in when the system starts up.

Some folks think that there's something magical about the way the system patches traps and that it's not something that ordinary humans can do. Although there are a few things to watch out for (see the "Patching Traps That Are Already Patched" section of Appendix B), patching traps is pretty straightforward.

Since virtually all of the Macintosh's personality is implemented through traps, you can do some impressive things by applying patches in the right places. For example, several developers were able to implement RAM caching schemes on the original 64K ROM by patching traps such as Read and Write. If you wanted to implement a fancy memory management watchdog system, you could patch NewHandle and NewPtr, and you would get control whenever a program allocated memory for a new heap object.

One problem to watch out for when patching traps is that trap addresses are required to be within the first 64K of RAM. This is because the trap dispatch table encodes trap addresses by packing them into an offset from the start of RAM (or ROM), and there's only enough space provided to give a 64K range.

To get around this limitation, most applications use a nifty technique. It works like this: they get a block in the application heap and put the patch there; then they get a small block in the system heap, which is always guaranteed to be completely within the first 64K of RAM, and install a single JMP instruction that jumps to the real patch, located elsewhere. This jump instruction in the system heap is then installed as the patch by calling SetTrapAddress. This only takes up six bytes in the system heap, a reasonable amount.

Since the JMP instruction is in the system heap, it's guaranteed to be in the first 64K of RAM, so its address is fine as a patch. Be sure to unpatch the patch when your application exits!

Macintosh Plus

In the Macintosh Plus, the trap dispatch table is not packed; each address in the table is a long word that points to the trap's address, so there's no restriction that the trap code must be in the first 64K of RAM. Also, future system heaps may be larger than 64K. If you're writing code that will only run on a Macintosh Plus, you need not use this technique. However, to be sure that you'll work on both 64K and 128K ROMs, you should use the "system heap jump" technique.

Updating Your Menu Items

Many applications have menu items that change during the course of a program's execution. Menu items may be either enabled or disabled (gray), depending on the frontmost window or other things; some menu items will have check marks next to them sometimes, again based on the state of things that usually are in the frontmost window.

The basic model of the Macintosh application doesn't really support changing menu items' appearance while the program is running. You can't really do everything in the code that handles activate events: what about when the last window on the screen is closed, and there is no activate event? Also, what about the changes that don't occur because a new window has been selected and so aren't related to activate events?

Many applications wind up with menu-fixing code scattered all over the place. One solution that some applications implement is to set up all the items in a menu at the time the user pulls it down. In principle, this is a great idea. The program doesn't have to bother fixing up menus that aren't pulled down. In practice, though, it can be a problem. If the menu has several items to be set, setting them may take just long enough to annoy the user with a delay before the menu is drawn. Macintosh users expect menus to come down as soon as they're clicked on and are bothered by having to wait even a moment. As someone once said, there must be a better way.

One radical solution is to invent a new kind of event: a menu-update event. Your application could cause a menu-update event to be posted whenever something happened that could cause a menu item (or its appearance) to change. For example, if a new window was opened, a menu-update event would be posted for the menus that had items whose appearance might change—the File and Edit menus, and maybe others, too.

The program's main event loop would then include code to handle these menu-update events. This event handler would set up the items in the appropriate menus. In fact, to simplify things, the menu-update event's message could be the menu ID number of the menu that needs updating.

Where will this menu-update event come from? The Event Manager thoughtfully leaves four events undefined so that applications can do their own things with them. These are events 12 through 15, called app1Evt, app2Evt, app3Evt, and app4Evt. We can use one of these for our menu-update event.

> **Switcher**
>
> Although these four events are left undefined by the Toolbox, the last two are used by Switcher to tell an application when it's being switched out and switched back in. Because of this, you should use app1Evt and app2Evt if you expect your users to run your application under Switcher.

Using menu-update events may seem like a clever idea, but we shouldn't use it just because it looks neat or feels right. If it really helps make the application better, it's a good idea; otherwise, it's not. Let's look at some of its advantages and disadvantages as implemented in the program shown in Listing 8-1, which is a generic multiwindow editing application (presented in the more conventional way in Chapter 7).

```pascal
program menuUpdate;

uses
   {$U HD:MPW:Interfaces.p:MemTypes.p } MemTypes,
   {$U HD:MPW:Interfaces.p:QuickDraw.p} QuickDraw,
   {$U HD:MPW:Interfaces.p:OSIntf.p   } OSIntf,
   {$U HD:MPW:Interfaces.p:ToolIntf.p } ToolIntf,
   {$U HD:MPW:Interfaces.p:PackIntf.p } PackIntf;

const
   appleID = 128;   {resource IDs/menu IDs for Apple, File and Edit menus}
   fileID  = 129;
   editID  = 130;

   appleM = 1; {index for each menu in myMenus (array of menu handles)}
   fileM  = 2;
   editM  = 3;

   menuCount = 3;        {total number of menus}

   aboutItem = 1;        {item in Apple menu}

   undoItem  = 1;        {Items in Edit menu}
   cutItem   = 3;
   copyItem  = 4;
   pasteItem = 5;
   clearitem = 6;

   newItem = 1;          {items in File menu}
   closeItem = 3;
   quitItem = 5;
```

Listing 8-1

```
   mUpdateEvt = app3Evt; {menu update event}

   wName = 'Window ';  {prefix for window names}

   windDX = 25;        {distance to move for new windows}
   windDY = 25;

   leftEdge = 10;      {initial dimensions of window}
   topEdge = 42;
   rightEdge = 210;
   botEdge = 175;

var
  myMenus: array [1..menuCount] OF MenuHandle; {handles to the menus}
  dragRect: Rect;          {rectangle used to mark boundaries for dragging window}
  txRect: Rect;            {rectangle for text in application window}
  textH: TEHandle;         {handle to Textedit record}
  theChar: char;           {typed character}
  extended: boolean;       {true if user is Shift-clicking}
  doneFlag: boolean;       {true if user has chosen Quit Item}
  myEvent: EventRecord;    {information about an event}
  wRecord: WindowRecord;   {information about the application window}
  myWindow: WindowPtr;     {pointer to wRecord}
  myWinPeek : WindowPeek;  {another pointer to wRecord}
  whichWindow: WindowPtr;  {window in which mouse button was pressed}
  nextWRect: Rect;         {portRect for next window to be opended}
  nextWTitle: Str255;      {title of next window to be opened}
  nextWNum: Longint;       {number of next window (for title)}
  savedPort: GrafPtr;      {pointer to preserve GrafPort}
  scrapErr: Longint;
  scrCopyErr: Integer;

procedure SetUpMenus;
{ set up menus and menu bar }

  var
    i: Integer;

  begin
    myMenus[appleM] := GetMenu(appleID); {read Apple menu}
    AddResMenu(myMenus[appleM],'DRVR');  {add desk accessory names}
    myMenus[fileM] := GetMenu(fileID);   {read file menu }
    myMenus[editM] := GetMenu(editID);   {read Edit menu }

    for i:=1 to menuCount do
      InsertMenu(myMenus[i],0); {install menus in menu bar }
    DrawMenuBar;  { and draw menu bar}
  end;   {SetUpMenus}
```

Listing 8-1 (*continued*)

```
procedure InvalMenu (menuID: Integer);

  var
    errCode: OSErr;

begin
  errCode := PostEvent (mUpdateEvt, menuID);   {post menu update event}
end; {procedure InvalMenu}


procedure OpenWindow;
{ Open a new window }

  begin
    NumToString (nextWNum, nextWTitle); {prepare number for title}
    nextWTitle := concat (wName, nextWTitle); {add to prefix}
    myWindow := NewWindow (Nil, nextWRect, nextWTitle, True, noGrowDocProc,
      Pointer (-1), True, 0);    {open the window}
    SetPort (myWindow);            {make it the current port}
    txRect := thePort^.portRect;{prepare TERecord for new window}
    InsetRect (txRect, 4, 0);
    textH := TENew (txRect, txRect);
    myWinPeek := WindowPeek (myWindow);
    myWinPeek^.refcon := Longint (textH); {keep TEHandle in refcon!}
    OffsetRect (nextWRect, windDX, windDY);{move window down and right}
    if nextWRect.right > dragRect.right   {move back if it's too far over}
      then OffsetRect (nextWRect, -nextWRect.left + leftEdge, 0);
    if nextWRect.bottom > dragRect.bottom
      then OffsetRect (nextWRect, 0, -nextWRect.top + topEdge);
    nextWNum := nextWNum + 1;   {bump number for next window}
    InvalMenu (editM);     {enable Edit menu if this is first window}
  end; {OpenWindow}


procedure KillWindow (theWindow: WindowPtr);
{Close a window and throw everything away}

  begin
    TEDispose (TEHandle (WindowPeek (theWindow)^.refcon));
                              {throw away TERecord}
    DisposeWindow (theWindow);  {throw away WindowRecord}
    textH := NIL;               {for TEIdle in main event loop}
    InvalMenu (fileM);          {disable close if no windows}
    Invalmenu (editM);          {set undo item properly}
  end; {KillWindow}
```

Listing 8-1 (*continued*)

```
function MyFilter (theDialog: DialogPtr; var theEvent: EventRecord;
    var itemHit: Integer): Boolean;

  var
    theType: Integer;
    theItem: Handle;
    theBox: Rect;
    finalTicks: Longint;

  begin
    if (BitAnd(theEvent.message,charCodeMask) = 13) {carriage return}
      or (BitAnd(theEvent.message,charCodeMask) = 3) {enter}
      then
        begin
          GetDItem (theDialog, 1, theType, theItem, theBox);
          HiliteControl (ControlHandle (theItem), 1);
          Delay (8, finalTicks);
          HiliteControl (ControlHandle (theItem), 0);
          itemHit := 1;
          MyFilter := True;
        end {if BitAnd...then begin}
      else MyFilter := False;
  end; {function MyFilter}



procedure DoAboutBox;

  var
    itemHit: Integer;

  begin
    myWindow := GetNewDialog (1000, Nil, pointer (-1));
    repeat
      ModalDialog (@MyFilter, itemHit)
    until itemHit = 1;
    DisposDialog (myWindow);
  end; {procedure DoAboutBox}



procedure DoCommand (mResult: LONGINT);
{Execute Item specified by mResult, the result of MenuSelect}

  var
    theItem: Integer; {menu item number from mResult low-order word}
    theMenu: Integer; {menu number from mResult high-order word}
    name: Str255;     {desk accessory name}
    temp: Integer;
```

Listing 8-1 (*continued*)

```
begin
  theItem := LoWord(mResult); {call Toolbox Utility routines to set }
  theMenu := HiWord(mResult);     { menu item number and menu number}

  case theMenu of              {case on menu ID}

     appleID:
       if theItem = aboutItem
         then DoAboutBox
         else
           begin
             GetItem(myMenus[appleM],theItem,name);
             scrapErr := ZeroScrap;
             scrCopyErr := TEToScrap;
             temp := OpenDeskAcc(name);
             InvalMenu (editM);       {enable Edit menu}
             InvalMenu (fileM);       {fix close & undo items}
          end;  {if theItem...else begin}
     fileID:
       case theItem of

          newItem:
            OpenWindow;

          closeItem:
            if WindowPeek (FrontWindow)^.windowKind < 0
              then
                begin
                  CloseDeskAcc (windowPeek (FrontWindow)^.windowKind);
                  InvalMenu (fileM); {if desk acc window, close it}
                  InvalMenu (editM);
                end {if WindowPeek...then begin}
              else KillWindow (FrontWindow);
              {if it's one of mine, blow it away}

          quitItem:
            doneFlag := TRUE; {quit}

        end; {case theItem}

     editID:
       begin
         if not SystemEdit(theItem-1)
           then
             case theItem of {case on menu item number}

               cutItem:
                 TECut(textH); {call TextEdit to handle Item}
```

Listing 8-1 (*continued*)

```
        copyItem:
           TECopy(textH);

        pasteItem:
           TEPaste(textH);

        clearItem:
           TEDelete(textH);

          end;     {case theItem}
        end;     {editID begin}

    end;     {case theMenu}
    HiliteMenu(0);
  end; {DoCommand}


procedure FixCursor;

  var
    mouseLoc: point;

begin
  GetMouse (mouseLoc);
  if PtInRect (mouseLoc, thePort^.portRect)
    then SetCursor (GetCursor (iBeamCursor)^^)
    else SetCursor (arrow);
end; {procedure FixCursor}


procedure FixMenus (menuID: Integer);

  var
    anyWindows: Boolean;
    frontKind: Integer;

begin
  anyWindows := (FrontWindow <> NIL);  {are there any windows displayed?}
  if anyWindows
    then frontKind := WindowPeek (FrontWindow)^.windowKind;
  case menuID of

    fileM: if anyWindows
             then EnableItem (myMenus [fileM], closeItem)
             else DisableItem (myMenus [fileM], closeItem);
```

Listing 8-1 (*continued*)

```
      editM: begin
              if anyWindows then
                begin
                  EnableItem (myMenus [editM], 0);
                  if frontKind < 0
                    then EnableItem (myMenus [editM], undoItem)
                    else DisableItem (myMenus [editM], undoItem);
                end {if anyWindows then begin}
                else
                  DisableItem (myMenus [editM], 0);
            end; {editM begin}
    end; {case menuID}
  end; {procedure FixMenus}


begin           {main program}

  InitGraf(@thePort);
  InitFonts;
  FlushEvents(everyEvent,0);
  InitWindows;
  InitMenus;
  TEInit;
  InitDialogs(NIL);
  InitCursor;

  SetUpMenus;
    with screenBits.bounds do
      SetRect(dragRect,4,24,right-4,bottom-4);
      doneFlag := false;

  nextWNum := 1;     {initialize window number}
  SetRect (nextWRect,leftEdge,topEdge,rightEdge,botEdge);
                     {initialize window rectangle}
  OpenWindow;        {start with one open window}

{ Main event loop }
  repeat
    SystemTask;
    if FrontWindow <> NIL
      then if WindowPeek (FrontWindow)^.windowKind >= 0
            then FixCursor;

    if textH <> Nil
      then TEIdle(textH);
```

Listing 8-1 (*continued*)

```
if GetNextEvent(everyEvent,myEvent)
  then
  case myEvent.what of

    mouseDown:
      case FindWindow(myEvent.where,whichWindow) of

          inSysWindow:
            begin
                SystemClick(myEvent,whichWindow);
                if FrontWindow = NIL {user just closed last window}
                  then begin
                          InvalMenu (fileM);
                          InvalMenu (editM);
                          end; {if FrontWindow...begin}
            end; {inSysWindow: begin}

          inMenuBar:
            DoCommand(MenuSelect(myEvent.where));

          inDrag:
            DragWindow(whichWindow,myEvent.where,dragRect);

          inContent:
            begin
              if whichWindow <> FrontWindow
                then SelectWindow(whichWindow)
                else
                  begin
                    GlobalToLocal(myEvent.where);
                    extended := BitAnd(myEvent.modifiers,shiftKey) <> 0;
                    TEClick(myEvent.where,extended,textH);
                  end;  {else}
            end;  {inContent}

          inGoAway:
            if TrackGoAway (whichWindow, myEvent.where)
              then KillWindow (whichWindow);

      end;    {case FindWindow}

    keyDown, autoKey:
      begin
        theChar := CHR(BitAnd(myEvent.message,charCodeMask));
        if BitAnd(myEvent.modifiers,cmdKey) <> 0
          then DoCommand(MenuKey(theChar))
          else TEKey(theChar,textH);
      end;  {keyDown, autoKey begin}
```

Listing 8-1 (*continued*)

```
    activateEvt:
      begin
      if BitAnd(myEvent.modifiers,activeFlag) <> 0
        then  {application window is becoming active}
          begin
            SetPort (GrafPtr (myEvent.message));
            textH := TEHandle (WindowPeek (myEvent.message)^.refcon);
            TEActivate(textH);
            if WindowPeek (FrontWindow)^.nextWindow^.windowKind < 0
              then scrCopyErr := TEFromScrap;
          end {if BitAnd...then begin}
        else  {application window is becoming inactive}
          begin
          TEDeactivate(TEHandle(WindowPeek(myEvent.message)^.refcon));
          if WindowPeek (FrontWindow)^.windowKind < 0
            then
              begin
                scrapErr := ZeroScrap;
                scrCopyErr := TEToScrap;
              end {if WindowPeek...then begin}
          end;  {if BitAnd...else begin}
        InvalMenu (editM);
        InvalMenu (fileM);
      end;  {activateEvt begin}

    updateEvt:
      begin
        GetPort (savedPort);
        SetPort (GrafPtr (myEvent.message));
        BeginUpdate(WindowPtr(myEvent.message));
        EraseRect(WindowPtr(myEvent.message)^.portRect);
        TEUpdate(WindowPtr(myEvent.message)^.portRect,
        TEHandle(WindowPeek(myEvent.message)^.refcon));
        EndUpdate(WindowPtr(myEvent.message));
        SetPort (savedPort);
      end;  {updateEvt begin}

    mUpdateEvt:
      FixMenus (myEvent.message);

    end;  {case myEvent.what}

  until doneFlag;
end.
```

Listing 8-1 (*continued*)

One obvious advantage is that having menu-update events gathers all the menu-modifying code together in the same place. Instead of having this code in lots of places throughout the application, it's all in one procedure. This makes the logic easy to follow and easy to modify as the program is modified.

A disadvantage of this method is that menu items are sometimes disabled (with DisableItem) when they've never been enabled and re-enabled when they're already enabled. This inefficiency is reduced because the overhead for setting a menu item as enabled or disabled is pretty low; that's a fancy way of saying that those calls are fast.

The final verdict on the menu-update event scheme is up to you. If you think it fits your application, you might want to use it and improve on it. If you don't like it, there are lots of other ways to do it, just like anything else on the Macintosh. Invent your own!

Which Registers You Can Use

If you're writing assembly language code you have to be concerned with register usage. Since your program must interact with ROM calls, desk accessories, definition procedures, and all the other lively inhabitants of Macintosh memory, and since all those guys have to use the same registers you do, you have to make sure that nobody steps on anybody else's toes.

To allow all the programs in the Macintosh to coexist, there are strict rules for register usage. You have to follow these rules when you're writing assembly language code; otherwise, some piece of code will expect a value in a register and crash when that value isn't right.

There are two points of view for register usage: either (1) you're about to call a routine that may change the value of registers (**trash** them, it's called) and you want to know which registers will not be changed, or (2) you're writing a routine that will be called by someone else (a patched trap, for example, or a VBL task), and you want to know which registers you may trash without upsetting the caller. We'll look at register conventions from both of these viewpoints.

First, let's introduce some general rules about register usage on the Macintosh. Register A7, which is the stack pointer, is special. A good rule is never to use it as anything but the stack pointer. If you do, you should save its value and restore it before calling any other code, such as ROM calls. Also, if you mess around with A7, you should disable the stack sniffer by saving location $110 (StkLowPt) and zeroing it to prevent system errors from ruining your day. Be sure to restore StkLowPt when you're done.

Register A5 is used to find lots of things in the Macintosh. It points to a list of things called the application parameters, the first of which is always a pointer to the QuickDraw global variable thePort. All the ROM routines that use QuickDraw globals (including QuickDraw itself) rely on A5 containing the value that it's initialized to at application startup time. It's also used to jump to routines in other segments, since jump table entries are expressed as A5-relative offsets.

Because A5 is so important, you should avoid changing it. If you must change it, be sure to restore it before calling any ROM routines or any routines in other segments. There's a system global called CurrentA5 at $904 that contains the "right" value of A5; it's set up when the application is launched.

Register A6 doesn't have any "official" use by the system. Many routines, especially Toolbox routines and compiled code, use A6 as a local frame pointer; in other words, they execute a LINK A6 instruction when they begin. Using A6 this way can help you debug, since it allows you to track down procedures' parameters and local variables. If you want, though, you can use A6 any way you wish.

There are several registers which are generally available for trashing by any routine. These registers are A0, A1, D0, D1, and D2. If you're writing an assembly language routine, you can usually destroy the contents of these registers. If you're calling a ROM routine from assembly language, in most cases you should count on these registers being modified.

Let's explain the "usually" and the "in most cases" in the previous paragraph. Calls to the Operating System preserve registers A1, D1, and D2. These extra registers are preserved by the trap dispatcher. In addition, all OS routines that don't return a result in A0 preserve the contents of A0. This is done through the use of a parameter bit in the trap word, bit 8. For calls that return a result in A0, bit 8 of the trap word is set; calls that don't return anything in A0 (which is most of them) have bit 8 clear. The saving and restoring of A0, if it's required, is done by the trap dispatcher.

Registers A2 through A4 and D3 through D7 are not preserved by the trap dispatcher, but all ROM routines and high-level language routines must preserve them. This means that an assembly language routine that's called by someone else (like a trap patch) can use these registers if it wants to, but it must save and restore them if it does.

If a routine uses registers that it must preserve, the easiest way to preserve them is with the 68000's Move Multiple instruction (spelled MOVEM). This single magic instruction moves the values of any combination of registers into a specified area of memory, or from memory back to the registers.

Let's say you're writing a patch for a Toolbox trap, and you want to use registers A0, A1, A2, A3, D0, D1, D2, D3, and D4. You don't have to worry about preserving the contents of A0, A1, D0, D1, or D2, since they're considered "trashable" and the programs that call your patch can't expect them to remain unchanged. You have to preserve A2, A3, D3, and D4. You can do this by saving their values on the stack with a MOVEM instruction when your routine begins, like this:

```
MOVEM.L D3/D4/A2/A3,-(A7)     ;save registers on stack
```

This instruction will save the specified registers on the stack. At the end of the routine, we can get them back with another MOVEM:

```
MOVEM.L (A7)+,D3/D4/A2/A3     ;restore contents of registers
```

That's all you have to do. You could save and restore lots more registers in your MOVEM instruction. That wouldn't hurt anything, but it wastes a little time and stack space to save and restore registers that you never use.

Here's a chart that summarizes what happens to registers in various situations:

If you call a:	These may be changed	These will be preserved
Toolbox trap	A0, A1, D0, D1, D2	A2-A6, D3-D7
OS trap	D0	A0-A6, D1-D7
OS trap with result in A0	A0, D0	A1-A6, D1-D7
Routine in an application	A0, A1, D0, D1, D2	A2-A6, D3-D7
If you write a:	You may change these	You must preserve these
Toolbox trap patch	A0, A1, D0, D1, D2	A2-A6, D3-D7
OS trap patch	A0, A1, D0, D1, D2	A2-A6, D3-D7
	(trap dispatcher preserves A0, A1, D1, D2 for OS traps)	
Callable application routine	A0, A1, D0, D1, D2	A2-A6, D3-D7
VBL task	A0-A3, D0-D3	A4-A6, D4-D7

Things to Remember

- You should try to anticipate your program's needs by preflighting situations before actually performing major actions.
- You can help avoid disk switching by understanding what's causing the disk switch to occur.
- Most Pascals that work on the Macintosh allow you to defeat Pascal's strong type checking with explicit type coercion.
- Any ROM call can be modified or replaced with your own version by using the `GetTrapAddress` and `SetTrapAddress` calls.
- An experimental technique for keeping menu items up to date involves using the user-defined events to signify an action that can cause a menu item to change.
- Well-defined register conventions dictate which of the 68000's registers can be used by different kinds of routines.

CHAPTER

9

Toolbox Techniques

In this chapter, we'll discuss some of the more interesting and obscure things that you can do with the Toolbox. Most of these things are accessible from assembly or high-level languages. Most of them are documented in **Inside Macintosh**, but are little known, little used, or not often asked about.

Writing a Definition Function in a High-level Language

As you probably know, the scheme used by the Toolbox for windows, menus, and controls is very flexible. The appearance of each of these things is controlled by a **definition function**. There are a few standard definition functions, which are stored in the system resource file as resources of type WDEF (for windows), CDEF (for controls), and MDEF (for menus).

There are two standard WDEFs. The first, WDEF 0, is the one that's almost always used. It draws the familiar square-cornered window in several varieties: with or without a title bar, with or without a grow box in the lower right corner, and several others. Virtually all the windows you see in Macintosh applications are drawn with this WDEF, including dialogs and alerts.

The other standard WDEF, which has resource ID 1, draws windows with rounded corners. The most common example of this type of window is the standard calculator desk accessory.

There are also two standard control definition functions. The first is CDEF 0, which is used to draw buttons, check boxes, and radio buttons. The other is CDEF 1, which draws scroll bars.

There's only one standard MDEF (menu definition). It has resource ID 0, and it can draw menus with textual items, check marks and icons to the left of the items, command key equivalents to the right, a style such as italic, bold, or underlined, and a dimmed appearance to show that the item is disabled.

Because of the nifty generality that's built into the Window, Control, and Menu Managers, you can write your own definition functions if you want to have things that don't behave like the standard ones. For example, if you want to define a menu that shows patterns or lines, like MacDraw's, you can write your own MDEF; if you want a window that's round, or shaped like California, you can write your own WDEF.

Warning

Rectangular windows are a good idea. As a window gets more jagged, its regions get more complex and take up more memory. Changing a window's shape affects several regions, including its VisRgn, StructRgn, and ContRgn, plus some regions maintained by the Window Manager. Funny-shaped windows usually take up a lot of memory, and they're usually useful for fun only.

The details for writing your own definition function (usually called a **defproc**, short for "definition procedure") are in **Inside Macintosh**. Although it's easiest to write them in assembly language, you can also write one in a high-level language. If you do, though, there are a couple of things that you have to be aware of (just like always).

The most important thing to remember is that the defproc must end up as a resource that runs on its own, with no global "world" set up off A5. This means that if you write your defproc in a high-level language it can't have any global variables. Since the compiler will allocate those global variables off A5, they won't be there when the defproc runs, because the application that loaded the defproc will have its global world defined.

Since most compilers, especially Pascal compilers, always assume that they're going to be compiling a complete program, they usually produce code that has the global world set up at the start and global world destruction at the end. Of course, this won't work for a defproc. Unfortunately, most compilers that do this don't have a way of turning this "feature" off.

What you'd really like to do is just write the defproc as a single function or procedure and simply compile that function or procedure all by itself. If you've got a compiler that lets you do this, as some C's do, you're in business. Just take the compiled output and make it a WDEF, CDEF, or MDEF resource with a resource-creating program like RMaker.

If you're stuck with a compiler that won't let you compile a single procedure or function, you'll have to find another alternative. If you're using Workshop Pascal, you can use the $ASM listing option to produce an assembly language source listing of your compiled code. It works like this: write your defproc as a single procedure or function, as defined in **Inside Macintosh**. Then write a dummy program to enclose the procedure. Here's how you would do it for a menu definition procedure, although the same technique will work for all defprocs:

```
program makeDefProc;

    procedure myDefProc (message: Integer; theMenu:
        MenuHandle; VAR menuRect: Rect; hitPt: Point)
        VAR whichItem: Integer);
        {as defined in Inside Macintosh}

        var x, y : someType; {local variables are OK}

    begin
        ... {code of myDefProc goes here}
            {don't use any globals!}
    end; {myDefProc}
begin    {dummy main program}
end.
```

If you then compile this "program" and instruct the compiler to give you an assembly language source listing (for example, using $ASM ONLY with Lisa Pascal), you'll get a source listing that can be sent directly to the assembler. You can then extract the part of this source listing that corresponds to the procedure MyDefProc (if it's Lisa Pascal, it will begin with a .PROC MyDefProc statement). You can then assemble this code and produce a file that you can make into an MDEF with a resource-making utility. Easy! In fact, before you run the assembler on this file, you can look it over and optimize the defproc's code if you want. Ten hacker points for every instruction that you're able to save by optimizing the compiler's output.

Logical Clipping

QuickDraw is one of the fastest and most flexible drawing packages available for any personal computer. It really has to be, since the Macintosh relies so heavily on QuickDraw for drawing things on the screen. If QuickDraw wasn't really quick, the whole user-interface metaphor would be in danger of breaking down.

QuickDraw's flexibility has an effect on the way applications are written. In particular, QuickDraw's clipping ability allows you to draw "outside the lines" and still have everything come out all right, since no lines will be drawn outside the clipRgn or the visRgn.

Many programs use QuickDraw's clipping ability in a lazy fashion. They know that nothing outside the visRgn will be drawn, so they don't bother trying to restrict the area that's drawn when an update event is processed. Of course, this doesn't cause anything incorrect to be drawn on the screen, since QuickDraw really does clip to the visRgn.

Although no extra lines are drawn, you do pay a penalty for this sort of sloppy drawing. QuickDraw takes some time to figure out what to clip, and if you do a lot of drawing commands that QuickDraw will clip, you'll pay a speed penalty. Although it's still fast, even with lots of clipping, you can really improve performance by using some logic about what should be drawn before calling the drawing commands. This technique is called **logical clipping**.

When you use logical clipping, you simply try to figure out the minimum amount of stuff that has to be drawn before calling any QuickDraw drawing commands. Usually, you'll find that you can logically decide that a lot of drawing isn't necessary, and it'll be faster for you to figure that out than to let QuickDraw clip it out. For example, before drawing a rectangle, you could test to see if the rectangle is within the region or rectangle to be drawn. If not, you wouldn't bother with the drawing command, and the nondrawing decision would probably be faster. Time it for yourself! Use the debugger to record traps, which will also record their time (the value of the global variable Ticks).

You can take the what-to-draw decision too far, of course. In general, it's a good idea to narrow the drawing down to the smallest possible rectangle you can figure. In fact, another handy tip for fast drawing is to use rectangles, rather than regions, whenever you want to draw fast and you don't mind drawing a little more than necessary. This is because nonrectangular regions are somewhat more complex than rectangles and so take a little longer to process.

For example, if you want to test a rectangle to see if it's within the update region after an update event, you could call RectInRgn. Remember, though, that every region has as a part of its data structure a field called rgnBBox, which is a rectangle that completely encloses the region. If you pull this field out of the region (by double-dereferencing the region's handle) and then test manually for inclusion in this *rectangle*, you'll almost certainly be faster. Again, the only way to find out is to time it for yourself.

Using ResErrProc

One of the stickiest problems to deal with in the Macintosh ROM is error detection. Most applications call the ROM thousands of times during their execution, and many calls can return errors. Few programs (and programmers) are disciplined enough to check the error result from every call, although you really should.

Some of the most common and deadly errors that an application has to deal with are errors returned by the Resource Manager. These errors are not reported directly in the calls, but instead are put into a global called ResErr, which you can read with the ROM call ResError. It's such a pain to have to check ResErr after every Resource Manager call that most applications don't bother to do so.

Compounding this problem is the fact that the Resource Manager sometimes returns errors when you least expect it. For example, when you call ChangedResource, the Resource Manager will return an error if, for example, the disk is locked or full and the resource can't be written to the disk. Very few applications plan for that one.

There's a way to make checking for resource errors much easier, though very few applications use it, probably because it's very obscure. There's yet another system global, this one called ResErrProc, which is a pointer to a resource error-handling procedure. If you install a pointer to a procedure in ResErrProc, the Resource Manager will call this procedure whenever a resource error occurs. So, instead of having to call ResError after every Resource Manager call, you can simply install a pointer to a procedure in ResErrProc. This is the principle of "don't call us, we'll call you."

One problem with this technique is that the error-handling procedure can only tell what the error was (by calling ResError). This procedure doesn't know any more about the call, such as which call it was or who called it. In fact, the procedure can't even be sure that it was a Resource Manager call from the application that caused the error; it might have been a desk accessory that did it.

You can learn at least a little more about the routine that caused the error by looking at the address on the top of the stack in your error-handling procedure (easier to do in assembly language, obviously). This address is the return address back to the instruction following the Resource Manager call that caused the error. From this, you can learn both the call that caused the error and the place the call was made.

While you're debugging your application, you can use this information to find places where strange things are going on by breaking into the debugger when a Resource Manager error occurs. After you've found the last bug (hah!) and your application is shipping, you can use ResErrProc instead of having to call ResError all the time. Be prepared to deal with errors that you didn't cause, though, since you'll get called for errors that desk accessories cause, too. A technique you might use to find out if you've got one of these would be to examine the windowKind field of the frontmost window. If it's negative, you should ignore the error and let the desk accessory handle it.

If you use ResErrProc, be careful of one common problem that's not reported in a ResError result. If GetResource fails to find the resource, it returns Nil, but no ResError is generated. So, if you install a ResErrProc, you'll still have to check for Nil handles upon return from GetResource.

Moving a Resource from One File to Another

If you ever have to write a program that puts resources in a file (an installer program, we'll call it), you'll need to know about moving a resource from one file to another. On the surface, this doesn't seem too hard. However, a few little traps are lurking beneath this innocent appearance, and you should be aware of them before you try moving resources.

To make sure that you're getting the resource out of the right file and putting it into the new file, you can use the UseResFile call. This call will make sure that the resource file that's being used is the right one. Be sure to call UseResFile before any resource getting (with GetResource) or resource adding (with AddResource).

A single resource in memory cannot belong to more than one resource file. This means that if you try to simply call GetResource to get the thing, UseResFile to set up the new file, and AddResource to add it to the new file, you'll fail. You must first call DetachResource to remove the resource's attachment to the file that it's coming from. Calling DetachResource does not remove the resource from the file; it just turns the copy that's in memory into an ordinary relocatable block, not a resource.

Another potential pitfall is in the copying of the resource's attributes. When you install the resource in the new file, you'd like it to have the same attributes as it had in the old file. Your first shot at doing this might be to simply call GetResAttrs on the old resource and SetResAttrs on the new one. Gotcha. After adding the resource to the new file, its resChanged attribute is set; this tells the Resource Manager that it needs to write this guy out to the file when the file is closed. If you call GetResAttrs to get the old resource's attributes and SetResAttrs on the new copy, you'll blast the resChanged flag back to "off" and the resource will never get written to the file! To get around this problem, you have to turn the resChanged attribute on after getting the old resource's attributes by adding the constant resChanged to the attributes before calling SetResAttrs.

If this is all getting a bit hairy, hang in there. We're almost done, and it's summarized at the end, with an example program.

The final killer in this operation is one that's not real obvious. When you add a resource to a file, the Resource Manager doesn't check to see if the file already has a resource with the type and ID you're trying to add. If you call AddResource and the current resource file already has a resource of that type and ID, the new one will be added to the file, but the old one will not be removed and no error will be reported. Worst of all, future GetResource calls will never return the new resource that you just added, since the one that was there previously comes before the new one in the resource file's map; and as soon as the Resource Manager finds it, it will use that one! This means that the new resource you just added to the file is impossible to access (see Figure 9-1).

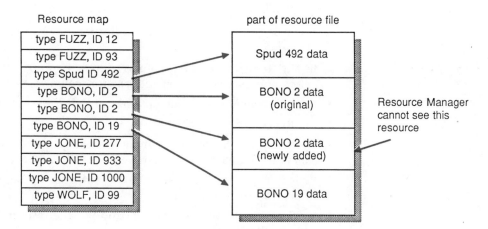

Figure 9-1 Orphaned resource

This is not good. To avoid this happening, before calling Add-Resource to put the resource in the new file, you must check to see if the file already has a resource of that type and ID (by calling GetResource), and if so, remove it with RmveResource. Then, when you add the new one, it'll be the only one in the file.

Picture this scenario: someone not as smart as you has called AddResource without checking to see if the file already had a resource with that type and ID, so a resource file already has two of, let's say, type FRED and ID 15. Then your installer program is run, and one of the resources it installs is FRED 15. Before calling AddResource, it finds that there's already a FRED 15 in the new file, so it calls RmveResource to take it away and then adds the new one. But wait—there's still one left in the old file, and the new one will be inaccessible! If you want to be paranoid, you should keep calling GetResource after your RmveResource until you're sure that there are no old copies remaining.

Different Names

There is one situation where two resources in the same file with the same type and ID can all be accessed. If they have different resource names, they can all be accessed with GetNamedResource. However, this is a pretty bizarre technique, and since it's not documented by Apple, it may not be supported in the future.

Now we can summarize the steps to go through to move a resource from one file to another.

1. Open both files (if one is the application, you don't have to open it, of course).

2. Be sure that you set the current resource file properly with UseResFile before any GetResource or AddResource calls.

3. Get the resource to be copied and call DetachResource on it.

4. Get the resource's attributes.

5. See if the new file already contains a resource of this type and ID (by calling GetResource); if so, remove it with RmveResource.

6. Repeat step 5 until the GetResource call returns Nil, meaning that it didn't find the resource.

7. Set the right file with UseResFile and put the resource in the new file with AddResource.

8. Call SetResAttrs with the value you got in step 4; then call Changed-Resource.

9. Close both resource files (unless one is the application—don't close it!).

By making sure you do all these nonobvious things, you'll be able to move resources around. Note that you actually don't have to close the resource files; when the application exits, they'll be closed automatically, but it's a good idea to force them closed before quitting in case the user reboots or something obnoxious like that.

The example program shown in Listing 9-1 shows you some real live code that moves a resource from one file to another.

```
program moveRes;

{$U+}
(*USES   {$U MemTypes.p } MemTypes,
         {$U QuickDraw.p} QuickDraw,
         {$U OSIntf.p  } OSIntf,
         {$U ToolIntf.p } ToolIntf,
         {$U PackIntf.p } PackIntf; *)
{$D+}

CONST
    DefaultVol = 0;      {vRef number of default volume}

VAR
  AddToFileName                    : Str255;
  AddToFileRefNum                  : integer;
  AppFileRefNum                    : integer;
  myWindow                         : WindowPtr;
  wRect                            : rect;
  replaced                         : Boolean;
  rType                            : ResType;
  rID                              : integer;
  copyErr                          : integer;
  err                              : integer;
  numStr                           : Str255;

{-------------------------------------------------------------------------------}
FUNCTION CopyAResource(rType: ResType; rID: integer;
        copyToFName: str255; vRef: integer): integer;

VAR
  HResToBeCopied                   : Handle;
  hResToCopyTo                     : Handle;
  attrs                            : integer;
  oldVol                           : integer;
```

Listing 9-1

```
Begin {CopyAResource}
    HResToBeCopied:= GetResource(rType,rID);
    If (ResError <> noErr) or (HResToBeCopied = NIL) or
                (HomeResFile(HResToBeCopied) <> AppFileRefNum)
    then Begin
        CopyAResource:= ResError;{copy failed}
        EXIT(CopyAResource);    {EXIT back to caller }
    End; {If (ResError....}

{NOTE: EXIT above -- at this point we know we've got}
{a resource of the desired type and id }

    attrs:= GetResAttrs(HResToBeCopied);
    replaced:= FALSE;                    {initialize this}

    DetachResource(HResToBeCopied); {so we can copy it}

    err:= GetVol(nil,oldVol); {get the default volume}
    err:= SetVol(nil,vRef);   {OpenResFile only opens files on default vol}
    AddToFileRefNum:= OpenResFile(copyToFName);
    If ResError <> noErr then Begin
        CopyAResource:= ResError;{copy failed}
        err:= SetVol(nil,oldVol);{restore default vol}
        EXIT(CopyAResource);    {EXIT back to caller }
    End;  {if}

{NOTE: EXIT above -- at this point we know we've}
{opened the desired resource file}

    UseResFile(AddToFileRefNum);   {in case the file was already open}

    repeat {repeat, stripping out all rTypes with rID in the target file}
        hResToCopyTo:= GetResource(rType,rID); {we know this won't fail here !!}
        If HomeResFile(hResToCopyTo) = AddToFileRefNum then Begin {it's in the file we want to copy to}
            RmveResource(hResToCopyTo); {remove from the resource file}
            DisposHandle(hResToCopyTo); { free up space in heap}
            replaced:= TRUE; {we found one}
        End;
    until (HomeResFile(hResToCopyTo) <> AddToFileRefNum);

    AddResource(hResToBeCopied,rType,rID,''); {put in the new one}
    if ResError <> noErr then {Copy was unsuccessful}
        CopyAResource:= ResError
    Else Begin
        SetResAttrs(hResToBeCopied,attrs);
            { set attributes, this clears, however,}
            { the resChanged (write) bit of the attributes, so we need to }
            { set it with the following ChangedResource call, or the resource }
            { will not get written, though the map will. }
        ChangedResource(hResToBeCopied);
```

Listing 9-1 *(continued)*

```
        If ResError = noErr then Begin
            CopyAResource:= noErr;  {successful!}
            CloseResFile(AddToFileRefNum);{ this updates too!!}
        End
        Else Begin{ChangedResource reported an error}
            CopyAResource:= ResError;
            CloseResFile(AddToFileRefNum);
        End; {else}
    End;  {Else}

    err:= SetVol(nil,oldVol);    {restore default vol}
End;  {CopyAResource}


{-----------------------------------------------------------------------------------}


Begin {main program}
    InitGraf (@thePort);
    InitFonts;
    InitWindows;
    TEInit;
    InitDialogs (nil);
    AddToFileName:= 'JimsResFile';
    rType:= 'DITL';            {resource type we want to copy}
    rID:= 5555;                {id of resource of type rType that we want to copy}

    SetRect(wRect,40,40,400,250);
    myWindow:= NewWindow(NIL,wRect,'Results',TRUE,rDocProc,pointer(-1),
                                FALSE,0); {create new window}

    SetPort(myWindow);


{here, for this example,  we'll create (or just open) the file
 that we're copying to.  In your program, this file may already exist}

    CreateResFile(AddToFileName);   {in real life -- check for errors after this}

    AppFileRefNum:= CurResFile;     {so we can restore later}

    {copy a resource into the file on the default volume}
    copyErr:= CopyAResource(rType,rID,AddToFileName,DefaultVol);

    UseResFile(AppFileRefNum);            {use our app's res file}
```

Listing 9-1 (*continued*)

```
{the following can be removed -- just for testing}
    MoveTo(20,20);
    If copyErr = noErr then Begin
        DrawString('Everything worked OK');
        If replaced then Begin
            MoveTo(20,40);
            DrawString('Resource was replaced');
        End; {if}
    End {if}
    else Begin
        NumToString(copyErr,numStr);
        DrawString(concat('Resource not copied [Error ',numStr,']'));
    End;  {Else}
    FlushEvents(everyEvent,0);
    repeat
    until button;

End.
```

Listing 9-1 *(continued)*

The Poor Man's Way to Smooth Animation

Or, smooth animation for the rest of us.

Programmers are always looking for a way to make their applications look better. If you've ever written an application that does animation or draws lots of rapidly changing graphics, you've probably come across the smooth animation problem.

The problem is this: if you're redrawing the screen a lot, you'd like the newly redrawn image to blend with the old one as smoothly as possible. Most programmers' first instinct on this is to do the redrawing as fast as possible, on the theory that this will help prevent the dreaded **screen flicker**: the awful effect you see a lot in poorly written animation programs.

If you try this, though, you'll soon see that no matter how fast you redraw the thing you're animating, even in assembly language, it still seems to flicker. Here is where a lot of programmers go astray, because the answer to this problem requires a little understanding of how the display hardware works (don't worry, the amount of understanding it takes isn't enough to be painful).

A computer does not redraw its entire screen instantaneously. Instead, it moves the electron beam across the screen, drawing as it goes—very fast, you bet, but not instantaneously! The beam starts at the upper-left corner of the screen and moves from left to right, drawing the image. When it reaches the right edge, it retraces its way back across the screen to the left edge without drawing. When it reaches the left edge, it moves down one row and starts drawing again. It repeats this drawing and retracing step for each line on the screen until it has drawn the last line.

After drawing the last line, the beam must retrace all the way back to the upper-left corner to start drawing the whole screen again. So it moves diagonally from the lower right, where it finished drawing the last line, to the upper left, where it begins drawing the first line again.

As the beam moves across and down the screen, the areas on the screen that it has already passed are refreshed as they change. If you change parts of the screen that the beam has already passed, the image is redrawn immediately and you get a flicker. The trick to avoiding flicker is to keep your drawing ahead of the beam; that is, draw the uppermost parts of the screen first and then the lower parts.

The time when the beam is retracing back to the beginning of the next line is called the **horizontal retrace period**. Similarly, the much longer time when the beam is traveling from the bottom of the screen back to the top is called the **vertical retrace period** (these are also called horizontal and vertical blanking periods). Any drawing that takes place during these blanking periods will result in a smooth display, since the changes will not actually take place until the beam comes out of the retrace period.

The horizontal blanking period is too short to do any drawing, but the vertical retrace period is, by computer standards, at least a pause, about 1.2 milliseconds (thousandths of a second). Any drawing that you can complete during that time will be flicker-free.

How do you know when the vertical retrace period begins? Aha! Good question! The Macintosh kindly provides an interrupt at the beginning of each and every vertical retrace period (called, as you might guess, the vertical retrace interrupt). This happens 60 times every second. What's more, when a vertical retrace interrupt occurs, the Macintosh executes a regular series of tasks that includes incrementing the Ticks counter (a system global), checking to see if the mouse has moved, and other stuff.

In addition to doing its built-in things at vertical retrace interrupt time, the Vertical Retrace Manager in the ROM will also execute any tasks that you have given it. You tell the ROM about these routines with the VInstall call. After you've installed a routine with VInstall, the ROM will call it when a vertical retrace interrupt occurs.

One inherent limitation of vertical retrace tasks is that they run at interrupt time. This means that they're really restricted: they can't make any calls that allocate or deallocate memory, they can't rely on unlocked handles, and so on (see Appendix B for more information). There's a way to get around this restriction.

The first thing the Macintosh does when a vertical retrace interrupt occurs is to increment the global variable Ticks, which you can read with the ROM call TickCount. This means that if your application waits patiently in a tight loop for Ticks to change (by calling TickCount repeatedly), you'll gain control very soon after the vertical retrace period has begun, and you'll have the advantage of not having to operate at interrupt time, freeing yourself from the interrupt-time restrictions. In practice, it looks like this:

```
{var tickValue : Longint;}
tickValue := TickCount;         {get value of Ticks}
repeat until (tickValue <> TickCount)
{start drawing, fast!}
```

With this technique, tickValue gets the value of TickCount. Then the repeat loop simply waits until TickCount changes. When it does, the program drops out of the loop. When this happens, the program knows that the vertical retrace interrupt has just occurred, and it should start updating its screen. It should start by redoing the upper part of the screen, since that's the place the beam will arrive first. It can be a little more leisurely about updating the lower part of the screen, since the beam has to travel a bit before getting there.

If your animation is fairly simple, you can use this technique to help prevent a flickering screen. Even if this doesn't eliminate your flicker completely, it should help, and it's really easy to implement.

Another handy way to create smooth animation is to use a technique known as the off-screen bitmap. In this technique, you create a Quick-Draw bitmap that uses heap or stack storage—not the screen—to keep its image. You set up the bitmap by making its baseAddr field point to the heap or stack storage that you've used for the image.

When you've created the image that you want, maybe by loading it from disk or by making it a GrafPort's bitmap and drawing into it, you can put it on the screen very quickly by using the CopyBits procedure. By synchronizing the call to CopyBits with a change in TickCount, you can get a smooth transition.

Automatic Window Updating

When your application creates windows, the Window Manager (via the Event Manager) lets you know whenever you should redraw part of a window, either because the window has changed or because a part of it just became visible. When you get an update event, you draw the update region in the specified window.

The Window Manager actually has another, simpler scheme for redrawing windows, but it works best with windows whose contents never change. Each window record has a field called windowPic. This field is usually not used and is set to zero. If you can use a QuickDraw picture to redraw the window, though, you can put the picture's handle in the windowPic field.

When the Window Manager sees a window that has to be updated, it checks to see if the window record has zero in its windowPic field. If so, it creates an update event; but if the field is not zero, the Window Manager uses the field as a handle to a picture and draws the picture.

Obviously, this isn't useful for all kinds of windows, but if you have some windows whose appearance doesn't change often (or ever), you can make your program simpler by using this technique. Windows with nonzero windowPic fields never get update events, since the Window Manager handles the updating by just drawing the picture. The program in Listing 9-2 demonstrates this technique.

```
windowPic;

uses
  {$U HD:MPW:Interfaces.p:MemTypes.p } MemTypes,
  {$U HD:MPW:Interfaces.p:QuickDraw.p} QuickDraw,
  {$U HD:MPW:Interfaces.p:OSIntf.p  } OSIntf,
  {$U HD:MPW:Interfaces.p:ToolIntf.p } ToolIntf,
  {$U HD:MPW:Interfaces.p:PackIntf.p } PackIntf;

const
  appleID = 128;   {resource IDs/menu IDs for Apple, File and Edit menus}
  fileID  = 129;
  editID  = 130;
  windowID= 131;

  appleM = 1; {index for each menu in myMenus (array of menu handles)}
  fileM  = 2;
  editM  = 3;
  windowM= 4;

  menuCount = 4;      {total number of menus}

  aboutItem = 1;      {item in Apple menu}

  undoItem  = 1;      {Items in Edit menu}
  cutItem   = 3;
  copyItem  = 4;
  pasteItem = 5;
  clearitem = 6;

  newItem = 1;      {items in File menu}
  closeItem = 3;
  quitItem = 5;
```

Listing 9-2

```
        textItem = 1; {items in Window menu}
        pictItem = 2;

        wName = 'Window ';  {prefix for window names}

        windDX = 25;        {distance to move for new windows}
        windDY = 25;

        leftEdge = 10;      {initial dimensions of window}
        topEdge = 42;
        rightEdge = 210;
        botEdge = 175;

        picResID = -15968

    var
        myMenus: array [1..menuCount] OF MenuHandle; {handles to the menus}
        dragRect: Rect;         {rectangle used to mark boundaries for dragging window}
        txRect: Rect;           {rectangle for text in application window}
        textH: TEHandle;        {handle to Textedit record}
        theChar: char;          {typed cnaracter}
        extended: boolean;      {true if user is Shift-clicking}
        doneFlag: boolean;      {true if user has chosen Quit Item}
        myEvent: EventRecord;   {information about an event}
        wRecord: WindowRecord;  {information about the application window}
        myWindow: WindowPtr;    {pointer to wRecord}
        myWinPeek : WindowPeek; {another pointer to wRecord}
        whichWindow: WindowPtr; {window in which mouse button was pressed}
        nextWRect: Rect;        {portRect for next window to be opended}
        nextWTitle: Str255;     {title of next window to be opened}
        nextWNum: Longint;      {number of next window (for title)}
        savedPort: GrafPtr;     {pointer to preserve GrafPort}
        menusOK: boolean;       {for disabling menu items}
        scrapErr: Longint;
        scrCopyErr: Integer;

    procedure SetUpMenus;
    { set up menus and menu bar }

      var
        i: Integer;

      begin
        myMenus[appleM] := GetMenu(appleID); {read Apple menu}
        AddResMenu(myMenus[appleM],'DRVR');  {add desk accessory names}
        myMenus[fileM] := GetMenu(fileID);   {read file menu }
        myMenus[editM] := GetMenu(editID);   {read Edit menu }
        myMenus[windowM] := GetMenu (windowID);

        for i:=1 to menuCount do
          InsertMenu(myMenus[i],0);  {install menus in menu bar }
        DrawMenuBar;  { and draw menu bar}
      end; {SetUpMenus}
```

Listing 9-2 (*continued*)

```
procedure OpenWindow;
{ Open a new window }

  begin
    NumToString (nextWNum, nextWTitle); {prepare number for title}
    nextWTitle := concat (wName, nextWTitle); {add to prefix}
    myWindow := NewWindow (Nil, nextWRect, nextWTitle, True, noGrowDocProc,
      Pointer (-1), True, 0);    {open the window}
    SetPort (myWindow);          {make it the current port}
    txRect := thePort^.portRect;{prepare TERecord for new window}
    InsetRect (txRect, 4, 0);
    textH := TENew (txRect, txRect);
    CheckItem (myMenus [windowM], textItem, true);
    CheckItem (myMenus [windowM], pictItem, false);
    myWinPeek := WindowPeek (myWindow);
    myWinPeek^.refcon := Longint (textH); {keep TEHandle in refcon!}
    OffsetRect (nextWRect, windDX, windDY);{move window down and right}
    if nextWRect.right > dragRect.right  {move back if it's too far over}
      then OffsetRect (nextWRect, -nextWRect.left + leftEdge, 0);
    if nextWRect.bottom > dragRect.bottom
      then OffsetRect (nextWRect, 0, -nextWRect.top + topEdge);
    nextWNum := nextWNum + 1;    {bump number for next window}
    menusOK := false;
    EnableItem (myMenus [editM],0); {in case this is the only window}
  end; {OpenWindow}


procedure KillWindow (theWindow: WindowPtr);
{Close a window and throw everything away}

  begin
    TEDispose (TEHandle (WindowPeek (theWindow)^.refcon));
                                 {throw away TERecord}
    DisposeWindow (theWindow);   {throw away WindowRecord}
    textH := NIL;                {for TEIdle in main event loop}
    if FrontWindow = NIL         {if no more windows, disable Close}
      then
        begin
          DisableItem (myMenus[fileM], closeItem);
          DisableItem (myMenus[windowM], 0);
        end; {then}
    if WindowPeek (FrontWindow)^.windowKind < 0 {desk acc coming up, enable undo}
      then
        begin
          EnableItem (myMenus[editM], undoItem)
          DisableItem (myMenus [windowM], 0);
      else DisableItem (myMenus[editM], undoItem);

end; {KillWindow}
```

Listing 9-2 (*continued*)

```
function MyFilter (theDialog: DialogPtr; var theEvent: EventRecord;
    var itemHit: Integer): Boolean;

  var
    theType: Integer;
    theItem: Handle;
    theBox: Rect;
    finalTicks: Longint;

  begin
    if (BitAnd(theEvent.message,charCodeMask) = 13) {carriage return}
      or (BitAnd(theEvent.message,charCodeMask) = 3) {enter}
      then
        begin
          GetDItem (theDialog, 1, theType, theItem, theBox);
          HiliteControl (ControlHandle (theItem), 1);
          Delay (8, finalTicks);
          HiliteControl (ControlHandle (theItem), 0);
          itemHit := 1;
          MyFilter := True;
        end {if BitAnd...then begin}
      else MyFilter := False;
  end; {function MyFilter}


procedure DoAboutBox;

  var
    itemHit: Integer;

  begin
    myWindow := GetNewDialog (1000, Nil, pointer (-1));
    repeat
      ModalDialog (@MyFilter, itemHit)
    until itemHit = 1;
    DisposDialog (myWindow);
  end; {procedure DoAboutBox}


procedure DoPicScrap (command: Integer);

  var
    thePicHandle: Handle;

  begin
    {command is ignored for now -- always acts like Copy}
    scrapErr := ZeroScrap;
    thePicHandle := Handle (GetWindowPic (FrontWindow));
    HLock (thePicHandle);
    scrapErr := PutScrap(GetHandleSize(thePicHandle),'PICT',thePicHandle^);
    HUnlock (thePicHandle);
  end; {procedure DoPicScrap}
```

Listing 9-2 (*continued*)

```
procedure DoCommand (mResult: LONGINT);
{Execute Item specified by mResult, the result of MenuSelect}

  var
    theItem: Integer; {menu item number from mResult low-order word}
    theMenu: Integer; {menu number from mResult high-order word}
    name: Str255;      {desk accessory name}
    temp: Integer;


  begin
    theItem := LoWord(mResult); {call Toolbox Utility routines to set }
    theMenu := HiWord(mResult);      { menu item number and menu number}

    case theMenu of              {case on menu ID}

      appleID:
        if theItem = aboutItem
          then DoAboutBox
          else
            begin
              GetItem(myMenus[appleM],theItem,name);
              {GetPort (savedPort);}
              scrapErr := ZeroScrap;
              scrCopyErr := TEToScrap;
              temp := OpenDeskAcc(name);
              EnableItem (myMenus [editM],0);
              {SetPort (savedPort);}
              if FrontWindow <> NIL
                then
                  begin
                    EnableItem (myMenus [fileM], closeItem);
                    EnableItem (myMenus [editM], undoItem);
                  end; {if FrontWindow then begin}
                menusOK := false;
              end; {if theItem...else begin}
      fileID:
        case theItem of

          newItem:
            OpenWindow;

          closeItem:
            if WindowPeek (FrontWindow)^.windowKind < 0
              then CloseDeskAcc (windowPeek (FrontWindow)^.windowKind)
              {if desk acc window, close it}
              else KillWindow (FrontWindow);
              {if it's one of mine, blow it away}

          quitItem:
            doneFlag := TRUE; {quit}

        end; {case theItem}
```

Listing 9-2 (*continued*)

```
     editID:
       begin
         if not SystemEdit(theItem-1)
           then
             case theItem of {case on menu item number}

                cutItem:
                  if GetWindowPic (FrontWindow) = Nil
                    then TECut(textH)  {call TextEdit to handle Item}
                    else DoPicScrap (cutItem);
                copyItem:
                  if GetWindowPic (FrontWindow) = Nil
                    then TECopy(textH)
                    else DoPicScrap (copyItem);

                pasteItem:
                  if GetWindowPic (FrontWindow) = Nil
                    then TEPaste(textH)
                    else DoPicScrap (pasteItem);

                clearItem:
                  if GetWindowPic (FrontWindow) = Nil
                    then TEDelete(textH)
                    else DoPicScrap (clearItem);


             end;     {case theItem}
         end;     {editID begin}

     windowID:
       case theItem of
         textItem:
           begin
             CheckItem (myMenus [windowM], textItem, true);
             CheckItem (myMenus [windowM], pictItem, false);
             SetWindowPic (FrontWindow, Nil);
             hText := TEHandle (GetWRefCon (FrontWindow));
             InvalRect (thePort^.portRect);
           end; {textItem case}
         pictItem:
           begin
             CheckItem (myMenus [windowM], textItem, false);
             CheckItem (myMenus [windowM], pictItem, true);
             SetWindowPic (FrontWindow, GetPicture (picResId));
             hText := Nil;
             InvalRect (thePort^.portRect);
           end; {pictItem case}


     end;     {case theMenu}
     HiliteMenu(0);
   end;   {DoCommand}
```

Listing 9-2 (*continued*)

```
procedure FixCursor;

  var
    mouseLoc: point;

begin
  GetMouse (mouseLoc);
  if PtInRect (mouseLoc, thePort^.portRect)
    then SetCursor (GetCursor (iBeamCursor)^^)
    else SetCursor (arrow);
end; {procedure FixCursor}


begin            {main program}

  InitGraf(@thePort);
  InitFonts;
  FlushEvents(everyEvent,0);
  InitWindows;
  InitMenus;
  TEInit;
  InitDialogs(NIL);
  InitCursor;

  SetUpMenus;
    with screenBits.bounds do
      SetRect(dragRect,4,24,right-4,bottom-4);
      doneFlag := false;

  menusOK := false;
  nextWNum := 1;    {initialize window number}
  SetRect (nextWRect,leftEdge,topEdge,rightEdge,botEdge);
                    {initialize window rectangle}
  OpenWindow;       {start with one open window}

{ Main event loop }
  repeat
    SystemTask;
    if FrontWindow <> NIL
      then
        if WindowPeek (FrontWindow)^.windowKind >= 0
          then FixCursor;
    if not menusOK and (FrontWindow = NIL)
      then
        begin
          DisableItem (myMenus [fileM], closeItem);
          DisableItem (myMenus [editM], 0);
          menusOK := true;
        end; {if FrontWindow...then begin}
    if textH <> Nil
      then TEIdle(textH);
```

Listing 9-2 (*continued*)

```
if GetNextEvent(everyEvent,myEvent)
  then
  case myEvent.what of

    mouseDown:
      case FindWindow(myEvent.where,whichWindow) of

          inSysWindow:
            SystemClick(myEvent,whichWindow);

          inMenuBar:
            DoCommand(MenuSelect(myEvent.where));

          inDrag:
            DragWindow(whichWindow,myEvent.where,dragRect);

          inContent:
            begin
              if whichWindow <> FrontWindow
                then SelectWindow(whichWindow)
                else if GetWindowPic (whichWindow) = Nil then
                  begin
                    GlobalToLocal(myEvent.where);
                    extended := BitAnd(myEvent.modifiers,shiftKey) <> 0;
                    TEClick(myEvent.where,extended,textH);
                  end;  {if}
            end;  {inContent}

          inGoAway:
            if TrackGoAway (whichWindow, myEvent.where)
              then KillWindow (whichWindow);

        end;    {case FindWindow}

    keyDown, autoKey:
      begin
        theChar := CHR(BitAnd(myEvent.message,charCodeMask));
        if BitAnd(myEvent.modifiers,cmdKey) <> 0
          then DoCommand(MenuKey(theChar))
          else
            if GetWindowPic (FrontWindow) = Nil
              then TEKey(theChar,textH);
      end;  {keyDown, autoKey begin}
```

Listing 9-2 (*continued*)

```
activateEvt:
  begin
  if BitAnd(myEvent.modifiers,activeFlag) <> 0
    then  {application window is becoming active}
      begin
        if GetWindowPic (WindowPtr (myEvent.message)) = Nil
        then begin
         textH := TEHandle (WindowPeek (myEvent.message)^.refcon);
          TEActivate(textH);
              end; {then}
        SetPort (GrafPtr (myEvent.message));
        EnableItem (myMenus[fileM],closeItem);
        DisableItem(myMenus[editM],undoItem);
        if WindowPeek (FrontWindow)^.nextWindow^.windowKind < 0
          then scrCopyErr := TEFromScrap;
      end {if BitAnd...then begin}
    else  {application window is becoming inactive}
      begin
      if GetWindowPic (WindowPtr (myEvent.message)) = Nil
        then TEDeactivate(TEHandle(WindowPeek(myEvent.message)^.refcon));
      if WindowPeek (FrontWindow)^.windowKind < 0
        then
          begin
            EnableItem (myMenus[editM], undoItem);
          if GetWindowPic (WindowPtr (myEvent.message)) = Nil
            then begin
              scrapErr := ZeroScrap;
              scrCopyErr := TEToScrap;
              end; {then}
            end {if WindowPeek...then begin}
          else DisableItem (myMenus[editM], undoItem);
        end;  {else begin}
    end;  {activateEvt begin}

updateEvt:
  begin
    GetPort (savedPort);
    SetPort (GrafPtr (myEvent.message));
    BeginUpdate(WindowPtr(myEvent.message));
    EraseRect(WindowPtr(myEvent.message)^.portRect);
    TEUpdate(WindowPtr(myEvent.message)^.portRect,
    TEHandle(WindowPeek(myEvent.message)^.refcon));
    EndUpdate(WindowPtr(myEvent.message));
    SetPort (savedPort);
  end;  {updateEvt begin}

end;  {case myEvent.what}

until doneFlag;
end.
```

Listing 9-2 (*continued*)

Using the refCon for Data

Each window record includes a Longint field called refCon. This field is left alone by the system. It's intended for whatever the application programmer wants to do with it. Often a window will have some data associated with it; for example, many programs associate TextEdit records with open windows. Although the refCon is declared as a Longint, it's no accident that the size of a Longint (4 bytes) is also the size of a handle. If your window has data associated with it, a good technique is to put the associated data together as a relocatable heap block (created by calling NewHandle) and to stash the handle in the window's refCon. You can do this in Workshop Pascal through the magic of explicit type coercion.

TextEdit Hooks

The TextEdit routines are really handy for doing text entry and editing on a small to medium scale within applications. Usually, when a tougher text editing job is at hand, many programmers will abandon TextEdit entirely and cook up their own text editing package.

Although this isn't always a bad idea, since TextEdit was designed for fairly simple tasks, it's got a lot of neat hooks that can be used to customize it and modify its behavior in various ways. All these hooks are pretty thoroughly documented, but not a lot of programs use them. This section will give you an idea of some of the fancy things you can do with TextEdit.

The first interesting TextEdit hook is called highHook. This hook is a field in each TextEdit record. The highHook field gives you a chance to customize the way TextEdit highlights a selection in that record. Usually, TextEdit just calls InvertRect to highlight a selection, causing the familiar white-on-black look. Let's say you're tired of that, and you want some sort of different appearance: maybe you want the selection enclosed in a box, or underlined, or maybe you want the Macintosh to speak the selection with some voice-synthesis software.

The highHook field allows you to change the highlighting to anything you want. If you install the address of a routine in a TextEdit record's highHook field, that routine will be called whenever TextEdit is asked to highlight a selection. When the routine is called, it has access to the TextEdit record and the rectangle that encloses the selection, so it can do whatever it wants.

Mostly for Assembly Language

Most of the TextEdit hooks provide information in registers rather than on the stack. For example, the highHook routine is passed a pointer to the TextEdit record in register A3, and teSelRect(A3) holds the rectangle to be highlighted. This means that it's fairly difficult to get to this information from a high-level language routine.

Another TextEdit hook, called caretHook, is similar to highHook. The caretHook field allows you to change the way the caret (the insertion point) is drawn. Normally, of course, TextEdit simply calls InvertRect on a one-pixel wide rectangle that is the insertion point. This makes the caret blink.

Let's say you're tired of blinking insertion points and you'd rather have a nonblinking insertion point, or one that flashes from top to bottom like a marquee, or maybe a little pointer sticking between the characters, or something else that you think of. You can do this with caretHook. If you install a pointer to a routine in the caretHook field of a TextEdit record, the ROM will call you whenever it wants to make the insertion point blink. You can then do whatever you want. Once again, register A3 will contain a pointer to the textEdit record.

When you double-click in text, TextEdit selects a word. TextEdit has a fairly simple definition of a word: it's anything that's surrounded by spaces or nonprinting characters (those with ASCII values less than $20). This definition of a word is also used when figuring out how to do word wrapping at the end of a line.

Sometimes you may want to define a word as something more sophisticated. For example, you may have an application in which you want to define hyphenated words as a single word, or you may want double-clicks to select words and a comma or period that follows the word. You can do these things by using the wordBreak hook in the TextEdit record.

When you install a routine in the wordBreak field, TextEdit will call you whenever it has to decide whether something is a word, either for a double-click or for word wrap. When you're called, TextEdit tells you the text that it's looking at and the character position that it's considering for the word break. You get to tell it whether you want to put a word break at that position or not.

When you call TEClick, TextEdit takes control and follows the user's mouse action until the mouse button goes up. This allows the user to drag the mouse around and select text. There's one problem with this arrangement: many applications like to implement **autoscrolling**; that is, when the user drags the mouse below the last line of text that's visible and there's more text below, a good application will automatically scroll the text up.

If your application calls TEClick when it sees a click in the text, it will lose control of things until the user releases the mouse button. This means that it has no chance to autoscroll while the user is dragging around. But, as you might have guessed, there's a nifty TextEdit hook that comes to the rescue. This is the clikLoop hook.

By setting this hook to point at a routine that you write, you can autoscroll or do anything else that you want while the user is dragging the mouse in text. The routine that you hook into the clikLoop will be called repeatedly by TextEdit after you call TEClick for as long as the user is holding down the mouse button.

Macintosh Plus

In the Macintosh Plus version of TextEdit, there's a default clikLoop that's supplied automatically when you create a new TextEdit record. This default clikLoop includes autoscrolling capability; however, you'll usually want to update a scroll bar in the window while you're autoscrolling along, and the default clikLoop supplied by TextEdit doesn't have any facility for updating a scroll bar. It's mainly designed to allow editable text that shows up in dialogs (usually without scroll bars) to be autoscrolled.

Using "Real" Fonts

The Macintosh ROM gives you a lot of flexibility when you're drawing text. In addition to having an incredible variety of fonts, you can draw in various styles that include bold and italic and in lots of different sizes.

Like just about every other piece of code or data that you use, fonts are stored as resources. FONT resources are basically little bitmaps of the characters within a font, along with other information used in drawing the characters, such as their widths.

One thing you get to specify when you draw text is the font's size, which is given in points. In the resource file, there can be copies of fonts in multiple sizes; for example, a resource file may have the bitmaps for a particular font in 9-, 12-, and 18-point sizes.

If you try to draw text in a point size that doesn't exist on disk, you might think that the Font Manager will give up and produce some kind of error. Actually, the Font Manager tries to be very accommodating. If it doesn't have the point size that you requested, it tries to grab another size and **scale** it, that is, stretch or shrink the bits that it has to the point size that you requested.

For example, let's say you tell the ROM that the user wants you to draw in New York font, 14-point size. You do this by calling `TextFont` (`newYork`) and `TextSize` (`14`). The ROM will attempt to find a FONT resource that has the bits for New York in 14-point size. If it doesn't find the font in this size, it will take the font in an available size and scale it. It will first try to find a size that's exactly twice the size or exactly half the size desired; in this case, that would be 28 point or 7 point. If it can't find a font that's twice or half the size, the Font Manager will next try for a larger point size; finally, it will settle for a smaller size.

When the Font Manager has to get a different size and scale it, the results can be ugly (see Figure 9-2 for some examples of scaled fonts). As you can see, scaled fonts are something you should avoid or you'll get a bad reputation. How can you prevent fonts from being scaled?

The best way to prevent fonts from being scaled is to help the user figure out which point sizes are present for each font. For example, if you let the user know that New York 9, 12, or 18 can be used without scaling, you'll at least be presenting enough information for an intelligent choice.

To support your noble efforts, the Font Manager includes a function called `RealFont`. This function takes a font number and a point size, and it returns a boolean value telling you whether the font really exists in that point size. If your application presents a choice of font sizes, you can call `RealFont` to determine which point sizes really exist. This is the technique used, for example, in MacPaint. The Font Size menu in MacPaint shows the sizes that are ''real'' in outlined type; the sizes that will have to be scaled are shown in plain type.

Four score and seven years ago,

our fathers brought forth upon this continent a
NEW nation conceived in liberty
and dedicated to the proposition that all men
are created equal.

Figure 9-2 Scaled fonts

By using RealFont, you can build a font size menu that tells the user which fonts will have nice-looking real bits and which will be scaled. The example program shown in Listing 9-3 demonstrates how to do this.

There's actually a way to disable font scaling completely. There's a system global called FScaleDisable located at $A63. This global is normally set to zero, which allows scaling. If this byte is set to anything other than zero, font scaling is disabled. If you try to draw in a font size that isn't there, the Font Manager just refuses and draws in a size that it does have.

```
program FontMenu;

{$U+}
{$D+}
(*  uses
    {$U HD:MPW:Interfaces.p:MemTypes.p } MemTypes,
    {$U HD:MPW:Interfaces.p:QuickDraw.p} QuickDraw,
    {$U HD:MPW:Interfaces.p:OSIntf.p    } OSIntf,
    {$U HD:MPW:Interfaces.p:ToolIntf.p } ToolIntf,
    {$U HD:MPW:Interfaces.p:PackIntf.p } PackIntf;*)

  const
      appleID = 128;   {resource IDs/menu IDs for Apple, File and Edit menus}
      fileID  = 129;
      editID  = 130;
      fontNameID = 131;
      fontSizeID  = 132;

      appleM = 1; {index for each menu in myMenus (array of menu handles)}
      fileM  = 2;
      editM  = 3;
      fontNameM  = 4;
      fontSizeM  = 5;

      menuCount = 5;      {total number of menus to be gotten from resource file}

      aboutItem = 1;      {item in Apple menu}

      undoItem  = 1;      {Items in Edit menu}
      cutItem   = 3;
      copyItem  = 4;
      pasteItem = 5;
      clearitem = 6;

      newItem = 1;       {items in File menu}
      closeItem = 3;
      quitItem = 5;

      nmFSizes = 6;       {number of Font Sizes}
      wName = 'Window ';  {prefix for window names}
```

Listing 9-3

```
      windDX = 25;          {distance to move for new windows}
      windDY = 25;

      leftEdge = 10;        {initial dimensions of window}
      topEdge = 42;
      rightEdge = 210;
      botEdge = 175;

  TYPE
    WDataRec = record
                   txEdH: TEHandle;
                   nChecked: integer;   {font name item checked}
                   sChecked: integer;   {font size item checked}
               End; {WdataRec}
    WDataPtr = ^WDataRec;
    WDataH = ^WDataPtr;

  var
    myMenus: array [1..menuCount] OF MenuHandle; {handles to the menus}
    dragRect: Rect;          {rectangle used to mark boundaries for dragging window}
    txRect: Rect;            {rectangle for text in application window}
    textH: TEHandle;         {handle to Textedit record}
    theChar: char;           {typed character}
    extended: boolean;       {true if user is Shift-clicking}
    doneFlag: boolean;       {true if user has chosen Quit Item}
    myEvent: EventRecord;    {information about an event}
    wRecord: WindowRecord;   {information about the application window}
    myWindow: WindowPtr;     {pointer to wRecord}
    myWinPeek : WindowPeek;  {another pointer to wRecord}
    whichWindow: WindowPtr;  {window in which mouse button was pressed}
    nextWRect: Rect;         {portRect for next window to be opended}
    nextWTitle: Str255;      {title of next window to be opened}
    nextWNum: Longint;       {number of next window (for title)}
    savedPort: GrafPtr;      {pointer to preserve GrafPort}
    menusOK: boolean;        {for disabling menu items}
    scrapErr: Longint;
    scrCopyErr: Integer;
    fontSizeChecked: Integer; {to keep track of which font size is checked}
    fontNameChecked: Integer; {to keep track of which font name is checked}
    AppFontItem: integer;
    AppSizeItem: integer;
    fSizes: array[1..nmFSizes] of Integer;  {to keep track of font sizes}
    WindowsOpen: integer;    { to keep track of how many windows are open}


procedure ChangeFontMenus(nmToCheck,szToCheck: integer);

Var
    i: integer;
    name: str255;
    fNum: integer;
```

Listing 9-3 (*continued*)

```
Begin {ChangeFontMenus}
    if nmToCheck <> fontNameChecked { if the font has changed...}
        then
            Begin
                myWinPeek := WindowPeek (myWindow);  {set MyWinPeek to the proper window}
                SetItemMark(myMenus[fontNameM],nmToCheck,chr(checkmark));
                SetItemMark(myMenus[fontNameM],fontNameChecked,chr(nomark));
                fontNameChecked:= nmToCheck;  {update this global}
                if WindowsOpen > 0  {we can only do this if we have a window open}
                    then
                        wDataH(myWinPeek^.refcon)^^.nChecked:= nmToCheck;
                            {update the nChecked field in the WDataRec for this window}

                GetItem(myMenus[fontNameM],nmToCheck,name);  {we need to get the font number}
                GetFNum(name,fNum);
                for i:= 1 to nmFSizes do
                    if RealFont(fNum,fSizes[i])
                        then
                            SetItemStyle(myMenus[fontSizeM],i,[outline])
                        else
                            SetItemStyle(myMenus[fontSizeM],i,[]);
            End; {if}

    if szToCheck <> fontSizeChecked { if the size has changed...}
        then
            Begin
                myWinPeek := WindowPeek (myWindow);{set MyWinPeek to the proper window}
                SetItemMark(myMenus[fontSizeM],szToCheck,chr(checkmark));
                SetItemMark(myMenus[fontSizeM],fontSizeChecked,chr(nomark));
                fontSizeChecked:= szToCheck; {update this global}
                if WindowsOpen > 0{we can only do this if we have a window open}
                    then
                        wDataH(myWinPeek^.refcon)^^.sChecked:= szToCheck;
                            {update the sChecked field in the WDataRec for this window}
            End; {if}
End;   {ChangeFontMenus}


    procedure SetUpMenus;
    { set up menus and menu bar }

        var
            i: Integer;
            ApplFName: str255;
            ApplFNum: integer;
            MenuFName: str255;
            FMDefaultSize: ^signedByte;
            DefSize: integer;
```

Listing 9-3 (*continued*)

```
begin
  myMenus[appleM] := GetMenu(appleID);  {read Apple menu}
  AddResMenu(myMenus[appleM],'DRVR');    {add desk accessory names}
  myMenus[fileM] := GetMenu(fileID);     {read file menu }
  myMenus[editM] := GetMenu(editID);     {read Edit menu }
  myMenus[fontNameM] := GetMenu(fontNameID);{read fName menu }
  myMenus[fontSizeM] := GetMenu(fontSizeID);{read fSize menu }
  AddResMenu(myMenus[fontNameM],'FONT');

  for i:=1 to menuCount do
    InsertMenu(myMenus[i],0);  {install menus in menu bar }
  GetFontName(ApplFont,ApplFName);
  GetFNum(ApplFName,ApplFNum);

  i:= 0;                    {initialize so we can step through the Font menu}
  repeat
    i:= i+1;
    GetItem(myMenus[fontNameM],i,MenuFName);{check each name, until..}
  until ApplFName = MenuFName;            {name matches the ApplFName}
  SetItemMark(myMenus[fontNameM],i,chr(checkMark));  {check that font}
  fontNameChecked:= i;  {update the global}
  AppFontItem:= i;      {update the global}


  FMDefaultSize:= pointer($987);
  for i:= 1 to nmFSizes do
    Begin
      if RealFont(ApplFNum,fSizes[i])
        then
          SetItemStyle(myMenus[fontSizeM],i,[outline]);
      if  fSizes[i] = FMDefaultSize^ {have we hit the default size ?}
        then
          Begin
            SetItemMark(myMenus[fontSizeM],i,chr(checkMark));  {check that size}
            fontSizeChecked:= i;  {update the global}
            AppSizeItem:= i;      {update the global}
          End; {if FMDefaultSize^...}
    End;  {for}
  DrawMenuBar;  { and draw menu bar}
end;  {SetUpMenus}



procedure OpenWindow;
{ Open a new window }

VAR
  newWDataH: WDataH;
```

Listing 9-3 (*continued*)

```
begin
   NumToString (nextWNum, nextWTitle); {prepare number for title}
   nextWTitle := concat (wName, nextWTitle); {add to prefix}
   myWindow := NewWindow (Nil, nextWRect, nextWTitle, True, noGrowDocProc,
      Pointer (-1), True, 0);   {open the window}
   SetPort (myWindow);            {make it the current port}
   txRect := thePort^.portRect;{prepare TERecord for new window}
   InsetRect (txRect, 4, 0);
   textH := TENew (txRect, txRect);
   myWinPeek := WindowPeek (myWindow);{set MyWinPeek to the proper window}
   newWDataH:= wDataH(NewHandle(SizeOf(wDataRec)));
   myWinPeek^.refcon := Longint (newWDataH); {keep Handle to our data struct in refcon!}
   with wDataH(myWinPeek^.refcon)^^ do
      Begin
         txEdH:= textH;
         nchecked:= AppFontItem;
         schecked:= AppSizeItem;
      End;  {with}

   OffsetRect (nextWRect, windDX, windDY);{move window down and right}
   if nextWRect.right > dragRect.right   {move back if it's too far over}
      then OffsetRect (nextWRect, -nextWRect.left + leftEdge, 0);
   if nextWRect.bottom > dragRect.bottom
      then OffsetRect (nextWRect, 0, -nextWRect.top + topEdge);
   nextWNum := nextWNum + 1;   {bump number for next window}
   menusOK := false;
   WindowsOpen:= WindowsOpen+1; {update the global}
   EnableItem (myMenus [editM],0); {in case this is the only window}
   if WindowsOpen = 1  {we just opened the first window, so we need to...}
      then             {redraw the menu bar to enable 'Edit' }
         DrawMenuBar;
end; {OpenWindow}


procedure KillWindow (theWindow: WindowPtr);
{Close a window and throw everything away}

begin
   myWinPeek := WindowPeek (theWindow);{set MyWinPeek to the proper window}
   TEDispose (wDataH(myWinPeek^.refcon)^^.txEdH);
                              {throw away TERecord}
   DisposHandle(Handle(WindowPeek(theWindow)^.refcon));{throw away recon handle}
   DisposeWindow (theWindow);  {throw away WindowRecord}
   textH := NIL;              {for TEIdle in main event loop}
   if FrontWindow = NIL then Begin   {if no more windows, disable Close}
      SetCursor(arrow);
      DisableItem (myMenus[fileM], closeItem)
   End {if}
```

Listing 9-3 (*continued*)

```
      else
          if WindowPeek (FrontWindow)^.windowKind < 0
                {if a desk acc is coming up, enable undo}
            then Begin
                SetCursor(arrow);
                EnableItem (myMenus[editM], undoItem);
            End {if}
            else DisableItem (myMenus[editM], undoItem);
      WindowsOpen:=WindowsOpen-1;{update the global}
      if WindowsOpen = 0 {if no windows are open, change menus to show defaults}
        then
          ChangeFontMenus(AppFontItem, AppSizeItem);
    end; {KillWindow}


function MyFilter (theDialog: DialogPtr; var theEvent: EventRecord;
    var itemHit: Integer): Boolean;

    var
      theType: Integer;
      theItem: Handle;
      theBox: Rect;
      finalTicks: Longint;

    begin
      if (BitAnd(theEvent.message,charCodeMask) = 13) {carriage return}
        or (BitAnd(theEvent.message,charCodeMask) = 3) {enter}
        then
          begin
            GetDItem (theDialog, 1, theType, theItem, theBox);
            HiliteControl (ControlHandle (theItem), 1);
            Delay (8, finalTicks);
            HiliteControl (ControlHandle (theItem), 0);
            itemHit := 1;
            MyFilter := True;
          end {if BitAnd...then begin}
        else MyFilter := False;
    end; {function MyFilter}


procedure DoAboutBox;

    var
      itemHit: Integer;

    begin
      myWindow := GetNewDialog (1000, Nil, pointer (-1));
      repeat
        ModalDialog (@MyFilter, itemHit)
      until itemHit = 1;
      DisposDialog (myWindow);
    end; {procedure DoAboutBox}
```

Listing 9-3 (*continued*)

```
procedure DoCommand (mResult: LONGINT);
{Execute Item specified by mResult, the result of MenuSelect}

  var
    theItem: Integer; {menu item number from mResult low-order word}
    theMenu: Integer; {menu number from mResult high-order word}
    name: Str255;      {desk accessory name}
    temp: Integer;
    i: integer;
    fontInf: fontInfo;

  begin
    theItem := LoWord(mResult); {call Toolbox Utility routines to set }
    theMenu := HiWord(mResult);      { menu item number and menu number}

    case theMenu of             {case on menu ID}

      appleID:
        if theItem = aboutItem
          then DoAboutBox
          else
            begin
              GetItem(myMenus[appleM],theItem,name);
              {GetPort (savedPort);}
              scrapErr := ZeroScrap;
              scrCopyErr := TEToScrap;
              temp := OpenDeskAcc(name);
              EnableItem (myMenus [editM],0);
              {SetPort (savedPort);}
              if FrontWindow <> NIL
                then
                  begin
                    EnableItem (myMenus [fileM], closeItem);
                    EnableItem (myMenus [editM], undoItem);
                  end; {if FrontWindow then begin}
              menusOK := false;
            end;   {if theItem...else begin}
      fileID:
        case theItem of

          newItem:
            OpenWindow;

          closeItem:
            if WindowPeek (FrontWindow)^.windowKind < 0
              then CloseDeskAcc (windowPeek (FrontWindow)^.windowKind)
              {if desk acc window, close it}
              else KillWindow (FrontWindow);
              {if it's one of mine, blow it away}
```

Listing 9-3 (*continued*)

```
        quitItem:
          doneFlag := TRUE; {quit}

     end; {case theItem}

  editID:
    begin
      if not SystemEdit(theItem-1) {we don't need to check OpenWindows...}
         then    {because edit menu is disabled if no active window exists}
           case theItem of {case on menu item number}
             cutItem:  TECut(textH); {call TextEdit to handle Item}
             copyItem: TECopy(textH);
             pasteItem:TEPaste(textH);
             clearItem:TEDelete(textH);
           end;    {case theItem}
    end;    {editID begin}

  fontNameID:
     Begin
        if (WindowsOpen > 0) and (theItem <> FontNameChecked)
          then
            Begin
              SetPort(myWindow);
              GetItem(myMenus[fontNameM],theItem,name);
              GetFNum(name,temp);
              TextFont(temp); {set Text Font to this}
              GetFontInfo(fontInf);{get info about font}
              with textH^^,fontinf do {manually stuff TERecord}
                Begin
                  txFont:= temp;
                  fontAscent:= ascent;
                  lineheight:= ascent+descent+leading;
                End;  {with}

              ChangeFontMenus(theItem,FontSizeChecked);   {update menus}
              TECalText(textH);   {tell TE that it needs to recalculate}
              InvalRect(textH^^.destRect); { to cause an update event }
            End;  {if}
     End;  {fontNameID Begin}

  fontSizeID:
     Begin
        if (WindowsOpen > 0) and (theItem <> FontSizeChecked)
          then
            Begin
              SetPort(myWindow);
              TextSize(fSizes[theItem]); {change the text size}
              GetFontInfo(fontInf);{get info about font}
              with textH^^,fontinf do {manually stuff TERecord}
```

Listing 9-3 (*continued*)

```
                 Begin
                   txSize:= fSizes[theItem];
                   fontAscent:= ascent;
                   lineheight:= ascent+descent+leading;
                 End;  {with}
               ChangeFontMenus(FontNameChecked,theItem);  {update menus}
               TECalText(textH);  {tell TE that it needs to recalculate}
               InvalRect(textH^^.destRect);  { to cause an update event }
             End; {if}
         End;  {fontSizeID Begin}
     end;     {case theMenu}


     HiliteMenu(0);
   end;  {DoCommand}



  procedure FixCursor;

    var
       mouseLoc: point;


  begin
    GetMouse (mouseLoc);
    if PtInRect (mouseLoc, thePort^.portRect)
      then SetCursor (GetCursor (iBeamCursor)^^)
      else SetCursor (arrow);
  end; {procedure FixCursor}



  begin          {main program}

    InitGraf(@thePort);
    InitFonts;
    FlushEvents(everyEvent,0);
    InitWindows;
    InitMenus;
    TEInit;
    InitDialogs(NIL);
    InitCursor;

    fSizes[1]:= 9; fSizes[2]:= 10; fSizes[3]:= 12;
    fSizes[4]:= 14; fSizes[5]:= 18; fSizes[6]:= 24;{initialize fSizes array}

    SetUpMenus;
      with screenBits.bounds do
        SetRect(dragRect,4,24,right-4,bottom-4);
    doneFlag := false;



    menusOK := false;
    nextWNum := 1;    {initialize window number}
    SetRect (nextWRect,leftEdge,topEdge,rightEdge,botEdge);
                    {initialize window rectangle}
```

Listing 9-3 (*continued*)

```
    WindowsOpen:= 0;   {initialize}
    OpenWindow;         {start with one open window}

{ Main event loop }
  repeat
    SystemTask;
    if FrontWindow <> NIL
      then
        if WindowPeek (FrontWindow)^.windowKind >= 0
          then FixCursor;
    if not menusOK and (FrontWindow = NIL)
      then
        begin
          DisableItem (myMenus [fileM], closeItem);
          DisableItem (myMenus [editM], 0);
          DrawMenuBar;  { dim the title "Edit" of the edit menu}
          menusOK := true;
        end; {if FrontWindow...then begin}
    if textH <> Nil
      then TEIdle(textH);

    if GetNextEvent(everyEvent,myEvent)
      then
      case myEvent.what of

        mouseDown:
          case FindWindow(myEvent.where,whichWindow) of

              inSysWindow:
                SystemClick(myEvent,whichWindow);

              inMenuBar:
                DoCommand(MenuSelect(myEvent.where));

              inDrag:
                DragWindow(whichWindow,myEvent.where,dragRect);

              inContent:
                begin
                  if whichWindow <> FrontWindow
                    then SelectWindow(whichWindow)
                    else
                      begin
                        GlobalToLocal(myEvent.where);
                        extended := BitAnd(myEvent.modifiers,shiftKey) <> 0;
                        TEClick(myEvent.where,extended,textH);
                      end;  {else}
              end;   {inContent}
```

Listing 9-3 (*continued*)

```
    inGoAway:
      if TrackGoAway (whichWindow, myEvent.where)
        then KillWindow (whichWindow);

  end;    {case FindWindow}


keyDown, autoKey:
  begin
    theChar := CHR(BitAnd(myEvent.message,charCodeMask));
    if BitAnd(myEvent.modifiers,cmdKey) <> 0
      then DoCommand(MenuKey(theChar))
      else
        if WindowsOpen > 0
          then
            TEKey(theChar,textH);
  end;   {keyDown, autoKey begin}


activateEvt:
  begin
    myWinPeek := WindowPeek (myEvent.message);{set MyWinPeek to the proper window}
    if BitAnd(myEvent.modifiers,activeFlag) <> 0
      then  {application window is becoming active}
        begin
          SetPort (GrafPtr (myEvent.message));
          myWindow:= GrafPtr(myEvent.message);
          with wDataH(myWinPeek^.refcon)^^ do
            Begin
              textH := txEdH;{ set textH to appropriate TEHandle }
              ChangeFontMenus(nChecked, sChecked); {update menus}
            End;   {with}

          TEActivate(textH);
          EnableItem (myMenus[fileM],closeItem);
          DisableItem(myMenus[editM],undoItem);
          if WindowPeek (FrontWindow)^.nextWindow^.windowKind < 0
            then scrCopyErr := TEFromScrap;
        end {if BitAnd...then begin}
      else  {application window is becoming inactive}
        begin
        TEDeactivate(wDataH(myWinPeek^.refcon)^^.txEdH);
        if WindowPeek (FrontWindow)^.windowKind < 0
          then
            begin
              EnableItem (myMenus[editM], undoItem);
              scrapErr := ZeroScrap;
              scrCopyErr := TEToScrap;
            end {if WindowPeek...then begin}
          else DisableItem (myMenus[editM], undoItem);
        end;   {else begin}
  end;  {activateEvt begin}
```

Listing 9-3 (continued)

```
    updateEvt:
      begin
        myWinPeek := WindowPeek (myEvent.message);{set MyWinPeek to the proper window}
        GetPort (savedPort);
        SetPort (GrafPtr (myEvent.message));

        BeginUpdate(WindowPtr(myEvent.message));
        EraseRect(WindowPtr(myEvent.message)^.portRect);
        TEUpdate(WindowPtr(myEvent.message)^.portRect,
        wDataH(myWinPeek^.refcon)^^.txEdH);
        EndUpdate(WindowPtr(myEvent.message));
        SetPort (savedPort);
      end;  {updateEvt begin}

    end;  {case myEvent.what}

  until doneFlag;
end.
```

Listing 9-3 (*continued*)

LaserWriter

The LaserWriter creates fonts in an entirely different way, with a technique called **splines**. In this scheme, the LaserWriter doesn't store a bitmap of the fonts in certain point sizes. Instead, it has a spline, or outline, of each character of the font. This takes up a lot more memory than a bitmap, but it allows the LaserWriter to print characters for any spline font that it has in ROM in any point size without scaling.

Macintosh Plus

The Font Manager is smarter in the Macintosh Plus. There's another resource type, FOND, that describes a "font family." This resource has information about all the fonts in the family. Also, the Macintosh Plus is better about scaling fonts, so they don't look as bad, especially when printed. If you still want to disable scaling, the Macintosh Plus ROM has a call that will take care of setting or clearing the FScaleDisable byte for you. The call is SetFScaleDisable, and it takes one parameter, a boolean indicating whether scaling should be disabled (True) or enabled (False).

Resuming from System Errors

A lot of this book is dedicated to helping you prevent your innocent users from ever seeing their Macintosh blow up with the dreaded system error alert. By understanding how your program works, testing it thoroughly, and debugging it, you'll greatly reduce the chance of your application dying with a system error.

However, even if you're really smart and very clever, you still might miss something and your program may crash. There's nothing more frustrating than losing work because you hadn't saved something before a crash. You may even have experienced this catastrophe yourself.

Sometimes, when a system error occurs, the system is in pretty sad shape. As we've already discussed, the heap and the stack may have been randomly trashed, the system globals may be invalid, and your program's code may have been overwritten. Often, though, things aren't all that bad. It may just be that you've attempted to dereference a handle that's been disposed of or maybe you passed a bad parameter to a ROM routine. It's possible that the system error actually caught the first sign of bad tidings and that the heap and stack are still reasonably valid.

Since there's a chance that the system is not completely broken when a system error occurs, there's also a chance that the user's data is intact. For example, if the user has been entering text into a word-processing document, it might still be readable even after a system error. It sure would be nice if you could save some of the document that the poor user has worked so hard on. Is there any way to do this?

Of course there is! On the Macintosh, there are ways to do all sorts of things, including recover from system errors. Almost every application calls InitDialogs (Nil) without the programmer thinking much about it. The parameter to InitDialogs is kind of out of place—it's actually more related to the System Error Handler than to the Dialog Manager. If you pass a pointer to a procedure in this field and a system error occurs while your program is running, the system error alert will have its "Resume" button enabled. If the user clicks it, the routine that you pointed to when you called InitDialogs will be called by the System Error Handler.

Once your procedure is called, you can try to do the user a favor, such as saving the document. If you succeed, as you have a reasonable chance of doing, you'll probably make the user very happy. Of course, there are a zillion things that could go wrong. Since a system error has occurred, all bets are off. There's no guarantee that your resume procedure itself hasn't been demolished by runaway code. It's even possible that your saving the document to the disk will damage things that are already saved on that disk.

Given all this, what can you possibly do to help the user in your resume procedure? One thing you can do is write a procedure that, requiring as little of the Operating System as possible, writes the user's document out to disk in some form. If it's a word-processing document, you might just mass-write it to disk and then worry about interpreting it after the user has restarted.

There's another problem. Since the System Error Handler will have reset the stack pointer, your global variables may no longer be valid. As a safety measure, you can use the system global variable called ApplScratch at $A78. This is a 12-byte space that's reserved for use by applications. If your application keeps its important data in a small number of relocatable blocks, you can store handles to these blocks in the ApplScratch area. Then, in your resume procedure: you can use these handles to find the data that you want to save. Of course, there's no guarantee that ApplScratch hasn't been smashed by runaway code before the system error occurred.

One more thing to remember about your resume procedure's efforts to save something to disk is this: if the system is broken in just the right way, you could clobber other stuff that's already on the disk you're saving to. Because of this, it's a good idea to ask the user to insert a disk that's blank or not "valuable" before you try to save. For this reason, it's a real good idea not to allow the attempted save to be to a hard disk.

Although trying to accomplish something useful after a system error has occurred is very tricky, it's sure nice to at least give the user the option. If you implement a resume routine, remember this important fact: the system is broken, maybe severely, maybe not. This means that you should try to do as little as possible: just try to save the user's work without making much fuss, and then have the user restart the Macintosh (going back to the Finder isn't good enough—system heap stuff or system globals may be damaged).

A good philosophy for resume procedures is "do it yourself." In other words, rely on the system as little as possible. If you want to ask the user a question, like whether to attempt saving his work, don't call GetNewDialog. Just call QuickDraw directly to draw the dialog. At this point, neatness doesn't count. You should also watch the mouse button yourself; don't rely on the Control Manager or the event queue.

If you design a useful, reasonably safe resume procedure that saves the user from disaster even once, you may be eligible for a medal, or at least large cash rewards from the person whose data you saved.

Things to Remember

- By observing some restrictions, you can use a high-level language to write a definition function, such as a window definition or menu definition.
- You can use the system global called ResErrProc to cause a procedure to be called automatically when a Resource Manager error occurs.
- When moving a resource from one file to another, there are several things to watch out for, including making sure that the destination file does not already contain a resource of the type and ID that you're copying.
- You can get some reasonably flicker-free drawing by simply looping until the vertical blanking period begins.
- The Window Manager defines a method for automatically updating windows by drawing pictures, instead of generating update events.
- TextEdit contains lots of hooks that you can grab onto to enhance its capabilities.
- You can determine whether a font will have to be scaled before using it by using the RealFont call.
- There's a hook in the System Error Handler to allow you to try to take some last-ditch action *after* a system error has occurred.

CHAPTER

10

Operating System Techniques

In this chapter, we'll discuss some tricks that you can do with the Operating System. We'll discuss the different kinds of File Manager calls, how ROM calls really work, what really happens when an application is launched, and other things.

High-level and Low-level Calls

Many parts of the Operating System define "low-level" and "high-level" calls. In general, the low-level calls are direct calls to the ROM. Many Operating System calls require extensive **parameter blocks**, and the low-level calls make the programmer specify the appropriate fields of the parameter block. The parameter block is also used to return values to the caller. For example, when you call PBOpen, you pass it a name and volume reference number, and it passes you a file reference number and an error result. In high-level languages, parameter blocks are implemented as records.

High-level language programmers are more used to dealing with routines that take a few distinct parameters, rather than one gigantic record with fields filled in. So there are a bunch of high-level calls that replace the parameter block with a short list of separate parameters. For example, the high-level version of PBOpen, a function called FSOpen, takes two parameters: a file name and a volume reference number. It returns the file reference number as a VAR parameter and returns the error code as the function result.

The high-level calls take care of all the dirty work of creating and filling in a parameter block. They're **glue** routines, as we discussed in Part Two. Although they're handy for making basic calls, they're designed to be general, and there are a lot of features of the sytem that can't be accessed with the high-level calls. For example, Operating System calls may be executed asynchronously. This means that the program is allowed to continue while the Operating System call is still going on. When the call is finished, it calls a **completion routine**, which is a routine that the programmer specified when the OS call was made. If you want to use asynchronous I/O, you'll have to use the low-level calls.

There are other advantages in using the low-level calls. Since the call is made directly, there's less overhead to make the call, so it's faster and less memory is used.

Although the high-level calls are adequate for many uses, it's important to know that the low-level calls are really very easy to use. If you want to try asynchronous I/O to speed up your application or give it some background-tasking capabilities, you can use the low-level calls to get access to more of the Operating System's power.

Printing Bitmaps

Sometimes you'll want to give your application the capability of printing a bitmap without the overhead of having to go through a normal printing job. The printer driver defines a very easy to use printer-independent way to print bitmaps. It's done with a control call to the printer driver, ".Print". The control call, which is call number four, takes three parameters: the bitmap to be printed, a rectangle specifying which part of the bitmap to print, and a parameter that allows bitmaps printed on the ImageWriter to have square dots, rather than the rectangular dots that are normally produced.

In a high-level language, you can use the PrCtlCall procedure to print a bitmap, like this Workshop Pascal example:

```
PrCtlCall (4, Longint(@myBitMap), Longint(@myRect), IPaintBits);
```

In this example, control call four is made to .Print, passing it pointers to the bitmap to be printed and to a rectangle within the bitmap. The last parameter specifies that the bitmap be printed in square pixels.

You can use this call to print the screen:

```
PrCtlCall (4, Longint (@screenBits), Longint (@screenBits.bounds), IPaintBits);
```

Using this printer control call, you can print bitmaps, including windows and the screen, very easily.

How ROM Calls Work

All personal computers provide some sort of operating system service routines that can be called by programmers. At the very least, these routines include creating, opening, closing, reading, and writing files, and most provide a lot more. There's probably no personal computer that has more callable routines than the Macintosh (something over 600 routines—everyone seems to have lost count).

One problem with having callable routines is that the computer's operating system is probably going to change. Even on the Macintosh, which has most of its callable routines in ROM, changes happen. Sometimes these changes require a whole new ROM, as with the Macintosh Plus; but changing the system routines can be as simple as using a new system disk that applies patches to the ROM. Since there are application programs depending on an unchanging ROM, the changers of the system have to be very careful.

On some systems, when applications call the operating system, they do so by jumping directly to an address in RAM or ROM. Obviously, this is a severe limitation on changes to the system; routines have to be in exactly the same place or the applications won't work any more.

The Macintosh uses a nifty scheme to make its ROM calls that doesn't have this problem. On the Macintosh, all ROM calls are single 68000 instructions. It works like this: when the 68000 sees an instruction that begins with the hex digit A, it immediately realizes that it doesn't want the instruction. Instead, it creates a 68000 **exception** and jumps to a routine whose address is stored at location $28. This address is called an **exception vector** and it's intended for just this purpose: taking control when an instruction starting with A is encountered.

The Macintosh ROM hooks itself into this vector when the system starts up. When the 68000 encounters an A-instruction, it winds up in the ROM, running a routine called the **trap dispatcher**. The trap dispatcher takes the A-instruction and, by looking at the remaining part of the word, determines which ROM routine is being called. It gets the address of the ROM routine from a table of addresses kept in the low memory global area.

After the trap dispatcher determines the address of the routine to be called, it simply jumps (JSR's, actually) to that location. This way, the application doesn't have to know where in the ROM the system routines are—it just calls things with an A-instruction. The trap dispatcher figures out where the routine really is.

The beauty of this scheme is that Apple can move routines around in the ROM all it wants. As long as the system sets up the trap dispatch table correctly when it starts up, applications don't have to care about the location of routines that they're calling. This helps ease compatibility as new and wonderful ROMs are made.

Speed Freaks

Those of you inclined to optimize your code for speed will no doubt have figured out that this trap dispatching business takes time. If you're calling a ROM routine over and over in a loop, you may wish that you knew the actual address of the routine in ROM so that you could JSR to it, which would be much faster than calling it via a trap.

The Macintosh actually provides you with a way to do this legally. There's a ROM call that will give you the absolute address of any call in the ROM. This call, GetTrapAddress, takes a ROM call number as a parameter and returns the address of that call. If you call GetTrapAddress once to find out the location of the call you want, you can then JSR to it all day long, and it will work fine. As long as you call GetTrapAddress in your application, you'll be OK, since Apple guarantees that the ROM will not change while your application is running.

Random Access File I/O

Most high-level language programmers are used to high-level, random access file I/O. This is a set of functions that allows access to logical records within a file. In Pascal, this is usually implemented with the reset and rewrite statements, which open a file; seek, which finds a specified record in the file; and put and get, which store and retrieve the file's records.

Most Macintosh languages provide libraries that implement these functions or something like them. These libraries provide code that's linked to your application. The code makes calls to the Macintosh File Manager in ROM to implement its functions.

Although you can use a language's library routines for random access file I/O, you should consider making direct calls to the File Manager yourself. There are several advantages to this. The File Manager ROM routines are well tested and reliable; some high-level language libraries, including early versions of Apple's own Pascal library, aren't as reliable. Another advantage to calling the ROM directly is better management of exactly what's going on when you work with files. If you make the calls directly to the ROM, your code will probably run faster, since you won't be going through a "middleman," and you'll gain the memory that would otherwise be used up by the library routines.

Random Access?

"Random access" is an interesting term here. It seems to suggest that no matter what record you ask for, you'll get a random one. Some code actually works this way (unintended by the programmer, of course). Some people prefer the term "direct access."

If making direct calls to the ROM is so great, why doesn't everyone do it? One reason is convenience: high-level language programmers know how to use the languages' file I/O instructions, and they're easy to use. Most programmers will stick with the familiar, comfortable way of doing things.

Doing file I/O by calling the ROM routines directly isn't that hard. In this section we'll discuss the basic algorithms for this technique. Each high-level language statement, such as reset, get, and put, can be simulated with a File Manager call.

The first thing to do to create a random access file is to declare the data type that you'll be using for things in the file. In Pascal, this is usually a record; in C, it's a struct. Let's say we want each item in our file to consist of two integers, a boolean and a long integer. The declaration would look something like this:

```
type
  MemberRecord = Record
                   height, weight: Integer;
                   active: Boolean;
                   idNum: Longint;
                 end; {myRecord}
```

This type will be used for records that go into the files. To maintain flexibility, we'll keep each record in the heap. That will allow us to dynamically create as many as we need during the execution of the program. Since these records will be heap objects, we should make them relocatable so that they won't cause fragmentation. That means that we'll need a couple more declarations:

```
type
  MemberPtr = ^MemberRecord;
  MemberHdl = ^MemberPtr;

var
  thisMemberHdl: MemberHdl;
```

Declaring these types simply gives us a way to manage the records as relocatable heap objects. Now we can use the statement

```
thisMemberHdl := MemberHdl (NewHandle (sizeOf (MemberRecord)))
```

to create a new record in the heap. Let's discuss each part of this statement. The sizeOf function is a handy Pascal built-in function that returns the size of any type or variable. NewHandle, of course, creates a new relocatable heap block. The MemberHdl in front of the NewHandle call is an explicit type coercion; it makes the compiler happy, since NewHandle returns a variable of type Handle that you cannot directly assign to the variable on the left—its type is MemberHandle (if this is puzzling you, see the section "How to Get around Pascal's Type Checking" in Chapter 8 for more on how it works).

Now we've created a relocatable heap block that's big enough to hold one of our records, and thisMemberHdl is a handle to that block. We can fill in the fields of this record with standard assignment statements, like this:

```
with thisMemberHdl^^ do
  begin
    height := 73;
    weight := 210;
    active := true;
    idNum := 5346633;
  end; {with}
```

This With Is OK

Remember from the section in Chapter 2 on implicit dereferencing that this type of with statement is dangerous, but only if there are any statements in the body of the with that can cause compaction. Since there aren't any here, we're OK. You can see Chapter 2 for a refresher course.

Next we need to create the file on disk. To do this, we use the File Manager call Create. This is analogous to (which means "pretty much like") Rewrite in standard Pascal and create in C. The Create call allows you to specify the file's name, the volume where it will live (in the vRef-Num parameter), and its creator and type:

errCode := Create (fileName, vRefNum, creator, type);

Notice that Create is a function that returns an error code. Don't ignore this error code—check it (even though we've ignored it here, of course). All the File Manager calls work this way. After we've created the file, we can open it with FSOpen (in C, it's open; in Pascal, it's Reset). We pass FSOpen the file's name and volume, and it returns something called a **file reference number,** which is what we use to refer to a file while it's open:

errCode := FSOpen (fileName, vRefNum, fileRefNum);

When a file is open, the File Manager remembers the current position in the file. This position is called the **mark**. Perhaps you know someone named Mark. In any case, when you read from the file, you read data starting at the mark; when you write to file, the data you write is put into the file starting at the mark. A newly opened file has its mark set at the beginning of the file.

To write out the record we've filled in, we'll use the FSWrite call (like Put in Pascal or write in C), which takes a file reference number, a pointer to the data to be written, and returns a number indicating how many bytes were actually written. The call will look like this:

errCode := FSWrite (fileRefNum, count, thisMemberHdl^);

This statement will write to the file specified by fileRefNum, which we got in the Create call. Since FSWrite requires a pointer to the data that's being written, we dereference thisMemberHdl by putting a ^ after it; thisMemberHdl is a handle to the record, so thisMemberHdl^ is a pointer to the data. The number of bytes written is returned in the count parameter.

> **Is This Dereference Safe?**
>
> The expression thisMemberHdl^ is a pointer to a relocatable object. If the object moves before this pointer is used, we'll be dead. What will happen to execute this line of code? The parameters will be pushed on the stack; there will be a JSR to a glue routine that takes the parameters off the stack, builds a parameter block for the Write call, and calls the ROM. Glue for ROM routines is put in the main segment, which is always loaded, so JSRing to it won't cause any new objects to be loaded. The Write call itself in ROM doesn't do anything to cause compaction (it's not listed in the **Inside Macintosh** list of calls that can cause compaction), so this call is safe.

After we call FSWrite, the File Manager will have advanced the mark to the end of the new data written. We can fill up the record with new data over and over again and write them out with more FSWrite calls.

When we want to read a record from the file, we need to position the mark manually. We can do this with the SetFPos File Manager call. This call, which acts kind of like Seek in Pascal or fseek in C, takes three parameters: a file reference number, an integer indicating the **positioning modes**, and a long integer indicating the offset we want. The positioning mode allows us to position the mark relative to the beginning of the file, the end of the file, or the current mark; in other words, we can tell the File Manager to put the mark a given number of bytes from the beginning of the file on a given number of bytes from the end of the file, or to move the mark a given number of bytes from its current position. Usually, you'll use the absolute positioning mode, which is called fsFromStart.

Let's say we've written 50 records to this file, and we want to read back record number 22. SetFPos doesn't know anything about our record; it only moves the mark in bytes. So we have to figure out what byte in the file starts record 22. We know that record 1 starts at the first byte in the file; record 2 starts at byte sizeOf (MemberRecord), record 3 starts at 2 * sizeOf (MemberRecord), record 4 starts at byte 3 * sizeOf (MemberRecord), and so on. It looks like the formula for setting the mark is (recordNumber − 1) * sizeOf (MemberRecord). So, to find record 22, we can write

```
errCode := SetFPos (fileRefNum, fsFromStart,
            21 * sizeOf (MemberRecord));
```

This will set the mark to the beginning of record 22. Now we can read it with an FSRead statement, like this:

```
errCode := FSRead (fileRefNum, count, thisMemberHdl^);
```

This call will fill up the record in the heap with the information from record 22 in the file, since we positioned the mark there with the preceding SetFPos statement. Like the FSWrite call, FSRead leaves the mark positioned at the end of the last byte it read, so we could have a sequence of FSRead statements that reads successive records from the file. If we want to modify a record that's already in the file, we can do so by first using SetFPos to point at the record, reading it with FSRead, changing the fields we want, setting the mark back to the record's position with SetFPos because the FSRead call automatically moved it forward, and writing out the new data with FSWrite.

Here's a program fragment that summarizes this technique:

```
program readnwrite;

  type
    MemberRecord = Record
                     height, weight: Integer;
                     active: Boolean;
                     idNum: Longint;
                   end; {myRecord}
    MemberPtr = ^MemberRecord;
    MemberHdl = ^MemberPtr;

  var
    thisMemberHdl: MemberHdl;
    errCode: OSErr;
    fileName: Str255;
    vRefNum, fileRefNum, recordNum: Integer;
    creator, fileType: OSType;
    count: Longint;


  {creating the record}
    thisMemberHdl := MemberHdl (NewHandle (sizeOf
(MemberRecord)));
    with thisMemberHdl^^ do
      begin
        height := 73;
        weight := 210;
        active := true;
        idNum := 5346633;
      end; {with}

  {creating and opening the file}
    errCode := Create (fileName, vRefNum, creator, fileType);
    errCode := FSOpen (fileName, vRefNum, fileRefNum);
```

```
{writing to the file}
    errCode := FSWrite (fileRefNum, count, thisMemberHdl^);
{assign new values and repeat for each record}

{reading record "recordNum" from the file}
    errCode := SetFPos (fileRefNum, fsFromStart,
                        (recordNum — 1) * sizeOf
                        (MemberRecord));
        errCode := FSRead (fileRefNum, count, thisMemberHdl^);

{modifying record "recordNum"}
    errCode := SetFPos (fileRefNum, fsFromStart,
                        (recordNum — 1) * sizeOf
                        (MemberRecord));
        errCode := FSRead (fileRefNum, count, thisMemberHdl^);
        {modify record in thisMemberHdl^^ with assignment
statements}
            errCode := SetFPos (fileRefNum, fsFromStart,
                                (recordNum — 1) * sizeOf
                                (MemberRecord));
            errCode := FSWrite (fileRefNum, count, thisMemberHdl^);
```

Of course, in real life, in your application, you'd check all these error codes. Wouldn't you?

When Your Application Ends

When your application ends, what happens? To answer this question, let's think about how your application was started up in the first place. Usually, applications are started when the Finder calls Launch. The Launch call loads in CODE 1, which is the application's main segment, and executes the main program.

The last thing a program does is usually an RTS instruction. But where is this RTS taking you? What's the return address that's left on the stack at this point? When an application is launched, the last thing the ROM does is JSR to the main program. This JSR, which is in the Segment Loader's Launch routine, puts a return address on the stack that is just beyond the JSR that started the application—it's "on the other side of the application," you might say.

When the application reaches its last instruction, which is an RTS, it will return control back to the Segment Loader part of the ROM. This code takes care of shutting down the application and automatically launching the Finder. In fact, the first instruction that's executed after the application does its final RTS has a trap entry point of its own. It's the ExitToShell trap. This trap simply closes the current application and launches the Finder.

When the application does its last RTS, it expects the return address to the ROM to be there. However, if you've done something really nasty in your application that's caused something to be pushed on the stack and never retrieved, the Macintosh will probably bomb when it tries to quit your application, since it will try to RTS to whatever is on the top of the stack. This is known as an unbalanced stack; that is, the stack isn't at the same level it was when the application started. This is pretty hard to do from a high-level language, even the permissive Workshop Pascal, but it's not hard at all from assembly language.

If you end your application by calling ExitToShell, it won't matter what's on the stack. This is because calling ExitToShell explicitly doesn't require anything at all to be on the stack; in fact, one of the things that ExitToShell does is initialize the stack and rebuild it for the new application that's being launched, the Finder.

If your application bombs on the way to the Finder if you don't call ExitToShell at the end of your application, you've probably got a stack balancing problem. You shouldn't rely on the ExitToShell to fix things, since the real problem will probably show up and kill you another way. Instead, you should find the code that's causing the unbalanced stack and fix it.

Play by Play: An Application Is Launched

This section describes what happens when the Finder (or any other program) calls Launch to start up a new application.

1. Move the new application's name and sound/video page options into the system globals CurApName and CurPageOption.

2. Check to see if any open drivers (which include desk accessories) have asked to be told when the application heap was being initialized (with the DNeedGoodBye flag). If so, send them the GoodBye message.

3. If there's an open application, close its resource file and set the system global CurApRefNum to zero.

4. Reinitialize the stack; this is done by moving the system global BufPtr (which normally points to the bottom of the screen) into register A7.

5. Disable the stack sniffer by setting StkLowPt to zero.

6. If there's anything in the scrap, save it on the stack; if its size is odd, an extra byte is saved to avoid address errors.

7. Reinitialize the application heap zone by calling InitApplZone.

8. If there was a scrap saved, call NewHandle to get space for it in the brand-new application heap and move the data in from the stack; put the new handle into the system global ScrapHandle.

9. Reinitialize the unit table by calling RDrvrInstall.

10. Clear the system globals DragHook, DeskHook, CloseOrnHook, RestProc, SaveProc, TaskLock, FScaleDisable, and ResErrProc.

11. Open the new application's resource file and save its reference number in the system global CurApRefNum.

12. If the open in step 11 returned an error, generate system error 26.

13. Load the application's CODE resource 0; if there's an error, generate system error 26.

14. If the call requested that page 2 video or sound be used, move the stack pointer down to just below page 2.

15. Allocate the "above A5" space by subtracting the "above A5" value in the CODE 0 from A7. This is where the jump table and application parameters will go. After this allocation, move A7 into A5.

16. Save register A5 in the system global CurrentA5.

17. Save A7 in the system global CurStackBase.

18. Enable the stack sniffer by putting A7 into StkLowPt.

19. Move the jump table from CODE 0 to its place above A5. Before moving it in, save the first address in the jump table in A3; it's the address of the start of the program.

20. Call ReleaseResource to get rid of CODE 0.

21. Set up the application parameters: clear the standard input and standard output hooks at $8(A5) and $C(A5) to zero; move the Finder information handle to its place at $10(A5); clear the word at $14(A5), since Workshop Pascal expects it that way.

22. Compute the address at the current stack pointer minus the amount specified in the system global DefltStack; call SetApplLimit to set the application heap's limit to this point. This usually reserves 8K for the stack beyond the end of the heap.

23. Clear register D7 to zero, since Workshop Pascal expects it that way.

24. Do a JSR(A3) to start the application (we set up A3 in step 19).

Macintosh Plus

The Launch routine in the Macintosh Plus is basically the same as this one. It does a few more things: it clears the system global EjectNotify, and it removes any VBL tasks that are in the application heap before calling InitApplZone. It also clears all data registers before launching the application. If the user has the RAM cache enabled, it reserves space for the cache before allocating the jump table.

Keeping Things Around between Applications

When you double-click an application in the Finder, the Finder calls Launch in the ROM to start up the new program. As part of the startup process, Launch reinitializes the application heap zone, and everything that's in it is lost. There are things that have to be preserved between applications, of course. Many of these things are kept in the system globals area. For example, the global Ticks, at $16A, is the number of ticks (sixtieths of a second) that have elapsed since the system was started up, and this value must be maintained even when new applications are launched.

Another area of memory that's preserved across applications is the system heap zone. Although the application heap is nuked when a new application is launched, the system heap is left alone. That's because the system heap is also filled with things that need to be kept alive when new applications are started. For example, the system heap contains the patches to the ROM, as well as the resource map for the system file, which is always open.

Sometimes you'll want something to stick around even when another application is launched. You'll need this, for example, if you're writing an application like a debugger or a RAM disk, or anything else that you don't want to be destroyed when an application quits. Where can you put your code?

You can't put it in the application heap, obviously. The system global space is already defined, so there's no room for it there. The apparent choice is the system heap. There's a problem, though: the system heap is jammed up pretty full already by regular system stuff. In fact, system heap space is so tight that you should avoid putting anything there except very small objects (as we did in the "Patching Traps" section in Chapter 8).

Where else can this "hang-around code" go? There's one other place that's custom made for this purpose. There's a system global called BufPtr; when an application is started, the Launch call uses the value in BufPtr as the place to begin building the application's "world," which consists of the jump table, the application parameters, and the application's global variables (see Figure 10-1).

The value in BufPtr is initialized to the highest usable RAM location, that is, the first byte below the screen (the video buffer in Figure 10-1) in memory. On a system with 1 megabyte of RAM, that's at $FA700; on a 512K system, BufPtr is initially set to $7A700. Other than this initial setup, the system never changes BufPtr, so it's a great place to put your code. If you want to install something that will hang around in memory, you can subtract the amount of memory that you need from BufPtr and then put your stuff in that memory.

When you use this technique, you have to be very careful about what's in the memory that you're taking. Often this installation is done by an INIT resource, which is a piece of code that executes at the time the system is started up. If you install your hang-around code from an INIT resource, there are no jump table, application parameters, or global variables that you have to worry about clobbering.

However, if you do this trick in an application, all those things are present, so you have to watch out. The memory that you're using to install your code in is already occupied by important things like the jump table and the global variables. To be absolutely sure that you're not bashing these things, you need to move them downward before putting your code in. The program shown in Listing 10-1 demonstrates how you can do this.

1M	512K	pointer	
$10000	$80000	(MemTop)	used by system error handler
FFFD0	7FFD0		sound/disk speed buffer
FFD00	7FD00		reserved for system
FFC80	7FC80		
			video buffer
FA700	7A700	(ScrnBase)	
		(BufPtr)	"hang-around" code
			jump table
			reserved for system
A5		(CurrentA5)	application global variables

Figure 10-1 Macintosh memory map

```
move BufPtr;

{$U+}
(*USES
      {$U HD:MPW:Interfaces.p:MemTypes.p } MemTypes,
      {$U HD:MPW:Interfaces.p:QuickDraw.p} QuickDraw,
      {$U HD:MPW:Interfaces.p:OSIntf.p   } OSIntf,
      {$U HD:MPW:Interfaces.p:ToolIntf.p } ToolIntf,
      {$U HD:MPW:Interfaces.p:PackIntf.p } PackIntf; *)
{$D+}


VAR
   BufPtr: ^Longint;
   CurA5 : ^Longint;
   myResource: Handle;
   BytesToMove: Longint;
   StartPtr: Ptr;
   A5,A7: Longint;


{-----------------------------------------------------------------------------------}
FUNCTION GetA5 :longint ;EXTERNAL;
FUNCTION GetA7 :longint ;EXTERNAL;
PROCEDURE DecrA5(amount:longint);EXTERNAL; {also takes care of currentA5}
PROCEDURE DecrA6(amount:longint);EXTERNAL;
PROCEDURE DecrA7(amount:longint);EXTERNAL;
 PROCEDURE Debug; INLINE $A9FF;


Begin {main program}

   {No "init"s needed}

   BufPtr:= Pointer($10C); { Pointer to low-memory global "BufPtr"}
   CurA5:= Pointer($904);  { Pointer to low-memory global "CurrentA5"}


   myResource:= GetResource('STR ',1);
   If ((ResError = 0) and (myResource <> NIL)) then Begin
       BytesToMove:= $1000;{GetHandleSize(myResource) -1;} {don't want the length}
       if odd(BytesToMove) then Begin
          BytesToMove:= BytesToMove + 1; {make it even}
          SysBeep(5);
       End; {if}

       startPtr:= Pointer(ord4(myResource^) +1); {skip length byte}
```

Listing 10-1 part 1

```
        A5:= GetA5;
        A7:= GetA7;
        BufPtr^:= BufPtr^ - BytesToMove;   {move it down }
        CurA5^:= CurA5^ - BytesToMove;

    {Move the world}
        BlockMove(pointer(A7),pointer(A7-BytesToMove),A5-A7);

    {update the world's registers}
    Debug; {look at registers A5,A6 and A7, they'll be changing soon!}
        DecrA5(BytesToMove);
        DecrA6(BytesToMove);
        DecrA7(BytesToMove);

    {Now move the string in}
        BlockMove(StartPtr,Pointer(BufPtr^),GetHandleSize(myResource) -1); {move in our data}
    End    {If ResError = 0 ...}
    Else
      Sysbeep(20);
End.
```

Listing 10-1 part 1 (*continued*)

```
            ;FUNCTION GetA5 :longint ;EXTERNAL;
        GetA5    FUNC     EXPORT
                 MOVE.L   A5,4(A7)
                 RTS


            ;FUNCTION GetA7 :longint ;EXTERNAL;
        GetA7    FUNC     EXPORT
                 MOVE.L   A7,4(A7)
                 RTS


            ;PROCEDURE DecrementA5(amount:longint);EXTERNAL;

        DecrA5   PROC EXPORT
                 SUB.L    4(SP),A5      ; subtract 'amount' from A5
                 MOVE.L   (SP)+,(SP)    ; put return 'on top of' param
                 RTS

            ;PROCEDURE DecrementA6(amount:longint);EXTERNAL;

        DecrA6   PROC EXPORT
                 SUB.L    4(SP),A6      ; subtract 'amount' from A6
                 MOVE.L   (SP)+,(SP)    ; put return 'on top of' param
                 RTS
```

Listing 10-1 part 2

```
;PROCEDURE DecrementA7(amount:longint);EXTERNAL;

; we have to do this the long way
DecrA7   PROC EXPORT
         MOVE.L   (SP)+,A0 ; return address
         SUB.L    (SP)+,A7    ; subtract 'amount' from A7
         MOVE.L   A0,-(SP)    ; put return 'on top of' param
         RTS

         END
```

Listing 10-1 part 2 (*continued*)

Warning

The program in Listing 10-1 is probably most useful as an example of just how weird a thing you can do if you really know what's going on. In practice, it's a good idea not to go moving BufPtr around from an application, but to do it at startup time, usually in an INIT resource.

One of the best things about putting your code above BufPtr is that any number of things can be installed there. Since everything that's installed there moves BufPtr downward, new things can be installed below the previously installed ones. Of course, removing things is a little more difficult; since you don't know if your code was the last one installed, you can't simply set BufPtr beyond your last byte. Instead, you have to move up everything that's below you and above the end of the jump table.

This technique for installing hang-around code is used by many debuggers, RAM disks, and RAM caches. It's also used by a great desk accessory called System Bugs. This desk accessory draws bugs that crawl up the screen, right over your windows. The bugs continue to crawl even when the application quits and another is launched, since the code is above BufPtr. With this technique, you can create something that's just as useful to society as System Bugs.

Things to Remember

- You can make low-level File Manager calls without much extra effort. These low-level calls give you access to more features than the high-level calls and also give you more direct control over what's actually happening.
- The Printing Manager includes device-independent methods for printing bitmaps.
- Macintosh ROM calls are implemented as illegal 68000 instructions. When the 68000 tries to execute one of them, a ROM routine called the trap dispatcher takes over and figures out what location in memory to jump to.
- You can use the high-level and low-level File Manager calls to simulate random access Pascal-style file I/O.
- When your application ends, it returns control to the Launch routine on the "other side" of the instruction that started the application.
- You can keep things around between applications by lowering the system global BufPtr and putting things above the address it points to.

Appendices

APPENDIX

Assembly Language Overview

T he goal of this appendix is to show you how to look at an assembly language program and understand what's going on. This appendix is designed to introduce the 68000 from the perspective of a high-level language programmer who's going to be debugging compiled object code—you, for example.

This appendix assumes no prior knowledge of assembly language. It assumes that you know how to program in Pascal or C, and it assumes you understand the basic principles behind the hexadecimal and binary numbering systems. You'll probably get more out of it if you understand Pascal and have written a Macintosh program, but it's not required.

Most likely, as you read this appendix, you'll find some facts that are new, while other sections may rehash stuff that you already know. Please try to stay awake through the parts you find boring; the information that's presented here is vital. If you already know it, that's fine.

After you've read and learned what's in this appendix, you should be able to look at an assembly language program, including your program after it's translated by the compiler, and at least understand what the instructions are doing. Chapters 5 and 6 will help you correlate your high-level source program with the object code that you're looking at.

To appreciate the difference between being able to write assembly language programs and being able to read them, imagine that you're trying to read and understand a sentence in a human language that you don't speak. If you understand a few words in a sentence, you may be able to glean some meaning without knowing about verb conjugation, noun declension, tense, voice, or other grammatical rules. For example, you can probably figure out what *La Quinta Sinfonia di Beethoven* means in Italian, but if you don't speak Italian, you probably couldn't have constructed the phrase yourself.

Terminology Corner

What's the difference between assembly language and machine language? Actually, these terms can be used almost interchangeably. The only difference is that machine language usually refers to the raw object code that the microprocessor executes, the actual byte-by-byte description of a program, like this: 53 4B. Assembly language is a little better, using mnemonic instruction and register names to make things more human-readable. The preceding machine language program is equivalent to this assembly language instruction: SUBQ.W #1,A3. Only people who are really twisted write program in machine language, since there's no benefit to it. One assembly language instruction translates directly into one machine language instruction, so you have absolute control over the assembler's output. Once in while, though, in a debugger, you may actually have to type in a word or two directly in machine language. It's interesting, but only in small doses.

Programming a Microprocessor

Assembly language programs generally show more attention to detail than high-level language programs. We usually think of high-level languages as being more powerful than assembly language, but this really depends on your definition of the word "powerful." Everything that can be done in a high-level language can also be done in assembly language—obviously, because every program that runs on a microprocessor must ultimately be in assembly language.

The Macintosh's 68000 microprocessor only understands assembly language. All communications with the 68000 must be done in its strict language. Every higher-level function that you see, every for statement, every case statement, every menu drawn on the screen, every application program, happens because of the execution of 68000 code.

The most fundamental capability of any microprocessor is the ability to accept and execute **instructions**. These instructions are stored in the computer's memory, either in RAM or ROM. The 68000 knows how to execute these instructions because of logic that's built into the chip itself.

Each 68000 instruction includes some **operands**, which are the values used by the instructions to perform their tasks. For example, the 68000 has an instruction that will add two numbers together. The two numbers are the operands for the instruction. Operands are roughly equivalent to parameters in high-level languages.

The instructions that the 68000 understands perform various operations. For example, one set of instructions is used to move data in memory. There's an instruction that will cause the 68000 to move data from one memory location to another; you specify the memory locations. Another set of instructions is used to perform math operations on data in memory; for example, there's an instruction that adds the contents of two memory locations together and puts the result in one of the locations.

Since 68000 instructions are stored in memory, they have numerical representations. The instruction that moves data from one memory location to another is encoded with the number $11F8; the instruction that adds the contents of two locations is $D178.

All 68000 instructions are two bytes long, like these, but some require additional bytes to specify the operands. If you use $11F8 to move a byte from one location to another, you must specify the source and destination addresses following the $11F8. Since different instructions require different numbers and formats of operands, a full 68000 instruction plus operands takes two to ten bytes.

Assembly language assigns names to each instruction. The example instruction, which moves a byte, is named MOVE in assembly language. These names are called **mnemonics** because they're more memorable (for humans) than things like $11F8. Mnemonics have no intrinsic meaning to the 68000; it only understands the numerical representation. Mnemonics are understood by assemblers, which translate programs expressed in mnemonics into raw 68000 instructions.

In addition to the memory provided by the computer's RAM and ROM, the 68000 contains a very important little chunk of its own memory. Like RAM, this memory can be read from and written to by the 68000. This memory consists of 16 sets of four bytes each; each set of four bytes is called a **register**. The registers are divided into two groups, the data registers and the address registers. Each register has a name: the data registers are named D0, D1, D2, and so on, through D7; the address registers are named A0 through A7.

Assembly language programs use the registers to hold various data and addresses, as you might have guessed by their names. The 68000 has instructions that work on registers. For example, the MOVE instruction can also be used to move data between two registers or between a register and memory.

In general, instructions that operate on registers are faster than those that operate on memory locations. This is because the registers are actually built into the 68000, so it doesn't have to read or write the computer's memory to do the operation.

There are only 16 registers, and some of them are dedicated to special purposes. One address register, A7, is used to control an extremely important part of memory known as the **stack**. The stack is a pile of data in memory that grows as things are added to it and shrinks as they're removed from it. Register A7, which is also called the **stack pointer**, or just SP, always points to the **top of the stack**, which is the location where the next thing to be added will go. The stack is used to hold lots of things, including a program's variables, temporarily saved values of registers, and more.

"Only" 16 Registers

As microprocessors go, a collection of 16 registers of 32 bits each is a huge group. You'll find few processors that have this much register space available.

Stack Grows Downward in Memory

A curious fact about most implementations of stacks on microprocessors, including the 68000 on the Macintosh, is that the stack grows downward in memory as it gets larger. This means that the so-called top of the stack is actually the address of the lowest byte on the stack.

Register A5 has a special significance in the Macintosh. A number of important values can be derived from the contents of A5. For example, A5 contains the address of a global value that points to QuickDraw's global variables; see **Inside Macintosh** for more information. Also, A5 is used to find the application's **jump table**, an important data structure that's described in Chapter 6.

In addition to these 16 general-purpose registers, there are a couple of other registers in the 68000. One register contains the address of the next instruction to be executed; this is called the **program counter**, or PC. As the program executes, the value in this register is automatically incremented by the amount necessary to get to the next instruction.

The last register holds various status information about the 68000, so it's called the **status register**. The most important part of the status register is the lowest byte (eight bits), which contains result information about instructions that have just been executed. One bit, called the Z bit, checks data for zero whenever an operation takes place; for example, if the 68000 executes a MOVE instruction, and the value that's moved is zero, the Z bit is set to 1.

There are five bits like this, called **condition codes**, and this byte of the status register is known as the **condition codes register**, or CCR. The 68000 includes a set of instructions that take various actions depending on the settings of the condition codes. These instructions are used to make the program do different things depending on the result of other operations. For example, there's an instruction that jumps to a different part of the program if the Z condition code is set. This is how if statements in high-level languages are implemented in compiled code.

Different Flavors of the 68000

The 68000 microprocessor is actually a family with several members. The most common ones are the 68000, the 68010, and the 68020. The higher the number, the faster, more powerful, and more expensive they get, just like BMWs. They have a large degree of upward compatibility; that is, most programs that run on a 68000 will work on the other two as well. The 010 and 020 models, as they're called, introduce additional instructions beyond those provided by the 68000. Macintosh 128K, 512K, XL, and Plus all have 68000 microprocessors.

Integer Arithmetic

In the 68000, the size of an instruction's data may be either a byte (eight bits), a word (16 bits, or two bytes), or a long word (32 bits, or four bytes). High-level languages define data types that correspond to these sizes. For example, the Pascal type integer and the C short are word sized; Pascal longints are long word sized.

The size of the data defines the range of values it can occupy. A value that must fit in a single bit can contain two different values: 0 and 1. This is enough to hold the value of a boolean variable, and some languages are capable of packing values this tightly.

Since one bit can hold two different values, the number of distinct values that can be represented in N bits is equal to 2^N. This means that eight bits can represent 2^8, or 256 different values; 16 bits can represent 2^{16}, or 65,536 different values; and 32-bit numbers can hold 2^{32}, which is 4,294,967,296 different values.

Programs usually need to represent negative as well as positive values. To implement this, most microprocessors use a mathematical scheme called **two's complement arithmetic**. In two's complement arithmetic, the highest bit of the value is used to indicate its sign: if this bit is a 1, the value is negative; if 0, it's positive.

If the value is positive, the lower bits simply give the value; if it's negative, these bits form the **two's complement** of the value. A value's two's complement is computed by subtracting the value from *zero plus a borrow* and *negating the result.*

What's a Borrow?

Remember the concept of borrowing from when you learned subtraction? For example, to subtract 52 from 161, you first subtract the one's column: 1 minus 2. Since you can't subtract 2 from 1, you borrow from the next column, making it 11 minus 2. It's the same idea here. If you're working with a byte, "zero plus a borrow" is $100; if it's a word, "zero plus a borrow" is $10000; for a long word, it's $100000000.

This somewhat arcane concept can be best explained with an example. Given the byte $FF, what two's complement value does it represent?

In binary, $FF is 1111 1111. Since its high bit is set, it's negative. To find out its value, we subtract $FF from zero plus a borrow; in other words, we subtract $FF from $100. The result of this subtraction is $1; negating this gives negative $1, or −1. Therefore, the byte $FF represents −1 in two's complement arithmetic.

Another example is the word $92D4. Its binary representation is 1001 0010 1101 0100. Again, the high bit is set, so this value is negative. Since it's a word and it's negative, we can find out its value by subtracting it from $10000. The result is $6D2C, or 27,948 decimal. So $92D4 is −27,948 decimal in two's complement form.

For positive numbers, we can get the value directly. The two's complement long word $40899610 is 0100 0000 1000 1001 1001 1010 0001 0000 in binary. The high bit is clear, so it's positive, and the value is simply $40899610, or 1,082,758,672 decimal.

Note that the size of the data is vital in determining its value. The value $A0 is −96 decimal (−$60) if it's a byte; if it's a word, $00A0, it's positive, and it's 160 decimal.

There's a neat shorthand way to figure a negative two's complement value. If you invert all the bits in the value, then add one, you'll get the correct *negative* value. Let's try this with the examples.

The byte $FF is 1111 1111 in binary; flipping all the bits gives 0000 0000; adding one gives 0000 0001; so $FF is −1.

The word $92D4 is 1001 0010 1101 0100 in binary; inverting the bits gives 0110 1101 0010 1011, which is $6D2B; adding one gives $6D2C, or 27,948 decimal; so $92D4 is −27,948 decimal.

Luckily, most disassemblers show you signed decimal values when they disassemble two's complement numbers. For example, an instruction that included the word-sized operand $FFE0 would usually show up in the disassembly as −32, which is more meaningful for humans.

Addressing Modes

Most 68000 instructions require operands, which are a lot like parameters to high-level language routines. For example, as we discussed earlier, the MOVE instruction requires two operands: the source of the data to be moved and its destination. In addition to specifying the operands, most instructions allow you to specify the size of the operands. Usually, the operands can be bytes, words, or long words.

At different times in an assembly language program, the operands will be found in different ways. For example, if the programmer wants to add 1000 to the value in register D0, there are two operands: the value 1000 and the register D0. Each of these operands is represented in assembly language instruction as a particular **addressing mode**. A particular instruction's addressing mode is the method used by that instruction to calculate the address of its operands.

This example, adding 1000 to the value in register D0, is written in assembly language like this: ADD.W #1000,D0. The name of the instruction is ADD. The suffix .W after ADD indicates that the size of the operand in this instruction is a word (two bytes). We could also use .B for a byte and .L for a long word (four bytes). An instruction with no suffix is assumed to have word-sized operands by default. The symbol # in front of the value 1000 indicates that the first operand is in the **immediate** addressing mode; in other words, the value specified in the instruction is the actual value to be used. It's not a memory location or a register specification, but the value itself.

Where Do the Bytes Come From?

If a .W suffix is used with a memory location, the word is taken from the byte addressed and the one immediately following it; if it's a long word operand in memory, the bytes are the one addressed and the next three bytes. If the operand is a register, the lower word of the register is used, ignoring the upper word; if a register is used as a byte-sized operand, the lowest byte is used, and the upper three bytes are ignored (see Figure A-1).

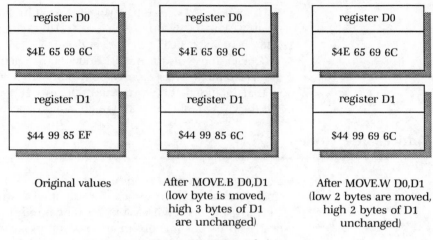

register D0	register D0	register D0
$4E 65 69 6C	$4E 65 69 6C	$4E 65 69 6C

register D1	register D1	register D1
$44 99 85 EF	$44 99 85 6C	$44 99 69 6C

| Original values | After MOVE.B D0,D1 (low byte is moved, high 3 bytes of D1 are unchanged) | After MOVE.W D0,D1 (low 2 bytes are moved, high 2 bytes of D1 unchanged) |

Figure A-1 Operand sizes

This instruction's second operand is register D0. This specification, simply the name of a register, is the **data register direct** mode. It just means that the instruction specifies a register that is to be used as the operand. By the way, the first operand is called the **source operand** and the second is called the **destination operand**.

These addressing modes, immediate and data register direct, are two of the 14 addressing modes that the 68000 provides. Some of these modes are rarely used. Not every instruction provides all the addressing modes; for most instructions, however, the most commonly desired addressing modes are available.

In an assembly language instruction, the address of the operand is known as the **effective address** of the operand. In some of the more powerful addressing modes, the effective address is calculated by adding several values together. We'll discuss how this works later in this section.

Let's take a look at the 68000's addressing modes. The 14 modes can be divided into six broad categories: register direct addressing, absolute data addressing, program counter relative addressing, register indirect addressing, immediate data addressing, and implied addressing.

Register Direct Addressing

In the register direct addressing modes, the operand is a 68000 register. In our preceding example, we saw an example of data register direct addressing. There's one other register direct mode, called **address register direct**. This mode works just like data register direct, except that an address register is used for the operand. An example of address register direct addressing is ADD A0,D0, which adds the values in A0 and D0 and puts the result in D0. In this instruction, the first operand is specified with address register direct addressing; the second uses the data register direct mode.

Absolute Data Addressing

In the absolute addressing modes, the effective address is the actual address specified in the instruction. There are two absolute addressing modes: absolute short and absolute long. The only difference between these two modes is the range of values allowed. Short addressing permits addresses in the range $0 through $FFFF forward or backward; long addresses can be in the range $0 through $FFFFFFFF.

If an absolute address will fit into a word, most compilers will automatically use the short mode, since it only requires one additional word per instruction, while the long mode takes two additional words.

Here's an example of short absolute addressing with the MOVE instruction: MOVE.L $7598,D0. In this instruction, the source (first) operand uses short absolute addressing; the destination (second) operand uses data register direct addressing. Note that the .L suffix on the MOVE instruction indicates the size of the operand; that is, a long word (32 bytes) of data will be moved from memory location $7598 into register D0. The .L does not mean that the long absolute mode is being used.

In the instruction MOVE.B D0,$DFF1FF, the destination operand is too large to fit into one word, so the absolute long addressing mode must be used for the address $DFF1FF.

The most common use of absolute data addressing in Macintosh programs is for references to low memory globals, which can always be found at fixed (absolute) addresses. In general, absolute addressing is not used a lot in Macintosh programs; because most objects are relocatable, absolute addressing can't be used, since the programmer doesn't know where the objects will be loaded. Other modes, which we'll discuss, let the program address these objects.

Watch That Mode

Be very careful when you're looking at assembly language code to see the difference between immediate and absolute addressing. If immediate addressing is specified (usually with a # symbol), take the value of the operand; if it's absolute addressing (there's no #), it's a memory reference, not an immediate value.

Program Counter Relative Addressing

On the Macintosh, lots of little pieces of code coexist in memory at the same time. These programs include the application's segments, desk accessories, definition procedures for menus, window, and controls, and others. Each of these objects is independently loaded into memory when it's needed. For maximum flexibility, they can be loaded virtually anywhere in RAM. In addition, they can be relocated if they're not locked.

The programmer has no way of knowing where the objects will be loaded at the time the code is written. This means that if the code has to use the address of a location within the object, it cannot be an absolute address. For example, if a desk accessory has stored a constant within the desk accessory's code, it cannot use absolute addressing to find the constant, since the programmer doesn't know the absolute address of the constant—it depends on where in memory the desk accessory was loaded.

To solve this problem, the 68000 implements a clever pair of addressing modes called **program counter relative**, usually known as PC-relative addressing. When a program uses PC-relative addressing, the effective address is computed by adding an offset to the current program counter. Since the program counter holds the address of the instruction currently being executed, PC-relative addressing works no matter where in memory the code is located.

The first and most common PC-relative mode is called **program counter relative with offset**. In this mode, the instruction includes an offset that is added to the current PC to produce the effective address. For example, an instruction like MOVE.W 244(PC),D4 will move the word that's 244 bytes from the instruction being executed into register D4.

Usually, you don't have to compute offsets like this yourself, even when writing assembly language programs. Most assemblers will automatically use PC-relative addressing when a code module refers to an address within the module itself. This mode is most commonly used for the JSR (jump to subroutine) instruction, which we'll talk about later. When a routine in a code module calls another routine in the same module, the JSR instruction can use PC-relative addressing.

The second and much more obscure kind of PC-relative addressing is called **program counter relative with index and offset**. In this mode, the assembly language instruction supplies an offset that is added to the program counter, just as in the previous mode. This mode, though, also adds another value, called the index, which can be any data or address register. In assembly language, it looks like this: JSR 2004(PC,A1.W). The effective address here is computed by adding the PC to the offset 2004 and the index, which is the word stored in register A1 (A1.W). Note that you can also use a long word index by specifying a .L suffix after the name of the address register to be used as an index.

This addressing mode is usually used for JSR's when a table of addresses has been built and the program must compute which one to take at runtime. For example, in a Pascal case or C switch statement, the compiler may construct a table consisting of addresses of the various cases. The program can then load the case selector into a register and execute a PC-relative JSR or JMP (jump) instruction with displacement and the index, using the register that has the case selector as the index.

Register Indirect Addressing

Often a programmer will want to compute an effective address based on an address that's in an address register. The 68000 provides five powerful addressing modes to specify addresses this way.

The first of these modes is called **register indirect**. In this mode, the effective address is simply the contents of the specified address register. For example, an instruction like MOVE.L $936,(A0) will move the long word that's stored in location $936 into the location *whose address* is in register A0. So, if A0 contained, say, $63448 before this instruction was executed, the contents of location $936 would be moved into location $63448. In this instruction, the destination operand uses register indirect addressing; the source operand uses short absolute addressing.

When the program manipulates objects on the stack, the stack pointer must be updated constantly to reflect the current top of the stack. Before a new object is placed on the stack, the stack pointer must be decremented to make room for the new object. When an object is removed from the stack, the stack pointer must be incremented past the old object.

Since this is such a common technique, the 68000 has defined an addressing mode to combine the two operations of pushing something on the stack and decrementing the stack pointer into a single instruction. Adding an object to the stack is accomplished with the addressing mode called **predecrement register indirect**. When a program uses this mode, the stack pointer is automatically decremented to make room for the new object before the object is placed on the stack. The assembly language looks like this: MOVE.W D0,−(A7). The minus sign indicates the predecrement mode.

This instruction will cause two things to happen in sequence; first, the stack pointer (register A7) will be decremented by two bytes (.W) to make room for the new value on the stack; then the word in D0 will be placed on the stack. This process is shown in Figure A-2.

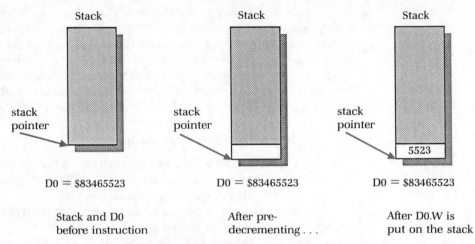

Figure A-2 Predecrement addressing mode

The 68000 automatically decrements the stack pointer by two bytes because the size of the operand is two bytes. If the operand were a long word, the stack pointer would be decreased by four. You would expect, then, that a byte-sized operand would decrement the stack pointer by one byte; actually, a byte-size operand will cause the stack pointer to be adjusted by two bytes. This ensures that the stack pointer stays even. Since word- and long-word-sized objects must begin at even addresses, this guarantees that future objects pushed on the stack will begin at even addresses.

The 68000 has a corresponding addressing mode for removing objects from the stack. It's called **postincrement register indirect**. In this mode, the instruction is executed first; then the stack pointer is incremented by the appropriate amount. Here's an example assembly language instruction that uses this mode: MOVE.L (A7)+,(A2). This instruction will move a long word from the top of the stack into the address pointed to by register A2. After the long word has been moved, the stack pointer will be incremented by four bytes, removing the value from the stack.

These modes are often called autopredecrement and autopostincrement. The position of the plus or minus sign in the assembly language reminds you that the decrement operation takes place before the instruction is executed, and the increment happens after the instruction is done. There are no preincrement or postdecrement modes—they wouldn't serve any useful purpose.

Other Uses for These Modes

Although these modes are most often used with the stack, any address register can be the one that's predecremented or postincremented. Postincrement is often used by compilers to move a small number of bytes from one location to another. To do this, the compiler first loads the location of the source of the bytes into one address register, typically A0. Then it loads the destination address into another address register, usually A1. It can then use MOVE instructions with postincrement to move bytes, four at a time, in this form: MOVE.L (A0)+,(A1)+. This instruction moves a long word (four bytes) from the address pointed to by A0 to the address pointed to by A1, and then increments both pointers by four. Four of these instructions in a row is a very fast way to move 16 bytes. This technique is often used for making local copies of procedure parameters in Pascal (see Chapter 6 for details).

The other register indirect modes are similar to the PC-relative modes. They're called **register indirect with offset** and **indexed register indirect with offset**. These modes allow the programmer or compiler to specify an address register and one or two values to be added to the address register to compute the effective address. In the instruction MOVE.W 8(A6),12(A1,D0.W), the source operand is specified using the register indirect with offset mode. The effective address will be computed by adding eight to the contents of register A6. This is usually spoken as "8 off A6" or "8 above A6." This addressing mode is used to specify global and local variables and parameters in high-level languages.

The destination operand uses indexed register indirect with offset. Its effective address is calculated by adding 12, the contents of A1, and the word-sized contents of D0. Once again, this mode is most useful when the program has built a table of addresses with A1+12 pointing to the table and D0 containing an index into the table. Indexed register indirect is one of the least often used 68000 addressing modes.

Immediate Data Addressing

We discussed immediate data addressing earlier in this section. Immediate addressing means that the data for the instruction is specified right after the instruction; there's no effective address to be computed. The instruction MOVE.B #$34,-$244(A5) puts the value of the source operand, $34, into the location at -$244 off A5 (also called "$244 below A5"). The # symbol in the source operand indicates that immediate addressing is being used. If the # were not present, the source operand would be in short absolute mode, and the contents of memory location $34 would be used instead of the value $34.

A variant of immediate data addressing is the **quick immediate data addressing** mode. This mode is just like standard immediate addressing, except that the source operand must fit into a single byte (for some instructions, the quick mode only permits values that can fit into three *bits*, which limits the values to zero through seven). When using this mode, the data is actually squeezed into the instruction word itself. So an instruction like MOVEQ #1,D3, which moves a one into D3, only takes two bytes in memory. Most assemblers will automatically produce a quick immediate operand if the instruction has this mode and the operand is a byte. In the 68000, only the ADD, SUB, and MOVE instructions allow quick immediate addressing.

Big Move

Although the MOVEQ instruction only permits operands that fit into a single byte, it actually moves a 32-bit sign extension of the operand. This means that a MOVEQ #1, D0 puts 0000 0001 into D0, and MOVEQ #−1, D1 puts FFFF FFFF (the 32-bit version of −1) into D1.

Implied Addressing

The final category of addressing modes is **implied addressing** or **implied register addressing**. In this mode, the instruction itself contains the address of the operands, and the operands are registers; the effective address is *implied* by the instruction itself. For example, the RTS instruction has only one form. It removes the address from the top of the stack, increments the stack pointer by four bytes, and then places the address in the program counter, causing execution to resume at that location. The stack pointer is the implied register in this instruction.

Another example of implied addressing is the PEA instruction. This instruction takes one operand. It calculates this operand's effective address and then pushes it on the stack after predecrementing the stack pointer. The source operand can use one of several 68000 instruction modes, but the destination is once again implied to be the stack pointer.

Figure A-3 68000 Addressing modes

Kind of addressing	Mode	Example
register direct	data register direct	MOVE D0,D1
	address register direct	MOVE A0,D0
absolute data	absolute short	MOVE $1024,D0
	absolute long	MOVE $2212348,D0
program counter relative	relative with offset	MOVE $200(PC),D0
	relative with index and offset	MOVE $342(PC,D1),D0
register indirect	register indirect	MOVE (A1),D0
	postincrement register indirect	MOVE (A7)+,D0
	predecrement register indirect	MOVE −(A0),D0
	register indirect with offset	MOVE $12(A6),D0
	indexed register indirect with offset	MOVE $20(A2,D1),D0
immediate data	immediate	MOVE #$7961,D0
	quick immediate	MOVE Q#$5,D0
implied addressing	implied register	MOVE CCR,D0

For example, PEA 1670(PC) will calculate the address of the location at 1670 off the PC and then predecrement the stack pointer and push this value; PEA (A3) will push the address that's in A3 (exactly like a MOVE.L A3,−(A7)); PEA $40FA82 will simply push the address $40FA82 on the stack.

The 14 addressing modes are summarized in Figure A-3.

68000 Instruction Set

The 68000 provides 56 different kinds of instructions. We've already discussed a few of them, including ADD, MOVE, JSR, and PEA. Many of these instructions work with byte, word, and long word data, and most of them allow various addressing modes to be used for operands. Some instruction types permit all 14 of the 68000's addressing modes to be used.

The 68000 instruction set can be broken up into eight categories: data movement, integer arithmetic, logical operations, shift and rotate, bit manipulation, binary-coded decimal, program control, and system control. We'll discuss each of these categories. We won't cover every 68000 instruction, just those that are most frequently used by compilers.

Data Movement Instructions

Data movement instructions are used to transfer data between memory locations and registers. The most common of these is the MOVE instruction. This instruction, which takes two operands, can be used to move data from one register to another, from one memory location to another, or between memory and a register in either direction. All addressing modes are allowed for the source; most are allowed for the destination. The data may be a byte, word, or long word.

Address Errors

Probably the most common system error on a Macintosh is an address error, system error 2. This error is usually the direct result of a MOVE instruction that fits these two qualifications: (1) the size of an operand is a word or long word, and (2) the address of the operand is odd. There's a lot more on address errors throughout this book, especially in Chapter 4.

Several variations of the standard MOVE instruction perform special-purpose functions. These include MOVEM (move multiple registers), which moves any set of registers to a specified memory location; MOVEA, which moves a value to an address register; and MOVEQ, which moves an embedded eight-bit number to a data register.

When a high-level language's assignment statement is compiled, the result is usually a MOVE instruction in the object code.

Instruction Variants

Many 68000 instructions have variants that extend their functionality or provide a smaller, special-purpose instruction to accomplish some function. For example, everything MOVEQ does can also be done with the generic MOVE, but MOVEQ is faster and takes less memory. Most assemblers will automatically produce the most efficient variant of an instruction. In general, from the viewpoint of an object code reader, an instruction and its variants do the same thing.

Figure A-4 Data movement operations

Instruction	Description
EXG	Exchange two registers
LEA	Load effective address into register
LINK	Create subroutine stack frame
MOVE	Move data in registers or memory
PEA	Push effective address on stack
SWAP	Swap high and low halves of a register
UNLK	Destroy subroutine stack frame

Other data movement instructions include LEA (load effective address), which computes an effective address and loads it into an address register; PEA, which pushes an effective address onto the stack; LINK and UNLK, which are used to manage data structures called **stack frames**; EXG, which exchanges the values in two registers; and SWAP, which trades the high and low words in a data register.

The data movement instructions are summarized in Figure A-4.

Integer Arithmetic Instructions

These instructions are used to perform two's complement math operations with data in registers and memory. These instructions are generated when the source program performs integer arithmetic. In general, addition, subtraction, multiplication, and division in a high-level language produce these instructions when both operands are integers or long integers.

The integer arithmetic instructions include ADD, which adds two operands and places the result in the second operand. The basic ADD instruction requires one operand to be a data register; the other operand may be specified with any of the 68000's addressing modes. The ADDA (add address) variant allows the destination to be an address register; there are also an ADDI (add immediate) variant, which allows an immediate value to be added to a memory location, and an ADDQ (add quick) variant, which is a fast way to add a quick immediate value.

There's a corresponding set of subtraction instructions. These include SUB, SUBA, SUBI, and SUBQ. Their functions are identical to their addition counterparts.

Short Take

The only possible values for the first operand in an ADDQ or SUBQ instruction are one through eight, since the value is jammed into three bits.

There are two multiplication instructions. MULU (unsigned multiply) multiplies two unsigned word-sized numbers. One of them must be in a data register. The result is an unsigned long word and is left in the specified data register, the second operand. The other operand can be specified with any 68000 addressing mode except address register direct.

The other multiplication instruction is MULS (signed multiply). This instruction is just like MULU, except that the values multiplied are treated as two's complement signed values, as is the long word result that's produced. Once again, the destination operand is a data register, and the source operand may be specified with any mode except address register direct.

The 68000 has a similar pair of division instructions. The DIVU instruction divides a long word destination operand by a word-sized source operand. The operation is an integer division. The quotient is put into the lower word of the destination, and the remainder is put into the upper word. Like the multiplication instructions, the destination operand must be a data register. There's also a DIVS instruction that treats the operands as signed numbers.

The CMP instruction is used to compare two values. The 68000's condition codes are set depending on the result of the comparison. This instruction is usually followed by a "branch conditionally" instruction (see "Program Control Instructions"). One of the values must be in a data register to use the generic CMP instruction. There are variants that compare a value to an address register (CMPA), an immediate value (CMPI), and a special variant that compares the values pointed to by two address registers (CMPM, compare memory).

Another instruction that sets the condition codes is TST (test), which compares a value with zero and sets the condition codes according to the result. This instruction, like CMP, is usually followed by a branch instruction.

The compare and test instructions are generated by the compiler as part of the implementation of high-level programs' "if" statements. In addition, they're used to test loop boundary conditions in "for", "repeat", and "while" statements.

The NEG instruction is used to negate an operand, that is, to convert a number to its two's complement. As we said earlier, the effect of this operation is to flip all the bits and add one. Mathematically, the NEG instruction multiplies a value by −1.

Sometimes a program must convert a value from a smaller type to a larger type; for example, when a Pascal program adds an integer to a long integer, the program must first convert the integer to a long integer.

Suppose that the integer's value was −14 and the long integer's value was 12. In hex, these numbers would be $FFF2 and $0000000C, respectively. Before they can be added, the integer must be converted to the

Figure A-5 Integer arithmetic instructions

Instruction	Description
ADD	Add operands and place result in destination
CLR	Clear operand to zero
CMP	Compare operands and set condition codes
DIVS	Divide destination by source (signed); result in destination
DIVU	Divide destination by source (unsigned); result in destination
EXT	Sign-extend operand
MULS	Multiply operands (signed); result in destination
MULU	Multiply operands (unsigned); result in destination
NEG	Negate operand
SUB	Subtract source from destination
TAS	Test and set a byte
TST	Compare operand with zero and set condition codes

long integer representation of −14, which is $FFFFFFF2. The 68000 provides an instruction to do this automatically; it's called EXT (sign extend). It automatically copies the operand's high bit (the sign bit) into all the bits of the high word, converting a word into a long word whether it's negative or positive. The EXT instruction also works on bytes being extended to words; it automatically figures out which to do based on the size of the operand.

The 68000 instruction CLR is used to clear the bits of the operand to zero. If the .W or .B suffix is used, only the specified bits will be cleared. This instruction is often used when an assignment statement assigns a value of zero.

Figure A-5 summarizes the integer arithmetic operations.

Logical Instructions

The 68000 defines a set of instructions to perform logical operations between operands. These instructions and variants allow an assembly language program to perform the four basic logical operations: **and**, **or**, **exclusive-or**, and **not**.

The AND instruction performs a "**logical and**" between two operands and puts the result in the destination operand. The "logical and" function compares corresponding bits in the operands; for example, it compares bit 0 of each operand. If both bits compared are set (have value 1), the corresponding bit in the result is 1. Otherwise, the result bit is cleared (set to 0).

Here's an example. In the instruction AND.B #$6B,D0, assume that register D0 contains the byte value $CA. In binary, $6B is 0110 1011, and $CA is 1100 1010. To logically and these two values, each bit is compared with its counterpart; if both bits are 1, a 1 is placed in the destination operand (D0). The first two bits are 0 in the source and 1 in the destination; this generates a 0. The next two are both 1; this generates a 1. Repeating this process for all the bits, the result is 0100 1010, or $4A. This instruction is used by the compiler to represent the Pascal logical operator "and" and the C logical operator "&" (the logical and operator). Figure A-6 demonstrates the logical and function.

The AND instruction has several variants. The most common is the ANDI variant, which can be used when one of the operands is an immediate value.

The 68000 instruction OR implements a **"logical or"** function. This function compares two operands, like logical and. If *either* the source or destination bit is 1, the result bit is 1. If both the source and destination bits are 1, the result bit is 1 also. If both source and destination bits are 0, the result bit is 0.

If we use the example OR.B #$6B,D0, with $CA in register D0, the 68000 will logically or the binary values 0110 1011 and 1100 1010. The result is 1110 1011, or $EB. The compiler generates an OR instruction when there's an "or" in the Pascal source or a "|" (vertical bar, the logical or operator) in a C program. Figure A-7 demonstrates how the logical or function works.

Like the AND instruction, OR has a variant called ORI that can be used if the source operand is in the immediate addressing mode.

The exclusive-or function is very much like logical or, except for one rule: if *both* the source and destination have a 1 in a bit position, that bit becomes a 0 in the result. As in the logical or function, if either the source or destination has a 1, the result is 1, and if both source and destination are 0, the destination is 0.

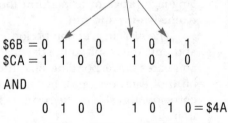

If both bits are ones, the result bit is a one; otherwise, the result bit is a zero.

```
$6B = 0  1  1  0    1  0  1  1
$CA = 1  1  0  0    1  0  1  0
AND
      0  1  0  0    1  0  1  0 = $4A
```

Figure A-6 Logical "and"

If either bit is one, the result bit is a one; otherwise, the result bit is a zero.

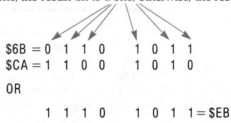

```
$6B = 0  1  1  0     1  0  1  1
$CA = 1  1  0  0     1  0  1  0
OR

      1  1  1  0     1  0  1  1 = $EB
```

Figure A-7 Logical "or"

The mnemonic for exclusive-or is EOR. In the instruction EOR #$6B,D0, with $CA in register D0, the result will be 1010 0001, or $A1. Figure A-8 shows exactly how this result was computed. The EOR instruction also has an EORI (exclusive-or immediate) mode.

Exclusive-or instructions are usually generated in object code when the exclusive-or logical operator has been used in the source. In C, for example, this operator is "^".

The fourth logical instruction is NOT. This operator causes all the operand's bits to be flipped: ones become zeros and zeros become ones. This instruction is generated when the source program uses the "not" operator (in Pascal) or the "~" operator (in C). Note that this operation differs from the mathematical NEG instruction in that it simply reverses all the bits of the operand. NEG multiplies the operand by −1. The 68000's logical instructions are summarized in Figure A-9.

If either bit, but not both, is one, the result bit is a one; otherwise, the result bit is a zero.

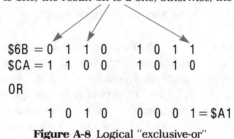

```
$6B = 0  1  1  0     1  0  1  1
$CA = 1  1  0  0     1  0  1  0
OR

      1  0  1  0     0  0  0  1 = $A1
```

Figure A-8 Logical "exclusive-or"

Figure A-9 Logical instructions

Instruction	Description
AND	Perform logical "and" on two operands
OR	Perform logical "or" on two operands
EOR	Perform logical "exclusive-or" on two operands
NOT	Perform logical "not" on one operand

Shift and Rotate Instructions

The 68000 defines a set of instructions that shift and rotate bits within operands. Although many of these instructions are rarely used by compiled object code, there are a few important ones.

The shift instructions cause the bits in an operand to be shifted a given number of positions, either to the left or the right. There are instructions that are designed for logical use and instructions designed for mathematical use (we'll discuss how). The shift instructions cause one or more bits to be "lost" when they're shifted out of the operand. The 68000 also defines a set of instructions that rotate bits so that bits shifted out of one end go back into the other end.

There are four instructions to shift bits: ASL (arithmetic shift left), ASR (arithmetic shift right), LSL (logical shift left), and LSR (logical shift right). The arithmetic shifts are used to multiply or divide integers. An integer can be multiplied by 2 by shifting it one bit to the left; shifting it one bit to the right divides it by 2. This works because each digit position in the binary numbering system represents the position to its right, multiplied by 2, just as in the decimal (base 10) system each position represents the position to its right multiplied by 10 (one, tens, hundreds, thousands, etc.).

Compilers use the arithmetic shift instructions as shortcuts for multiplication and division when the divisor or one of the multiplication operands is a power of 2. For example, the high-level language expression N * 8 would probably be compiled into an ASL instruction that shifted the operand by three bits (because 8 is 2*2*2=2^3).

The logical shift instructions are used when the high-level source program specifically uses a logical shift operator, like "<<" in C. The only difference between the arithmetic shifts and the logical shifts is that the arithmetic-right shift makes the sign bit stay the same after the shift takes place. This ensures that the arithmetic shift instructions do proper integer math and respect the sign bit.

Figure A-10 demonstrates the execution of the instruction ASL.W #1,D0, where D0 contains $534B.

ASL.W #1,D0
(shift all bits left
by one position)

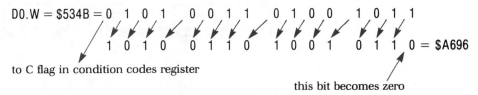

Figure A-10 Operation of shift instruction

Figure A-11 Shift and rotate
instructions

Instruction	Description
ASL	Arithmetic shift left
ASR	Arithmetic shift right
LSL	Logical shift left
LSR	Logical shift right
ROL	Rotate left
ROR	Rotate right
ROXL	Rotate left with extend
ROXR	Rotate right with extend

The rotate instructions defined by the 68000 are not generally used for compiler code generations. Figure A-11 lists the shift and rotate instructions.

Bit Manipulation Instructions

The 68000 instruction set includes a group of instructions that are used to test and manipulate single bits within operands. There are four bit manipulation instructions: bit test (BTST), bit test and set (BSET), bit test and clear (BCLR), and bit test and change (BCHG). The bit manipulation instructions operate on byte or long word operands.

The bit test instruction is used to determine if a bit is one or zero. The Z condition code is set based on the result; Z is set if the bit tested is 0; Z is cleared if the bit tested is 1. In the instruction BTST #3,D3, the fourth-lowest bit (bit 3, numbering from zero) is checked. If the bit is 0, the Z flag is set; if the bit is 1, the Z flag is cleared. Figure A-12 shows how this works.

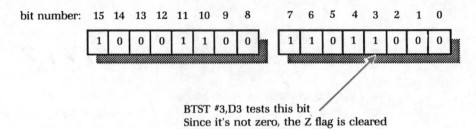

register D3 (low word)

BTST #3,D3 tests this bit
Since it's not zero, the Z flag is cleared

Figure A-12 BTST instruction

The BSET instruction first tests a bit and sets the Z condition code, just as in the BTST instruction, but it then sets the bit to 1 after the test. For example, the instruction BSET #12,(A7) will test bit 2 of the first word on the stack and then set that bit. The fact that this instruction tests the bit before setting it is usually incidental; often the programmer or compiler will just want to set the bit and will not care about the result of the test.

The bit test and clear instruction, BCLR, is similar to the BSET instruction. It first tests the bit, setting the Z condition code; then, instead of setting the bit to 1, like BSET, it clears the bit to 0. Once again, the initial testing of the bit is often ignored. Usually, the programmer or compiler just wants to clear the bit and doesn't care about its previous setting.

The last bit manipulation instruction is used to test a bit and then flip it. If the bit is 0, BCHG changes it to 1 after testing it; if it's 1, BCHG tests it and then changes it to 0. Like the two preceding instructions, BCHG is often used just to flip a bit's value, with no regard to the previous value that's tested before the change.

There's a summary of bit manipulation instructions in Figure A-13.

Figure A-13 Bit manipulation instructions

Instruction	Description
BCHG	Test a bit, set Z condition code, then change the bit
BCLR	Test a bit, set Z condition code, then clear the bit
BSET	Test a bit, set Z condition code, then set the bit
BTST	Test a bit and set Z condition code

Binary Coded Decimal Instructions

Two's complement arithmetic is not the only kind of math supported by the 68000. There's another mode, called **binary-coded decimal**, or BCD. In this mode, each hexadecimal digit represents one decimal digit. Only hex values from 0 to 9 are allowed; A through F are illegal, since they're not used in the decimal system. In this representation, for example, the hex value $28 represents the decimal number 28. Instructions are provided to add, subtract, and negate BCD numbers.

This mode is rarely used, since two's complement integers are more efficient. A single BCD byte can represent 100 different values (0 through 99); a two's complement byte can represent 0 through $FF, or 255 different values. Very few compilers use BCD arithmetic, so we won't list the instructions or discuss them here.

Program Control Instructions

The 68000 has a group of instructions that allows the flow of the program to be changed. These instructions are analogous to instructions like "goto" in Pascal and C: they cause execution of the program to continue at another location. In assembly languge, there are three groups of program control instructions: conditional instructions, unconditional instructions, and return instructions. All these are important in compiled object code.

The first conditional instruction is the conditional branch instruction. This instruction tests the condition codes for a given condition; if the condition is true, it branches to another location. The general form of this instruction is written Bcc, which means "branch on condition codes." There are actually 14 different branches, each of which tests a different condition. For example, BEQ means "branch if equal." The 14 conditional branches are listed in Figure A-14.

Usually, a Bcc instruction follows a CMP instruction, which sets the condition codes. For example, a program can compare two values for equality and then branch if they're equal by executing a CMP instruction followed by a BEQ instruction. This sequence can be used for any of the 14 tests.

Compilers use Bcc instructions to implement "if" statements. First, the comparison is performed; then, if the comparison was false, there's a branch past the "then" clause to the "else" clause, if any. Conditional branches after CMP instructions are also used in testing loop boundaries.

Figure A-14 Branch on condition codes instructions

Instruction	Description
BCC	Branch if carry clear (C flag clear)
BCS	Branch if carry set (C flag set)
BEQ	Branch if equal to (Z flag set)
BGE	Branch if greater than or equal to
BGT	Branch if greater than
BHI	Branch if high (C and Z flags are clear)
BLE	Branch if less than or equal to
BLS	Branch if low or same (C or Z flag set)
BLT	Branch if less than (also sandwich)
BMI	Branch if minus (N flag set)
BNE	Branch if not equal to (Z flag clear)
BPL	Branch if plus (N flag clear)
BVC	Branch if overflow clear (V flag clear)
BVS	Branch if overflow set (V flag set)

Comparison Is "Backwards"

When reading code with CMP instructions followed by conditional branches, note that the source operand is compared to the destination. This means that conditional branches appear to have the comparison "backwards." For example, let's look at this sequence of instructions:

```
CMP.B #24,D0    ; compare the byte in D0 to #24
BGT label       ; branch if D0 > 24
```

Although the immediate value 24 is written before the D0, the "greater than" comparison in the BGT instruction compares them the other way, (D0 > 24). Be sure you follow this rule when you're looking at conditional instructions.

There's a more sophisticated form of conditional branch, called DBcc (decrement and branch). This single instruction actually performs three functions. First, it tests a condition; if the condition is false, a given data register is decremented, and if the data register is not equal to -1, the branch is taken. If the initial condition is true or if the decremented data register equals -1, no branch is taken, and the next instruction is executed. This means you can have a loop that can be terminated in two ways: either the condition is true or the data register's value goes below zero.

This instruction can be used by compilers to optimize loops. The conditions for the branch can be any of the 14 listed for Bcc, plus two more: DBT (decrement and branch until true), which will always fail the conditional test, and DBF (decrement and branch until false), which will always cause the branch to be taken. Since this condition is always taken, it's usually written as DBRA (decrement and branch always). This means that the only thing that can terminate the loop is the data register going below zero. The DBRA instruction is by far the most commonly used and is just about the only one you'll ever see.

The third and last conditional instruction is Scc (set byte conditionally). This instruction tests a given condition. If the condition is true, the byte specified as an operand is set to all ones ($FF); if the condition is false, the byte is set to all zeros ($00). In addition to the standard 14 conditions, there's a ST (set if true) instruction that always sets the operand to all ones, and a SF (set if false) instruction that always sets the operand to all zeros.

The first unconditional instruction is BSR, branch to subroutine. This instruction causes an unconditional branch to the specified location, but before branching, it saves the address of the next instruction. This allows the called routine to return to the caller by executing an RTS (return from subroutine) instruction, which is discussed later.

Another unconditional instruction very similar to BSR is JSR, jump to subroutine. Like BSR, JSR saves a return address that is used later when the called routine does an RTS. In fact, the only difference between these two subroutine-calling instructions is the available addressing modes for the operand. The JSR instruction allows the effective address to be specified with any of several addressing modes, including address register indirect, program counter relative, short and long absolute, and several others. The BSR instruction always takes a program counter relative displacement, either a byte-sized value (called a **short branch**) or a word-sized value (called a **long branch**).

Most compilers implement procedure and function calls as JSR instructions. Some compilers will automatically use a BSR if it's available and if it's more efficient than the equivalent JSR.

The third unconditional instruction is similar to the Bcc instructions. It's the BRA (branch always, or unconditional branch) instruction. This instruction is used to cause a branch to another location in the program without any conditions. Unlike the BSR and JSR instructions, this instruction does not save a return address, so it's used to transfer control without returning.

The fourth and last unconditional instruction, like the BRA instruction, causes an unconditional branch without a return. This instruction is JMP (jump). Again, the only difference between these two instructions is the set of available addressing modes. The JMP instruction allows the

Figure A-15 Program control instructions

Instruction	Description
Bcc	Branch on condition codes
DBcc	Test condition, decrement counter, and branch on condition codes
Scc	Set byte on condition codes
BRA	Branch always
BSR	Branch to subroutine
JMP	Jump
JSR	Jump to subroutine
RTS	Return from subroutine

same set of addressing modes as JSR, including address register indirect and program counter relative, while BRA takes a program counter relative displacement, which can be a byte (**short jump**) or a word (**long jump**).

Many compilers use the BRA instruction to force a branch to the "else" clause of an "if" statement. The BRA instruction is also frequently used in implementing loops. The JMP instruction is used in a Macintosh system data structure called the **jump table**, used for cross-segment communication.

The 68000 also defines a return instruction that is used frequently in compiled object code. This instruction is RTS, return from subroutine. The RTS instruction is used to return to a routine that called another routine with a BSR or JSR.

The BSR and JSR instructions save the address of the following instruction, called the **return address**, on the stack before jumping to the new location. Then, when the called routine executes an RTS, the saved address is pulled from the stack and placed into the program counter. In compiled high-level language code, procedures and functions end with an RTS, which causes control to return to the instruction immediately following the JSR or BSR.

The program control instructions are summarized in Figure A-15.

System Control Instructions

The system control instructions are operations that affect the state of the system. Only one of these instructions normally appears in compiled object code: the CHK (check register) instruction.

The CHK instruction is used if the compiler has a range-checking feature, like the $R+ option in Workshop Pascal. Range checking verifies that values are within legal ranges; for example, it checks to see that a value declared in Pascal as 0..1000 is actually within that range. On the 68000, range checking is implemented with the CHK instruction.

The CHK instruction takes two operands. The first (source) specifies the effective address that holds the maximum allowable value. The second operand is a data register that holds the value to be checked. If the value in the data register is less than zero or is greater than the value in the source operand, the 68000 generates a **check exception**. On the Macintosh, this exception is reported as a system error 5; if a debugger is installed, the debugger takes control.

Summary

This isn't a complete list of 68000 instructions, but it covers the instructions that are generated by most Pascal and C compilers on the Macintosh. When you're debugging, you should have a copy of the 68000 Programmer's Reference Manual so that you can see exactly what an instruction or addressing mode does. If you see an instruction that's not discussed in this section, you can look it up in the 68000 manual.

For lots more information on the code that compilers put out, see Chapters 5 and 6. If you want to learn more about assembly language, you should get a tutorial book on the subject, and you can use TMON's built-in assembler and disassembler feature to try things easily.

APPENDIX

Common Problems

This appendix gathers together some common, easy-to-create problems that can kill your program. They're listed by problem, not by symptom, since almost all of them can cause almost any crash imaginable. For each gotcha listed here, we discuss what you have to do to cause the problem, explain exactly why the problem occurs, and then tell how to avoid the situation.

Nested Procedure Pointers

There are lots of ROM routines that take a procedure pointer (procPtr) as a parameter. For example, ModalDialog takes a parameter of type procPtr, which is a pointer to the dialog's filter procedure; the Track-Control call takes a pointer to a control's action procedure; the Window Manager's DragGrayRgn function also calls an action procedure, given a procedure pointer.

In Workshop Pascal, these calls usually look something like this:

```
ModalDialog (@myFilter, itemHit)
```

In this example, myFilter is the name of the filter procedure, which is declared somewhere else in the program.

Since myFilter is only called by ModalDialog, you might be tempted to be a real disciplined programmer and nest myFilter's declaration within the procedure that calls ModalDialog, like this:

```
procedure CallDialog;
    function myFilter (theDialog: DialogPtr; var
        theEvent:EventRecord; var itemHit: Integer): Boolean;

    begin
        {whatever myFilter does}
    end; {function myFilter}
begin {procedure CallDialog}
    ModalDialog (@myFilter, itemHit);
end; {procedure CallDialog}
```

This looks like a good idea: since CallDialog is the only place that myFilter will be referenced, nesting its declaration within CallDialog makes sure that no other procedures can call it.

Unfortunately, the compiler is playing hidden tricks on you again. One feature of nested procedures and functions is that they're able to access the outer procedure's local variables. To do this, the compiler pushes an extra long word on the stack when it calls the inner routine. This extra long word, called a **static link**, allows the inner routine to find the outer routine's locals.

When procPtr-passed routines are called, they're called by ROM routines (ModalDialog calls myFilter, for example). These ROM routines know nothing about the compiler's static link; they just create a standard stack frame by pushing the parameters and then calling the routine.

If the called routine's declaration was nested, the compiled code will have been generated assuming that the static link will be on the stack. This will screw up all references to parameters in the routine—they'll be off by four bytes, the size of the static link. Any possible death of the system may result.

The fix: don't nest declarations of routines passed by procPtr.

Figure B-1 has a list of ROM calls, fields of records, and system globals that are pointers to procedures and functions. Any routine pointed to by one of these must not have its declaration nested.

Figure B-1 Procedure pointers associated
with the ROM

system calls		
DragGrayRgn	InitDialogs	ModalDialog
SetCtlAction	Alert	StopAlert
TrackControl	NoteAlert	CautionAlert
ErrorSound	InitZone	SetGrowZone
StartSound	SFPutFile	SFPPutFile
SFGetFile	SFPGetFile	

fields of records

wordBreak, clikLoop, highHook, caretHook fields
   of TERec record
ioCompletion field of O. S. call parameter blocks
vblAddr filed of VBLTask record
pIdleProc field of TPrJob record
all fields of QDProcs record
contrlAction field of ControlRecord
gzProc, purgeProc fields of Zone record

system globals		
CloseOrnHook	DABeeper	DeskHook
DragHook	EjectNotify	IAZNotify
MBarHook	MenuHook	ResErrProc
ResumeProc	SaveProc	TEDoText
TERecal		

Register Being Trashed by PACKs

Some early versions (released in 1984) of the system file included a real flaming bug in two packages, SANE and International Utilities. The bug was that some routines in those packages were using register D3 without preserving its value.

As you may remember from Chapter 8, register D3 is not up for grabs. All system calls are expected to preserve it. This means that code that calls one of these nasty PACK routines may have a value in D3 that it assumes will be left alone, but in fact is getting trashed.

One common symptom of this is a scroll bar that seems to forget which part of it is being clicked; for example, you hold the mouse down in the up-arrow, and it scrolls once and stops, keeping the arrow highlighted. The reason this happens is that your application calls TrackControl, which figures out which part of the control is being highlighted and puts that part code in D3. The TrackControl routine then calls your ActionProc, which was one of the parameters that you passed to TrackControl. If, in your ActionProc, you make a call to SANE or International Utilities that trashes D3, TrackControl will forget which part the mouse was in when it takes over again.

The fix: make sure you're using the latest system file, which fixes the bug.

Implicit Dereferencing in With Statements

As we discussed in depth in Chapter 2, Workshop Pascal will sometimes implicitly dereference a handle. In a statement like this,

```
with myHdl^^ do begin   {saves a copy of pointer to the record
                            that myHdl is a handle to}
  myNum := 10;     {myNum is a field of the record}
  aHandle := GetResource ('DAVE', 27);
        {GetResource can cause compaction}
  myBool := true;    {saved pointer to the record may be invalid!}
end; {with}
```

the apparently safe double-dereferenced handle causes the compiler to save a pointer in a register for optimization. This means that if there are any statements in the body of the with statement that can cause heap objects to move, like the GetResource call, this pointer may become invalid, since the object it points to may have moved.

The fix: try to keep compaction-causing calls out of with statements that look like this; otherwise, before executing the compaction-causing call, call MoveHHi on the record whose handle is being double-dereferenced in the with statement and then HLock it, like this:

```
MoveHHi (myHdl);
HLock (myHdl);
```

Be sure to HUnlock it right after the compaction-causing call.

Implicit Dereferencing in Procedure Calls

This is another one that's discussed in Chapter 2. If you pass a double-dereferenced handle as a procedure parameter, and that parameter is a VAR parameter or a parameter larger than 4 bytes (in other words, it's passed by pointer), *and* the procedure called is in another segment that must be loaded from disk, you could have problems. Here's an example:

```
SetToZero (myHdl^^.myNum)
```

In this example, the parameter is declared by SetToZero to be a VAR parameter, and SetToZero is in another segment. So, by the time the segment containing SetToZero is loaded, the object that myHdl is a handle to may have been relocated, and the pointer passed on the stack may be invalid.

The fix: don't pass double-dereferenced handles as procedure parameters, unless you want to be responsible for ensuring that (1) the parameter isn't a VAR parameter, (2) the parameter isn't larger than four bytes, and (3) the called procedure isn't in another segment. Instead, copy the parameter into a variable before making the call, like this:

```
localNum := myHdl^ .myNum;
SetToZero (localNum);
```

This way, you're safe, because localNum is a stack object and can't move.

Implicit Dereferencing in Function Calls

Once again, this problem was discussed in Chapter 2. If you assign a function result to a double-dereferenced handle and the function is in another segment, you could wind up in deep trouble with a bad pointer. In this call

```
myHdl^^ .myNum := SomeFunction (anyParam)
```

the compiler generates code that constructs a pointer to the variable on the left side and then calls the function. If the function is in another segment, or if there are any relocation-triggering calls in the function, memory compaction could occur, and the pointer could be left pointing into space.

The fix: don't assign function results to double-dereferenced handles, unless you want to be sure that the function called isn't in another segment and that there are no relocation-triggering calls in the function. The safest thing to do is to call the function with a variable and then assign that variable to the desired record field, like this:

```
localNum := SomeFunction (anyParam);
myHdl^^ .myNum := localNum;
```

Since localNum is on the stack and can't move, this method avoids the problem.

Register A5 at Interrupt Time

Register A5 is an important global pointer that's used to find several system data structures, including all the application's global variables, the QuickDraw global variables (thePort, the cursor arrow, the patterns black and white, etc.), and the jump table. If you have code that executes in response to an interrupt, A5 may be invalid, since the routine that was interrupted may have preserved its value while using the register for something else. A problem like this can be extremely hard to find, since A5 will sometimes be valid. It all depends on what code was interrupted.

Because the "real" value A5 is so important, ROM routines that use A5 save its value in the global called CurrentA5 at $904. If you have a routine that executes at interrupt time, be sure that you preserve A5, load A5 from CurrentA5, and then restore A5 before exiting. Examples of routines that execute at interrupt time include VBL tasks and I/O completion routines.

This problem can bite you when you're debugging, too. If you interrupt the ROM, be sure that the contents of A5 match CurrentA5.

If you're writing in Workshop Pascal, you can use the OS Utilities SetUpA5 and RestoreA5 to preserve, set up, and restore A5 for you.

The fix: from assembly language, preserve A5 and load it from CurrentA5 for interrupt-time routines like VBL tasks and completion routines, and then restore it when you're done; from Pascal, call SetUpA5 at the beginning of the procedure and RestoreA5 at the end.

Relying on Handles at Interrupt Time

Code that executes in response to an interrupt may be called after virtually any task has been interrupted. For example, a heap compaction may be taking place when the interrupt occurs, calling your routine.

What if your routine has a handle to the object that's being relocated? The state of the object may be invalid; it's right in the middle of being moved! If you're writing code that executes at interrupt time, such as a VBL task or an I/O completion routine, you can't rely on handles being valid, since their objects might be in the middle of a relocation. This is the only time that a master pointer might be invalid.

The only way around this problem is to ensure that any handles you might need in your interrupt-time routine are locked. You can't lock them in the routine itself; it's too late by then.

The fix: don't rely on handles being valid at interrupt time, unless the handles are to locked objects.

Calling the ROM at Interrupt Time

Interrupt-time code may be interrupting the Memory Manager while it's allocating a new object. Because of this, interrupt-time code can't call the Memory Manager to allocate new objects.

A more general problem is lack of **reentrancy**; that is, what happens if a ROM routine, say PackBits, is interrupted, and the interrupt-time code calls PackBits? What if the original, interrupted PackBits call was keeping a temporary value in a system global location? The PackBits called from the interrupt-time code might destroy that value, and the original, interrupted call would be messed up.

In practice, this doesn't happen too much, because most ROM routines don't change system globals that often; instead, they keep their variables in stack frames, which are preserved if the routine is interrupted. The ROM routines' level of reentrancy is not well explored. The only hard rule is that interrupt-time code must not make any Memory Manager calls that rely on a consistent heap zone; most calls do rely on the heap zone being good.

This also means that interrupt-time code may not call any ROM routines that call the Memory Manager, for the same reason. There's a list of ROM routines that are no-nos at interrupt time in **Inside Macintosh.**

The fix: interrupt-time code can't call make Memory Manager calls; it also can't call ROM routines that call the Memory Manager; it should be cautious about calling any ROM routines at all, since the routine called may have been interrupted and may not be reentrant.

Calling UnloadSeg with a Routine in the Same Segment

When you call UnloadSeg, the ROM expects the parameter to be a pointer to a routine in another segment. How are routines referenced from other segments? Cross-segment references are really pointers to entries in the jump table. Consider this source and object code:

```
ProcInOtherSeg;      { JSR address(A5) }
```

As we saw in Chapter 6, calls to routines in other segments produce A5-relative JSRs. These are really JSRs to entries in the jump table, which is located above A5. UnloadSeg expects its parameter to be a jump table entry, as in this call:

```
UnloadSeg (@ProcInOtherSeg);       { PEA address(A5) }
                                   { _UnloadSeg }
```

The effective address that's pushed on the stack by the PEA instruction is the address of ProcInOtherSeg's jump table entry. When Unload-Seg gets control, it starts doing all the stuff needed to unload the segment: unlocking it, marking the jump table entries unloaded, and so on.

What if you inadvertently call UnloadSeg on a routine in the same segment? Same-segment routines look like this:

```
ProcInSameSeg;          { JSR address(PC) }
```

You might remember from Chapter 6 that same-segment calls produce PC-relative JSRs, like this one. So a same-segment UnloadSeg would look like this:

```
UnloadSeg (@ProcInSameSeg);          { PEA address(PC) }
                                     { _UnloadSeg }
```

The address that's pushed here isn't a jump table entry—it's the actual address of the procedure! UnloadSeg won't know the difference, unfortunately. It will assume that the address is really a jump table entry. You'd think that this would cause a disaster, but not so. The UnloadSeg routine is smart enough to do one reality check before it unloads the segment. It checks to see that the word pointed to by the parameter passed to it is $4EF9, which is the opcode for the JMP instruction. If it's not $4EF9, UnLoadSeg assumes that this is a segment that is already unloaded, and returns without doing anything.

Since JMP instructions almost never occur in application code, this "feature" of UnloadSeg will render most inadvertent same-segment calls harmless. This just makes these errors harder to find. The easiest way to catch them is with a Discipline feature in a debugger (see Chapter 4).

The fix: calling UnloadSeg with a procedure that's in the same segment usually does nothing at all, but you should still avoid doing it, of course.

Applications That Change Globals or Trap Addresses

When an application quits, the application heap and stack are reinitialized, so any information there is lost (except the scrap, which the system preserves). The ROM code that takes control when an application quits also resets many system globals. However, some changes that the application makes to system globals are still in effect.

To avoid ruining the lives of the applications that follow, an application should take care to clean up after itself by undoing any changes it made to system globals that won't be undone by the ROM. The ROM clears the globals DragHook, DeskHook, CloseOrnHook, ResumeProc, SaveProc, ResErrProc, and EjectNotify. This takes care of most of the globals that point to routines, so you probably won't have to worry about any others.

Warning

See the section "ResLoad Set to False" in this Appendix about another important system global that you should watch out for.

The most important thing your application should do to clean up after itself is to remove any patches to ROM calls that it may have installed. It can do this by calling SetTrapAddress to restore the address to its original value, which the application should have saved somewhere. Since trap patches are usually in the application heap, and the application heap is reinitialized when the application quits, failure to reset patched traps usually results in disaster.

The fix: if you've intercepted any traps, always reset them back to their original addresses when your application quits.

Misspelling CODE in the Resource Compiler

Don't laugh. CODE is most frequently misspelled like this: code or Code. Remember that resource types are case sensitive, so CODE and code are not the same type.

How do you spell CODE? The Launch routine in the ROM spells it with all uppercase letters. When an application is launched, the ROM looks for the file's CODE resource number 0. If it can't find it, it puts up a system error 26. Some versions of the Lisa-based RMaker program automatically forced all resource types to uppercase; other versions did not. This means that you can have an RMaker input file that contains the word code that will kill you with some versions of RMaker and not with others.

If you launch an application and get an instant system error 26, use ResEdit to see if you've got a CODE 0—not Code, or code.

The fix: change your RMaker input file to spell CODE in all uppercase.

Patching Traps That Are Already Patched

Many applications like to customize the function of one or more of the Macintosh ROM traps. For example, a program that wants to monitor its usage of NewHandle might patch the NewHandle call so that it can execute its own code before calling the ROM. The system provides the GetTrapAddress and SetTrapAddress calls to help you do this.

There are four ways you can handle patches: (1) you can execute your code (a **prolog**) and then call the original routine; (2) you can call the original routine first and then execute your code (an **epilog**); (3) you can start with your own code, execute the original routine and then some more of your own code; or (4) you can ignore the original routine entirely, using only your own code. Which of these you choose depends on exactly what you want to do.

The technique for running your code first is obvious: just use SetTrapAddress to point to your code and then jump to the original routine when you're done. To run the original first and then your code, you can JSR to the original routine; when it ends with an RTS, it will come back to your code. This technique looks like this:

```
Patch    JSR origAddr  ;we got this address with GetTrapAddress
         {patch is here}  ;RTS at end of original returns here
```

Some "ROM" calls are already patched so that bugs in ROM can be fixed in RAM. You might think that patching these traps is no problem, as long as you're sure to call the original routine whose address you got with GetTrapAddress. This isn't always the case.

Some traps are patched in a strange and clever way. In some cases, instead of patching a given trap, Apple patched a trap that was *called by* the trap with the bug. Here's an example. MenuSelect has a bug: it should be incrementing a global value, and it's not doing so. Just one additional line of code, ADDQ.W #4,$9FA, would fix the problem. To do this, though, we'd have to replace the entire MenuSelect routine, which is over 700 bytes long. That would cost us a significant amount of disk space and RAM.

While it's executing, MenuSelect calls InsetRect. Instead of spending over 700 bytes to patch MenuSelect, we'll do this: we'll patch InsetRect. In the InsetRect patch, we'll examine the return address on the stack to determine if we were called by MenuSelect. If so, we'll apply the fix; if not, we'll just jump back to the ROM. Ingenious! Total size of the patch: 18 bytes. It looks like this:

```
         CMPI.L #40CB92,(A7)  ;called from this address in MenuSelect?
         BNE.S goBack    ;    no, return to ROM now
         ADDQ.W #4,$9FA       ;  yes, do the fix
goBack   JMP $40718C     ;go to original InsetRect in ROM
```

This technique is used for many ROM patches, especially in the 64K ROM. It can cause problems if you attempt to put in your own patches. If you're trying to put in an epilog, you push your return address on the stack and then call the original patch. If it's one like the InsetRect patch, it will look at the return address on the top of the stack, but instead of seeing the ROM address that called it, it sees the return address to your patch. Even if it were really called by MenuSelect, it won't be able to tell.

If you want to add an epilog, the only safe way to patch a trap that's already patched is to look at the patch with a debugger and see if it looks at the stack for a return address to ROM. If not, you're probably OK. If it does, you'll need to duplicate the functionality of the existing patch in your patch. Just add the code that's already there and then execute your code.

Adding a prolog to a trap that's already patched is no problem, since you don't modify the stack.

The fix: to add an epilog to a trap that's already patched, look at the existing patch; if it examines the stack for a return address, you'll need to duplicate its code in your custom patch.

ResLoad Set to False

There's a very important global call ResLoad that is maintained by the Resource Manager. Whenever a call takes place that might cause a resource to be loaded, such as GetResource, the Resource Manager first checks the state of ResLoad, which is kept at $A5E. If ResLoad is False, the Resource Manager will go through all the motions, but it will not load in the resource. If you're not expecting this, boy, are you in for a surprise. Having ResLoad false inadvertently is one of the quickest ways to kill an application. You can change the state of ResLoad with the SetResLoad call.

There are several ROM calls that leave ResLoad set to True as a side effect of calling them; for example, the Font Manager's RealFont routine sets ResLoad to true while executing and leaves it that way when it returns. You shouldn't depend on side effects to fix ResLoad for you, though. If your application sets it False, you should be sure to set it back to True as soon as possible.

You should be especially sure to set ResLoad to true before quitting your application. With the current ROM (64K and 128K), there's a side effect that occurs when the ROM launches the application after yours that sets ResLoad to true, but you shouldn't count on this always happening. Instead, if you set ResLoad to False in your application, you should be sure to restore it to true before your application ends or you'll poison the Apple for the next program.

The fix: set ResLoad to true before quitting your application.

Purgeable MENU Resources

The Menu Manager assumes that MENU resources are not purgeable. Once it gets a handle to a MENU, it expects it to be in memory until the application quits. On the 64K ROM, the Menu Manager never checks to see if a MENU has been purged, so your program can crash in any way.

Macintosh Plus

The Macintosh Plus (128K) ROM checks to see if a MENU has been purged before trying to use it. If it has been purged, it generates a system error 84.

The fix: don't make MENUs purgeable.

Applications That Won't Work without the Finder

The Finder's Special menu has an item called Set Startup. With this item, you can make any application start up immediately when the disk is booted, bypassing the Finder. This is especially handy if you don't have a hard disk and want to make your applications come up faster.

Sometimes an application will not run correctly as the startup application. It might bomb with an address error or display a funny screen when it comes up. If an application does this, it's probably not initializing something correctly; maybe it's using a variable that is has never assigned a value to. When the Finder is run first, the variable's memory happens to be initialized to the proper value, but if the Finder isn't run first, the value is wrong.

All applications should be able to run as the startup. If yours doesn't, you should track down the problem with normal debugging techniques and fix it.

The fix: debug your program, looking especially for uninitialized variables.

Disposing of System Objects

The Operating System and Toolbox create various heap objects that you use in your application. For example, if you use TextEdit, there's a TextEdit scrap that holds cut or copied information from a Text-Edit record. Another system object is the information pointed to by AppParmHandle, which the Finder sets up when it launches an application.

Be sure you don't call `DisposHandle` to get rid of these objects! The system expects these objects to be around and isn't real robust about checking to see if they've been destroyed. If you call `DisposHandle` on them, you'll find your system crashing in extremely bizarre ways. Often your application will seem to run OK, but the system will crash after you've returned to the Finder. The rule of thumb is this: if you didn't directly allocate the object, don't dispose of it.

The fix: don't dispose of heap objects that you didn't allocate.

Macintosh Plus

In January 1986, Apple introduced the Macintosh Plus. This computer differs from its predecessor, the Macintosh 512K, in several ways. The most important changes are:

- Macintosh 512K had 64K bytes of ROM; Macintosh Plus has 128K bytes of ROM. This new ROM implements bug fixes, performance enhancements, and new features. Also, some frequently used system resources are now in ROM.

- Macintosh Plus has 1 megabyte of RAM as a standard feature, expandable to 4 megabytes with high-density RAM chips.

- Macintosh 512K had a built-in 400K, single-sided disk drive; Macintosh Plus has a built-in disk drive that holds 800K bytes on double-sided disks. Both computers can support an external drive: 400K for the Macintosh 512K, 400K or 800K for the Macintosh Plus.

- Macintosh Plus has an expanded keyboard that includes a built-in numeric pad and arrow keys.

- Macintosh Plus has a built-in SCSI (small computer system interface) port for connection to third-party devices, especially hard disks.

You can get an upgrade kit from Apple to convert your Macintosh 128K or 512K into a Macintosh Plus. Everything in this book that applies to a Macintosh Plus is also applicable to an upgraded Macintosh 128K or 512K.

The rest of this appendix is a very brief discussion of the ROM, piece by piece, with highlights of the changes and a listing of new calls. We'll distinguish between the two ROMs by calling them the "original ROM" and the "Macintosh Plus ROM." You may also hear the original ROM referred to as the "64K ROM," the "old ROM," and by its version number, which is version $69. The Macintosh Plus ROM is also called the "128K ROM," the "new ROM," and its official version number, $75. The ROM version number is a byte at location ROMBase + 9 ($400009).

Because the Macintosh Plus has space for many more traps (see "Trap Dispatcher", which follows), not all trap numbers were used by ROM calls. Many of these leftover calls were used by Apple as vectors to core routines in the ROM to facilitate patching these routines if bugs were discovered. Since these calls aren't generally useful and since their interface isn't guaranteed, they probably won't be documented by Apple. Because they aren't documented, they may change in the future, so you should use them at your own risk.

For more complete information on the Macintosh Plus ROM and the new calls in particular, you should write to Apple about getting the most current documentation and technical note updates.

There's a special memory location that you can test to determine if you're running under 128K ROMs. This is location $28E, called ROM85. You should check the high bit of this location. If the high bit is zero, new ROMs are present; otherwise, the computer has the old ROM.

Warning

If you don't check this flag before doing things that require the presence of the Macintosh Plus ROM, your program will die in amazing and spectacular ways. Consider yourself warned.

Trap Dispatcher

Under the original ROM, there is a table of trap addresses at $400–7FF. This table is used to figure out what address to go to when the system encounters a trap. To save space, each address is packed into a single word (two bytes).

The Macintosh Plus ROM does not pack the addresses in the trap dispatch table; each one takes four bytes and is an actual address. This makes the trap dispatch table larger, but simplifies and speeds up the dispatching code.

Although the trap dispatching mechanism provides for a bit in the trap word to distinguish between Toolbox and Operating System traps (bit 11), the original ROM does not use this bit. For example, the trap word for the OS call MoreMasters is $A036 (called "trap number $36").

In theory, there should be a corresponding Toolbox trap number $36 with bit 11 set: $A836. However, to save space in the trap dispatch table under the original ROM, bit 11 is ignored; each trap number is either a Toolbox trap or an OS trap, but not both, so there is no trap $A836.

On the Macintosh Plus, bit 11 of the trap word is used to distinguish between Toolbox and OS traps. Each trap number may have both an OS trap and a Toolbox trap associated with it. For example, the Macintosh Plus defines $A036 as MoreMasters, and it also defines a Toolbox trap number $36, the new QuickDraw call GetMaskTable, which is $A836.

Since there are now 512 different Toolbox traps ($0-1FF) and 256 different OS traps ($0-FF), the size of the trap dispatch table is (512 + 256) entries * 4 bytes per entry, or 3072 (3K) bytes. To accommodate this, the table has been split into two pieces: the OS traps at $400-7FF and the Toolbox traps at $C00-13FF.

Of course, the Macintosh Plus ROM does not change the trap numbers for any traps that exist in the original ROM. Without this consideration, applications that were written before Macintosh Plus would have no shot at running on the newer machine.

Resource Manager

The Resource Manager has benefited from the experience of the hundreds of Macintosh applications that were written in 1984 and 1985. After examining the behavior of lots of Macintosh applications, the Resource Manager was modified to make it faster, especially for important functions like starting up an application and updating a resource file. The Resource Manager also uses various caching techniques to speed things up.

The Resource Manager searches through all open resource files when looking for a resource. It starts in the current resource file, which is usually the last opened file; if the requested resource can't be found in that file, it then searches through the next file, and so on, until the resource is found or the last opened file has been searched.

Sometimes you only want to search the current file for a resource and just give up if it can't be found there. The Resource Manager now implements a set of calls to help you do this. These calls are known as "one-deep" calls because they only search the current resource file. You should use them in any situation in which you're certain that you only want to search the current file.

Several commonly used resources are now in ROM. This gives you several benefits: for example, applications run faster, since they don't have to load these resources, and there's more room in RAM that's not taken up by the ROM-based resources.

These resources that used to be loaded from disk are in the Macintosh Plus ROM:

- MDEF 0 (text menus)
- WDEF 0 (standard windows)
- PACK 4 (SANE)   PACK 5 (Elems)   PACK 7 (Binary-Decimal)
- SERD 0 (serial drivers)
- DRVR 9 (.MPP, AppleTalk driver)
- DRVR 10 (.ATP, AppleTalk driver)
- DRVR 2 (.Print, printer driver shell)
- CURS 1, 2, 3, 4 (standard cursors)
- FONT 12 (system font)

In addition, two drivers were present in the 64K ROM that have now become part of the ROM resource file. This really doesn't change them functionally. They are DRVR 4 (.Sony) and DRVR 3 (.Sound).

New Calls

Function MaxSizeRsrc (theResource:Handle): Longint;

This call determines a resource's size without having to read the size from the disk (it does this by looking at the resource map and seeing the difference between the start of this resource and the next). The resource may actually be smaller than the number reported by MaxSizeRsrc if the file hasn't been compacted.

Function RsrcMapEntry (theResource:Handle): Longint;

You can use this function to find a resource's entry in its resource map. The function result is an offset from the start of the resource map to the desired entry. This is mainly useful if you're writing resource or file editing utilities, or if you just want to hack around. Can you do damage with this if you don't know what you're doing? You betcha.

Function OpenRFPerm (fileName: Str255; vRefNum: Integer;
    permission: byte;): Integer;

This call is similar to OpenResFile in that it opens a resource file. It provides more options, though: you can specify a volume or HFS folder with the vRefNum parameter, and there's a permission parameter that allows you to specify file attributes such as read only.

QuickDraw

QuickDraw has also been improved in the Macintosh Plus ROM. Various functions have been made up to four times faster while retaining compatibility with existing applications.

Several infamous QuickDraw bugs have been fixed. These include:

- RectInRgn sometimes returned True even if the rectangle was not in the region (it checked to see if the rectangle was in the region's bounding box instead).
- Various region calculation calls (SectRgn, UnionRgn, DiffRgn, XorRgn, and FrameRgn) could cause stack overflows when complex regions were used.
- PtToAngle sometimes didn't work right if the angle parameter was 90.
- CopyBits sometimes destroyed the source bitmap if the source and destination bitmaps overlapped.
- Text drawing would cause a stack overflow if a large amount of text was drawn in a large point size and with a complex style, such as shadowing.
- DrawText recorded in a picture did not work correctly if the byteCount parameter was greater than 255.

QuickDraw's text drawing capability has been expanded to allow all eight transfer modes; previously, only srcOr, srcBic, and srcXor worked.

QuickDraw and the Font Manager have now been enhanced to support fractional pixel spacing for characters. This and other Font Manager enhancements make bitmapped fonts look better when they're printed.

Picture sizes are now a long word instead of a word. This means that pictures can be over four gigabytes (if you've got the storage, of course). The picSize field of the picture record contains the low word of the real picture size. To determine a picture's true size, you can call GetHandleSize.

New Calls

```
Procedure SeedFill (srcPtr,dstPtr: Ptr; srcRow,dstRow,height,
    words: Integer; seedH,seedV: Integer);

Procedure CalcMask (srcPtr,dstPtr: Ptr; srcRow,dstRow,height,
    words: Integer);
```

These calls provide the foundation for the paint bucket and lasso tools found in MacPaint. The SeedFill procedure "leaks paint" from the point specified by seedH and seedV through the source bitmap. It produces a bitmap that will have black bits in the appropriate places.

The CalcMask procedure can be used to add the capability of MacPaint's lasso tool. CalcMask produces a bitmap that has been "lassoed" after scanning the input bitmap.

Procedure CopyMask (srcBits,maskBits,dstBits: BitMap; srcRect,maskRect,dstRect: Rect);

This procedure is a variation on CopyBits. It uses another parameter, maskBits, which "masks" the output bitmap; in other words, only bits that correspond to a one in maskBits can be set in dstBits.

Procedure MeasureText (count: Integer; textAddr,charLocs: Ptr);

This procedure is similar to TextWidth in that it measures the width of characters; instead of measuring an entire string and adding the results, it puts the width of each character into an array of integers, pointed to by charLocs. Since this procedure doesn't use QuickDraw's StdText procedure, it can only be used for text displayed on the screen, not text to be printed.

Function GetMaskTable: Ptr;

This function returns a pointer to three tables in ROM that can be used as masks, such as for the CopyMask procedure.

Font Manager

As mentioned previously, the Font Manager now supports fractional character spacing. Also, a new resource type called FOND has been invented and is used to specify an entire family of related fonts instead of just one point size.

New Calls

Procedure SetFScaleDisable (scaleDis: Boolean);

This procedure is used to disable or enable font scaling. It does so by setting or clearing the low-memory global called FScaleDisable at $AB2. This global also exists under the original ROM. The SetFScaleDisable call is all that's new. If scaling is disabled, text will be drawn in the size that would normally be scaled.

```
Procedure FontMetrics (var theMetrics: FontMetricRec);

{type FontMetricRec = Record
                    ascent: Fixed;
                    descent: Fixed;
                    leading: Fixed;
                    widMax: Fixed;
                    wTabHandle: Handle;
                  end;}
```

You can use FontMetrics to get information about the current GrafPort's font, that is, the font in thePort.

Window Manager

The Window Manager now supports a new feature, zooming windows. This feature appears as a box on the right edge of the title bar. Clicking in this box causes a window to zoom to full screen size; clicking again sets the window back to the size it was before zooming. Zooming is supported by a new WDEF 0 (standard window definition function) in the ROM and two new calls in the Window Manager.

New Calls

```
Function TrackBox (window: WindowPtr; thePt: Point;
    partCode: Integer) : Boolean;
```

If you create a window with window definition ID 8, the window will have a zoom box on the right edge of the title bar. If there's a mouse-down event in this box, FindWindow will return code 8, which is inZoomOut. If you get this response, you should call TrackBox with partCode equal to 8. If the user released the mouse button while still in the zoom box, TrackBox will return True and you should call ZoomWindow.

If the window has previously been zoomed out, a mouse-down event in the zoom box will return code 7 (inZoomIn) when you call FindWindow. Calling TrackBox with partCode set to 7 will track the mouse, and calling ZoomWindow if TrackBox returns True will cause the window to be zoomed back to its previous size.

```
Procedure ZoomWindow (window: WindowPtr; partCode: Integer;
    front: Boolean);
```

If TrackBox returns True, you should call ZoomWindow with the appropriate part code (inZoomIn or inZoomOut). The front parameter is used to specify if the window should also be brought to the front. If it's True, the window will be made the frontmost; otherwise, it's position will not change.

Control Manager

New Calls

```
Procedure UpdateControls (theWindow: WindowPtr;
    update: RgnHandle);
```

This procedure draws all the controls in the given window that intersect the given region. This can be used, for example, to redraw controls in a window whose contents have just scrolled.

Menu Manager

The AddResMenu and InsertResMenu calls now automatically alphabetize the resources they get when they build their menus, like the Apple and Font menus, for example. InsertResMenu alphabetizes within the range that it inserts.

The Menu Manager still doesn't like purged menus. In the original ROM, the Menu Manager simply assumed that menus would not be purged. If one was purged, it wasn't detected until a future system error, such as an address error, occurred. In the Macintosh Plus, a purged menu is detected as soon as the system tries to read it, and a system error 84 (called MenuPrgErr) is generated.

If a menu is too long to fit on the screen when it's pulled down, the Menu Manager will draw as many items as it can, up to 19. If the user drags down from the last item, the menu will scroll up, showing more items at the bottom. Dragging up from the top item will make the menu scroll back the other way. There's a new MDEF 0 (standard menu definition procedure) that implements this feature.

New Calls

```
Procedure InsMenuItem (menuHandle: Handle; itemString: str255;
    itemNum: Integer);
```

This procedure inserts the items specified in the itemString parameter following the item given in itemNum. If the string contains multiple items, they're inserted in the reverse of their order in itemString.

Procedure DelMenuItem (menuHandle: Handle; itemNum: Integer);

Use this procedure to remove an item from the specified menu.

TextEdit

When you create a TextEdit record, there is a field included for you to implement your own procedure to be called during calls to TEClick, that is, whenever the user clicks in the text (you put a pointer to this procedure in the clikLoop field). In the Macintosh Plus, the default behavior for a new TextEdit record implements autoscrolling in the text; that is, if the user drags the mouse up or down, left or right, past the edge of the rectangle, the text will automatically scroll in that direction.

Since the ROM updates the text and its display, there's no way to correctly update a scroll bar while the user is dragging the mouse. For this reason, the main use for this feature is to provide autoscrolling in dialogs that have editable text items and other text that doesn't have a scroll bar.

New Calls

Procedure TEAutoView (auto: Boolean; hTe: TEHandle);

This procedure sets the TextEdit record's autoView field. If autoView is false, autoscrolling is turned off for this record's default clickLoop; if true, autoscrolling is enabled. Also, this field enables and disables automatic scrolling to show the selection in a TextEdit record (see TESelView, which follows).

Procedure TESelView (hTe: TEHandle);

Calling TESelView will make sure that the selection is displayed, scrolling if necessary. It's called by the default clikLoop if autoView is true.

Procedure TEPinScroll (dh, dv: Integer; hTe: TEHandle);

This procedure is very similar to TEScroll; the only difference is that it stops scrolling when the last line of text is drawn in the window. Normally, this is the behavior that you'd want, so you should use this call where you used TEScroll previously.

Dialog Manager

New Calls

Procedure HideDItem (dialog: DialogPtr; itemNo: Integer);

This procedure can be used to "hide" the specified item in a dialog. It hides the item by forcing its display rectangle to be off screen. It also erases the item and calls InvalRect to generate an update event.

Procedure ShowDItem (dialog: DialogPtr; itemNo: Integer);

Use this procedure to bring back an item that you've hidden with HideDItem.

Procedure UpdtDialog (dialog: DialogPtr; updateRgn: RgnHandle);

Calling UpdtDialog causes all the items that are in the specified region to be drawn. Before calling this procedure, you should call BeginUpdate, and after calling it, you should call EndUpdate.

Function FindDItem (dialog: DialogPtr; thePoint: Point): Integer

You can use this function to find out which item in a dialog contains a given point. If there's no item in the dialog that contains the point, FindDItem returns −1; otherwise, the function result is the item number that contains the point. The thePoint parameter must be in local coordinates.

Desk Manager

Under the original ROM, the Desk Manager only passed events 0 through 8 to desk accessories. The Macintosh Plus passes events 0 through 11 to desk accessories, which includes networkEvt (10) and driverEvt (11). Event 9 is undefined.

Scrap Manager

The Scrap Manager in the Macintosh Plus ROM writes the scrap to the disk specified by the low-memory global BootDrive at $210 when UnloadScrap is called. If it's an HFS volume, the scrap is put in the System Folder. The original ROM put the scrap on the default volume, which is not necessarily the same as BootDrive.

Toolbox Utilities

There is now a set of calls that provides very accurate fixed-point math with numbers that have a small absolute value (numbers between −2 and 2). These numbers are represented by a type called Fract. This type is four bytes long. The highest bit, bit 31, is the sign: 0 for positive, 1 for negative. The next bit, bit 30, represents the integer portion of the number: 0 or 1. The lowest 30 bits represent the fractional portion of the number.

The ROM provides two sets of calls to support this type: conversion routines, which convert between Fract, the SANE type Extended, and the type Fixed; and math routines.

New Calls

```
Function Long2Fix (x: Longint): Fixed;
Function Fix2Long (x: Fixed): Longint;
Function Fix2Frac (x: Fixed): Fract;
Function Frac2Fix (x: Fract): Fixed;
Function Fix2X (x: Fixed): Extended;
Function X2Fix (x: Extended): Fixed;
Function Frac2X (x: Fract): Extended;
Function X2Frac (x: Extended): Fract;
```

These functions all provide the indicated conversions. There's also a bunch of calls to perform math on these numbers:

```
Function FracCos (x: Fixed): Fract;
Function FracSin (x: Fixed): Fract;
Function FracSqrt (x: Fract): Fract;
Function FracMul (x, y: Fract): Fract;
Function FracDiv (x, y: Fract): Fixed;
Function FixAtan2 (x, y: Longint): Fixed;
Function FixDiv (x, y: Fixed): Fixed;
```

Package Manager

The Package Manager now supports 16 packages; the 64K ROM was limited to 8. The new slots are reserved for future use by Apple. The existing packages have undergone some changes, and there's one whole new package, the List Manager.

Standard File

Standard File now supports the Hierarchical File System, which is in the Macintosh Plus ROM. Most programmers who were good boys and girls when using Standard File with the 64K ROM found that their code worked fine with the new Standard File. The key to this is in Standard File's reply record. There's a vRefNum field in the reply record, and under HFS a vRefNum can specify a volume and a folder (subdirectory). Old programs that used this value as a volume reference number in an Open call generally work fine under HFS.

Binary-Decimal Conversion

The old-system version of this little package contained calls that converted both ways between Pascal strings and long integers. The Macintosh Plus version has been enhanced in two ways: calls have been added and the whole package is now in ROM.

New Calls

```
Procedure PStr2Dec (s: DecStr; var index: Integer; var d:
decimal; var validPrefix: Boolean);

Procedure CStr2Dec (s: DecStr; var index: Integer; var d:
decimal; var validPrefix: Boolean);
```

These two procedures are used to convert between strings and SANE decimals. You should set the index parameter to the first character in the string that you want the routine to look at. After making this call, index will be set to the first character after the end of the string that was converted, and validPrefix will be set to true if the remainder of the string contains a valid SANE decimal.

The first call starts with a Pascal string, and the second takes a C string.

```
Procedure Dec2Str (f: DecForm; d: Decimal; var s: DecStr);
```

This procedure converts a SANE decimal to a Pascal string.

Disk Initialization

When you insert a disk to be initialized on a Macintosh Plus, the Disk Initialization package figures out whether the drive being used is single- or double-sided; if it's double-sided, it gives the user a choice of formatting the disk as single- or double-sided. Single-sided volumes have old-style (flat) catalogs. Double-sided disks are formatted with hierarchical catalogs.

List Manager

This new package is used to help you draw and manage lists of data. The resource editor ResEdit uses the List Manager to draw its lists of files, resource types, and resources, and to handle their selection and scrolling.

Memory Manager

As we learned way back in Chapter 3, every master pointer contains a byte of flags that give information about its relocatable object. Only three of these bits are defined: bit 5, which tells whether the object is a resource, bit 6, which tells if the object is purgeable, and bit 7, which indicates if the object is locked.

Since the highest byte of a master pointer is used for flags, there's really only 3 bytes worth of "pointer" in a master pointer. This means that the maximum "pointable" address is $FFFFFF, which is 16 megabytes of memory. When the system was being designed, and 128K RAM was standard, 16 meg probably seemed like a lot; now, with four-megabyte Macintosh Pluses making the scene, 16 megabytes is close to being a real limitation.

To help prepare for the day when the Macintosh will go beyond 16 megabytes of RAM, the Macintosh Plus implements some new calls designed to allow master pointers to expand to four bytes. The new calls, together with some old ones, allow programmers to examine and set all the flags in the flags byte without depending on them being in the master pointer's high byte.

For example, the new call HGetState returns a master pointer's flags byte. In the Macintosh Plus, this is simply the master pointer's high byte; in the future, it may fetch the flags byte from somewhere else. The important thing to know is that Apple will ensure that these calls always work; by calling HGetState to find out about the flags byte instead of trying to access it directly, your code will work on future systems.

Warning

If you don't use these calls to get to the flags byte, and instead rely on the flags being in the master pointer's high byte, you'll be sunk if Apple decides to move the flags byte on future systems to support 32-bit master pointers.

New Calls

```
Procedure HSetRBit (h: Handle);
Procedure HClrRBit (h: Handle);
```

The original ROM defined calls to set and clear the lock bit and the purgeable bit in a master pointer (HLock, HUnlock, HPurge, HNoPurge). These new calls allow you to set and clear the other bit in the flags byte, the resource bit. Normally, you'd never call these routines, since setting and clearing the resource bit is usually done through the Resource Manager.

```
Function HGetState (h: Handle): Byte;
Procedure HSetState (h: Handle, flags: Byte);
```

These calls are used to examine and modify the flags byte in one chunk. Calling HGetState gives you a master pointer's flags byte; bit 5 is the resource bit, bit 6 is the purgeable bit, and bit 7 is the lock bit. If you want to set one or more of these flags, you can do so with the HSetState call. These calls are guaranteed to always find the flags byte, no matter where it might travel to in future systems.

How Much Is Enough?

Expanding master pointers to 32 bits will allow them to address up to four *gigabytes* of memory. Will this seem like a limitation someday?

```
Function MaxBlock: Longint;
```

This function tells you the largest free block that could be created in the heap before it would be necessary to grow the zone or purge some blocks. If you call MaxApplZone when your application starts up, this call will tell you the largest block that's available without doing any purging.

Function PurgeSpace (var totalSpace: Longint): Longint;

This function tells you two things: first, it gives you the total number of purgeable and free bytes in a heap zone (in the totalSpace parameter), and, second, it returns the maximum possible contiguous space that would be available in the heap after purging and compacting (in the function result). This function returns both of these values without actually relocating or purging anything.

Function StackSpace: Longint;

You can use this call to determine how much space you have remaining on the stack. The result will be the number of bytes that can be added to the stack before it would crash into the heap.

In addition to these new calls, the MaxApplZone and MoveHHi calls, which were previously available in Pascal glue, are now in the ROM.

Segment Loader

The Segment Loader has been tweaked in the Macintosh Plus. Now, when LoadSeg loads a segment, it checks to see if the segment is locked. If it's not, it calls MoveHHi on it, trying to move it to the highest part of the heap. Remember that unloaded segments are unlocked, so LoadSeg in the 128K ROM will always move segments high when reloading them if they're still in memory.

The effect of this is that code segments don't get locked down in the middle of the heap anymore, thus solving one of the most difficult of all fragmentation problems. To benefit from this scheme, you should call MaxApplZone early in your application so that segments are moved high.

There's one problem here. By setting the "locked" attribute on CODE resources, the Memory Manager is smart enough to try to force them low in memory when they're loaded. This is what you want on 64K ROM systems. But if segments are marked locked in the resource file, they don't get moved high when they're first loaded under the new ROM; if they're marked unlocked in the file, they don't get loaded low under the old ROM.

Remember that LoadSeg checks to see if a segment is locked in memory before deciding whether to move it high. The effect is that if a segment's "locked" attribute is set it will be loaded low. When you call UnloadSeg on it, it becomes unlocked. The next time LoadSeg loads it, if it's still in memory and marked unlocked, it will be moved high; if it's been purged, it will be loaded low again.

What should you do? Since the goal with locked relocatable objects is to have them gathered together at either the low or high end of the heap, having your CODE segments marked locked is the wisest thing to do.

Another possibility is to implement the automatic moving-high of segments as a patch to LoadSeg if you're running under old ROMs and to mark all your segments unlocked. This way you'll get the benefit of the moving-high technique whether under old ROMs or new. The patch is available in a technical note from Apple.

Warning

No matter what technique you use, you should make sure that CODE 1, the main segment, is locked in the resource file. This is because CODE 1 is loaded when the heap is at its default 6K size. If it's unlocked in the file and the new LoadSeg is running, it'll be moved "high" to the top of the tiny 6K heap. Then, as the heap expands, it'll stay where it is, never being unlocked and causing some fragmentation.

File Manager

The Macintosh Plus File Manager is the Hierarchical File System. This file system allows disks to be divided into tree-structured collections of catalogs and subdirectories. In addition to implementing this new functionality, the File Manager supports all the old "flat" file system calls.

Operating System Utilities

The SetTrapAddress and GetTrapAddress calls have some new features to support the new trap dispatching extensions. Of course, calls in existing applications that don't know about the new traps still have to work the same way, but the calls must also have the power to allow you to specify "Toolbox trap #n" or "Operating System trap #n", since trap numbers can now refer to both a Toolbox and an OS trap, as we discussed at the start of this section.

To do this, GetTrapAddress and SetTrapAddress have defined a couple of new parameter bits in the trap word. The first, bit 10, lets you specify whether you want a Toolbox trap or an OS trap. If you want to use this bit to explicitly specify Toolbox or OS, you must also set bit 9 to show that you're using the new trap numbering. If bit 9 is zero, the ROM will assume that you're setting a trap according to the old ROM's trap numbering; for example, any trap word that refers to trap number $50 will mean InitCursor, the only trap in the old ROM corresponding to trap number 50.

New Calls

```
Function RelString(str1,str2: Str255;caseSens,diacSens: Boolean):
Integer;
```

This function is very similar to the CmpString call, which compares two strings for alphabetical order, but this call tells which string comes first when sorting, while CmpString just tells if they're equal.

This call is used to create an ordering that is used for alphabetizing file names, such as in the Finder's text views. This ordering does not depend on local rules that are specified in the international (INTL) resources; it's always the same. This means that you should continue to use the International Utilities to sort strings according to the user's expectations.

Macintosh 512K Enhanced

In April 1986, Apple introduced the Macintosh 512K Enhanced. This computer is functionally equivalent to a Macintosh 512K with a new ROM and 800K built-in disk drive. The "512K Enhanced" ROM is identical to the "Plus" ROM.

APPENDIX

D

A Guided Tour of Macsbug

In this appendix we'll take an in-depth look at Macsbug, the object code debugger that Apple provides for the Macintosh. The discussion here is very similar to the one given in the Chapter 4 section entitled "A Guided Tour of TMON." In fact, some of the exact wording is used to discuss similar commands. You should read this section if you're using Macsbug or if you want to learn more about how it works.

There are several versions of Macsbug, which differ mainly in the number of lines of information that they display on the screen and whether they communicate with an external terminal. The version that's used for this appendix is the standard one, which displays 40 lines of information and does not use an external terminal. Figure D-1 contains a list of some of the most common variants of Macsbug.

When you enter Macsbug, the first line of the display tells what caused Macsbug to take control. For our guided tour, we'll assume that Macsbug was invoked because an address error occurred, as denoted by the only slightly cryptic message "ADDR ERR00000715.", which you can see in Figure D-2. Then the instruction at the current program counter is displayed (that's the line that starts with "116A8:..."), followed by a list of all the 68000's registers and their contents.

The "ADDR ERR00000715." message means that an address error occurred (ADDR ERR) and that error caused Macsbug to be invoked. It also says that the odd value that caused the address error was 00000715.

Figure D-1 Some common versions of Macsbug debugger

Version	Target system	Features
Macsbug	not XL	Displays 10 lines
Maxbug	512K or more, not XL	Displays 40 lines, trap names
Termbug A	not XL	Sends display information to port A
Termbug B	not XL	Sends display information to port B
Lisabug	XL	Displays 40 lines, trap names
Ladybug	Ladybug	Fly away home
MacXLbug	XL	New name for Lisabug
Midibug	not XL	Displays 20 lines
Tinybug	not XL	Displays 8 lines, doesn't preserve screen

```
ADDR ERR00000715
116A8:                    OR.B (A2),A4
PC=000116A8 SR=00002000 TM=00002340
D0=10020040 D1=00003000 D2=FFFFFFFF D3=80008000
D4=0000CB34 D5=FFFFFF84 D6=0000E230 D7=00000001
A0=00021446 A1=00401F4E A2=01003044 A3=00000715
A4=0040B628 A5=00070FA6 A6=00070D7C A7=00070D64
```

Figure D-2 Macsbug display

Help Is Available

If you're not real familiar with 68000 assembly language, don't forget about Appendix A. It's designed for high-level language programmers who want to know more about assembly language. If you fit into this category, you might want to go read it right now.

The next line says "116A8: OR.B (A2),A4". It says that the current program counter (PC) is at 116A8, and that the instruction at that location is OR.B (A2),A4, which means "logically-or the byte pointed to by register A2 with the contents of register A4," or "take the contents of the lowest byte of register A4, perform a logical-or between those contents and the byte pointed to by register A2, and put the result of this operation back into A4." The debugger seems to be saying that the address error occurred after executing this statement.

Great. There's only one thing wrong with this information: there's absolutely no way that instruction could have caused an address error. Why? Well, we said that address errors occur when word-size or long-word-size data is accessed at an odd address. In this instruction, the size of the operand is a byte (the .B part of OR.B). Address errors cannot occur on instructions that do not have word or long word operands.

So what's going on? Is Macsbug playing tricks on us? Is there really an address error? Yes, there is, but debuggers often misplace the program counter by a couple of instructions following an error. Part of the reason is that debuggers actually take control before executing the instruction at the current program counter. How do you find the real location of the address error?

The address error actually occurs just before the instruction displayed by Macsbug, and you can use Macsbug's **disassembly** feature to list the instructions just before the one that's displayed, allowing you to see the one that caused the error. The disassembly feature is invoked with the IL (instruction list) command, followed by the address at which you want the disassembly to begin.

To have Macsbug show the instruction that caused the address error, you have to enter the IL command with the address of the offending instruction. There's one problem: we know that the error occurred just before the current instruction, but instructions on the 68000 can be anywhere from two to ten bytes long, so we're not sure just how far back to look for the preceding instruction. If we look at 2 bytes before the program counter, which we can specify to the debugger by typing IL PC-2, we'll see the correct instruction only if it happens to be two bytes long.

The easy way to get around this problem is to enter the command IL PC-10. This will guarantee that the instruction that caused the address error is displayed, even if it's the (rare) maximum-length 10 byter. If the preceding instruction is not 10 bytes long, the IL PC-10 command will display two or more instructions. That's OK; we'll just look at the instruction that immediately precedes the current program counter.

Instructions out of Synch

Since 68000 instructions are of different lengths, it's possible to use the IL instruction to start disassembling right in the middle of an instruction. This will cause a single "garbage" instruction to be displayed; then the debugger will usually get back in synchronization and start listing instructions properly. If you use IL PC-10 to look at instructions that precede the program counter, be aware that the first one displayed may not be a valid instruction. For example, if the three instructions that immediately precede the program counter are all 4 bytes long, IL PC-10 will display one garbage instruction as it attempts to interpret the second half of a four-byte instruction as a real instruction. If you're looking backwards from the program counter to find the culprit in an address error, you're usually not interested in the first instruction displayed by the IL PC-10; you're interested in the last one before the current program counter.

When we enter the IL PC-10 command to the debugger, it displays the instructions that immediately precede the program counter. The listing produced is shown in Figure D-3. The instruction we're interested in is the one right before the program counter, the line that reads MOVE.L (A3),A4. Is this instruction the one that caused the address error? Let's take a look.

```
IL PC-10
11698:                     MOVE.W $0018(A7),D0
1169C:                     MOVE.L $0016(A7),D1
116A0:                     BNE *+$0020          ; 000116C2
116A2:                     MOVE.L D2,$0012(A7)
116A6:                     MOVE.L (A3),A4
116AA:                  PC SUBQ.W #2,A3
```

Figure D-3 Macsbug IL PC-10 command

The instruction says to move the long word (32-bit value) pointed to by register A3 into register A4. Since this instruction says that A3 is pointing at a long word, its contents must be even. But, if we look at the contents of A3, as shown in the register dump that's at the bottom of Figure D-2, we see that the contents of A3 are $00000715, which is indeed an odd number. This instruction is the one that caused the address error. In fact, if you recall, the first line displayed in the debugger after the address error occurred included this number, $00000715, indicating that it was the specific odd address that caused the address error. Notice, however, that it doesn't tell you which instruction caused the error.

When a program crashes into the debugger, the first thing you'll do is find out what instruction caused the error by using the IL command. The next important thing to learn is what routine was being executed when the crash occurred. To figure this out, you first have to determine if the offending instruction is in your application's code, in the ROM, or somewhere else (in a desk accessory, for example).

The most common case is that the instruction is in the ROM. Remember, this doesn't necessarily mean that there's a bug in the ROM. In fact, it rarely indicates that. Most of the ROM routines trust their callers to pass them reasonable parameters and often fail with system errors if the parameters are not valid. You can easily tell if the instruction is in the ROM just by looking at its address. If the address is in the range $400000 through $40FFFF, the instruction is in the ROM.

Macintosh Plus

On a Macintosh Plus, the ROM is 128K bytes long, so the range for ROM addresses is $400000 through $41FFFF.

If the crash did indeed occur in the ROM, Macsbug provides a handy tool for finding out which ROM routine was being executed. This is the WH command, which means "where." If you enter this command followed by an address, such as PC for "program counter," Macsburg will tell you the name of the ROM call that was interrupted by the error. At first thought, you might think that this information will enable you to determine the last ROM routine called by your application. For example, if the crash is in the ROM, and the WH command tells you that the offending instruction is in the DrawText ROM routine, you might think that all you have to do is figure out where your program called DrawText.

Unfortunately, it's not that easy (you probably guessed that I was going to tell you that). The complication is that routines in the ROM frequently call other ROM routines to get their jobs done, sometimes several levels deep. For example, when you call DisposeWindow, it calls CloseWindow, which calls DisposPtr. So, if your application crashes and the WH command tells you that the error occurred in DisposPtr, you really don't know where the DisposPtr call came from. However, a little bit later in this appendix we'll discuss another Macsbug command that *will* tell you the last ROM call your application made at any point.

So the result of the WH command is another clue you can use in your debugging, but it won't automatically tell you the last thing your application did. You can use your knowledge of the Macintosh ROM to guess at what your application's last ROM call was. For example, in the preceding discussion we said that DisposeWindow eventually calls DisposPtr. If you suspect that you may have passed a bad window pointer to a DisposeWindow call, a crash in DisposPtr fits right in with that suspicion. It seems reasonable that DisposeWindow would take the window pointer you pass to it and call DisposPtr on it. If you passed an invalid pointer, an error in DisposPtr is a reasonable expectation.

What if the instruction that caused the crash is not located in the ROM? Obviously, this is the case if the offending instruction's address does not fall in the range $400000 through $41FFFF. If the crash is in RAM, which means anywhere in the vast four-megabyte range from $0 through $3FFFFF, the offending instruction is probably in your application's code, but it may not be. Remember that there are lots of other little programs running around the Macintosh's memory with your application, and the crash may have been in one of them, too. Later in this section we'll discuss debugger commands that will tell you how to find out just what thing owns the offending instruction.

It's also possible to use the WH command with your application's code. In this case, Macsbug will respond with the name of the procedure or function that the instruction resides in. How does it know this name? Some development systems, Apple's Pascal and C in particular, have an option to embed procedure and function names in the object code at the end of each procedure or function. If you invoked this option when you built the program, Macsbug will be able to find these names and use them in the WH command. In Lisa Pascal, this feature is invoked with the D+ option. If your development system doesn't have this ability to embed procedure names, you won't be able to use this feature. Some development systems do this automatically. To find out if yours does, just try the WH command!

The WH command has another use, too. Given the name of a trap, Macsbug will display the trap's number and its address. This also works with embedded procedure and function names. For example, to find the location of a procedure named DoCommand, you could enter the Macsbug command WH DOCOMMAND and Macsbug would respond with the address of the routine in memory.

Macsbug Features

Macsbug and other object code debuggers provide lots of different commands and displays to help you track your program's progress. Let's look at these commands now.

Many Macsbug commands require numbers as input, and these numbers are usually addresses. For example, the DM (display memory) command displays bytes in memory at an address that you specify. To allow maximum flexibility, Macsbug will accept expressions that include numbers in a variety of forms whenever it wants a number as input. You can enter numbers either in hexadecimal or in decimal; decimal numbers should be preceded by an ampersand (&). You can precede hex numbers with a dollar sign if you really want to, but Macsbug will assume hex unless you use the ampersand. You can also enter ASCII strings by enclosing them in single quotes (known to punctuation fanatics as apostrophes).

You can also use symbols to represent the contents of the 68000 registers. You specify the contents of a data register by using the notation RDn, where n is the number of the register; address registers are indicated with RAn. For example, if you want to display memory that register A2 points to, you can enter the command DM RA2, which literally means "display memory beginning at the address pointed to by register A2." Since A7 is the stack pointer, you can look at bytes on the stack by typing DM RA7. You can also refer to the program counter by using the symbol PC, as we saw earlier in the IL PC command.

Macsbug will also let you perform some arithmetic in the numbers that you pass to commands. You can do addition and subtraction in your expression by using + and −. For an example, remember the IL PC-10 command we used earlier. Macsbug also defines the @ symbol as an "indirection operator"; in other words, it dereferences a pointer. This is most useful with system global locations that contain pointers. For example, we know that location $9D6, which is called WindowList, contains a pointer to the frontmost window. To look at the contents of the frontmost window's windowRecord, we can use the command DM @9D6, which means "display memory at the address pointed to by location $9D6." You can use multiple @ symbols to dereference handles.

For example, ScrapHandle at $964 contains a handle to the scrap (you may have guessed that). To examine the scrap, you could enter DM @@964.

As we've shown, the DM command allows you to "display memory" anywhere in the Macintosh. The memory that you look at is displayed both in hexadecimal and ASCII form. This command is useful for looking at your program's data structures in memory. Some sample DM commands and their displays are shown in Figure D-4.

The other side of the DM command is SM, which is "set memory." The SM command allows you to change the values of bytes in memory. This is handy when you want to modify the value of a variable or change one of the Macintosh global variables. You have to be careful with SM, of course, since it will let you write over anything in RAM. It assumes you know what you're doing, so make sure that you do!

Macsbug includes a set of commands that allow you to examine and change the contents of the 68000's registers. When you enter the debugger, either with a system error or by pressing the interrupt button, Macsbug displays the contents of all the registers. You can get this display at any time by entering the TD (total display) command.

Macsbug also lets you display the value of any single register. To get this display, just enter the name of the register. This command can be used with any of the address or data registers (A0 through A7 and D0 through D7), as well as the program counter (PC) and the status register (SR). You can also set the value of any register. To do this, simply enter the name of the register, followed by the value that you want to set. For example, to put a hexadecimal 12 in register A0, you would type A0 12. That's certainly easy enough. You can use any of the operators described previously when you set register values; for example, you can increment the value of D5 by 2 with the command D5 D5+2.

```
>DM 12D
00012D     0000 0000 06ED 9600   0017 02FF FFFF FFFF     ................
>DM 12040
12040      0100 0202 4405 8832   0000 0000 3004 5450     ....D..2....0.TP
>DM RA7
70D82      0041 1136 0000 09FA   0000 001C 0102 3172     .A.6.........1R
```

Figure D-4 Macsbug DM command

Execution Commands

Macsbug contains a set of commands for controlled execution of code. One that's frequently used is the T (trace) command. This command executes a single 68000 instruction and then returns control to the debugger. The trace command is invaluable in playing Mr. Computer as you step through your program. This command also has the handy feature of treating ROM calls as a single instruction. In other words, if you're tracing along and you come to a ROM call, such as GetNextEvent, typing T will not trace all the 68000 instructions that GetNextEvent executes in the ROM. It will act as if GetNextEvent is a single 68000 instruction and will come back to the debugger after GetNextEvent returns.

Usually, when you're tracing through your program, you'll want the debugger to execute ROM calls as single instructions, since their actions are usually well known and well defined. Sometimes, though, you want to actually trace through the ROM code, maybe to check subtleties of behavior, to learn more about how the call works, or perhaps just to amuse yourself (if you're a little unusual). You can do this with the S (step) command in Macsbug. It works just like the trace command, unless the program counter is at a ROM call instruction, in which case it descends into the ROM and traces the call there.

After every step or trace command that you execute, Macsbug will display the program counter and disassemble the current instruction. In addition, it will display the contents of all the registers, which is something that really gets to be a drag if you're doing a lot of tracing. You can turn off this register display with the RX (register clear) command. This command is actually a toggle; if you use it a second time, you'll turn the automatic register display back on. Even if the display is off, you can always get a register display whenever you want by entering the TD command.

If you're doing a lot of tracing, you'll soon get very tired of typing T, return, T, return, hundreds or thousands of times. Macsbug defines a nice shorthand: if you just press return, it repeats the previous command. So if you're tracing through a program, you can just keep pressing return after entering the first T command.

If you entered the debugger by pressing the interrupt button and not because your application crashed, you may want to have your application resume executing without any further debugging. To do this, you can use the G (go) command, which simply tells the Macintosh to resume normal execution at the current program counter.

Warning

Step Lightly

When you're in the debugger and you have access to registers and memory, it's pretty easy to step on some important value and completely destroy any chance of resuming your application. If you're playing around in the debugger, make sure that you haven't got any unsaved valuable data in a document in the application. When you enter G to go back to the application after you're done messing around, you may find that you accidentally destroyed an important register value and that your application quickly crashes you right back into the debugger, this time with a real error.

A couple of variations on the go and step commands are GT (go till) and ST (step till). Go till is like the go command, except that it specifies an address; when the program counter reaches that address, the application will drop back into the debugger. This is useful when you're tracing through your application and you want to skip ahead to a point past some code.

The step till command is a slight variation of go till. The only real difference is that step till allows the address specified to be in the ROM, and go till does not. Be careful of this: if you're stepping through the ROM and you want to skip ahead by using the go till command, the debugger won't warn you that it's not going to work, but it's not going to work. It'll just ignore the address you specified and continue executing. To get around this problem, use step till.

Sometimes when you're tracing, particularly if you're tracing through the ROM, you'll come to instructions that execute subroutines (JSR and BSR, jump to subroutine and branch to subroutine). Often, tracing through these subroutines is very tedious, and what you're really interested in is the main line code. If you get into a subroutine that you really don't want to trace through, you can use Macsbug's MR (magic return) command. This command causes execution to continue until the address on the top of the stack is reached. If you enter MR immediately after executing a JSR or BSR, the processor will resume executing instructions until it finishes the subroutine, and then it will reenter the debugger.

Often when you're debugging an application you want the debugger to be invoked when a specified part of your application's code is executed. In Macsbug, this is accomplished through the use of **breakpoints**. A breakpoint is an address that, when reached by the program counter, causes entry into the debugger (a "break"). To set a breakpoint, you have to know the address in your code where you want the break to occur. You'll be able to determine this by examining your code with the IL command or by seeing code when you're tracing.

To set a breakpoint, type BR followed by an address. The address that you enter following the BR becomes a breakpoint; the next time the computer tries to execute the instruction at that address, you'll fall into the debugger. You can set up to eight breakpoints. If you want to see all the breakpoints that are currently set, enter BR with no address. Remember that the debugger also knows about embedded procedure names, so if you have a procedure named Ginger and you want to set a breakpoint on its first instruction, you can simply enter BR Ginger.

You'll also need a way to clear breakpoints when you no longer need them. To clear a breakpoint, enter CL followed by an address; any breakpoints at that address will be cleared. You can also clear all breakpoints by just entering CL.

You should realize that breakpoints are forever: if you set a breakpoint, it will stay set, even if you leave the application that you're debugging. If you don't want other programs, like the Finder, to stop unexpectedly, clear breakpoints before quitting an application.

No Breakpoints in ROM

When you set a breakpoint, the debugger replaces the instruction at the breakpoint address with a special instruction that calls the debugger. It saves the real contents of the location and restores them whenever you examine the location with the debugger. Since breakpoints are created this way, you can't set a breakpoint in the ROM.

The ES ("exit to shell") command leaves the debugger and starts the Finder. Similarly, EA ("exit to application") causes the current application to be restarted. These commands are kind of fragile if the application has crashed, since the state of the machine is undefined after a crash (system globals can have bad values, for example); so you'll sometimes find that EA or ES crash right back into the debugger with an error. If this happens, your safest option is to use RB, which means "reboot." This is virtually the same as pressing the reset button. In fact, if you prefer the physical exercise, you can press the reset button yourself instead of typing RB, or if RB doesn't seem to work (sometimes he doesn't).

The last command for controlled execution of code is the most esoteric and one of the least used. It's the SS ("step spy") command. It's a variation on the standard step command. Step spy lets you specify a range of memory to be watched closely by the debugger. If any bytes in the memory range are modified, the debugger is invoked. Obviously, this command can be very useful if you want to let your application run until a specified value in memory is changed.

Honesty Department

Actually, the debugger doesn't specifically watch each byte in the memory range passed to the step spy command. Instead, it uses a very effective technique called **checksumming**. This technique involves adding all the values in the memory range, coming up with a value (a checksum), and then saving this checksum. After each instruction is executed, the debugger recomputes the checksum. If it has changed, the debugger is invoked. Note that memory could be changed without the checksum changing, but for this to happen two bytes would have to be changed by one instruction in such a way as leave their total value the same—an extremely unlikely occurrence.

One of the most important things to know about the step spy command is that it slows the Macintosh to an almost unbearable crawl. Since the debugger is examining memory after every instruction, it's taking up a lot of the machine's time, and you can sure tell by watching. The poor performance will probably lead you to use step spy sparingly, if at all. It is kind of fun, though, to watch things drawn on the screen at this snail's pace. You get to see things you never saw before, such as the way that dimmed text in menus is actually drawn black and then dimmed; how a scroll bar is completely filled with gray before the white box for the thumb is filled in; and the order in which things are drawn when a new window appears. I highly recommend that you try this exercise at least once, for the educational value if nothing else.

Macsbug defines a couple of commands to help you disassemble code. We've already used the IL command to get a disassembly of 16 instructions. You can specify the number of instructions to disassemble with the IL command simply by typing it after the address you give to IL. There's a special instruction, ID ("instruction disassemble"), that displays a single 68000 instruction.

The Dot

Macsbug defines a useful variable that always remembers the last address you entered. To specify this address, you use a period (called the "dot"). For example, if you type DM 77842 to examine a value and then want to change its value, you can type SM . NNNN, where NNNN is the new value for location 77842; the dot represents that address, since it's the last address you entered.

Heap Commands

Macsbug provides a collection of commands to give you information about the system and application heap zones. The most commonly used heap command is HD ("heap dump"). This command produces a display that provides you with a dizzying amount of information. Let's take a look at the sample heap dump in Figure D-5 and discuss what secrets it reveals.

The first line in the display, 0000CB00, is the address of the start of the heap zone. As we discussed in Chapter 2, the first thing in the heap zone is a heap zone header. Following the header are the objects, or blocks, in the heap. Each heap block gets one line of display.

```
>HD

0000CB00

0000CB34  P  00000108              *
0000CC3C  H  000011EA  A 0000CC1C  * .1C 0001 CODE
0000DE26  P  00000166              *
0000DF8C  P  00000208              *
0000E194  P  00000074              *
0000E208  H  0000003A
0000E242  H  000100B8
0001E2FA  F  000000A4
0001E39E  H  000001BA  A 0000E150  * 1C 0002 CODE
0001E558  P  000000B2              *
0001E60A  P  000000A4              *
0001E6AE  F  00000012
0001E6C0  F  000000BA

HLP PF 0018 0002 0003 00001D56  0009 00000676
```

Figure D-5 Macsbug HD command

The first number in the line, 0000CB34 for the first line, is the address of the beginning of the heap block. Remember that each heap block starts with an eight-byte block header and that the block's contents come after the header. The address given here is the address of the block header, so you have to add eight to get the address of the contents.

The next column contains a single letter, either H, P, or F. These mnemonics indicate the type of block: relocatable (H for handle), non-relocatable (P for pointer), or free (F, logically enough). The number in the third column gives the physical size of the heap block in bytes. This size includes the eight-byte block header; so if you're looking for a specific object that should have $100 bytes of contents, its size will be $108.

The single digit in the fourth column displays the master pointer flags. Only relocatable blocks have master pointers, of course, so this column is blank for free and nonrelocatable blocks. Since only three of these bits are currently used, a single digit is enough. To refresh your memory (no pun intended), the flags digit will have the "twos" bit set if the object is a resource (that is, it will be 2, 6, A, or E); the "fours" bit means the block is purgeable (digit is 4, 6, C, or E); the "eights" bit means that the block is locked (digit is 8, A, C, or E). The chart in Figure D-6 can be used to translate the flags digit into the correct attributes.

Figure D-6 Interpreting the master pointer flags byte

Flags byte	Meaning
0	unlocked, not purgeable, not a resource
2	unlocked, not purgeable, a resource
4	unlocked, purgeable, not a resource
6	unlocked, purgeable, a resource
8	locked, not purgeable, not a resource
A	locked, not purgeable, a resource
C	locked, purgeable, not a resource
E	locked, purgeable, a resource

> **Low Bit Set?**
>
> If you're looking at someone else's heap, the Macintosh Programmer's Workshop, for example, you may find some master pointer flag digits with the low bit set; in other words, you'll see odd digits like 1, 3, and F in this field. This indicates that the application is using this "unused" bit. In general, you should avoid using any of the bits in this byte for your own applications, since they're all officially reserved by Apple for future use.

The fifth column, which also is filled in only for relocatable blocks, gives the address of the block's master pointer. This is useful if you want to check the validity of a handle, since the handle is the address of the master pointer. The next column either has an asterisk or nothing. An asterisk indicates an immobile object, that is, either a nonrelocatable block or a locked relocatable block.

A quick glance down this column can tell you a lot about a program's memory management. A well-managed heap will have all the asterisks gathered in two groups, one at the beginning of the heap and one at the end. If you see lots of asterisks scattered throughout the heap, you've got a fragmentation problem.

The last three columns are only used if the block is a resource. If so, these columns indicate the resource's type, ID number, and the file reference number of the resource file that it's in (the first number shown is the resource file reference number). Usually, as in our example, the first resource in the heap will be a master pointer block, which is a nonrelocatable block with a size of $108 bytes. The next thing is almost always a CODE resource with ID 1. This is the application's main segment, and, as you know, it's always loaded and always locked.

The last line of the heap dump display is a rather hard to understand summary of some useful information about the heap zone. The five letters at the left, HLP PF, are there as mnemonics to help you remember what the numbers mean. The first number, 0018, is the number of relocatable blocks in the heap (the mnemonic H means "handles"); the next number, 0002, is the number of locked relocatables (as the L reminds you); the next two numbers, as indicated by the mnemonics P and the space, are the number of purgeable blocks and purgeable bytes ("purgeable space") in the heap (0003 and 00001D56 in our example); the next number, 0009, gives you the number of nonrelocatable blocks in the heap (the P means "pointers"); and the last number, the 00000676, is the amount of free space in the heap (as the F reminds you). Figure D-7 lists all the mnemonics for the heap summary and their meanings.

Figure D-7 Macsbug heap summary mnemonics

Mnemonic	Meaning
H	Number of relocatable blocks ("handles")
L	Number of locked relocatable blocks ("locked")
P	Number of purgeable blocks ("Pizzuti")
	Number of purgeable bytes ("space")
P	Number of nonrelocatable blocks ("pointers")
F	Number of free bytes ("free")

Macsbug defines a special command if you just want to see the summary line. This command is HT, for heap totals.

If you're only interested in getting heap information about a particular resource type, you can use a special form of the heap dump command. If you enter a resource type after the HD, the heap dump searches for and displays blocks of that type only. For example, if you just want to see the CODE resources that are currently in the heap, you can use the command HD 'CODE'. This displays the same information as the regular heap dump command, but for CODE resources only. The summary line is slightly different: it shows the number of blocks of that type and the number of bytes those blocks take up. There's an example of this display in Figure D-8.

There are other values that you can use with the HD command to display only specific blocks. If you want to see all the blocks that contain resources, you can enter 'R' after the HD (you need the single quotes). You can also use 'P' to show all the nonrelocatable blocks ("pointers"), 'H' to list all the relocatable blocks ("handles"), and 'F' to display all the free blocks.

```
>HD 'CODE'

0000CB00

0000CC3C H 000011EA A 0000CC1C * 1C 0001 CODE
0001E39E H 000001BA A 0000E150 * 1C 0002 CODE
00020404 H 00001340 2 0000E15C   1C 0005 CODE
0003064C H 00000982 2 0000E160   1C 0009 CODE

CNT ### 0004 00003066
```

Figure D-8 Macsbug HD 'CODE' command

If you're using one of the varieties of Macsbug that communicates with an external terminal (usually called "Termbug"), there's a command that will send the heap dump to the "other" serial port, that is, the one that's not being used to talk to the terminal. This command, which is HP (heap print), is used to print the heap dump.

You can use the heap check command (HC) to perform a consistency check on the heap zone. This check attempts to make sure that all the block sizes given in the block headers are correct and that the heap hasn't been damaged. Of course, it can't check everything; but if it says that there's a bad block, you can be pretty sure that something has trashed the heap.

Note that all these commands operate on the application heap. If you want to look at the system heap instead, you can use the HX command, which means "heap exchange." This command is a toggle, so you can return to the application heap by typing it again.

A-trap Commands

Another important set of Macsbug commands are the A-trap commands. These let you work with the Macintosh's A-traps, which are the mechanisms used to implement calls to the ROM- and RAM-based system software. The name comes from the fact that these calls are implemented as single 16-bit words having $A as the first digit. For the complete story on how the Macintosh implements A-traps, see the "How ROM Calls Work" section of Chapter 10.

The A-trap commands in Macsbug tell the debugger to take some action when A-traps are encountered. Macsbug includes commands that cause the debugger to display traps as they're executed, remember the last trap executed, check the heap zone after traps, cause relocatable blocks to move, make the program break into the debugger, and perform a checksum after traps.

All these commands allow you to qualify when you want the specified action taken. Most let you specify the range of traps that you want the debugger to watch for. Most of them also let you designate a specific memory range in which the traps must be located. Finally, a few of these commands also let you specify a range of values to check for in register D0, which is a parameter to many operating system traps. The syntax for commands that allow all three of these ranges is this:

Ax LOWTRAP HITTRAP LOWADDRESS HIADDRESS LOWD0 HID0

All the parameters except LOWTRAP are optional. If you want to specify the address range or the D0 range, you must specify both a low trap and a high trap; if you're only interested in one trap, you must enter its name twice. Only one A-trap command may be active at any time.

The AT command (A-trap trace) allows you to see which traps are being executed. You can specify a range of traps to watch for, a memory range to look for them in, and a range of D0 values to watch for. All the parameters except the trap numbers are optional. If a trap is executed and not all the conditions you specified are met, the trap call won't be displayed.

For example, if you enter the command AT GETNEXTEVENT, the debugger will display all the calls to GetNextEvent. When it encounters a call to GetNextEvent, it will display a line like the one in Figure D-9. The MACTRAP A970 GETNEXTEVE part means, of course, that it has come across a trap call that you asked to check for. The next four values give the contents of the program counter, the A0 and D0 registers, and the value of the system variable Ticks, which is the number of sixtieths of a second that have elapsed since the system was started up (it's indicated by TM: in this display, which stands for "time").

Often you'll want to use the optional parameters to restrict the display of trap calls. For example, let's say you want to know about every call your application makes to GetResource. If you simply enter AT GETRESOURCE, the debugger will show you every time GetResource is called, whether it's by your application or by another ROM routine. Since ROM routines frequently make this call, you'll see lots of trap calls that you're not really interested in.

The way to get just the calls you want is to use the address range parameter to specify addresses in RAM only when you use the AT instruction. All RAM addresses fall into the range 0 through $7FFFF for a 512K Macintosh (up to $FFFFF for a one-megabyte machine). You can further narrow it down by knowing that your application's code resides in the application heap. The address of the beginning of the application heap is kept in the system global ApplZone at $2AA; a global called ApplLimit at $130 contains the address of the end of the application heap's growable space. So you can specify that you're only interested in trap calls that take place between the addresses pointed to by $2AA and $130.

```
MACTRAP A970 GETNEXTEVE PC:0000E28A A0:0000D836 D0:0000A970 TM:00006604
```

Figure D-9 Macsbug AT command

Given all this information, we can now enter a command to tell Macsbug to display all the calls to GetResource made from code in the application heap zone:

AT GETRESOURCE GETRESOURCE @2AA @130

Note that, as mentioned previously, we have to enter the name of the trap twice, because Macsbug expects a range of traps if we specify a range of addresses.

Other Code in RAM

Remember that there's code in the application heap other than your application's CODE resources. The system puts definition functions for controls, windows, and menus (CDEF, WDEF, and MDEF resources) in the application heap, as well as desk accessories (DRVR resources). Any of these may make ROM calls. So Macsbug may still report some calls that you're not interested in, but there's no easy way to prevent these.

When would you need to use the D0 range parameter? One of the most important uses of D0 in a trap is in the NewHandle call, where D0 contains the size of the handle that's being requested. Let's say you have several NewHandle (2000) calls in your application and you want those calls displayed. You can do so by specifying 2000 (which is $7D0 in hex) as the low and high value for D0, like this:

AT NEWHANDLE NEWHANDLE @2AA @130 7D0 7D0

In English, this means "display calls to NewHandle, if the call comes from the application heap and if D0 contains exactly $7D0 at the time of the call."

Often you don't just want to watch the traps fly by. You want the program to fall into the debugger when a certain trap is executed. You can do this with the AB ("A-trap break") command. Its syntax and function are exactly like AT, except that, instead of simply displaying the trap name and associated information, it enters the debugger when the trap is encounted and the conditions specified by the optional parameters are met.

The AB command is very useful when you're tracing through a program that you know is going to crash at a certain point. For example, if you know that the last trap an application executed before crashing was GetNewDialog, you could tell Macsbug to break when it saw a GetNewDialog call. Then you could examine the parameters that were passed to GetNewDialog and do further tracing, if necessary. The optional address range and D0 range parameters are available for the AB command.

Another A-trap command you may find useful is AH, which is "A-trap heap check." This command causes the heap to be checked (as with HC) when the given conditions are met. It can optionally take the standard address range and D0 range parameters.

A particularly interesting A-trap command, only available on versions of Macsbug dated May 1985 or later, is AR, or A-trap record. This command records the last A-trap executed that met the specifications of the parameters. It never causes the program to break. When you reenter the debugger after having used this command, you can obtain information about the most recent trap call by just typing AR.

The information you get includes the standard name of the trap, program counter where it was executed, and contents of A0, D0, and Ticks. You also get some additional information: if the last trap was an Operating System call, you'll see the first 32 bytes pointed to by A0 at the time of the trap call. This is particularly useful for OS calls that use A0 as a pointer to a parameter block, such as file system calls. If the last trap was a Toolbox call, the additional information displayed will be the top 32 bytes of the stack when the call was executed. Since Toolbox calls are stack based, this information will tell you the parameters to the call when it was made.

As you might imagine, this command can be incredibly powerful in telling you what the last trap call was before the application crashed. If you suspect that your application will crash (unlikely as it may seem), you can enter an AR command just in case. Then, if it does crash, you can examine the most recent trap call, an extremely valuable piece of information in the detective work of debugging.

One drawback to the use of AR is the restriction that only one A-trap command may be active at any time. If you're using one of the other A-trap commands, such as AB, you can't use AR. But once you know how to make your application crash, AR will help you determine why it's crashing.

These are the most commonly used A-trap commands, but there are a couple of others that come in handy sometimes. The HS command, "heap scramble," is used to help you find invalid uses of handles. Even though it doesn't really do anything with A-traps, it's mentioned here because it takes the same parameters as the other A-trap commands. This is the syntax:

HS LOWTRAP HITTRAP LOWADDRESS HIADDRESS

This command causes the relocatable blocks in the heap to be moved. No matter what range of traps you give it, HS will only scramble the heap upon encountering NewHandle, NewPtr, and ReallocHandle calls and SetHandleSize and SetPtrSize calls that cause the specified heap object to grow. The A-trap range that you specify can only be used to further restrict the set of traps that cause scrambling; for example, HS NEWHANDLE NEWHANDLE will cause the heap scramble to occur only upon encountering NewHandle calls.

This fits in nicely with what we talked about in Chapter 2: these are the only normally used traps that can cause relocation. When the specified trap and address conditions are met, the heap's unlocked relocatable blocks will be moved, thus ensuring that, if you're using any improperly dereferenced handles, you'll now have pointers that are no longer valid.

The HS command is a way of enforcing a worst-case memory scenario on your heap, since you should be prepared for heap compaction whenever HS might scramble things. So, if turning heap scrambling on causes your application to break, you're probably doing something like dereferencing a handle when it's not safe to do so. Running under normal circumstances, everything may have worked OK, but turning on heap scrambling is like simulating an almost full heap zone, and bad handle dereferences that may escape normal testing are often caught.

Another A-trap command you can use is the AS ("A-trap spy") command. Like the step spy command that we talked about earlier, this command calculates a checksum for a given memory range, recomputes the checksum periodically, and compares it to the original. If the checksums don't match, it breaks into the debugger. For AS, the debugger checksums memory every time an A-trap within the given range is encountered. Unlike most of the other A-trap commands, AS only allows a range of traps as parameters; it will not take an address range or a D0 range.

When you're using the A-trap commands, you'll eventually want to turn all of them off. You can accomplish this with the AX ("A-trap clear") command.

An important tip about using the A-trap commands: when you have a command like AT active, which displays information on the debugger's screen and then immediately returns to the application's screen, you may find it difficult to break into the debugger by pressing the interrupt switch. The problem is that the debugger is in control while it draws onto its screen, and it doesn't respond to the interrupt switch if it's already in control. When this happens, just hold down the interrupt switch for a second or so and you'll enter the debugger.

Miscellaneous Commands

There are a few more commands defined by Macsbug that don't fall into any single category, so we'll gather them together here as a miscellaneous group. The "find" command (F) can be used to search through memory for a desired value. The thing you're looking for can be 1, 2, or 4 bytes long, and you can search through any desired memory range for it. The syntax for the find command is this:

F ADDRESS COUNT DATA MASK

The ADDRESS parameter specifies the place to begin the search. The COUNT parameter tells how many bytes to search. Note that this command asks you to specify a starting address and a number of bytes, like the DM command, and unlike the addresses given in the A-trap commands, which are starting and ending memory addresses.

The DATA parameter specifies the value that you want to search for. This value can be 1, 2, or 4 bytes long. You can use any of Macsbug's expression-specifying features to denote the value; for example, you can search for a 4-byte string by enclosing it in single quotes, and you can specify indirection by using the @ operator.

The mask parameter can be used to create one or more "wild-card" bits in the search. Let's say you need to search for two-byte patterns that have "12" as the first two digits and "4" as the fourth digit, but you don't care what the third digit is. You can do this with Macsbug like this: in the DATA parameter, specify a zero for the bits that you don't care about (in this case, the bits in the third digit). So the DATA parameter in our example would be 1204.

Then, in the MASK parameter, use all ones for the bits you really want to search for and zero for the "don't-care" bits. In this example, the don't-care bits are the bits in the third digit. So our MASK parameter becomes FF0F, with the F's indicating digits that should be matched and the zero specifying the don't-care or wild card digit. So you can use the command F 3000 5000 1204 FF0F to search through addresses starting at

$3000 and continuing for $5000 bytes for two-byte sequences that begin with 12, have a 4 as the fourth digit, and contain any value at all in the third digit.

There's a generic checksum command that you can use to determine if any bytes in a given range of memory have changed (although like the other checksum commands, it won't tell you which bytes have changed). The generic checksum command is CS. If you enter CS followed by a starting and ending address, the debugger will compute the checksum for that range of memory and save it. Then, if you later enter just CS, Macsbug will recompute the checksum and compare the new result to the previous result. If they match, Macsbug will print CHKSUM T and, if they're different, CHKSUM F.

Macsbug provides a handy utility to convert between decimal, hex, and ASCII. This is the CV, or convert, command. To use it, you just enter CV, followed by a value. As usual, the value you enter can be formed with any of Macsbug's wonderful expression-forming parts, like the @ symbol for indirectly using the contents of a memory location, + and − for addition and subtraction, the dot symbol for the most recently referenced address, and so on.

Macsbug will respond to the CV command with the value in unsigned hex, signed hex, decimal, and ASCII text. For example, if you enter CV 3350, Macsbug will respond with this line:

```
$00003350 00003350 &13136 '..3P'
```

The first two values are simply signed and unsigned hexadecimal reflections of the value you already entered, $3350 (remember that by default Macsbug assumes values you type in are hexadecimal). The third number is the same value, represented in decimal, as indicated by the prefixed ampersand (&), Macsbug's symbol for decimal numbers. The last thing on the line is the ASCII representation of the value. In this case, 33 is the ASCII value for a 3, and 50 represents an uppercase letter P.

Macsbug Case Limitation

Note that Macsbug is slightly brain damaged when it comes to the Macintosh extended ASCII character set. In particular, Macsbug only understands ASCII characters with values of $20 through $7A. In addition, Macsbug does not properly recognize ASCII characters $5B through $5F; these are the left and right square brackets, backslash, circumflex ("^"), and underscore. Macsbug also does not distinguish between upper- and lowercase when echoing input or converting values, using just uppercase when text is printed.

You can also use the CV command as a simple hex calculator. For example, if you want to add two hex numbers, you can type them into a CV command, and it will respond with the hexadecimal sum (as well as the decimal sum and the ASCII representation, which you would probably just want to ignore). This is handy to remember when you've accidentally left your HP-16 hex calculator in another country.

We discussed the WH command earlier, so we'll just summarize it here for completeness. Typing WH followed by a trap name or number will give you the name of the trap and its address; if you type in an address, you'll get the name and number of the nearest preceding trap; if you type in an address that's within the application heap zone, Macsbug will try to find a function or procedure name, if the application was created with a development system that embeds names within object code, such as Apple's development systems.

Sometimes you may want to enter the debugger programatically; that is, somewhere in your program, you may want to force the debugger to take control. You can do this with a special A-trap, $A9FF. If your program executes this special trap, the debugger will be invoked.

If you're using a language that allows you to generate assembly language code from your source, you can easily generate this special trap. For example, in Workshop Pascal, you can declare a procedure like this:

```
PROCEDURE Debugger; Inline $A9FF;
```

Then, whenever you want to cause your program to invoke the debugger, you can simply call this procedure.

Spinning Wheel

Often, when you enter the debugger, the disk drive is still spinning and it just won't stop, not ever (almost). Well, don't go for your shotgun. If you type the magic incantation DM DFF1FF, the disk drive will shut off. Here's why: on the Macintosh, I/O devices like the disk drives are memory mapped. That means that their functions are controlled by just referencing the correct bytes in memory. Address $DFF1FF is the switch that turns off the disk drive.

There may be a lot of features in TMON that Macsbug doesn't have (Figure D-10 has a comparison of commands), but Macsbug is still a very powerful debugger with some unique features of its own, and you can't beat the price.

Figure D-10 Macsbug and TMON commands

Macsbug	TMON	Description
DM	Dump	Shows memory at desired address
SM	Dump	Changes memory at desired address
Dn,An,PC,SR,TD	Registers	Displays or changes a register
BR,CL	Breakpoint	Sets or clears a breakpoint
G	Exit	Leaves the debugger
GT	-----	Sets a breakpoint and leaves the debugger
T	Step	Executes one instruction, which may be a trap
S	Trace	Executes one instruction, traces into ROM
SS	-----	Steps and computes checksum
ST	-----	Like GT, but can be used in ROM
MR	-----	Finishes subroutine and returns to caller
RB	Shut Down	Restarts the system
ES	Finder	Launches the Finder
EA	-----	Relaunches the current application
SC	Stack Crawl	Examines stack frames
AR	Trap Record	Records traps: 1 in Macsbug, any number in TMON
IL	Assembly	Disassembles memory at desired address
AB	Trap Intercept	Enters debugger when a system call is executed
AT	-----	Displays each trap as it's executed
AH	Trap Check	Checks heap when a system call is executed
HS	Heap Scramble	Scrambles heap
AS	Trap Checksum	Computes checksum before each system call
HD	Heap	Displays heap zone
F	Find	Searches for a specified byte or bytes
WH	Assembly	Shows closest label to an address
CS	Checksum	Calculates checksum
CV	Number	Does math in hex and decimal
-----	File	Displays contents of a resource map
-----	Assembly	Assembles 68000 instructions
-----	Block Move	Moves bytes in memory
-----	Block Compare	Compares two ranges of bytes
-----	Fill	Fills memory with a specified value
DM	Template	Displays Window, ParamBlock, TERecord
-----	Stack Addresses	Looks on stack for return addresses
-----	Load Resource	Loads a resource into memory

APPENDIX

Debugging Quick Reference Guide

This appendix is useful for finding out things when you're debugging. There are three parts to this appendix. First is a list of system globals in low memory, sorted alphabetically. Next is the same list, but arranged in numerical order. These lists are useful for observing the low-memory locations when you're tracing a program. In both lists, the addresses are in hexadecimal.

The third part of this appendix is a list of common ROM data types. You can use this to examine data structures in memory while your application is running.

System Globals: Alphabetical Listing

Name	Address	Type	Comment
ABusVars	2D8	8 bytes	Local variables used by AppleTalk
ACount	A9A	Integer	Number of times this alert called
AddrErr	C	Pointer	Address error vector
AlarmState	21F	Byte	Bit 7=Apple logo on/off, Bit 6=beeped, Bit 0=enabled
ANumber	A98	Integer	Active alert ID
ApFontID	984	Integer	Resource ID of application font
App2Packs	BC8	8 Handles	+handles for Pack8 - Pack15
ApplLimit	130	Pointer	End of application heap if fully grown
ApplScratch	A78	12 Bytes	Reserved for use by application
ApplZone	2AA	Pointer	Start of application heap zone
AppPacks	AB8	8 Handles	Handles to Pack0 through Pack7
AppParmHandle	AEC	Handle	Handle to Finder information on Launch
AtalkHk1	B14	Pointer	+Appletalk hook
AtalkHk2	B18	Pointer	+Appletalk hook
AtMenuBottom	B28	Integer	+Flag used by scrolling menus
AutoInt1	64	Pointer	Level 1 interrupt auto-vector
AutoInt2	68	Pointer	Level 2 interrupt auto-vector

Name	Address	Type	Comment
AutoInt3	6C	Pointer	Level 3 interrupt auto-vector
AutoInt4	70	Pointer	Level 4 interrupt auto-vector
AutoInt5	74	Pointer	Level 5 interrupt auto-vector
AutoInt6	78	Pointer	Level 6 interrupt auto-vector
AutoInt7	7C	Pointer	Level 7 interrupt auto-vector
BasicGlob	2B6	Pointer	Basic globals
BootDrive	210	Integer	Drive number of boot drive
BootMask	B0E	Integer	+Used by boot code
BootTmp8	B36	8 Bytes	+Temp space needed by StartBoot
BtDskRfn	B34	Integer	+Refnum of boot disk driver
BufPtr	10C	Pointer	Top of application memory (end of jump table)
BufTgDate	304	Integer	Time stamp
BufTgFBkNum	302	Integer	Logical block number
BufTgFFlg	300	Integer	Buffer tag flags
BufTgFNum	2FC	Longint	Buffer tag file number
BusError	8	Pointer	Bus error vector
CaretTime	2F4	Longint	Ticks between caret blinks
ChkError	18	Pointer	Vector CHK, CHK2 instruction error
ChooserBits	946	Byte	Bit 7=0, don't run; Bit 6=0, gray out AppleTalk
CkdDB	340	Integer	Used when searching the directory
CloseOrnHook	A88	Pointer	Routine called when closing desk accessories
Coproces	34	Pointer	Vector for coprocessor protocol violation
CoreEditVars	954	12 Bytes	Core edit variables
CPUFlag	12F	Byte	+$00=68000, $01=68010,$02=68020
CrsrAddr	888	Pointer	Screen-memory address covered by cursor
CrsrBusy	8CD	Byte	Cursor locked out?
CrsrCouple	8CF	Byte	Cursor coupled to mouse?
CrsrNew	8CE	Byte	Cursor changed?
CrsrObscure	8D2	Byte	Cursor obscure flag
CrsrPin	834	Rect	Cursor pinning rectangle
CrsrRect	83C	Rect	Cursor hit rectangle
CrsrSave	88C	64 Bytes	Saved data under the cursor
CrsrScale	8D3	Byte	Cursor scaled?
CrsrState	8D0	Integer	Cursor nesting level
CrsrThresh	8EC	Integer	Delta threshold for mouse scaling
CrsrVis	8CC	Byte	Cursor visible?
CurActivate	A64	Pointer	Window which will get activate event
CurApName	910	String[31]	Name of current application
CurApRefNum	900	Integer	RefNum of application's resource file
CurDeactive	A68	Pointer	Window which will get activate event
CurDeKind	A22	Integer	WindowKind of deactivated window
CurDragAction	A46	Pointer	Implicit actionProc for DragControl
CurFMDenom	994	Point	Current denominator of scale factor
CurFMDenom	9AE	Point	Point for denominators of scale factor
CurFMDevice	98E	Integer	Current font device
CurFMFace	98C	Byte	Current font face
CurFMFamily	988	Integer	Current font family
CurFMInput	988	Pointer	Quickdraw FMInput Record
CurFMNeedBits	98D	Boolean	Does Font Manager need bits?
CurFMNumer	990	Point	Current numerator of scale factor
CurFMSize	98A	Integer	Current font size
CurJTOffset	934	Integer	Ofiset from A5 to start of jump table
CurMap	A5A	Integer	Reference number of current resource file
CurPageOption	936	Integer	Current page 2 video/sound configuration
CurPitch	280	Integer	Current pitch value
CurrentA5	904	Pointer	Correct value of A5
CurStackBase	908	Pointer	Current stack base

Name	Address	Type	Comment
DABeeper	A9C	Pointer	Beep routine for ModalDialog
DAStrings	AA0	4 Handles	ParamText substitution strings
DefltStack	322	Longint	Default size of stack
DefVCBPtr	352	Pointer	Default volume control block
DeskHook	A6C	Pointer	Routine which will be called to paint the desk
DeskPattern	A3C	Pattern	Desktop pattern
DiskVars	222	62 Bytes	Variables used by .SONY driver
DispatchTab	400	1024 Bytes	Trap dispatch table (64K ROM)
DlgFont	AFA	Integer	Default dialog font ID
DoubleTime	2F0	Longint	Allowed ticks between clicks of a double-click
DragFlag	A44	Integer	Implicit parameter to DragControl
DragHook	9F6	Pointer	Routine called during dragging
DragPattern	A34	Pattern	Dragged by DragTheRgn
DrMstrBlk	34C	Integer	Master directory block in a volume (MFS)
DrvQHdr	308	10 Bytes	Header of system's drive queue
DSAlertRect	3F8	Rect	Rectangle for disk-switch alert
DSAlertTab	2BA	Pointer	System error alerts
DSDrawProc	334	Pointer	Alternate SysError draw procedure
DSErrCode	AF0	Integer	Last system error alert ID
DskErr	142	Integer	Disk routine result code
DskRtnAdr	124	Pointer	Used by disk driver
DskSwtchHook	3EA	Pointer	Hook for disk-switch dialog
DskVerify	12C	Byte	Used by .SONY driver for read/verify
DSWndUpdate	15D	Byte	Used by disk switch hook
EjectNotify	338	Pointer	Routine called when a disk is ejected
ErCode	3A2	Integer	Disk driver async errors
EventQueue	14A	10 Bytes	Event queue header
EvtBufCnt	154	Integer	Maximum number of events in SysEvtBuf - 1
ExtFSHook	3E6	Pointer	Used by external file system
ExtStsDT	2BE	16 Bytes	SCC ext/sts secondary dispatch table
FCBSPtr	34E	Pointer	File control blocks
FDevDisable	BB3	Byte	+$FF to disable device-defined style extra
FileVars	340	184 Bytes	File system variables
Finder	261	Byte	Private Finder flags
FinderName	2E0	String[15]	Filename of the Finder
FLckUnlck	348	Byte	Flag used by SetFilLock,RstFilLock
FlEvtMask	25E	Integer	+Mask of allowable events to flush at FlushEvents
FlushOnly	346	Byte	Flag used by UnMountVol,FlushVol
FMDefaultSize	987	Byte	Default size of Font Record
FMDotsPerInch	9B2	Point	Dots per inch of current device
FMgrOutRec	998	Pointer	Quickdraw font output record
FMStyleTab	9B6	18 bytes	Style heuristic table supplied by device
FmtErrVect	38	Pointer	+Format error vector for 68010 and 68020
FONDID	BC6	Integer	+ID of last font definition record (FOND)
FontFlag	15E	Byte	Font manager loop flag
FormatEr	38	Pointer	Format error vector
FOutAscent	9A5	Byte	Height above baseline
FOutBold	99E	Byte	Bolding factor
FOutDescent	9A6	Byte	Height below baseline
FOutError	998	Integer	Error code
FOutExtra	9A4	Byte	Extra horizontal width
FOutFontHandle	99A	Handle	Font bits
FOutItalic	99F	Byte	Italic factor
FOutLeading	9A8	Byte	Space between lines
FOutNumer	9AA	Point	Numerators of scaling factors
FOutRec	998	Pointer	Font Manager output record
FOutShadow	9A3	Byte	Shadow factor

Name	Address	Type	Comment
FOutULOffset	9A0	Byte	Underline offset
FOutULShadow	9A1	Byte	Underline "halo"
FOutULThick	9A2	Byte	Underline thickness
FOutWidMax	9A7	Byte	Maximum width of character
FPState	A4A	6 Bytes	Floating point state
FractEnable	BF4	Byte	+Flag for fractional font widths
FrcSync	349	Byte	When set, all File System calls are synched
FSBusy	360	Integer	Non-zero when the file system is busy
FScaleDisable	A63	Byte	Disable font scaling?
FScaleHFact	BF6	Longint	+Horizontal font scale factor
FScaleVFact	BFA	Longint	+Vertical font scale factor
FSQHdr	360	10 Bytes	File system queue header
FSQHead	362	Pointer	First queued command in File System queue
FSQTail	366	Pointer	Last File System queue element
FSQueueHook	3E2	Pointer	Hook to capture all FS calls
FSTemp4	3DE	Longint	Used by File System
FSTemp8	3D6	8 bytes	Used by File System
fsVarEnd	3F6		End of file system variables
GetParam	1E4	20 Bytes	System parameter scratch space
GhostWindow	A84	Pointer	Window hidden from FrontWindow
GotStrike	986	Byte	Do we have the strike? (Font Manager)
GrafBegin	800		QuickDraw system globals area
GrafEnd	8F2		End of QuickDraw system globals
GrayRgn	9EE	Handle	Rounded gray desk region
GZMoveHnd	330	Handle	Moving handle for GrowZone
GZRootHnd	328	Handle	Block which must not be moved by GrowZone function
GZRootPtr	32C	Pointer	Root pointer for GrowZone
HeapEnd	114	Pointer	End of application heap
HeapStart	B00		Start of the system heap (64K ROM)
HiHeapMark	BAE	Pointer	+Highest address used by a heap zone below A7
IAZNotify	33C	Pointer	Routine called when application heap is reinitialized
IconBitmap	A0E	BitMap	Used by PlotIcon
Illegal	10	Pointer	Illegal instruction vector
IntFlag	15F	Byte	Reduce interrupt disable time when bit 7 = 0
IntlSpec	BA0	Pointer	+Extra international data
IWM	1E0	Pointer	IWM base address
JAdrDisk	252	Pointer	Disk driver vector
JBlockMove	4B8	Pointer	+Vector used by Memory Manager
JControl	242	Pointer	Disk driver vector
JCrsrObscure	81C	Pointer	Vector used by QuickDraw
JCrsrTask	8EE	Pointer	Address of CrsrVBLTask
JDCDReset	B48	Pointer	+Disk driver vector
JDiskPrime	226	Pointer	Disk driver vector
JDiskSel	B40	Pointer	+Disk driver vector
JFetch	8F4	Pointer	Fetch a byte routine for drivers
JFigTrkSpd	222	Pointer	Disk driver vector
JFontInfo	8E4	Pointer	Jump entry for FMFontMetrics
JGNEFilter	29A	Pointer	GetNextEvent filter proc
JHideCursor	800	Pointer	Vector used by QuickDraw
JInitCrsr	814	Pointer	Vector used by QuickDraw
JIODone	8FC	Pointer	IODone vector
JKybdTask	21A	Pointer	Keyboard VBL task hook
JMakeSpdTbl	24E	Pointer	Disk driver vector
JournalFlag	8DE	Integer	Journaling state
JournalRef	8E8	Integer	Journaling driver's refnum
JRdAddr	22A	Pointer	Disk driver vector
JRdData	22E	Pointer	Disk driver vector

Name	Address	Type	Comment
JRecal	23E	Pointer	Disk driver vector
JReSeek	24A	Pointer	Disk driver vector
JScrnAddr	80C	Pointer	Vector used by QuickDraw
JScrnSize	810	Pointer	Vector used by QuickDraw
JSeek	236	Pointer	Disk driver vector
JSendCmd	B44	Pointer	+Disk driver vector
JSetCrsr	818	Pointer	Vector used by QuickDraw
JSetSpeed	256	Pointer	Disk driver vector
JSetUpPoll	23A	Pointer	Disk driver vector
JShell	212	Integer	Journaling shell state
JShieldCursor	808	Pointer	Vector used by QuickDraw
JShowCursor	804	Pointer	Vector used by QuickDraw
JStash	8F8	Pointer	Stash a byte routine for drivers
JSwapFont	8E0	Longint	Jump entry for FMSwapFont
JUpdateProc	820	Pointer	Vector used by QuickDraw
JWakeUp	246	Pointer	Disk driver vector
JWrData	232	Pointer	Disk driver vector
KbdType	21E	Byte	Keyboard model number
KbdVars	216	Longint	Keyboard driver variables
Key1Trans	29E	Pointer	Keyboard mapping procedure
Key2Trans	2A2	Pointer	Numeric keypad mapping procedure
KeyLast	184	Integer	ASCII for last valid keycode
KeyMap	174	2 Longints	Bitmap showing keys up/down
KeyMVars	B04	Integer	+ROM KEYM procedure variables
KeypadMap	17C	Longint	Bitmap for numeric pad-18 bits
KeyRepThresh	190	Integer	Key repeat speed
KeyRepTime	18A	Longint	Tickcount when key was last repeated
KeyThresh	18E	Integer	Threshold for key repeat
KeyTime	186	Longint	Tickcount when last keystroke was received
LastFOND	BC2	Handle	+Last font definition record (FOND)
LastLGlobal	944		Last Segment Loader global
LastPGlobal	954		Last Printing Manager global
LastSPExtra	B4C	Longint	+Most recent value of space extra
LaunchFlag	902	Byte	Used by Launch and Chain
LGrafJump	824	Pointer	Vector used by QuickDraw
Line1010	28	Pointer	1010 emulator trap (vector for A-traps)
Line1111	2C	Pointer	1111 emulator trap (reserved)
Lo3Bytes	31A	Longint	Constant $00FFFFFF
LoaderPBlock	93A	10 Bytes	parameter block for ExitToShell
LoadTrap	12D	Byte	If non-zero, enters debugger before entering new segment
LoadVars	900	68 Bytes	Segment Loader variables
Lvl1DT	192	32 Bytes	Interrupt level 1 dispatch table
Lvl2DT	1B2	32 Bytes	Interrupt level 2 dispatch table
MAErrProc	BE8	Pointer	+MacApp error procedure
MaskBC	31A	Longint	Memory Manager byte count mask (also called Lo3Bytes)
MASuperTab	BEC	Handle	+MacApp superclass table
MBarEnable	A20	Integer	menuBar enable for desk accessories
MBarHeight	BAA	Integer	+Height of menu bar (usually 20)
MBarHook	A2C	Pointer	User hook before MenuHook
MBState	172	Byte	Current mouse button state
MBTicks	16E	Longint	Tickcount at last mouse button
MemErr	220	Integer	Last memory manager error
MemTop	108	Pointer	Top of RAM
MenuFlash	A24	Integer	Flash feedback count
MenuHook	A30	Pointer	User hook during menuSelect
MenuList	A1C	Handle	Current menuBar list structure
MicroSoft	A78	12 bytes	Old name for ApplScratch

Name	Address	Type	Comment
MinStack	31E	Longint	Minimum size of stack
MinusOne	A06	Longint	Constant $FFFFFFFF
MMDefFlags	326	Integer	Default zone flags
MmInOK	12E	Byte	Initial memory mgr checks ok?
MonkeyLives	100	Integer	Monkey tester in use if >= 0
MouseMask	8D6	Point	Mask for ANDing with mouse
MouseOffset	8DA	Point	Offset for adding after ANDing
MrMacHook	A2C	Pointer	Old name for MBarHook
MTemp	828	Longint	Low-level interrupt mouse location
NewMount	34A	Integer	Used by MountVol to flag new mounts
NiblTbl	25A	Pointer	Used by disk driver
OldContent	9EA	Handle	Saved content region
OldStructure	9E6	Handle	Saved structure region
OneOne	A02	Longint	Constant $00010001
PaintWhite	9DC	Integer	Erase newly drawn windows?
Params	3A4	50 bytes	Used by Device Manager for I/O parameter blocks
PollProc	13E	Pointer	SCC poll data procedure
PollRtnAddr	128	Pointer	'Other' driver locals
PollStack	13A	Pointer	SCC poll data start stack location
PortAUse	290	Byte	Bits 0-3: port type; bit 7: 0 = in use
PortBUse	291	Byte	Port B use, same format as PortAUse
PrintErr	944	Integer	Current print error
PrintVars	944	16 Bytes	Print code variables
Privileg	20	Pointer	Privilege violation vector
PWMBuf1	B0A	Pointer	+PWM buffer pointer
PWMBuf2	312	Pointer	PWM buffer 1 (or 2 if sound)
PWMValue	138	Integer	Current PWM value
QDExist	8F3	Byte	Quickdraw is initialized if zero
RAMBase	2B2	Pointer	Lowest address for trap routines in RAM
RawMouse	82C	Point	Un-jerked mouse coordinates
RegRsrc	347	Byte	Flag used by File Manager
ReqstVol	3EE	Pointer	VCB of off-line or external volume
ResErr	A60	Integer	Resource Manager error code
ResErrProc	AF2	Pointer	Routine called whenever Resource Manager error occurs
ResetSPPC	0	8 bytes	Reset vector
ResLoad	A5E	Integer	Load resources on GetResource if non-zero
RestProc	A8C	Pointer	Old name for ResumeProc
ResumeProc	A8C	Pointer	Resume procedure for system errors
RgSvArea	36A	38	Register save area used by system
RMGRPerm	BA4	Byte	+Permission byte for OpenResFile
RndSeed	156	Longint	Random number seed
ROM85	28E	Integer	+$FFFF = 64K ROM, $7FFF = 128K ROM or newer
ROMBase	2AE	Pointer	Start of ROM
RomFont0	980	Handle	System font
ROMMapHndl	B06	Handle	+ROM resource file's map
RomMapInsert	B9E	Byte	+$FF = look in ROM resource file, $00 = don't look in ROM
SavedHandle	A28	Handle	Saved bits under a menu
SaveProc	A90	Pointer	Address of Save failsafe procedure
SaveSegHandle	930	Handle	CODE resource 0 (used by Launch)
SaveSP	A94	Longint	Safe SP for restart or save
SaveUpdate	9DA	Integer	Enable window update accumulation?
SaveVisRgn	9F2	Handle	Temporarily saved visRegion
SCCASts	2CE	Byte	SCC read reg 0 last ext/sts rupt - A
SCCBSts	2CF	Byte	SCC read reg 0 last ext/sts rupt - B
SCCRd	1D8	Pointer	SCC base read address
SCCWr	1DC	Pointer	SCC base write address

Name	Address	Type	Comment
ScrapCount	968	Integer	Count changed by ZeroScrap
ScrapEnd	980		End of scrap variables
ScrapHandle	964	Handle	Desk scrap
ScrapInfo	960	Longint	Old name for ScrapSize
ScrapName	96C	Pointer	Scrap file name
ScrapSize	960	Longint	Length of desk scrap
ScrapState	96A	Integer	Is scrap on disk?
ScrapTag	970	String[15]	Scrap file name
ScrapVars	960	32 Bytes	Scrap manager variables
scratch20	1E4	20 Bytes	Application scratch area
scratch8	9FA	8 Bytes	Application scratch area
ScrDmpEnb	2F8	Byte	Screen dump enabled if non-zero
ScrDmpType	2F9	Byte	$FF dumps screen, $FE dumps front window
ScreenRow	106	Integer	rowBytes of screen
ScreenVars	292	8 Bytes	Screen driver variables (MacsBug)
ScrHRes	104	Integer	Screen horizontal dots per inch
ScrnBase	824	Pointer	Base address of screen
ScrVRes	102	Integer	Screen vertical dots per inch
SCSIDrvrs	B2E	Integer	+Bitmap for loaded SCSI drivers
SCSIFlag	B22	Integer	+Configuration flag for SCSI
SdVolume	260	Byte	Global volume control
SegHiEnable	BB2	Byte	+0 to disable MoveHHi in LoadSeg
SerialVars	2D0	16 Bytes	Async driver variables
SEvtEnb	15C	Byte	If zero, SystemEvent will always return False
SFSaveDisk	214	Integer	Last vRefNum seen by standard file
SonyVars	134	Pointer	Variables for .SONY driver
SoundActive	27E	Byte	Sound is active?
SoundBase	266	Pointer	Free-form synthesizer buffer
SoundDCE	27A	Pointer	Sound driver device control entry
SoundLast	282		End of sound driver variables
SoundLevel	27F	Byte	Amplitude in sound buffer
SoundPtr	262	Pointer	Four-tone record
SoundVars	262	32 Bytes	Sound driver variables
SoundVBL	26A	16 Bytes	Vertical retrace control element for sound
SPAlarm	200	Longint	Alarm time setting
SPATalkA	1F9	Byte	AppleTalk node ID hint for port A (modem port)
SPATalkB	1FA	Byte	AppleTalk node number hint for port B (printer port)
SPClikCaret	209	Byte	Double-click and caret-blink times (in 4-tick units)
SPConfig	1FB	Byte	Serial port type-use bits
SPFont	204	Integer	Application font number minus 1
SPKbd	206	Byte	Auto-key threshold and rate (in 4-tick units)
SPMisc1	20A	Byte	Miscellaneous parameter RAM
SPMisc2	20B	Byte	Mouse scaling, startup disk, menu blink
SPPortA	1FC	Integer	Port A (modem) configuration
SPPortB	1FE	Integer	Port B (printer) configuration
SPPrint	207	Byte	Printer connection
Spurious	60	Pointer	Spurious interrupt vector
SPValid	1F8	Byte	Parameter RAM validation field ($A7 if valid)
SPVolCtl	208	Byte	Speaker volume setting
StkLowPt	110	Pointer	Lowest stack as measured by stack sniffer
Switcher	282	8 Bytes	Used by Switcher
SwitcherTPtr	286	Pointer	+Switcher's switch table
SysEvtBuf	146	Pointer	System event queue element buffer
SysEvtMask	144	Integer	System event mask
SysFontFam	BA6	Integer	+System font family ID or zero
SysFontSize	BA8	Integer	+System font size (or zero for 12 point)

Name	Address	Type	Comment
SysMap	A58	Integer	Reference number of system resource file
SysMapHndl	A54	Handle	System resource file map
SysParam	1F8	20 Bytes	Low-memory copy of parameter RAM
SysResName	AD8	String[15]	Name of system resource file
SysVersion	15A	Integer	Version number of RAM-based system
SysZone	2A6	Pointer	Start of system heap zone
T1Arbitrate	B3F	Byte	+$FF if VIA timer T1 is available
TagData	2FA	14 Bytes	Sector tag info for disk drivers
TaskLock	A62	Byte	Re-entering SystemTask
TEDoText	A70	Pointer	TextEdit doText hook
TempRect	9FA	8 Bytes	Scratch rectangle used by system
TERecal	A74	Pointer	TextEdit routine to recalculate line starts
TEScrpHandle	AB4	Handle	TextEdit scrap
TEScrpLength	AB0	Integer	Size of TextEdit scrap
TESysJust	BAC	Integer	+System justification for international
TEWdBreak	AF6	Pointer	Default TextEdit word break routine
TheCrsr	844	68 Bytes	Cursor data, mask and hotspot
TheMenu	A26	Integer	ID of currently highlighted menu
TheZone	118	Pointer	Current heap zone
Ticks	16A	Longint	Number of ticks since boot
Time	20C	Longint	Seconds since midnight, January 1, 1904
TimeVars	B30	Pointer	+Time Manager variables
TmpResLoad	B9F	Byte	+Temporary ResLoad value
Tocks	173	Byte	Lisa sub-tick count
ToExtFS	3F2	Pointer	Hook for external file systems
ToolScratch	9CE	8 Bytes	Scratch area used by Toolbox
TopMapHndl	A50	Handle	Most recently opened resource file's map
TopMenuItem	B26	Integer	+Used for menu scrolling
Trace	24	Pointer	Trace vector
TrapAgain	B00	4 bytes	+Used by disk switch hook to repeat File System call
TRAPtble	80	16 pointers	TRAP #0-15 instruction vectors
TrapVErr	1C	Pointer	cpTRAPcc, TRAPcc, TRAPV instruction error
Unassig2	40	32 bytes	Unassigned, reserved by Motorola
Unassig3	C0	64 bytes	Unassigned, reserved by Motorola
Unassigned	30	4 bytes	Unassigned, reserved by Motorola
Uninited	3C	Pointer	Uninitialized interrupt vector
UnitNtryCnt	1D2	Integer	Number of entries in unit table
UserFWidths	BF5	Byte	+Flag saying if we used fractional widths
UTableBase	11C	Pointer	Start of unit table
VBLQueue	160	10 Bytes	VBL queue header
VCBQHdr	356	10 bytes	VCB queue header
VIA	1D4	Pointer	VIA base address
WidthListHand	8E4	Handle	+List of extra width tables, or nil
WidthPtr	B10	Longint	+Used by Font Manager
WidthTabHandle	B2A	Handle	+Font width table for measure
WindowList	9D6	Pointer	Pointer to first window in window list
WMgrPort	9DE	Pointer	Window manager's GrafPort
WordRedraw	BA5	Byte	+Used by TextEdit RecalDraw
WWExist	8F2	Byte	If zero, Window Manager is initialized
ZeroDiv	14	Pointer	Zero divide vector

+ valid only if ROM85 = $7FFF (i.e., Macintosh Plus or newer)

System Globals: Numeric Listing

Address	Name	Type	Comment
0	ResetSPPC	8 bytes	Reset vector
8	BusError	Pointer	Bus error vector
C	AddrErr	Pointer	Address error vector
10	Illegal	Pointer	Illegal instruction vector
14	vZeroDiv	Pointer	Zero divide vector
18	ChkError	Pointer	Vector CHK, CHK2 instruction error
1C	TrapVErr	Pointer	cpTRAPcc, TRAPcc, TRAPV instruction error
20	Privileg	Pointer	Privilege violation vector
24	Trace	Pointer	Trace vector
28	Line1010	Pointer	1010 emulator trap (vector for A-traps)
2C	Line1111	Pointer	1111 emulator trap (reserved)
30	Unassigned	4 bytes	Unassigned, reserved by Motorola
34	Coproces	Pointer	Vector for coprocessor protocol violation
38	FormatEr	Pointer	Format error vector
38	FmtErrVect	Pointer	+Format error vector for 68010 and 68020
3C	Uninited	Pointer	Uninitialized interrupt vector
40	Unassig2	32 bytes	Unassigned, reserved by Motorola
60	Spurious	Pointer	Spurious interrupt vector
64	AutoInt1	Pointer	Level 1 interrupt auto-vector
68	AutoInt2	Pointer	Level 2 interrupt auto-vector
6C	AutoInt3	Pointer	Level 3 interrupt auto-vector
70	AutoInt4	Pointer	Level 4 interrupt auto-vector
74	AutoInt5	Pointer	Level 5 interrupt auto-vector
78	AutoInt6	Pointer	Level 6 interrupt auto-vector
7C	AutoInt7	Pointer	Level 7 interrupt auto-vector
80	TRAPtble	16 pointers	TRAP #0-15 instruction vectors
C0	Unassig3	64 bytes	Unassigned, reserved by Motorola
100	MonkeyLives	Integer	Monkey tester in use if >= 0
102	ScrVRes	Integer	Screen vertical dots per inch
104	ScrHRes	Integer	Screen horizontal dots per inch
106	ScreenRow	Integer	rowBytes of screen
108	MemTop	Pointer	Top of RAM
10C	BufPtr	Pointer	Top of application memory (end of jump table)
110	StkLowPt	Pointer	Lowest stack as measured by stack sniffer
114	HeapEnd	Pointer	End of application heap
118	TheZone	Pointer	Current heap zone
11C	UTableBase	Pointer	Start of unit table
124	DskRtnAdr	Pointer	Used by disk driver
128	PollRtnAddr	Pointer	'Other' driver locals
12C	DskVerify	Byte	Used by .SONY driver for read/verify
12D	LoadTrap	Byte	If non-zero, enters debugger before entering new segment
12E	MmInOK	Byte	Initial memory mgr checks ok?
12F	CPUFlag	Byte	+$00=68000, $01=68010,$02=68020
130	ApplLimit	Pointer	End of application heap if fully grown
134	SonyVars	Pointer	Variables for .SONY driver
138	PWMValue	Integer	Current PWM value
13A	PollStack	Pointer	SCC poll data start stack location
13E	PollProc	Pointer	SCC poll data procedure
142	DskErr	Integer	Disk routine result code
144	SysEvtMask	Integer	System event mask
146	SysEvtBuf	Pointer	System event queue element buffer
14A	EventQueue	10 Bytes	Event queue header
154	EvtBufCnt	Integer	Maximum number of events in SysEvtBuf -1
156	RndSeed	Longint	Random number seed
15A	SysVersion	Integer	Version number of RAM-based system

Address	Name	Type	Comment
15C	SEvtEnb	Byte	If zero, SystemEvent will always return False
15D	DSWndUpdate	Byte	Used by disk switch hook
15E	FontFlag	Byte	Font manager loop flag
15F	IntFlag	Byte	Reduce interrupt disable time when bit 7 = 0
160	VBLQueue	10 Bytes	VBL queue header
16A	Ticks	Longint	Number of ticks since boot
16E	MBTicks	Longint	Tickcount at last mouse button
172	MBState	Byte	Current mouse button state
173	Tocks	Byte	Lisa sub-tick count
174	KeyMap	2 Longints	Bitmap showing keys up/down
17C	KeypadMap	Longint	Bitmap for numeric pad-18 bits
184	KeyLast	Integer	ASCII for last valid keycode
186	KeyTime	Longint	Tickcount when last keystroke was received
18A	KeyRepTime	Longint	Tickcount when key was last repeated
18E	KeyThresh	Integer	Threshold for key repeat
190	KeyRepThresh	Integer	Key repeat speed
192	Lvl1DT	32 Bytes	Interrupt level 1 dispatch table
1B2	Lvl2DT	32 Bytes	Interrupt level 2 dispatch table
1D2	UnitNtryCnt	Integer	Number of entries in unit table
1D4	VIA	Pointer	VIA base address
1D8	SCCRd	Pointer	SCC base read address
1DC	SCCWr	Pointer	SCC base write address
1E0	IWM	Pointer	IWM base address
1E4	GetParam	20 Bytes	System parameter scratch space
1E4	scratch20	20 Bytes	Application scratch area
1F8	SPValid	Byte	Parameter RAM validation field ($A7 if valid)
1F8	SysParam	20 Bytes	Low-memory copy of parameter RAM
1F9	SPATalkA	Byte	AppleTalk node ID hint for port A (modem port)
1FA	SPATalkB	Byte	AppleTalk node number hint for port B (printer port)
1FB	SPConfig	Byte	Serial port type-use bits
1FC	SPPortA	Integer	Port A (modem) configuration
1FE	SPPortB	Integer	Port B (printer) configuration
200	SPAlarm	Longint	Alarm time setting
204	SPFont	Integer	Application font number minus 1
206	SPKbd	Byte	Auto-key threshold and rate (in 4-tick units)
207	SPPrint	Byte	Printer connection
208	SPVolCtl	Byte	Speaker volume setting
209	SPClikCaret	Byte	Double-click and caret-blink times (in 4-tick units)
20A	SPMisc1	Byte	Miscellaneous parameter RAM
20B	SPMisc2	Byte	Mouse scaling, startup disk, menu blink
20C	Time	Longint	Seconds since midnight, January 1, 1904
210	BootDrive	Integer	Drive number of boot drive
212	JShell	Integer	Journaling shell state
214	SFSaveDisk	Integer	Last vRefNum seen by standard file
216	KbdVars	Longint	Keyboard driver variables
21A	JKybdTask	Pointer	Keyboard VBL task hook
21E	KbdType	Byte	Keyboard model number
21F	AlarmState	Byte	Bit 7=Apple logo on/off, Bit 6=beeped, Bit 0=enabled
220	MemErr	Integer	Last memory manager error
222	DiskVars	62 Bytes	Variables used by .SONY driver
222	JFigTrkSpd	Pointer	Disk driver vector
226	JDiskPrime	Pointer	Disk driver vector
22A	JRdAddr	Pointer	Disk driver vector
22E	JRdData	Pointer	Disk driver vector
232	JWrData	Pointer	Disk driver vector
236	JSeek	Pointer	Disk driver vector

Address	Name	Type	Comment
23A	JSetUpPoll	Pointer	Disk driver vector
23E	JRecal	Pointer	Disk driver vector
242	JControl	Pointer	Disk driver vector
246	JWakeUp	Pointer	Disk driver vector
24A	JReSeek	Pointer	Disk driver vector
24E	JMakeSpdTbl	Pointer	Disk driver vector
252	JAdrDisk	Pointer	Disk driver vector
256	JSetSpeed	Pointer	Disk driver vector
25A	NiblTbl	Pointer	Used by disk driver
25E	FlEvtMask	Integer	+Mask of allowable events to flush at FlushEvents
260	SdVolume	Byte	Global volume control
261	Finder	Byte	Private Finder flags
262	SoundPtr	Pointer	Four-tone record
262	SoundVars	32 Bytes	Sound driver variables
266	SoundBase	Pointer	Free-form synthesizer buffer
26A	SoundVBL	16 Bytes	Vertical retrace control element for sound
27A	SoundDCE	Pointer	Sound driver device control entry
27E	SoundActive	Byte	Sound is active?
27F	SoundLevel	Byte	Amplitude in sound buffer
280	CurPitch	Integer	Current pitch value
282	SoundLast		End of sound driver variables
282	Switcher	8 Bytes	Used by Switcher
286	SwitcherTPtr	Pointer	+Switcher's switch table
28E	ROM85	Integer	+$FFFF = 64K ROM, $7FFF = 128K ROM or newer
290	PortAUse	Byte	Bits 0-3: port type; bit 7: 0 = in use
291	PortBUse	Byte	Port B use, same format as PortAUse
292	ScreenVars	8 Bytes	Screen driver variables (MacsBug)
29A	JGNEFilter	Pointer	GetNextEvent filter proc
29E	Key1Trans	Pointer	Keyboard mapping procedure
2A2	Key2Trans	Pointer	Numeric keypad mapping procedure
2A6	SysZone	Pointer	Start of system heap zone
2AA	ApplZone	Pointer	Start of application heap zone
2AE	ROMBase	Pointer	Start of ROM
2B2	RAMBase	Pointer	Lowest address for trap routines in RAM
2B6	BasicGlob	Pointer	Basic globals
2BA	DSAlertTab	Pointer	System error alerts
2BE	ExtStsDT	16 Bytes	SCC ext/sts secondary dispatch table
2CE	SCCASts	Byte	SCC read reg 0 last ext/sts rupt - A
2CF	SCCBSts	Byte	SCC read reg 0 last ext/sts rupt - B
2D0	SerialVars	16 Bytes	Async driver variables
2D8	ABusVars	8 bytes	Local variables used by AppleTalk
2E0	FinderName	String[15]	Filename of the Finder
2F0	DoubleTime	Longint	Allowed ticks between clicks of a double-click
2F4	CaretTime	Longint	Ticks between caret blinks
2F8	ScrDmpEnb	Byte	Screen dump enabled if non-zero
2F9	ScrDmpType	Byte	$FF dumps screen, $FE dumps front window
2FA	TagData	14 Bytes	Sector tag info for disk drivers
2FC	BufTgFNum	Longint	Buffer tag file number
300	BufTgFFlg	Integer	Buffer tag flags
302	BufTgFBkNum	Integer	Logical block number
304	BufTgDate	Integer	Time stamp
308	DrvQHdr	10 Bytes	Header of system's drive queue
312	PWMBuf2	Pointer	PWM buffer 1 (or 2 if sound)
31A	Lo3Bytes	Longint	Constant $00FFFFFF
31A	MaskBC	Longint	Memory Manager byte count mask (also called Lo3Bytes)
31E	MinStack	Longint	Minimum size of stack

Address	Name	Type	Comment
322	DefltStack	Longint	Default size of stack
326	MMDefFlags	Integer	Default zone flags
328	GZRootHnd	Handle	Block which must not be moved by GrowZone function
32C	GZRootPtr	Pointer	Root pointer for GrowZone
330	GZMoveHnd	Handle	Moving handle for GrowZone
334	DSDrawProc	Pointer	Alternate SysError draw procedure
338	EjectNotify	Pointer	Routine called when a disk is ejected
33C	IAZNotify	Pointer	Routine called when application heap is reinitialized
340	CkdDB	Integer	Used when searching the directory
340	FileVars	184 Bytes	File system variables
346	FlushOnly	Byte	Flag used by UnMountVol,FlushVol
347	RegRsrc	Byte	Flag used by File Manager
348	FLckUnlck	Byte	Flag used by SetFilLock,RstFilLock
349	FrcSync	Byte	When set, all File System calls are synched
34A	NewMount	Integer	Used by MountVol to flag new mounts
34C	DrMstrBlk	Integer	Master directory block in a volume (MFS)
34E	FCBSPtr	Pointer	File control blocks
352	DefVCBPtr	Pointer	Default volume control block
356	VCBQHdr	10 bytes	VCB queue header
360	FSBusy	Integer	Non-zero when the file system is busy
360	FSQHdr	10 Bytes	File system queue header
362	FSQHead	Pointer	First queued command in File System queue
366	FSQTail	Pointer	Last File System queue element
36A	RgSvArea	38	Register save area used by system
3A2	ErCode	Integer	Disk driver async errors
3A4	Params	50 bytes	Used by Device Manager for I/O parameter blocks
3D6	FSTemp8	8 bytes	Used by File System
3DE	FSTemp4	Longint	Used by File System
3E2	FSQueueHook	Pointer	Hook to capture all FS calls
3E6	ExtFSHook	Pointer	Used by external file system
3EA	DskSwtchHook	Pointer	Hook for disk-switch dialog
3EE	ReqstVol	Pointer	VCB of off-line or external volume
3F2	ToExtFS	Pointer	Hook for external file systems
3F6	fsVarEnd		End of file system variables
3F8	DSAlertRect	Rect	Rectangle for disk-switch alert
400	DispatchTab	1024 Bytes	A-Trap dispatch table (64K ROM)
4B8	JBlockMove	Pointer	+Vector used by Memory Manager
800	GrafBegin		QuickDraw system globals area
800	JHideCursor	Pointer	Vector used by QuickDraw
804	JShowCursor	Pointer	Vector used by QuickDraw
808	JShieldCursor	Pointer	Vector used by QuickDraw
80C	JScrnAddr	Pointer	Vector used by QuickDraw
810	JScrnSize	Pointer	Vector used by QuickDraw
814	JInitCrsr	Pointer	Vector used by QuickDraw
818	JSetCrsr	Pointer	Vector used by QuickDraw
81C	JCrsrObscure	Pointer	Vector used by QuickDraw
820	JUpdateProc	Pointer	Vector used by QuickDraw
824	LGrafJump	Pointer	Vector used by QuickDraw
824	ScrnBase	Pointer	Base address of screen
828	MTemp	Longint	Low-level interrupt mouse location
82C	RawMouse	Point	Un-jerked mouse coordinates
834	CrsrPin	Rect	Cursor pinning rectangle
83C	CrsrRect	Rect	Cursor hit rectangle
844	TheCrsr	68 Bytes	Cursor data, mask and hotspot
888	CrsrAddr	Pointer	Screen-memory address covered by cursor
88C	CrsrSave	64 Bytes	Saved data under the cursor

Address	Name	Type	Comment
8CC	CrsrVis	Byte	Cursor visible?
8CD	CrsrBusy	Byte	Cursor locked out?
8CE	CrsrNew	Byte	Cursor changed?
8CF	CrsrCouple	Byte	Cursor coupled to mouse?
8D0	CrsrState	Integer	Cursor nesting level
8D2	CrsrObscure	Byte	Cursor obscure flag
8D3	CrsrScale	Byte	Cursor scaled?
8D6	MouseMask	Point	Mask for ANDing with mouse
8DA	MouseOffset	Point	Offset for adding after ANDing
8DE	JournalFlag	Integer	Journaling state
8E0	JSwapFont	Longint	Jump entry for FMSwapFont
8E4	JFontInfo	Pointer	Jump entry for FMFontMetrics
8E4	WidthListHand	Handle	+List of extra width tables, or nil
8E8	JournalRef	Integer	Journaling driver's refnum
8EC	CrsrThresh	Integer	Delta threshold for mouse scaling
8EE	JCrsrTask	Pointer	Address of CrsrVBLTask
8F2	GrafEnd		End of QuickDraw system globals
8F2	WWExist	Byte	If zero, Window Manager is initialized
8F3	QDExist	Byte	Quickdraw is initialized if zero
8F4	JFetch	Pointer	Fetch a byte routine for drivers
8F8	JStash	Pointer	Stash a byte routine for drivers
8FC	JIODone	Pointer	IODone vector
900	CurApRefNum	Integer	RefNum of application's resource file
900	LoadVars	68 Bytes	Segment Loader variables
902	LaunchFlag	Byte	Used by Launch and Chain
904	CurrentA5	Pointer	Correct value of A5
908	CurStackBase	Pointer	Current stack base
910	CurApName	String[31]	Name of current application
930	SaveSegHandle	Handle	CODE resource 0 (used by Launch)
934	CurJTOffset	Integer	Offset from A5 to start of jump table
936	CurPageOption	Integer	Current page 2 video/sound configuration
93A	LoaderPBlock	10 Bytes	parameter block for ExitToShell
944	LastLGlobal		Last Segment Loader global
944	PrintErr	Integer	Current print error
944	PrintVars	16 Bytes	Print code variables
946	ChooserBits	Byte	Bit 7=0, don't run; Bit 6=0, gray out AppleTalk
954	CoreEditVars	12 Bytes	Core edit variables
954	LastPGlobal		Last Printing Manager global
960	ScrapInfo	Longint	Old name for ScrapSize
960	ScrapSize	Longint	Length of desk scrap
960	ScrapVars	32 Bytes	Scrap manager variables
964	ScrapHandle	Handle	Desk scrap
968	ScrapCount	Integer	Count changed by ZeroScrap
96A	ScrapState	Integer	Is scrap on disk?
96C	ScrapName	Pointer	Scrap file name
970	ScrapTag	String[15]	Scrap file name
980	RomFont0	Handle	System font
980	ScrapEnd		End of scrap variables
984	ApFontID	Integer	Resource ID of application font
986	GotStrike	Byte	Do we have the strike? (Font Manager)
987	FMDefaultSize	Byte	Default size of Font Record
988	CurFMFamily	Integer	Current font family
988	CurFMInput	Pointer	Quickdraw FMInput Record
98A	CurFMSize	Integer	Current font size
98C	CurFMFace	Byte	Current font face
98D	CurFMNeedBits	Boolean	Does Font Manager need bits?

Address	Name	Type	Comment
98E	CurFMDevice	Integer	Current font device
990	CurFMNumer	Point	Current numerator of scale factor
994	CurFMDenom	Point	Current denominator of scale factor
998	FMgrOutRec	Pointer	Quickdraw font output record
998	FOutError	Integer	Error code
998	FOutRec	Pointer	Font Manager output record
99A	FOutFontHandle	Handle	Font bits
99E	FOutBold	Byte	Bolding factor
99F	FOutItalic	Byte	Italic factor
9A0	FOutULOffset	Byte	Underline offset
9A1	FOutULShadow	Byte	Underline "halo"
9A2	FOutULThick	Byte	Underline thickness
9A3	FOutShadow	Byte	Shadow factor
9A4	FOutExtra	Byte	Extra horizontal width
9A5	FOutAscent	Byte	Height above baseline
9A6	FOutDescent	Byte	Height below baseline
9A7	FOutWidMax	Byte	Maximum width of character
9A8	FOutLeading	Byte	Space between lines
9AA	FOutNumer	Point	Numerators of scaling factors
9AE	CurFMDenom	Point	Point for denominators of scale factor
9B2	FMDotsPerInch	Point	Dots per inch of current device
9B6	FMStyleTab	18 bytes	Style heuristic table supplied by device
9CE	ToolScratch	8 Bytes	Scratch area used by Toolbox
9D6	WindowList	Pointer	Pointer to first window in window list
9DA	SaveUpdate	Integer	Enable window update accumulation?
9DC	PaintWhite	Integer	Erase newly drawn windows?
9DE	WMgrPort	Pointer	Window manager's GrafPort
9E6	OldStructure	Handle	Saved structure region
9EA	OldContent	Handle	Saved content region
9EE	GrayRgn	Handle	Rounded gray desk region
9F2	SaveVisRgn	Handle	Temporarily saved visRegion
9F6	DragHook	Pointer	Routine called during dragging
9FA	scratch8	8 Bytes	Application scratch area
9FA	TempRect	8 Bytes	Scratch rectangle used by system
A02	OneOne	Longint	Constant $00010001
A06	MinusOne	Longint	Constant $FFFFFFFF
A0E	IconBitmap	BitMap	Used by PlotIcon
A1C	MenuList	Handle	Current menuBar list structure
A20	MBarEnable	Integer	menuBar enable for desk accessories
A22	CurDeKind	Integer	WindowKind of deactivated window
A24	MenuFlash	Integer	Flash feedback count
A26	TheMenu	Integer	ID of currently highlighted menu
A28	SavedHandle	Handle	Saved bits under a menu
A2C	MBarHook	Pointer	User hook before MenuHook
A2C	MrMacHook	Pointer	Old name for MBarHook
A30	MenuHook	Pointer	User hook during menuSelect
A34	DragPattern	Pattern	Dragged by DragTheRgn
A3C	DeskPattern	Pattern	Desktop pattern
A44	DragFlag	Integer	Implicit parameter to DragControl
A46	CurDragAction	Pointer	Implicit actionProc for DragControl
A4A	FPState	6 Bytes	Floating point state
A50	TopMapHndl	Handle	Most recently opened resource file's map
A54	SysMapHndl	Handle	System resource file map
A58	SysMap	Integer	Reference number of system resource file
A5A	CurMap	Integer	Reference number of current resource file
A5E	ResLoad	Integer	Load resources on GetResource if non-zero

Address	Name	Type	Comment
A60	ResErr	Integer	Resource Manager error code
A62	TaskLock	Byte	Re-entering SystemTask
A63	FScaleDisable	Byte	Disable font scaling?
A64	CurActivate	Pointer	Window which will get activate event
A68	CurDeactive	Pointer	Window which will get activate event
A6C	DeskHook	Pointer	Routine which will be called to paint the desk
A70	TEDoText	Pointer	TextEdit doText hook
A74	TERecal	Pointer	TextEdit routine to recalculate line starts
A78	ApplScratch	12 Bytes	Reserved for use by application
A78	MicroSoft	12 bytes	Old name for ApplScratch
A84	GhostWindow	Pointer	Window hidden from FrontWindow
A88	CloseOrnHook	Pointer	Routine called when closing desk accessories
A8C	RestProc	Pointer	Old name for ResumeProc
A8C	ResumeProc	Pointer	Resume procedure for system errors
A90	SaveProc	Pointer	Address of Save failsafe procedure
A94	SaveSP	Longint	Safe SP for restart or save
A98	ANumber	Integer	Active alert ID
A9A	ACount	Integer	Number of times this alert called
A9C	DABeeper	Pointer	Beep routine for ModalDialog
AA0	DAStrings	4 Handles	ParamText substitution strings
AB0	TEScrpLength	Integer	Size of TextEdit scrap
AB4	TEScrpHandle	Handle	TextEdit scrap
AB8	AppPacks	8 Handles	Handles to Pack0 through Pack7
AD8	SysResName	String[15]	Name of system resource file
AEC	AppParmHandle	Handle	Handle to Finder information on Launch
AF0	DSErrCode	Integer	Last system error alert ID
AF2	ResErrProc	Pointer	Routine called whenever Resource Manager error occurs
AF6	TEWdBreak	Pointer	Default TextEdit word break routine
AFA	DlgFont	Integer	Default dialog font ID
B00	HeapStart		Start of the system heap (64K ROM)
B00	TrapAgain	4 bytes	+Used by disk switch hook to repeat File System call
B04	KeyMVars	Integer	+ROM KEYM procedure variables
B06	ROMMapHndl	Handle	+ROM resource file's map
B0A	PWMBuf1	Pointer	+PWM buffer pointer
B0E	BootMask	Integer	+Used by boot code
B10	WidthPtr	Longint	+Used by Font Manager
B14	AtalkHk1	Pointer	+Appletalk hook
B18	AtalkHk2	Pointer	+Appletalk hook
B22	SCSIFlag	Integer	+Configuration flag for SCSI
B26	TopMenuItem	Integer	+Used for menu scrolling
B28	AtMenuBottom	Integer	+Flag used by scrolling menus
B2A	WidthTabHandle	Handle	+Font width table for measure
B2E	SCSIDrvrs	Integer	+Bitmap for loaded SCSI drivers
B30	TimeVars	Pointer	+Time Manager variables
B34	BtDskRfn	Integer	+Refnum of boot disk driver
B36	BootTmp8	8 Bytes	+Temp space needed by StartBoot
B3F	T1Arbitrate	Byte	+$FF if VIA timer T1 is available
B40	JDiskSel	Pointer	+Disk driver vector
B44	JSendCmd	Pointer	+Disk driver vector
B48	JDCDReset	Pointer	+Disk driver vector
B4C	LastSPExtra	Longint	+Most recent value of space extra
B9E	RomMapInsert	Byte	+$FF = look first in ROM resource file, $00 = don't look in ROM
B9F	TmpResLoad	Byte	+Temporary ResLoad value
BA0	IntlSpec	Pointer	+Extra international data
BA4	RMGRPerm	Byte	+Permission byte for OpenResFile
BA5	WordRedraw	Byte	+Used by TextEdit RecalDraw

Address	Name	Type	Comment
BA6	SysFontFam	Integer	+System font family ID or zero
BA8	SysFontSize	Integer	+System font size (or zero for 12 point)
BAA	MBarHeight	Integer	+Height of menu bar (usually 20)
BAC	TESysJust	Integer	+System justification for international
BAE	HiHeapMark	Pointer	+Highest address used by a heap zone below A7
BB2	SegHiEnable	Byte	+0 to disable MoveHHi in LoadSeg
BB3	FDevDisable	Byte	+$FF to disable device-defined style extra
BC2	LastFOND	Handle	+Last font definition record (FOND)
BC6	FONDID	Integer	+ID of last font definition record (FOND)
BC8	App2Packs	8 Handles	+handles for Pack8 - Pack15
BE8	MAErrProc	Pointer	+MacApp error procedure
BEC	MASuperTab	Handle	+MacApp superclass table
BF4	FractEnable	Byte	+Flag for fractional font widths
BF5	UserFWidths	Byte	+Flag saying if we used fractional widths
BF6	FScaleHFact	Longint	+Horizontal font scale factor
BFA	FScaleVFact	Longint	+Vertical font scale factor

+ valid only if ROM85 = $7FFF (i.e., Macintosh Plus or newer)

Data Structures

Name	Type	Hex Offset	Dec Offset
AlertTemplate			
boundsRect	Rect	0	0
itemsID	Integer	8	8
stages	StageList	A	10
(size)		C	12
BitMap			
baseAddr	Pointer	0	0
rowBytes	Integer	4	4
bounds	Rect	6	6
(size)		D	14
CInfoPBRec			
qLink	QElemPtr	0	0
qType	Integer	4	4
ioTrap	Integer	6	6
ioCmdAddr	Pointer	8	8
ioCompletion	ProcPtr	C	12
ioResult	OSErr	10	16
ioNamePtr	StringPtr	12	18
ioVRefNum	Integer	16	22
ioFRefNum	Integer	18	24
filler1	Integer	1A	26
ioFDirIndex	Integer	1C	28
ioFlAttrib	SignedByte	1E	30
filler2	SignedByte	1F	31
hFileInfo:			
ioFlFndrInfo	FInfo	20	32
ioFlNum	Longint	30	48
ioFlStBlk	Integer	34	52
ioFlLgLen	Longint	36	54

Name	Type	Hex Offset	Dec Offset
ioFlPyLen	Longint	3A	58
ioFlRStBlk	Integer	3E	62
ioFlRLgLen	Longint	40	64
ioFlRPylLen	Longint	44	68
ioFlCrDat	Longint	48	72
ioFlMdDat	Longint	4C	76
ioFlBkDat	Longint	50	80
ioFlXFndrInfo	FInfo	54	84
ioFlParID	Longint	64	100
ioFlClpSiz	Longint	68	104
dirInfo:			
ioDrUsrWds	Array[1..8] of Integer	20	32
ioDrDirID	Longint	30	48
ioDrNmFls	Integer	34	52
filler3	Array[1..9]of Integer	36	54
ioDrCrDat	Longint	48	72
ioDrMdDat	Longint	4C	76
ioDrBkDat	Longint	50	80
ioDrFndrInfo	Array[1..8] of Integer	54	84
ioDrParID	Longint	64	100
CMovePBRec			
qLink	QElemPtr	0	0
qType	Integer	4	4
ioTrap	Integer	6	6
ioCmdAddr	Pointer	8	8
ioCompletion	ProcPtr	C	12
ioResult	OSErr	10	16
ioNamePtr	StringPtr	12	18
ioVRefNum	Integer	16	22
filler1	Longint	18	24
ioNewName	StringPtr	1C	28
filler2	Longint	20	32
ioNewDirID	Longint	24	36
filler3	Array[1..2] of Longint	28	40
ioDirID	Longint	30	48
ControlRecord			
nextControl	ControlHandle	0	0
contrlOwner	WindowPtr	4	4
contrlRect	Rect	8	8
contrlVis	Byte	10	16
contrlHilite	Byte	11	17
contrlValue	Integer	12	18
contrlMin	Integer	14	20
contrlMax	Integer	16	22
contrlDefProc	Handle	18	24
contrlData	Handle	1C	28
contrlAction	ProcPtr	20	32
contrlrfCon	Longint	24	36
contrlTitle	Str255	28	40
(size without title)		28	40

Name	Type	Hex Offset	Dec Offset
Cursor			
data	Bits16	0	0
mask	Bits16	20	32
hotSpot	Point	40	64
(size)		68	104
DialogRecord			
window	WindowRecord	0	0
Items	Handle	9C	156
textH	TEHandle	A0	160
EditField	Integer	A4	164
EditOpen	Integer	A6	166
ADefItem	Integer	A8	168
(size)		AA	170
DialogTemplate			
boundsRect	Rect	0	0
procID	Integer	8	8
visible	Boolean	A	10
goAwayFlag	Boolean	C	12
refCon	Longint	E	14
ItemsID	Integer	12	18
title	Str255	14	20
(size)			
EventRecord			
what	Integer	0	0
message	Longint	2	2
when	Longint	6	6
where	Point	A	10
modifiers	Integer	E	14
(size)		10	16
FCBPRec			
qLink	QElemPtr	0	0
qType	Integer	4	4
ioTrap	Integer	6	6
ioCmdAddr	Pointer	8	8
ioCompletion	ProcPtr	C	12
ioResult	OSErr	10	16
ioNamePtr	StringPtr	12	18
ioVRefNum	Integer	16	22
ioRefNum	Integer	28	24
filler	Integer	1A	26
ioFCBIndex	Longint	1C	28
ioFCBFlNm	Longint	20	32
ioFCBFlags	Integer	24	36
ioFCBStBlk	Integer	26	38
ioFCBEOF	Longint	28	40
ioFCBPLen	Longint	2C	44
ioFCBCrPs	Longint	30	48
ioFCBVRefNum	Integer	34	52
ioFCBClpSiz	Longint	36	54
ioFCBParID	Longint	3A	58

Name	Type	Hex Offset	Dec Offset
GrafPort			
device	Integer	0	0
portBits	BitMap	2	2
portBits.baseAddr	Pointer	2	2
portBits.rowBytes	Integer	4	4
portBits.Bounds	Rect	6	6
portRect	Rect	10	16
visRgn	RgnHandle	18	24
clipRgn	RgnHandle	1C	28
bkPat	Pattern	20	32
fillPat	Pattern	28	40
pnLoc	Point	30	48
pnSize	Point	34	52
pnMode	Integer	38	56
pnPat	Pattern	3A	58
pnVis	Integer	42	66
txFont	Integer	44	68
txFace	Style	46	70
txMode	Integer	48	72
txSize	Integer	4A	74
spExtra	Longint	4C	76
fgColor	Longint	50	80
bkColor	Longint	54	84
colrBit	Integer	58	88
patStretch	Integer	5A	90
picSave	Handle	5C	92
rgnSave	Handle	60	96
polySave	Handle	64	100
grafProcs	QDProcsPtr	68	104
(size)		6C	108
HParamBlockRec			
qLink	QElemPtr	0	0
qType	Integer	4	4
ioTrap	Integer	6	6
ioCmdAddr	Pointer	8	8
ioCompletion	ProcPtr	C	12
ioResult	OSErr	10	16
ioNamePtr	StringPtr	12	18
ioVRefNum	Integer	16	22
ioParam:			
ioRefNum	Integer	18	24
ioVersNum	SignedByte	1A	26
ioPermssn	SignedByte	1B	27
ioMisc	Pointer	1C	28
ioBuffer	Pointer	20	32
ioReqCount	Longint	24	36
ioActCount	Longint	28	40
ioPosMode	Integer	2C	44
ioPosOffset	Longint	2E	46
fileParam:			
ioFRefNum	Integer	18	24
ioFVersNum	SignedByte	1A	26
filler1	SignedByte	1B	27

Name	Type	Hex Offset	Dec Offset
ioFDirIndex	Integer	1C	28
ioFlAttrib	SignedByte	1E	30
ioFlVersNum	SignedByte	1F	31
ioFlFndrInfo	FInfo	20	32
ioDirID	Longint	30	48
ioFlStBlk	Integer	34	52
ioFlLgLen	Longint	36	54
ioFlPyLen	Longint	3A	58
ioFlRStBlk	Integer	3E	62
ioFlRLgLen	Longint	40	64
ioFlRPyLen	Longint	44	68
ioFlCrDat	Longint	48	72
ioFlMdDat	Longint	4C	76
volumeParam:			
filler4	Longint	18	24
ioVolIndex	Integer	1C	28
ioVCrDate	Longint	1E	30
ioVLsMod	Longint	22	34
ioVAtrb	Integer	26	38
ioVNmFls	Integer	28	40
ioVBitMap	Integer	2A	42
ioVAllocPtr	Integer	2C	44
ioVNmAlBlks	Integer	2E	46
ioVAlBlkSiz	Longint	30	48
ioVClpSiz	Longint	34	52
ioAlBlSt	Integer	38	56
ioVNxtCNID	Longint	3A	58
ioVFrBlk	Integer	3E	62
ioVSigWord	Integer	40	64
ioVDrvInfo	Integer	42	66
ioVDRefNum	Integer	44	68
ioVFSID	Integer	46	70
ioVBkUp	Longint	48	72
ioVSeqNum	Integer	4C	76
ioVWrCnt	Longint	4E	78
ioVFilCnt	Longint	52	82
ioVDirCnt	Longint	56	86
ioVFndrInfo	Array[1..8] of Longint	5A	90

MenuInfo

Name	Type	Hex Offset	Dec Offset
menuID	Integer	0	0
menuWidth	Integer	2	2
menuHeight	Integer	4	4
menuProc	Handle	6	6
enableFlags	Longint	A	10
menuData	Str255	E	14
(size)		E	14

Name	Type	Hex Offset	Dec Offset
ParamBlockRec			
qLink	QElemPtr	0	0
qType	Integer	4	4
ioTrap	Integer	6	6
ioCmdAddr	Pointer	8	8
ioCompletion	ProcPtr	C	12
ioResult	OSErr	10	16
ioNamePtr	StringPtr	12	18
ioVRefNum	Integer	16	22
ioParam:			
ioRefNum	Integer	18	24
ioVersNum	SignedByte	1A	26
ioPermssn	SignedByte	1B	27
ioMisc	Pointer	1C	28
ioBuffer	Pointer	20	32
ioReqCount	Longint	24	36
ioActCount	Longint	28	40
ioPosMode	Integer	2C	44
ioPosOffset	Longint	2E	46
fileParam:			
ioFRefNum	Integer	18	24
ioFVersNum	SignedByte	1A	26
filler1	SignedByte	1B	27
ioFDirIndex	Integer	1C	28
ioFlAttrib	SignedByte	1E	30
ioFlVersNum	SignedByte	1F	31
ioFlFndrInfo	FInfo	20	32
ioFlNum	Longint	30	48
ioFlStBlk	Integer	34	52
ioFlLgLen	Longint	36	54
ioFlPyLen	Longint	3A	58
ioFlRStBlk	Integer	3E	62
ioFlRLgLen	Longint	40	64
ioFlRPyLen	Longint	44	68
ioFlCrDat	Longint	48	72
ioFlMdDat	Longint	4C	76
volumeParam:			
filler2	Longint	18	24
ioVolIndex	Integer	1C	28
ioVCrDate	Longint	1E	30
ioVLsBkUp	Longint	22	34
ioVAtrb	Integer	26	38
ioVNmFls	Integer	28	40
ioVDirSt	Integer	2A	42
ioVBlLn	Integer	2C	44
ioVNmAlBlks	Integer	2E	46
ioVAlBlkSiz	Longint	30	48
ioVClpSiz	Longint	34	52
ioAlBlSt	Integer	38	56
ioVNxtFNum	Longint	3A	58
ioVFrBlk	Integer	3E	62

Name	Type	Hex Offset	Dec Offset
cntrlParam:			
ioCRefNum	Integer	18	24
csCode	Integer	1A	26
csParam	Array [0..10] of Integer	1C	28

Point

Name	Type	Hex Offset	Dec Offset
v	Integer	0	0
h	Integer	2	2
(size)		4	4

Rect

Name	Type	Hex Offset	Dec Offset
top	Integer	0	0
left	Integer	2	2
bottom	Integer	4	4
right	Integer	6	6
topLeft	Point	0	0
botRight	Point	4	4
(size)		8	8

SFReply

Name	Type	Hex Offset	Dec Offset
good	Boolean	0	0
copy	Boolean	1	1
fType	OSType	2	2
vRefNum	Integer	6	6
version	Integer	8	8
fName	String[63]	A	10
(size)			

TERec

Name	Type	Hex Offset	Dec Offset
destRect	Rect	0	0
viewRect	Rect	8	8
selRect	Rect	10	16
lineHeight	Integer	18	24
fontAscent	Integer	1A	26
selPoint	Point	1C	28
selStart	Integer	20	32
selEnd	Integer	22	34
active	Integer	24	36
wordBreak	ProcPtr	26	38
clikLoop	Procptr	2A	42
clickTime	Longint	2E	46
clickLoc	Integer	32	50
caretTime	Longint	34	52
caretState	Integer	38	56
just	Integer	3A	58
TELength	Integer	3C	60
hText	Handle	3E	62
recalBack	Integer	42	66
recalLines	Integer	44	68
clikStuff	Integer	46	70
crOnly	Integer	48	72
txFont	Integer	4A	74
txFace	Style	4C	76
txMode	Integer	4E	78
txSize	Integer	50	80

Name	Type	Hex Offset	Dec Offset
inPort	GrafPtr	52	82
highHook	ProcPtr	56	86
caretHook	ProcPtr	5A	80
nLines	Integer	5E	94
lineStarts	Array of Integer	60	96
(size of new TERecord)		68	104
VCB			
qLink	QElemPtr	0	0
qType	Integer	4	4
vcbFlags	Integer	6	6
vcbSigWord	Integer	8	8
vcbCrDate	Longint	A	10
vcbLsMod	Longint	E	14
vcbAtrb	Integer	12	18
vcbNmFls	Integer	14	20
vcbVBMSt	Integer	16	22
vcbAllocPtr	Integer	18	24
vcbNmAlBlks	Integer	1A	26
vcbAlBlkSiz	Longint	1C	28
vcbClpSiz	Longint	20	32
vcbAlBlSt	Integer	24	36
vcbNxtCNID	Longint	26	38
vcbFreeBks	Integer	2A	42
vcbVN	String[27]	2C	44
vcbDrvNum	Integer	4B	75
vcbDRefNum	Integer	4A	74
vcbFSID	Integer	4C	76
vcbVRefNum	Integer	4E	78
vcbMAdr	Pointer	50	80
vcbBufAdr	Pointer	54	84
vcbMLen	Integer	58	88
vcbDirIndex	Integer	5A	90
vcbDirBlk	Integer	5C	92
vcbVolBkUp	Longint	5E	94
vcbVSeqNum	Integer	62	98
vcbWrCnt	Longint	64	100
vcbXTClpSiz	Longint	68	104
vcbCTClpSiz	Longint	6C	108
vcbNmRtDirs	Integer	70	112
vcbFilCnt	Longint	72	114
vcbDirCnt	Longint	76	118
vcbFndrInfo	Array[1..8] of Longint	78	120
vcbVCSize	Integer	98	152
vcbVBMCSiz	Integer	9A	154
vcbCtlCSiz	Integer	9C	156
vcbXTAlBlks	Integer	9E	158
vcbCTAlBlks	Integer	A0	160
vcbXTRef	Integer	A2	162
vcbCTRef	Integer	A4	164
vcbCt1Buf	Longint	A6	166
vcbDirIDM	Longint	AA	170
vcbOffsM	Integer	AE	174
(size)			

Name	Type	Hex Offset	Dec Offset
WDPBRec			
qLink	QElemPtr	0	0
qType	Integer	4	4
ioTrap	Integer	6	6
ioCmdAddr	Pointer	8	8
ioCompletion	ProcPtr	C	12
ioResult	OSErr	10	16
ioNamePtr	StringPtr	12	18
ioVRefNum	Integer	16	22
filler1	Integer	18	24
ioWDIndex	Integer	1A	26
ioWDProcID	Longint	1C	28
ioWDVRefNum	Integer	20	32
filler2	Array[1..7] of Integer	22	34
ioWDDirID	Longint	30	48
WindowRecord			
port	GrafPort	0	0
windowKind	Integer	6C	108
visible	Boolean	6E	110
hilited	Boolean	6F	111
goAwayFlag	Boolean	70	112
strucRgn	RgnHandle	72	114
contRgn	RgnHandle	76	118
updateRgn	RgnHandle	7A	122
windowDefProc	Handle	7E	126
dataHandle	Handle	82	130
titleHandle	StringHandle	86	134
titleWidth	Integer	8A	138
ControlList	ControlHandle	8C	140
nextWindow	WindowPeek	90	144
windowPic	PicHandle	94	148
refCon	Longint	98	152
(size)		9C	156
Zone			
BkLim	Pointer	0	0
PurgePtr	Pointer	4	4
HFstFree	Pointer	8	8
ZCBFree	Longint	C	12
GZProc	ProcPtr	10	16
MoreMast	Integer	14	20
Flags	Integer	16	22
CntRel	Integer	18	24
MaxRel	Integer	1A	26
CntNRel	Integer	1C	28
MaxNRel	Integer	1E	30
CntEmpty	Integer	20	32
CntHandles	Integer	22	34
MinCBFree	Longint	24	36
PurgeProc	ProcPtr	28	40
SparePtr	Pointer	2C	44
AllocPtr	Pointer	30	48
HeapData	Integer	34	52
(size of header)		34	52

Glossary

Address register direct—A 68000 addressing mode in which the operand is the contents of an address register.

Addressing mode—Any of several methods used by a microprocessor to determine an operand.

And—See *logical and.*

Application heap—The area of memory that contains the application's code and its resources. It usually begins at $CB00 and extends for much of the Macintosh's RAM, but you should find its start by examining the global variable ApplZone.

A-trap—A call to the Macintosh User Interface Toolbox or Operating System. Same as *system call, ROM call,* and *trap.*

Autoscrolling—The technique used by many text-editing applications of automatically scrolling the window's contents when the user is selecting something and drags the mouse below the window.

Binary-coded decimal—A numbering scheme used by the 68000 that uses one hexadecimal digit to represent one decimal digit.

Blank segment—See *main segment.*

Block header—The first 8 bytes of a heap block, which give information about the block. Also called heap block header.

Breakpoint—A location within a program set by the person debugging at which the debugger will interrupt and take control.

Case label—The name of a part of a Pascal case statement that can be branched to by the case statement.

Case selector—The value used to determine which part of a case statement to execute.

Check exception—A 68000 exception caused by a failed CHK instruction. It usually indicates a Pascal value range error.

Checksum—A partial sum of a range of values, used to determine if any values in the range have changed.

Completion routine—A section of code that is executed when an asynchronous I/O operation is finished.

Condition codes—A group of flags in the 68000 that give information about the previous instruction, such as whether an operand or result was zero or whether an overflow occurred.

Condition codes register—The 68000 register that contains the condition codes. This register, called CCR, is the lower half of the status register.

Contents—The bytes in a heap block that contain the data stored there by the program; that is, everything in a heap block except the header.

Data fork—The part of a file that does not contain resources. The data fork contains a stream of bytes that has no meaningful format to the system.

Data register direct—A 68000 addressing mode in that the operand is the contents of a data register.

Debugger—A program that assists a programmer in finding and removing bugs.

Definition function—A routine that is used by one of the Toolbox Managers to draw and maintain a user-interface item, such as a control, menu, window, or list (for the List Manager). Also called a defproc, short for definition procedure.

Defproc—See *definition function.*

Desk accessory—A program whose name appears in the Apple menu and which can be used while an application is running.

Destination operand—The second operand in a 68000 assembly language instruction. This operand receives the results of arithmetic instructions.

Device driver—A program that controls the operation of a hardware device, such as a disk drive or the audio output, or that implements a special input or output feature, such as sound output or graphics pad input.

Diagnostic output—A debugging technique in which the programmer inserts instructions to write information to a printer, the screen, or an external terminal.

Dialog box—A window that a Macintosh program can display to report or request information.

Dialog record—A data structure that contains information about a dialog box. Dialog records cannot be relocatable objects.

Disassembly—The process of decoding machine language instructions into assembly language, the reverse of assembly.

Double bus fault—A catastrophic failure of the 68000 in which an exception occurs while a previous exception is being processed. A double bus fault causes the system to restart.

Double-dereferencing—The technique of deriving the address of an object from its handle, which contains the address of a master pointer.

Dynamically allocated—Created in memory at the time a program is run, rather than reserving space at the time the program is created by a compiler or assembler.

Effective address—The location of an operand in a 68000 instruction. An operand's effective address is computed with one of the 68000's addressing modes.

Epilog—1. The end of a procedure or function, which destroys the stack frame with an UNLK instruction, saves the return address, pops the parameters, and returns to the caller. 2. The part of a ROM patch that is executed following the original ROM call's code.

Exception—A special situation detected by the 68000 which causes a predetermined routine to execute. Examples of 68000 exceptions include address error, nonmaskable interrupt, and line 1010 exception (A-trap).

Exception vector—A low-memory location that contains the address of a routine to be executed when an exception occurs.

Exclusive-or—See *logical exclusive-or*.

Explicit dereferencing—The action of writing an instruction that uses the value of a handle to obtain a pointer to a relocatable block. A pointer obtained this way is only valid until a heap compaction occurs.

Explicit type coercion—A technique in C and Lisa Pascal that allows a variable to be used in an expression that requires a different type. Also called typecasting.

External reference—A call to a procedure or function that is not in the caller's code segment.

File reference number—An integer, assigned when a file is opened, that is used to refer to that file in File Manager calls.

Flags (master pointer)—The first byte of a master pointer, which contains information about the master pointer.

Format code—An integer that specifies whether a SANE call uses an extended-precision, double-precision, single-precision, integer, long integer, or computational value.

Fragmentation—The situation that occurs when free space in a heap is divided into several pieces. Since heap objects must consist of contiguous bytes, fragmentation causes applications to run out of memory while free memory is still available in the heap.

Frame pointer—A 68000 address register that is used to point to a program or procedure's variables and parameters.

Free (block)—A type of heap block that contains unused bytes.

Generic application—An application defined by MacApp that implements the standard behavior of Macintosh applications, including resizable windows, menus, and desk accessories.

Global frame pointer—The address register A5, which is used to locate an application's global variables.

Glue routine—A procedure or function that allows a high-level language to call the ROM. Also simply called glue.

GrafPort—A QuickDraw data structure that defines a complete environment for drawing, including a bitmap, pen and pattern information, and font information. GrafPorts cannot be relocatable objects.

Gross bug—A massive error in a program that completely prevents the intended feature from functioning.

Grow—To enlarge a heap by moving its end higher in memory.

Grow zone function—A function that is called by the Memory Manager when it can't find enough memory to fulfill a request for memory in a heap. The function, which is usually implemented by the application, should try to free some memory.

Growable heap space—The memory above the end of a heap and below the top of the stack that a heap can claim by moving its limit pointer. The `MaxApplZone` procedure automatically claims all of a heap's growable space.

Handle—The address of a master pointer to a relocatable block in the heap.

Heap zone—An area in memory that may be allocated in relocatable and non-relocatable pieces, called heap blocks or heap objects. A heap zone is also simply called a heap.

Heap zone header—A 52-byte data structure that precedes every heap and gives information about the heap, such as the address of the first available master pointer, the number of free bytes, and the address of the last block in the heap.

Hook—A pointer, usually in the system globals area, to a routine that is called in specified situations and through which a programmer can provide special features.

Horizontal retrace period—The period after the electron beam stops drawing a line of dots on the screen and moves back to the left edge of the screen. Also called the horizontal blanking period (HBL).

ID—An integer that is used to identify a resource of a particular type.

Immediate addressing—A 68000 addressing mode in which the operand is specified right after the instruction.

Implicit dereferencing—The action of obtaining a pointer to a relocatable block without the programmer having written an instruction to obtain the pointer. This can occur in Pascal "with" statements and function and procedure calls. A pointer obtained this way is only valid until a heap compaction occurs.

Implied addressing—A 68000 addressing mode in which the operand is a register specified in the instruction itself. Also called implied register addressing.

Indexed register indirect addressing—A 68000 addressing mode in which the operand's address is obtained by adding the contents of an address register to an index and an offset.

Instruction—A command that is understood and carried out by a microprocessor.

Jump table—A data structure that an application's procedures and functions use to call routines outside their own code segment.

Last in, first out—A data structure that is capable of adding and removing objects, and in which the last object added will be the first one removed. The 68000's stack is a last in, first out structure. Also called LIFO.

Library—A collection of routines that are gathered together and compiled or assembled and that can then be linked to an application.

Loaded—Currently in memory and locked (refers to a code segment).

Local frame pointer—An address register, usually A6, that is specified in a LINK instruction and is used to locate a procedure or function's local variables and parameters.

Lock—An attribute of relocatable objects that temporarily prevents them from moving in the heap.

Logical and—An operation in which the bit of both the source and destination operands must be set in order to set the result bit.

Logical clipping—A drawing technique in which the program attempts to narrow the amount of drawing as much as possible before performing any QuickDraw drawing operations.

Logical exclusive-or—An operation in which the bit of either the source or the destination operand, but not both, must be set in order to set the result bit.

Logical not—An operation in which the state of each bit of the source operand is changed. The result is called the complement, or one's complement, of the operand.

Logical or—An operation in which the bit of either the source or the destination operand, or both, must be set in order to set the result bit.

Logical size—The number of bytes in a heap block requested by the caller. The actual number of bytes used by the block will be larger (see *physical size*).

Long branch—A relative branch in a 68000 instruction that is specified by a 16-bit displacement.

Long jump—A 68000 JMP instruction that uses a 32-bit address as its destination.

Main event loop—The part of an application that continuously waits for user action, usually by calling GetNextEvent. Also simply called the main loop.

Main segment—The code segment of an application that contains the main body of the program. The main segment is also called the blank segment and is always CODE resource 1.

Mark—The position in a file from which the next read will get information or into which the next write will put information.

Master pointer—A data structure in a heap that contains the address of a relocatable block. The Memory Manager will update a master pointer after it relocates a block.

Master pointer block—A group of master pointers allocated together as a single heap block. There are usually 64 master pointers in an application heap's master pointer block.

Memory Manager—The part of the Operating System that controls the allocation of heap blocks.

Menu bar—The list of menu titles across the top of the Macintosh screen.

Mnemonic—An Englishlike code that represents a 68000 instruction. Assemblers translate mnemonics into machine language instructions.

Nonpurgeable—An attribute of a heap block that prevents it from being removed from memory by the Memory Manager unless the application explicitly deallocates it. A nonpurgeable heap block may be made purgeable by calling the Memory Manager procedure HPurge.

Nonrelocatable—An attribute of a heap block that prevents it from being moved. A nonrelocatable heap block, once allocated, can never be made relocatable.

Not—See *logical not.*

Operand—A value that is used by a 68000 instruction to perform its operation. An operand is similar to a parameter of a high-level language procedure.

Operation code—An integer that specifies which mathematical function will be performed by a SANE call.

Optimization—The practice of improving on a compiler's standard output by including techniques that make the object code faster or smaller, or both.

Opword—An integer that is formed by computing the logical or of a SANE format code and an operation code. The opword specifies the complete SANE operation to be performed.

Or—See *logical or.*

Package—A collection of related routines that performs some function in the Toolbox or Operating System. The Macintosh Plus includes some packages in ROM; previously, all packages were loaded into RAM.

Parameter block—A data structure used when calling the File Manager or Device Manager that specifies all the relevant information for a call, including the file and the volume or directory.

Patch—1. An addition or correction to a ROM routine that is applied by using SetTrapAddress. 2. Any addition or correction to a previously written routine.

Physical size—The number of bytes actually used by a heap block, including its header. See also *logical size.*

Positioning mode—The method when moving a file's mark that allows the programmer to specify that the mark should be positioned relative to the beginning of the file, the end of the file, or the current mark.

Postincrement register indirect addressing—A 68000 addressing mode in which the operand's address is obtained from an address register, following which the contents of the address register are incremented by the size of the operand (byte, word, or long word).

Predecrement register indirect addressing—A 68000 addressing mode in which the operand's address is obtained from an address register after first decrementing the contents of the address register by the size of the operand (byte, word, or long word).

Preflighting—The practice of trying to ensure that an operation has a good chance of success before starting the operation.

Preserving the port—The practice of saving the current GrafPort (the QuickDraw global variable thePort) before changing it, and then restoring it.

Program counter—A 68000 register that contains the address of the next instruction to be executed.

Program counter indirect with offset—A 68000 addressing mode in which the operand's address is obtained by adding an offset to the current program counter.

Program counter relative addressing—A 68000 addressing mode in which the operand's address is obtained from the current program counter.

Program counter relative addressing with index and offset—A 68000 addressing mode in which the operand's address is obtained by adding an offset and an index to the current program counter.

Prolog—1. The beginning of a procedure or function, which creates the stack frame with a LINK instruction and makes local copies of any parameters, if necessary. 2. The part of a ROM patch that is executed before running the original ROM call's code.

Purgeable—An attribute of a heap block that allows the Memory Manager to remove it if its space is needed for a memory allocation. A purgeable heap block may be made nonpurgeable by calling the Memory Manager procedure HNoPurge.

Quick immediate data addressing—A 68000 addressing mode in which the operand is a 1-byte value specified in the instruction itself.

Range checking—The process used by a Pascal compiler to verify that a value is within its allowed range, such as string length and subrange values. Failed range checks result in system error 5, check exception.

Reentrancy—The capability of a routine to be interrupted and allow the interrupt-handling code to call the routine before the original call has completed.

Register—A memory location within the 68000 itself.

Register indirect addressing—A 68000 addressing mode in which the operand's address is obtained from an address register.

Register indirect with offset—A 68000 addressing mode in which the operand's address is obtained by adding the contents of an address register to an offset.

Relative handle—A specially encoded handle used by the Memory Manager in a relocatable block's header.

Relocatable—An attribute of a heap block that allows the Memory Manager to move it at certain well-defined times. A relocatable heap block, once allocated, can be made temporarily immobile by locking it with the HLock call and can be made relocatable again with the HUnlock call.

Resource—A piece of data that be accessed by its type and ID and is stored in a resource file.

Resource attribute—A set of properties that a resource has that includes whether it will be locked when loaded, whether it will be loaded into the system heap, and whether it will be made purgeable when loaded.

Resource fork—The part of a file that contains specially indexed data called resources.

Resource map—An index that contains information that tells how to find the resources in a resource file.

Return address—The address, saved by the 68000 when a subroutine is called, to which the subroutine will return when it finishes.

ROM call—A call to the Macintosh User Interface Toolbox or Operating System. Same as system call, A-trap, and trap.

Runtime library—A collection of routines that is necessary for the basic functioning of a compiled program.

SANE—The Standard Apple Numerics Environment, a set of arithmetic features and capabilities provided on all Apple computers; it conforms to the IEEE Standard 754 for Binary Floating-Point Arithmetic.

Scale—The Font Manager's technique for resizing the bits of a font in an existing size to display it in a different size.

Screen flicker—The ugly flashing of the screen caused by the interaction between a program's drawing and the movement of the electron beam that is placing dots on the screen.

Short branch—A relative branch in a 68000 instruction that is specified by an 8-bit displacement.

Short jump—A 68000 JMP instruction that uses a 16-bit address as its destination.

Signature—A pattern of bytes that is common to all occurrences of a certain data structure and that allows the person debugging to identify the structure.

Single-dereferencing—The technique of using a handle to obtain a pointer to a relocatable block. A pointer obtained this way is only valid until a heap compaction occurs. Also simply called dereferencing.

Size correction—The difference between a heap block's physical size and its logical size plus its 8-byte header. A block's size correction is the number of unused bytes past the end of the block's logical size.

Skew—To begin a disassembly in the middle of an instruction, causing at least one garbage instruction to be displayed.

Source operand—The first operand in a 68000 assembly language instruction.

Spline—A mathematical outline of a font, used by the LaserWriter to create high-resolution characters that are not scaled. The LaserWriter stores splines for four fonts in its ROM: Times, Helvetica, Courier, and Symbol. The LaserWriter Plus has seven more: Avant Garde, Bookman, New Century Schoolbook, New Helvetica Narrow, Palatino, Zapf Chancery, and Zapf Dingbats.

Stack—The 68000's LIFO data structure that is used for local and global variables, parameter passing, return addresses, saved register values, and more.

Stack frame—The data on a specified part of the stack associated with the address in a specific address register. See *local frame pointer* and *global frame pointer*.

Stack pointer—The address register A7, which points to the top of the stack. The stack pointer is usually referred to as SP.

Static link—A value pushed on the stack by the compiler that allows a procedure or function to access the local variables of an outer procedure or function.

Status register—A 68000 register that includes the condition codes register and various status information about the 68000, including the current interrupt level. The status register is called SR.

Switch launch—A technique that the Finder uses that changes the boot volume when launching an application off a volume that's not currently the boot volume.

System call—A call to the Macintosh User Interface Toolbox or Operating System. Same as ROM call, A-trap, and trap.

System globals—The area of low memory that contains global variables used to indicate the state of the system.

System heap—The heap zone that is used mostly by operating system data structures. This heap zone usually begins at $B00 ($1400 on a Macintosh Plus) and extends to $CAFF, but you should not count on those addresses being correct.

Tag byte—The first byte of a heap block header, which contains information about the heap block.

Top of the stack—The address pointed to by the stack pointer. The top of the stack is the lowest address in the stack, since the stack grows downward in memory.

Trap—A call to the Macintosh User Interface Toolbox or Operating System. Same as system call, A-trap, and ROM call.

Trap dispatcher—The part of the Macintosh Operating System that determines the proper address that ROM calls should jump to.

Trap recording—A debugger feature that records the occurrence of ROM calls for later examination.

Trap word—The instruction word that constitutes a call to the Macintosh ROM.

Trash—To change the contents of, especially a register.

Two's complement arithmetic—A scheme for representing positive and negative numbers, used by most microprocessors, in which setting the high bit indicates that a number is negative.

Type—The general kind of a resource. A resource can be found by its type and ID.

Type coercion—In a high-level language, causing a variable to be used where a different type variable is specified. Also called typecasting.

Unloaded—Possibly in memory; if so, unlocked and possibly purgeable (refers to a code segment).

User Area—The part of the TMON debugger that is extensible by writing additional code.

Vertical retrace period—The period after the electron beam stops drawing the last line of dots on the screen and moves back to the top left edge of the screen. Also called the vertical blanking period (VBL).

Video/sound buffer—The area of RAM that is displayed as bits on the screen and played as sound from the speaker.

Whizzy—Neat, fancy, cool.

Window—An area on the screen, usually rectangular, in which most information in Macintosh applications is displayed.

Window record—A data structure that contains information about a window. Window records cannot be relocatable objects.

Index